CAMBRIDGE GREEK AND LATIN CLASSICS

TACITUS
ANNALS
BOOK IV

EDITED BY

R. H. MARTIN

Emeritus Professor of Classics,
University of Leeds

AND

A. J. WOODMAN

Professor of Latin,
University of Durham

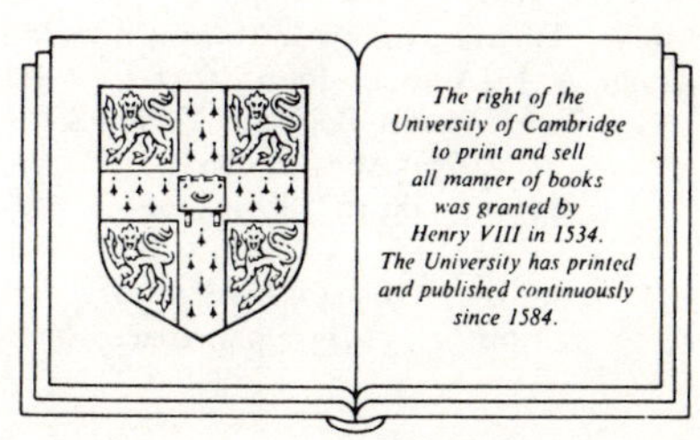

CAMBRIDGE UNIVERSITY PRESS

CAMBRIDGE

NEW YORK PORT CHESTER MELBOURNE SYDNEY

Published by the Press Syndicate of the University of Cambridge
The Pitt Building, Trumpington Street, Cambridge CB2 1RP
40 West 20th Street, New York, NY 10011, USA
10 Stamford Road, Oakleigh, Melbourne 3166, Australia

First published 1989

Printed in Great Britain at The Bath Press, Avon

British Library cataloguing in publication data

Tacitus, Cornelius
Tacitus Annals book IV. – (Cambridge Greek and Latin Classics)
1. Roman Empire. Historiography. Tacitus, Cornelius
I. Title II. Martin, Ronald
III. Woodman, A. J. (Anthony John)
937'.0072024

Library of Congress cataloguing in publication data

Tacitus, Cornelius.
[Annales. Liber 4]
Annals. Book IV / Tacitus: edited by R. H. Martin and A. J. Woodman
p. cm. – (Cambridge Greek and Latin classics)
Text in Latin: commentary in English.
Bibliography.
Includes indexes.
ISBN 0 521 30504 7 – ISBN 0 521 31543 3 (pbk.)
1. Rome – History – Tiberius, 14–37. I. Martin, Ronald H., 1915– .
II. Woodman, A. J. (Anthony John), 1945– . III. Title.
IV. Title: Annals. Book 4. V. Series.
PA6705.A6B4 1989
937'.07—dc 19 89-545 CIP

ISBN 0 521 30504 7 hard covers
ISBN 0 521 31543 3 paperback

ETA

CONTENTS

PREFACE

'Book iv of the *Annales*, it may be asserted, is the best that Tacitus ever wrote.' Such is the judgement of this century's leading Tacitean scholar, Sir Ronald Syme (*Roman papers* (1984) III 1031); yet no commentary on the Latin text has been published in English since the time of the First World War. In the seventy-five years which have elapsed between then and now, our knowledge of classical literature has greatly increased, there have been several revolutions in the way literary texts may be read, and readers have become accustomed to expect more from classical commentaries than the elucidation of points of grammar and syntax.

We have devoted our Introduction to explaining both the nature of Latin historical writing and Tacitus' place within the historiographical tradition. By analysing the structure and various other aspects of the composition and style of Book 4, we have tried to show how Tacitus capitalised on that tradition to produce a dramatic work of literature which would be found compelling by his readers in the second century A.D.

In the Commentary we have had two principal aims: first, to help the modern reader understand Tacitus' Latin and, second, to illustrate the intrinsic fascination of his writing. On the relatively few occasions when we have been unable to put forward an agreed interpretation, our separate views are identified by our initials – a practice which we hope may stimulate further discussion amongst readers. We have not attempted to give an account of the broader historical background, which is available in two reliable and relatively recent biographies of Tiberius by R. Seager and B. Levick. Though we hope that the Commentary will make a contribution to Tacitean scholarship and be useful to professional classicists, we also hope that it will be found 'user-friendly' by the sixth-formers and university students for whom it is primarily intended. We have tried to avoid much of the conventional panoply of scholarship, preferring instead to refer to such works as E. C. Woodcock's *New Latin syntax* or the *Oxford Latin dictionary*, to which our readers may reasonably be expected to have access.

We are jointly indebted to the generosity of Dr D. C. Braund and Mr K. Wellesley, who supplied us with valuable information on buffer states and Tacitean emendations respectively, and of Professor W. S. Watt, who volunteered a series of textual notes on Book 4. In addition AJW is grateful to a number of friends and colleagues in the North East, who have cheerfully tried to answer the questions with which they have been pestered and amongst whom Dr E. D. Hunt deserves a special mention. He also wishes to express his appreciation to the University of Durham for allowing him an extended period of research leave, during which the bulk of the book was written, and for a research grant to help with the purchase of a book by the Durham University Library.

September 1988

R.H.M.
A.J.W.

INTRODUCTION

1. LATIN HISTORIOGRAPHY TO TACITUS

'It is foreign locations, the suspense of battles, and heroic deaths which keep the readers' attention and whet their appetites for more.' This statement from Book 4 of Tacitus' *Annals* (33.3) indicates a basic truth about the works of ancient historians: they were not written to be read as text-books or as source-material for a modern discipline called 'history'; they were written to be enjoyed as works of literature in their own right, containing the same kinds of compulsive topic which today we associate more readily with historical novels or war films. Of course that is not the whole story, as we shall see below; but unless we are aware of the spirit in which works of ancient historiography were written, we have no chance of appreciating them properly.

In his dialogue *De Oratore*, the dramatic date of which is 91 B.C., Cicero makes one of the speakers, M. Antonius, express disappointment that hitherto Latin historiography had entirely failed to match the standards set by the Greek masters Herodotus and Thucydides. Maintaining that earlier historians had done little more than transmit in continuous prose the kind of year-by-year record (*annales*) kept by the *pontifex maximus* at Rome (2.52),[1] Antonius complained that as a result earlier historiography comprised 'only plain notices of dates, persons, places and events' (2.53). Similar complaints had already been made by two of the early historians themselves, Cato the Elder (234–149 B.C.) and Sempronius Asellio (flor. 133 B.C.),[2] the latter adding that jejune annals 'cannot in any way make people more enthusiastic to defend their country or more reluctant to do wrong' (fr. 2). This statement reveals two other important characteristics of Latin historiography: its political and its moral dimensions. On the one hand

For an explanation of our system of references and abbreviations see below, pp. 264–7.

[1] Almost everything connected with these records is problematic and controversial: see B. W. Frier, *Libri annales pontificum maximorum* (1979).

[2] Cato, fr. 77, Sempr. fr. 2. These and other fragments of the earlier Roman historians are in H. Peter, *Historicorum Romanorum reliquiae* I (2nd edn, 1914). For discussion see E. Badian, 'The early historians', *Latin historians* (ed. T. A. Dorey, 1966), 1–38; Wiseman 9–26.

historians were expected to treat Roman history with a patriotic bias and to demonstrate that Rome's greatness was something admirable and worthwhile. On the other hand they were expected to use their works as a medium for reinforcing the moral code of the upper sections of society to which they and their readers largely belonged.[3]

Slightly later in Cicero's dialogue Antonius suggests how Roman historiography can be brought up to Greek standards. He argues that earlier historians had failed to exploit the rhetorical potential of the genre: that is, they had not approached their task as if they were writing a speech (2.62), the aim of which was to move and persuade an audience. If historiography is to be raised above the level of a merely perfunctory record, Antonius says that it requires a 'superstructure' (*exaedificatio*) which 'consists of content (*res*) and style (*uerba*)':

> It is in the nature of content, on the one hand, that you require a chronological order of events and topographical descriptions; and also that you need – since in the treatment of important and memorable achievements the reader expects (i) intentions, (ii) the events themselves, and (iii) consequences – in the case of (i) to indicate whether you approve of the intentions, of (ii) to reveal not only what was said or done but also in what manner, and of (iii) to explain all the reasons, whether they be of chance or intelligence or impetuousness, and also to give not only the achievements of any famous protagonist but also his life and character. The nature of style and type of discourse, on the other hand, require amplitude and mobility, with a slow and regular fluency and without any of the roughness and prickliness associated with the law-courts. (2.63–4)

This is the most important substantial text for our understanding of how Latin historiography worked.[4]

[3] See D. Earl, *The moral and political tradition of Rome* (1967); T. P. Wiseman (ed.), *Roman political life 90 B.C.–A.D. 69* (1985).

[4] See *RICH* 78–95, of which the following is a summary. Readers should be warned at this point that the view of Roman historiography offered here differs substantially from that found in other books both on the ancient historians in general (e.g. S. Usher, *The historians of Greece and Rome* (1969), M. Grant, *The ancient historians* (1970), C. W. Fornara, *The nature of history in ancient Greece and Rome* (1983); but not Wiseman) and on Tacitus in particular (e.g. those listed by Martin (2) 271–2).

Antonius' distinction between content and style confirms that he approaches historiography as he would a speech. For example Quintilian, a professor of rhetoric and older contemporary of Tacitus, was only expounding conventional doctrine when he said (8 pref. 6) that 'every speech consists of content and style (*rebus et uerbis*)'. But the implications of this approach become clear when Quintilian adds: 'with reference to content (*in rebus*) we must study *inuentio*'. For *inuentio*, one of the five techniques in which orators were supposed to be expert, is defined as 'the "discovery" of what requires to be said in a given situation, the implied theory being that this is somehow already "there" though latent'.[5] This means that when an orator was confronted by a particular situation or case which demanded his attention, he would draw on his rhetorical training, as well as on his knowledge of literature and experience of life, to provide his audience with a convincing and persuasive presentation. In the context of historiography, it means that when a historian was provided by his sources with an item of information, however small, he would immediately be aware of the various ways in which he could 'build up' its presentation into an episode which his readers would enjoy.[6] This parallelism between oratory and historiography is confirmed by the fact that each of the elements listed by Antonius under 'content' (for example, topographical descriptions, the revelation of how a person spoke, or the attribution of reasons based on chance or character) is drawn from the theoretical instructions which were provided in rhetorical handbooks for *inuentio*. It follows, and is implicit in the term *inuentio* itself, that any element so 'discovered' need only be plausible: as Cicero himself said, *inuentio* is 'the devising of matter true or plausible which will make a case appear convincing' (*Inu.* 1.9). Since it was axiomatic that rhetoric should be persuasive, the minimal criterion for an ancient historian was, therefore, that his work should be realistic.[7]

Since there is a rapid increase in the numbers of volumes written by

[5] D. A. Russell, 'Rhetoric and criticism', *G. & R.* 14 (1967) 135.

[6] See *RICH* 88–93. Of course the amount of source material available to a historian can vary greatly depending on circumstances: for Tacitus see below, pp. 26–7.

[7] This criterion forms the basis for Tacitus' excursus on the death of Drusus (see below, p. 123 and 11.3n.). He also introduces realistic elements into Tiberius' speeches (8.2n.).

historians later in the first century B.C., the signs are that they wrote history in accordance with Antonius' views on its content (*res*).[8] By the time Livy began writing in the mid-30s, the early centuries of Rome had acquired an entire history, equipped with precise names of individuals and items of state business, for which there was virtually no source material whatsoever. As M. I. Finley has remarked, 'the ability of the ancients to invent and their capacity to believe are persistently underestimated'; but this does not mean that their historians are 'liars': it simply means, to quote Finley again, that 'we start from the wrong premise by assuming that the Greeks and Romans looked upon the study and writing of history essentially as we do'.[9]

Though Cicero himself never wrote a history, his name was firmly associated with the views expressed by his character Antonius: in another dialogue Cicero's great friend Atticus is represented as saying to the author that historiography 'is singularly well suited to an orator – or so it has always seemed to you at least' (*Leg.* 1.5). Yet the qualification 'to you *at least*' (*tibi quidem*) serves to remind us that the Greeks and Romans had an alternative way of viewing historiography which was extremely ancient and which Quintilian later expressed when he said (10.1.31): 'historiography is very close to poetry and is rather like a poem in prose'.[10] To us these alternative ways of looking at historiography may seem irreconcilable, since we tend to regard oratory and poetry as separate activities with little in common; but this was not so in the ancient world, where both genres were regarded equally as species of rhetoric: that is, the presentation of language in its most persuasive form, whether in prose or verse.[11] And the very fact that the ancients defined historical writing in such terms is a convenient and telling indication of the gulf which exists between the ancient genre and its modern namesake.

[8] Badian (above, n. 2) 11–12, Wiseman 9–12. We refer to Antonius' views (rather than to Cicero's) to underline that they are attributable to 91 B.C., the dramatic date of the dialogue (rather than to 55 B.C., when the *De Oratore* was published). Antonius' other area of concern, style (*uerba*), is discussed below, pp. 6–8, apropos of Sallust and Livy.

[9] M. I. Finley, *Ancient history: evidence and models* (1985) 9, 14.

[10] So Herodotus, the first Greek historian, was thought to have imitated Homer: see [Long.] *Subl.* 13.3 and Russell's n.; *RICH* 1–5.

[11] See *RICH* 98–101.

Cicero's own general attitude to historiography was expressed in a letter he wrote in 55 B.C. to a friend who was also a historian, L. Lucceius. The purpose of the letter was to ask Lucceius to deal with the Catilinarian conspiracy of 63 B.C., and Cicero's own role therein, in an appropriate manner (*Fam.* 5.12.3–6):

> Elaborate my activities even against your better judgement . . .: that prejudice (*gratiam*), which you discussed quite beautifully in one or other of your prefaces . . ., well, please don't suppress it if it nudges you strongly in my favour. . . . My experiences will provide you with plenty of variety (*uarietatem*) when you come to write – variety mixed with the kind of pleasure (*uoluptatis*) which can hold the attention of your readers. For nothing is more calculated to entertain a reader (*ad delectationem lectoris*) than changes of circumstance and the vicissitudes of fortune (*temporum uarietates fortunaeque uicissitudines*). . . . The monotonous regularity of the annals has as much effect on us as if we were reading through official calendars; but the unpredictable and fluctuating circumstances surrounding a great figure induce admiration, anticipation, delight, misery, hope and fear. And if they have a memorable outcome (*exitu notabili*), the reader feels a warm glow of pleasure (*iucundissima uoluptate*). So . . . you'll find that [the drama of my own experiences] has various 'acts' (*actus*) and many reversals of plan and circumstance (*multasque mutationes et consiliorum et temporum*).

These extracts of course confirm the view which Tacitus himself expressed in the sentence with which we began (p. 1); but they also bear on Asellio's remark about the patriotic function of historical writing. When Cicero suppressed the conspiracy of Catiline during his consulship, he identified his own interests with those of the *res publica.* He therefore expected Lucceius to treat him personally with the same enthusiasm as he would the state.

This was not, however, the line taken by Sallust (*c.* 86–35 B.C.) in his first work of history, the *Bellum Catilinae*, in which he deals with the very subject pressed on Lucceius by Cicero but treats Cicero himself with studied ambiguity.[12] Indeed Sallust also fails to display any broader patriotism: his work constitutes a savage indictment of

[12] For all aspects of Sallust's life and works see R. Syme, *Sallust* (1964).

contemporary society.[13] The same element recurs in his second work, the *Bellum Iugurthinum*, and in his now fragmentary *Historiae*, in which he dealt with the period from 78 B.C. onwards in the annalistic format which had now been consecrated by generations of Roman historians. Nevertheless Sallust's *œuvre* demonstrates how Antonius' theoretical prescriptions could be put into practice. For example, Antonius had required historians to expand on 'the character of any famous protagonist' and 'to reveal not only what was said but in what manner': Sallust begins each of his first two works with a full description of the villain of the piece (*C.* 5.1–8, *J.* 6–7.1) and puts full speeches, invented by himself, into the mouths of various characters.

Antonius had also required 'topographical descriptions': this was unnecessary in Sallust's first work, where the events were domestic, but in his second he included a full description of Africa (*J.* 17–19), where much of the action takes place. This is a particularly good example of ancient historiography in action. Since Sallust had actually been governor of Africa in 46 B.C., he presumably knew what the place was like; but, as Syme has said, his description scarcely seems 'to benefit from that fact'. Syme continues that to Sallust's readers 'a man's own experience might seem less attractive and convincing than what stood in literary tradition, guaranteed by time and famous names'.[14] The phrase 'attractive and convincing' goes to the heart of the matter and aptly sums up the criteria by which historiography was judged. And if traditional literary material was preferred to first-hand experience when autopsy was available, that has obvious implications for the infinitely more numerous occasions when it was not. For these quintessential characteristics of ancient historiography are not restricted to set-piece descriptions or speeches in character but can permeate the whole of a narrative.

Yet if Sallust followed Antonius in the matter of content (*res*), he did not do so in the other area to which Antonius had directed attention, that of style (*uerba*). In Antonius' view history should be written in a style which displayed 'amplitude and mobility, with a slow and regular fluency' (above, p. 2), and it is clear from one of Cicero's other works that this is an allusion to the style of Herodotus, which 'flows along like

[13] Sallust 'attacks his own times and criticises their failings', according to the second-century A.D. historian Granius Licinianus (36).

[14] Syme 126; see also Thomas 2–5.

a calm stream without any choppiness' (*Or.* 39). Sallust's style, however, is the opposite of this, being seen by ancient readers themselves in terms of brevity, speed, irregularity and the unexpected.[15] These indeed were the characteristics of the style of Thucydides, and several readers actually saw Sallust as a 'second Thucydides'.[16]

It was not until the work of Livy (64 B.C.–A.D. 17) that Antonius' prescriptions for both content *and* style were fulfilled.[17] In a vast work of one hundred and forty-two volumes Livy described the history of Rome from its foundation to the year 9 B.C. Though only thirty-five of the earlier volumes now survive, we can see that Livy adopted Antonius' theory of content to expand on the works of his immediate predecessors in the same way as they had expanded on those of theirs (above, pp. 3–4).[18] Livy seems to have organised his material in groups of five books or 'pentads', and he often devotes an individual book to the projection of some moral theme such as *pietas* or *libertas*.[19] Within each book the narrative consistently evokes tradition and the past by being annalistic in format: each year tends to begin with the names of the consuls, after which Livy normally moves from domestic to foreign affairs, returning again to domestic affairs at the year's end.[20] This repeated patterning itself acts as a regularising device, suggesting the constancy with which domestic and foreign affairs ebbed and flowed during the major portions of Rome's earlier history.[21]

As for Livy's style, which Quintilian (10.1.32, 101) likened to that of Herodotus and contrasted with that of Sallust, it displayed an

[15] See Syme (above, n. 12) 240–73 for Sallust's style, and 288–301 for readers' reactions to it.

[16] Sen. *Contr.* 9.1.13, Vell. 36.2, Quint. 10.1.101.

[17] For all aspects of Livy's work see P. G. Walsh, *Livy: his historical aims and methods* (1961).

[18] For ex., Livy's account of T. Manlius Torquatus (7.9.6–10.4) is exactly double the length of that of Claudius Quadrigarius (fr. 10), on which it is based: see, briefly, *The Blackwell dictionary of historians* (ed. J. Cannon, R. H. C. Davis, W. Doyle, J. P. Greene, 1988) under 'Livy'.

[19] See esp. Luce 3–32; also R. M. Ogilvie, *A commentary on Livy Books 1–5* (1965) 17–18.

[20] See A. H. McDonald, *J.R.S.* 47 (1957) 155–7; Ginsburg 10–14 (109 n. 35 for exceptions).

[21] Ginsburg 86.

amplitude and fluency of which Antonius would have approved. The result was a monumental achievement which in literary form and patriotic intent matched the achievement of the Roman people themselves, tracing their development during the expansionist era of the mid-republic, through the social disturbances of the second and first centuries and the two dark decades of civil war under Julius Caesar and Octavian, to the triumphant resurgence under Rome's first emperor, now named Augustus. In its scale Livy's work represents the culmination of republican historiography at Rome; in its enthusiastic endorsement of Augustus it looks forward to the historiography of the empire.[22]

Yet we know little for certain of the historians who lived in the century immediately after Livy's death, as the works of most of them have not survived.[23] One exception is Velleius Paterculus, who had been elected praetor just before the death of Augustus in A.D. 14 and had served with the future emperor Tiberius on campaign in Germany and Illyricum between A.D. 4 and 9.[24] No doubt reacting to the bulk of Livy's work, Velleius in A.D. 30 published a two-volume summary of Roman history which covers, in neo-Ciceronian style, events to the death of Augustus' wife, Livia, in 29. His terms of reference as a summarist necessarily restricted his scale;[25] but his eyewitness account of the foreign campaigns is relatively expansive (2.104.2–115), and his abbreviated record of Tiberius' first fifteen years as emperor is of course contemporary with events (2.124–30). Velleius' devotion to Tiberius is what one would expect of an old soldier towards his former commander, but needs to be seen in the content of the patriotic historians of the republic. With the advent of the empire, the interests of the emperor and the state enjoyed an even closer identification than that which

[22] Tacitus at *H.* 1.1.1 says that after 31 B.C. people were motivated by *odio aduersus dominantes* as well as by *libidine adsentandi* and implies that historians before his time had been susceptible to both. Yet it is not clear that he has any specific cases in mind (the commentators suggest no names); and the treatment meted out to Cremutius Cordus and some other historians under the first two emperors (see below, 34–5nn.) makes it likely that 'opposition historians' remained relatively scarce.

[23] The fragments are collected by H. Peter (above, n. 2) II (2nd edn, 1967). For discussion see Syme 132–56; J. Wilkes, *C.W.* 65 (1972) 177–203.

[24] For Velleius' life and career see G. V. Sumner, *H.S.C.P.* 74 (1970) 265–79.

[25] See A. J. Woodman, *C.Q.* 25 (1975) 273–87.

Cicero had proposed many years earlier (above, p. 5): 'res est publica Caesar', as Ovid said (*Tr.* 4.4.15). It was therefore only natural that a loyal historian like Velleius should transfer his traditional enthusiasm for the *res publica* to the *princeps* himself. It is, however, significant that Velleius' devotion to Tiberius seems not to extend to the emperor's minister, Sejanus, whose position in the state he goes to uncomfortable and elaborate lengths to excuse (2.127–8); and Velleius' decision to end his narrative with a brief glance at the disappointments of Tiberius' reign (2.130.3–5) is decidedly curious.[26] It is difficult to resist the inference that his loyalty was sorely tested by the emperor's withdrawal from Rome in 26 and the even greater influence which Sejanus wielded thereafter.

The only other historian of this period whose work has survived is Curtius Rufus, whose neo-Livian account of Alexander the Great probably belongs to Claudius' reign. The one extant fragment of Aufidius Bassus, a younger contemporary of Tiberius, deals with Cicero's death and presumably derives from a general work of Roman history whose precise scope is now unknown. His *libri belli Germanici* are referred to by Quintilian (10.1.103), but we know neither whether this is a separate work or part of his general history nor what is meant by 'the German war'.[27] The elder Pliny (A.D. 23/4–79), according to his nephew (*Ep.* 3.5.6), wrote a work of thirty-one volumes entitled *A fine Aufidii Bassi*, about which speculation is hampered by our ignorance of Aufidius' work; he also wrote a twenty-one volume *Bella Germaniae* (ibid. 4), to which Tacitus once refers (1.69.2) but of which we otherwise know little.[28] Tacitus elsewhere (*D.* 23.2), like Quintilian (10.1.102–3), pairs Aufidius with Servilius Nonianus (consul in A.D. 35), another historian whose work is obscure to us. Quintilian does, however, say that Servilius' style was 'less condensed than historiography demands', from which Syme has rightly inferred that he cannot have modelled himself on the abbreviated style of Sallust.[29] And from the scraps of information which we possess, the same seems to be true of most other first-century historians.[30] Yet the period is

[26] See W.'s introductions to both sections.

[27] See Syme 697–700 for the issues and various suggestions.

[28] See Sherwin-White's commentary on Plin. *Ep.* 3.5.4, 6. Also below, p. 26.

[29] *TST* 102–3 (91–109 for a full discussion of Servilius' life and work).

[30] See *RICH* 140–6.

admittedly one of uncertainty – which only serves to enhance our impression that Tacitus' emergence as a historian was explosive.

2. TACITUS' CAREER

T. was born probably in northern Italy or modern Provence, in France, in A.D. 56 or 57;[31] twenty years later, in 77, he married a daughter of Iulius Agricola, who had just been appointed governor of Britain (*Agr.* 9.6). His political career, as summed up allusively in his own words, was 'started by Vespasian [69–79], enhanced by Titus [79–81] and carried further by Domitian [81–96]' (*H.* 1.1.3). The first of these references is taken to mean that he had Vespasian's blessing to seek and hold some of the minor offices of a public career; the second that *c.* 81 he was elected to the quaestorship, which entitled him to membership of the senate. Elsewhere (11.11.1) he tells us that he was praetor in 88, and at the same time a member of the priestly quindecimviral college. In 97 he was suffect consul, his election having evidently been blessed by Domitian before his death in the previous year. This, then, was a career in which T. held office at roughly the earliest ages conventional for each position, but no earlier; and his friend Pliny testifies that during this period of his life his reputation rested on his oratory (*Ep.* 2.1.6, 11.17).

The year after his consulship T. published the *Agricola*, a biography of his father-in-law who had died in 93.[32] In accordance with the conventions of ancient biography, the work acts as a vehicle for praise of its subject; but it also provides a savage indictment of Domitian's tyranny, experience of which is thought by scholars to have scarred T. for life.[33] From this tension between praise and blame there emerges a question which informs most of T.'s writing: namely, 'what is to be the public behaviour of a Roman under what is nominally a republic, but in

[31] Also uncertain is his *praenomen* (Gaius or Publius). For a fuller account of his career and related issues see Martin (2) 26–35; more specialised is Syme 59–74, 611–24 and the appropriate Appendices.

[32] See esp. the commentary by R. M. Ogilvie and I. A. Richmond (1967); also Syme 121–5.

[33] His experience is held to explain his savage treatment of other emperors such as Tiberius and Nero in the *Annals*: see below, pp. 32–3.

fact an autocracy?'[34] In Agricola's case the answer is *moderatio* (e.g. *Agr.* 42.3): aware of the realities of the times, 'quibus inertia pro sapientia fuit' (6.3), he practised *quies* and *otium* (ibid.) but nevertheless enjoyed an influential, successful and honourable career. He was a living proof that 'posse etiam sub malis principibus magnos uiros esse' (42.4), and his are virtues whose praise will echo through the remainder of T.'s work (e.g. below, 20.2–3nn.).

Shortly afterwards T. published a second monograph, the *Germania*, in which, alongside some valid comments on the land and its peoples, contrasting their integrity with contemporary Roman decadence, there is included a great deal of what other authors at other times had said about other lands and peoples.[35] Thus the work is scarcely more accurate than the *Agricola* is impartial; but to expect otherwise is to misunderstand the nature of these types of ancient writing. The third of T.'s so-called 'minor' works is the *Dialogus*, the date of which is uncertain but which has a dramatic date of A.D. 75.[36] Its subject is the perennial problem of the decline in oratorical standards; and since it is written in conscious imitation of Cicero's oratorical dialogues, T. adopts an appropriately neo-Ciceronian style. The work thus serves as a reminder of the way ancient writers were trained in the ability to change their styles at will to suit their immediate needs.

It is again Pliny who tells us that by 106/7 T. was writing the full-scale work which we know as the *Histories*.[37] Hardly more than the first four of its original books survive, but in its complete state it covered almost twenty-eight years to the death of Domitian in 96. Although it had been Nero's death in June 68 which brought to an end the Julio-Claudian dynasty and precipitated civil war, T. chose to begin his work with the consuls who took up office on 1 January 69, a choice which gives some indication that the annalistic format had lost none of its influence or traditional appeal. The six preceding months are accommodated in a retrospective section (1.4.2–11.3) of the elaborate

[34] Martin (2) 9. For *Agr.* see esp. W. Liebeschuetz, *C.Q.* 16 (1966) 126–39; also W. on Vell. 88.2.

[35] See esp. the commentary by J. G. C. Anderson (1938); also Syme 125–9.

[36] See Syme 100–11; G. Williams, *Change and decline: Roman literature in the early Empire* (1978) 26–51.

[37] Whether this was its original title is uncertain: see G. on the titulature of the *Annals* (1 85–7). The original length of *H.* is also unknown: see below, n. 41.

preface, of which another section (1.2.1–4.1) is designed to assure prospective readers that T. will be dealing with many of the topics which, as we know from Cicero and T. himself (above, pp. 1, 2, 5), were guaranteed to hold their attention.[38] Among other items T. mentions foreign countries, battles, heroic deaths and captured cities; and in the surviving narrative he handles these topics with all the rhetorical skill one would expect of an author whose application of historiographical theory (above, pp. 2–3) was sharpened by his own acknowledged excellence as a practising orator. It was for his eloquence that T. had praised Livy less than ten years before (*Agr.* 10.3), and the influence of Livy is detectable throughout the *Histories*.[39] The result was a work which Pliny, who at T.'s own request had sent an account of his uncle's death during the eruption of Mt Vesuvius in 79 (*Ep.* 6.16), was convinced would be immortal (*Ep.* 7.33.1).

Although we do not know the date by which the *Histories* was completed, we know that in 112/13 or 113/14 T. held the proconsulship of Asia, which, along with that of Africa, was the summit of a senator's political career. The former year is perhaps more likely, since it seems that T. was engaged with Book 4 of his next work, the *Annals*, in 115 (see 5.2n. *qui magnitudine*). After this, the rest is silence; the date of his death is unknown.

3. THE *ANNALS*

In the preface to his *Histories* T. had predicted that in a future work he would describe the years from 96 onwards, 'a period of rare delight, when you can think what you want and say what you think' (1.1.4). But in his final work, the *Annals*, he went back in time and described events from the death of Augustus in 14 to that of Nero in 68. Whether his decision was based on increasing disillusion about the limits of free speech, or on a realisation that the civil war of 68–9 and its aftermath could not be seen without the perspective of the post-Augustan age, or on a combination of these and other considerations, is unknown.[40] Equally uncertain is the precise length of the *Annals*, which, in addition

[38] *RICH* 160–7.

[39] See Syme 200–1 and App. 34.

[40] Syme has argued that T. came to see even A.D. 14 as a mistaken starting-point (e.g. 369–71); but see Martin (2) 108.

to having lost all of Books 5 (except a small fragment) and 7–10, breaks off midway through Book 16. All we know is what we are told by St Jerome, that *Histories* and *Annals* together amounted to thirty books;[41] and the treatment of eighty-three years of Roman history on such a scale suggests that T. wished to acquire for himself the monumental status which Livy had enjoyed a century earlier. Yet whereas Livy had written in pentads (above, p. 7), the first twelve books of the *Annals* comprise two 'hexads': 1–6 for Tiberius, 7–12 for Gaius Caligula and Claudius. Whether that arrangement was continued thereafter is unknown; but it is generally acknowledged that it is in the first, Tiberian, hexad that T.'s idiosyncratic brilliance is best sustained.

The preface to the *Annals* is extremely short (1.1.1–3) and gives no explicit hint of the nature of the work apart from a brief list of its contents: 'inde consilium mihi pauca de Augusto et extrema tradere, mox Tiberii principatum et cetera'.[42] This is quite different from the elaborate preface to the *Histories*, but it is only one of several significant differences between the openings of the two works. The very first sentence of the *Annals* ('Vrbem Romam a principio reges habuere') comprises a double allusion to Sallust (*C.* 6.1 '*urbem Romam . . . habuere* initio Troiani', *H.* 1.8 '*a principio* urbis') and indicates unambiguously to T.'s readers that his work is to be modelled on Sallust (below, pp. 24, 32). Second, although Augustus died in August A.D. 14, T. does not on this occasion defer the start of his narrative until the January of the following year. On the contrary, as the list of contents makes clear, the transmission of power from Augustus to Tiberius was an essential component which took precedence over any claims made by the annalistic format: Tiberius' represented a dynastic succession, after which there could be no return to republican government. The third difference follows on from the second. Whereas the first full-length character sketch in the *Histories* is devoted to Licinius Mucianus, the 'king-maker' of the civil war (1.10.1–2), at the outset of the *Annals* it is the future emperor Tiberius himself whose character is described, albeit in reported speech (1.4.3–5). His character dominates the

[41] *Comm. Zach.* 3.14. Scholars apportion the books hypothetically as follows: *H.* 12 or 14, *A.* 18 or 16. Jerome does not use the title *Annales*, which is not attested before the sixteenth century: see G. (above, n. 37).

[42] This sentence refers respectively to: (*a*) 1.2.1–1.4.1; (*b*) 1.4.2–1.5.4; (*c*) 1.6.1–6.51.3; (*d*) Book 7 onwards.

principate, and the Tiberian hexad closes with a full-length obituary notice of the emperor (6.51).

Tiberius died on 16 March 37 after twenty-two and a half years in power. T. presents the period as falling into two unequal halves, of which the first lasted just over eight years (14–22) and was relatively laudable, whereas the second lasted just over fourteen years (23–37) and was increasingly reprehensible. This dichotomy is reflected in the disposition of the narrative: the first half of the first hexad (Books 1–3) is devoted to the former period, and the second half (Books 4–6) to the latter. This artistic division into two 'acts' naturally serves to emphasise the change which allegedly took place in A.D. 23;[43] but it also has the interesting consequence that T., renowned for his critical presentation of the emperor, in fact devotes as much space to the admirable but shorter period as he does to the reprehensible but longer period.[44] At any rate, the division of the first hexad into two sets of three books naturally places great emphasis on Book 4, the book which opens the second half.

4. *ANNALS* BOOK 4

That Book 4 marks a new beginning is plain at the outset from its dramatic opening. Its first sentence, like that of Book 1, contains a clear allusion to Sallust ('turbare fortuna coepit, saeuire ipse', cf. Sall. *C.* 10.1 '*saeuire fortuna* ac miscere omnia *coepit*'). Again, while Book 4 begins with a reference to the consular year, this annalistic convention is combined with a unique reference to the number of years during which Tiberius had so far held power ('nonus Tiberio annus erat': see n.). Third, there is a full-length character sketch of Tiberius' minister Sejanus (1.2–3), the evil genius allegedly responsible for the emperor's deterioration from this year onwards. To these three features, which exhibit similarities to those with which Book 1 opens (above, p. 13), there may be added a fourth. Shortly after Book 4 has opened, T. interposes a double digression (5–6) which both suspends the narrative and looks back over the years 14–22. The pivotal nature of the book could hardly have been underlined more emphatically.

[43] Cicero too had seen the history of his friend Lucceius as falling into 'acts' (above, p. 5).

[44] T. also spends more time on the earlier years of Claudius than on the later.

Structure and narrative

While it was Tiberius' principate which dictated the content of the first hexad and its bipartite division, T.'s role as an annalistic historian means that within individual books he usually operates in units consisting of a single consular year. Book 4 contains six such units, seemingly arranged in three pairs. The first pair, whose end is marked off by the familiar device of a digression (32–3), consists of a year devoted exclusively to home affairs (A.D. 23) followed by another (A.D. 24) in which foreign affairs are 'framed', in the Livian manner (above, p. 7), by two sections on home affairs. The structure of the central pair is chiastic, home and foreign affairs in the first year (A.D. 25) being followed by foreign and home affairs in the second (A.D. 26); moreover, a comparison is invited between Tiberius' relationship with Sejanus in the former (39–41: three communications) and with Agrippina, Sejanus' victim, in the latter (52–4: three vignettes). The pattern of the third pair (A.D. 27 and 28) exactly repeats that of the first pair, and on both occasions the second year has *amicitia* as the main theme of its domestic frame and moral reversal as that of its foreign section.[45] This carefully symmetrical arrangement can best be illustrated schematically.[46]

1–16 (A.D. 23)

HOME AFFAIRS

1–3 Sejanus and a seduction

4–6 Senatorial business (5–6 double digression on the state of the empire)

7–12 Death of Drusus (10–11 excursus)

13–16 The end of the year

17–33 (A.D. 24)

HOME AFFAIRS: 17–22

17 Priests

[45] See intro. to 17–22, 23–6, 27–31, 68–71, 72–3 and 74.

[46] The scheme does not correspond either with those proposed for individual years by Ginsburg or with that for the book as a whole by G. Wille, *Der Aufbau der Werke des Tacitus* (1983).

17–33 (A.D. 24) (*continued*)

18–20 Trials of Silius and Sosia
21–2 Three further trials
FOREIGN AFFAIRS: 23–6 Victory over Tacfarinas in Africa
23 Flashback
24–5 Fighting
26 Sequel
HOME AFFAIRS: 27–31
27 Slave revolt
28–30 Trial of Vibius Serenus
31 Three further cases
DIGRESSION: 32–3 T.'s historiography of Tiberius

34–45 (A.D. 25)

HOME AFFAIRS: 34–44
34–6 Cremutius Cordus and other trials
37–8 Tib. and the imperial cult
39–41 Sejanus and Tib. (three communications)
42–4 The end of the year
FOREIGN AFFAIRS: 45 Death in Spain

46–61 (A.D. 26)

FOREIGN AFFAIRS: 46–51 War in Thrace
HOME AFFAIRS: 52–61
52–4 Agrippina and Tib. (three vignettes)
55–6 Senatorial business
57–60 Tib.'s departure from Rome exploited by Sejanus
61 The end of the year

62–7 (A.D. 27)

HOME AFFAIRS
62–3 Disaster at Fidenae
64–5 Disaster at Rome
66 Trial of Quintilius Varus
67 Tib. withdraws to Capri

68–75 (A.D. 28)

HOME AFFAIRS: 68–71 Case of Sabinus and other events
FOREIGN AFFAIRS: 72–3 Revolt of the Frisii
HOME AFFAIRS: 74–5
74 Sejanus
75 The end of the year: a marriage

It will be seen that the symmetrical arrangement of annual units does not determine the amount of space devoted to each year. The first two are the longest and exactly comparable in length; the third and fourth are slightly shorter but again comparable with each other; the fifth and sixth are remarkably short and together comparable with either of the two preceding years. These disproportions mean that the communications between the two major figures, Tiberius and Sejanus (39–41), appropriately occupy what is virtually the mathematical centre of the book;[47] they also mean that, whereas the overall structure of the shortest year (A.D. 27) is very simple and consists of two sets of paired episodes (the first pair exhibiting precise parallelism: below, pp. 232–3), that of one of the longest years (A.D. 24) displays an elaborate series of triads. Triadic arrangement is indeed one of T.'s favourites, being also evident at 32–3 and 42–4 (see pp. 170 and 200).

There are also links between the various divisions of the book. In addition to cases where the events of an earlier year are resumed straightforwardly in a later (e.g. 15.3 ~ 55–6), T. juxtaposes items to provide transitions between sections, annual units, and paired years.[48] Thus, for example, the foreign affairs at 23–6 and 46–51 are linked to the home affairs of the same years at 27.1 and 52.1 respectively; the final chapters of A.D. 23 and 25 (16, 45) are linked to the opening chapters of A.D. 24 and 26 respectively (17, 46); and just as the first pair of years is linked to the second by the theme of free speech (at both 33.4 and 34–5), so the second pair is linked to the third by an elaborate sequence of events of which Tiberius' departure from Rome and arrival at Capri are the most significant.[49]

[47] See intro. to 39–41.
[48] See the Commentary for the examples which follow.
[49] See below, p. 233; more detail in Woodman (1) 150–4.

The above scheme also reveals some of the dynamics of the narrative. The book opens with a section on Sejanus: his character, his military base, his *clientela*, his relationship with Tiberius and position as his minister, his statues, and his ambitions – which lead him to seduce Livi(ll)a with hopes of marriage.[50] It is on the subject of that marriage that Sejanus writes to Tiberius in the central section of the book (39); but Tiberius' rejection of the proposal, focusing on his *clientela* (40.5), frightens Sejanus and leads him to try persuading the emperor to leave Rome in the hope that access to him may be controlled by Sejanus himself (41). In the following year Tiberius leaves for Campania and in the next withdraws to Capri; and the narrative closes with two final sections which mirror the very first in the book. In the penultimate section (74) Sejanus' position as Tiberius' minister is consolidated by the erection of an *ara amicitiae*, flanked by statues of himself and the emperor; and the relationship of the two men is eloquently attested by Sejanus' now inflated and more extreme *clientela*, for whom he represents the only means of access to Tiberius. In the last section (75) there is a final twist: the emperor, having rejected Sejanus' own marriage plans, gives official blessing to another union – the offspring of which will be the future emperor Nero.

Another perspective is offered by foreign affairs, the appeal of which was recognised by Cicero (p. 2) and by T. himself both in the *Histories* (p. 12) and in the present book of the *Annals* (32.1, 33.3). Book 4 takes the reader to all points of the compass: the south (23–6 Africa), the west (45 Spain), the near east (46–51 Thrace) and the far north (72–3 Germany). The first three of these episodes draw, in varying degrees, on the language and events of episodes in Sallust, although only the third of them is a full-scale military narrative;[51] and whereas the first and third of them result in victory for Rome, the second involves the murder of a local Roman governor and the fourth an ignominious defeat. The frequency with which such episodes appear, while in no way comparing with their regularity and scale in Livy's work (above, p. 7), is nevertheless somewhat surprising, since in the digression at 32–3 T. maintains that Tiberius' reign offers no opportunity at all to describe such events. Such paradoxes are, however, a recurrent feature of Tacitean narrative.

[50] For this form of her name see 3.3n.

[51] See the intro. to each section.

With the exceptions of A.D. 24 and 27, T. concludes each annual unit with a section on 'the end of the year',[52] in which he gathers together, often in no apparent order, miscellaneous items of a formal nature. These sections afford him the chance of recalling his annalistic ancestors while at the same time introducing new types of material of his own: sometimes these link with the preceding narrative, or anticipate the following narrative, or provide a total contrast with both.[53] The most familiar of such items is the obituary notice (15.1–2, 44 [another death follows in 45], 61, cf. 71.4), although its regular placing at the year's end inevitably induces some scepticism: 'that so many distinguished men should happen to die as the year closed strains coincidence'.[54] Yet the implication is that when T. writes *Fine anni excessere insignes uiri* . . ., as he does at 61, he is employing a form of metonymy: he refers not to the historical year A.D. 26 but to the narrative record of that year, since it is the latter which groups together deaths which doubtless took place at random intervals during the former. This predisposition to see history as text, rather than as whatever reality lies behind the text, explains why T. can manipulate the structure of his narrative for maximum effect and further confirms the literary nature of ancient historical writing.[55]

Language and expression

Though T.'s reputation as a historian has fluctuated during the course of time,[56] his masterly manipulation of language has never been in dispute. It would scarcely be possible to select two consecutive sentences of Book 4 which did not carry the individual stamp of his style, but his distinctiveness is not the result of uniformity. On the contrary, he gains and holds his reader's attention by adjusting his style

[52] A.D. 28 is a special case. While elsewhere too marriages belong to 'the end of the year' (e.g. 3.29.3–4), that at 75 is clearly intended to appear significant since T. has retrojected to 71.4 the obituary of Julia which might otherwise have accompanied it.

[53] See Ginsburg 31–52.

[54] G. on 2.41.1.

[55] For related topics see A. Cameron (ed.), *History as text* (1989).

[56] See e.g. P. Burke, 'Tacitism', *Tacitus* (ed. T. A. Dorey, 1969) 149–71; Martin (2) 236–43. On his treatment of Tiberius note the assessment of Seager 255–62.

to suit the variations in subject-matter which have been surveyed in the previous section (pp. 14–19): for example, foreign and domestic affairs, descriptions of character (1.2–3) and of place (67.1–2), speech both direct (8.4–5, 34.2–35.3, 37.2–38.3, 40.4–7) and indirect (8.3, 39.2–4), and dialectic (10–11, 32–3).[57] In the following paragraphs we provide a brief introduction to some of the more notable stylistic features of T.'s writing.[58]

Vocabulary. Until the publication of the *Histories* T. was best known for his oratory (above, pp. 10–11), the style of which was described by his friend Pliny as 'solemn' or 'dignified'.[59] The same description might be applied also to his historical style, particularly with reference to his choice of words (*delectus uerborum*), one of the areas to which ancient stylists devoted considerable attention.[60] Cicero in his *De Oratore* makes Crassus, one of the contributors to the dialogue, say that in vocabulary there are three elements which bring illumination and decoration to a speech (3.152 'ad illustrandam atque exornandam orationem'): the rare word (*inusitatum uerbum*), the new coinage (*nouatum*), and metaphor (*translatum*). Rare words, he continues (153), 'are mostly archaisms'.

Now archaisms are a regular feature of Latin historical prose, because historians often wish their narrative to reproduce something of the flavour of the past ages with which they are concerned. But whereas T.'s main model, Sallust, had been criticised by Asinius Pollio for his excessive affectation of archaisms (Suet. *Gramm.* 10), T. himself prefers 'mild archaisms' to those which are obtrusively odd.[61] Examples are *deum* for *deorum* (1.2n.), *apiscor* for *adipiscor* (1.3n.),

[57] A further element of variation is the number of different authors to whom T. is indebted at various points in his work: see the index esp. under 'Cicero', 'Livy', 'Sallust' and 'Virgil'. It is sometimes the case that T. relies on such authors to provide him with material in episodes for which genuine sources were scarce: this seems particularly true of the war in Thrace at 46–51 (below, p. 206). For this aspect of *inuentio* see *RICH* 193 n. 42.

[58] We make no attempt at a comprehensive analysis of T.'s style: see Syme 340–63 and Appendices 42–60; Martin (2) 214–35. Walker remains the only general guide to T. exclusively as a literary artist.

[59] *Ep.* 2.11.17. Pliny uses the Greek word σεμνός, which is customarily translated as 'solemn'.

[60] See Russell on [Long.] *Subl.* 43, W. on Vell. 41.3.

[61] The phrase is G.'s (1 334–5, where he also explains his use of 'choice' and 'colourful' to describe T.'s language).

claritudo for the Ciceronian *claritas* (6.2n.),[62] and *tempestas* for *tempus* (14.1n.).[63] An archaism such as *praetor* for *proconsul* (15.2n.), already anachronistic in the first century A.D., can be used pointedly to evoke an age which predates that which T. is describing; *duint* for *dent* (38.3n.) can give verisimilitude to a speech of Tiberius. But most often T.'s use of archaisms seems designed to avoid a commoner word or phrase: such avoidance is indeed one of the most characteristic features of his writing, being particularly clear in his aversion to standard terminology (1.1n. *cohortibus*).

Newly coined words, in the strictest sense, very often originate in verse authors; but the rate at which they are incorporated into the language of the educated classes depends to a great extent on the practice of prose authors. There are in fact comparatively few words, or meanings of words, which are first attested in T.: see, for example, *intectus* (1.2n.), *intutus* (3.1n.), *praegracilis* (57.2n.) and *peramoenus* (67.2n.); *criminator* (1.3n.) and *condemnator* (66.1n.) additionally illustrate T.'s fondness for verbal nouns in *-tor* or *-sor*. Nevertheless T., along with other prose authors of the first and second centuries A.D., is a beneficiary of the considerable expansion of Latin vocabulary which resulted from the explosion of poetic activity in the late republic and the age of Augustus. Examples are *iuuenta* for *iuuentus* (1.2n.) and *grates* for *gratias* (15.3n.); even so small a mannerism as *-que ac* (3.4n.) belongs to this category, appearing first with Virgil in verse and with Livy in prose. As will be clear from the Commentary, a similar pattern of usage can be posited for a great many individual words, since historiography was regarded as a close relative of poetry (above, p. 4) and thus historians enjoyed a greater freedom than other prose writers in incorporating poeticisms into their narratives.[64] If T. seems even more free with such vocabulary than might have been expected, one reason

[62] Cf. Gellius' comment that *sanctitudo* has more *dignitas* than *sanctitas* (17.2.19).

[63] At *De Or.* 3.153 *qua tempestate*, like the phrase *non rebar* (see below, 4.3n.), is said to have *dignitas*.

[64] It should be noted that distinctions between 'poeticisms' and 'archaisms' are often artificial and unhelpful, since archaisms (as is pointed out at *De Or.* 3.153) tend to be used relatively more frequently in poetry and hence are themselves 'poetic'. This qualification should be borne in mind while reading the Commentary, where our categorisation of individual words is intended as shorthand and designed to indicate merely their predominant flavour.

is the paucity of first-century A.D. historiography with which to compare him (above, pp. 8–10): had more of the post-Livian tradition survived, T.'s innovativeness might be found less startling than it now appears.[65]

Metaphor is generally thought to be more a feature of Latin poetry than prose, but T.'s narrative teems with metaphorical life in the manner of the most suggestive of Latin poets.[66] Thus, for example, life for a senator at Rome is a hazardous road bordered by cliffs and wasteland (20.3n.), Tiberius' resentment is a chronic illness (21.1n.), Sejanus is a master puppeteer (59.3–60.2nn.), the young Drusus a fierce dog (60.2n.), the collapse of an amphitheatre is a military disaster (62.1, 63.2), the spread of criminal accusations is an epidemic (66.1n.), spies are snakes (69.1n.), waiters serve Tiberius with crimes till he is glutted (71.1n.), and Sejanus is worshipped as a god with altar, prayers and devotees (74.2–5nn.). Sometimes related metaphors extend over considerable portions of the narrative. Thus Sejanus is presented as a general addressing his troops before the battle for the principate (2.2n.), from which he later diverts attention by alleging that it is his own opponent Agrippina who is intent on civil war (17.3n.). Similarly Tiberius himself withdraws from Rome to self-imposed exile (58.2n.) on the island of Capri, which is described as if it were a foreign country (below, p. 242; 67.1–3nn.); but he sometimes returns to assault by siege the very city of Rome from which he was supposed to govern (58.3n.).[67] These typical examples indicate that metaphor provides the vehicle for much of T.'s narrative power and characteristic view of events.

Syntax. As with vocabulary, T. profits from the general loosening of syntax which was largely derived from poetic practice and exploited in the first century A.D. by prose writers. No comprehensive survey of Tacitean syntax will be offered here, since individual points are annotated fully throughout the Commentary;[68] but it should be

[65] See Goodyear 23.

[66] Though scholars have often commented on T.'s use of metaphor (e.g. Walker 62–6), they have usually restricted themselves to the more obvious or superficial cases.

[67] See Keitel for the recurrent metaphor of civil war and its various manifestations.

[68] Note esp., e.g., adjectives followed by a genitive (as 7.1 *occultus*, 12.2 *ferox*)

stressed that our syntactical notes are not provided merely for their own sake: besides being an aid to translation, such notes, like those on vocabulary, are intended to illustrate a significant element of T.'s manner of expression and the extent to which he is similar to, or (more often) differs from, other Latin writers. Without such information the picture of his style would be incomplete.

Sentence structure. It is in sentence structure more than in any other aspect of style that T.'s distinctiveness is most visible. In all Latin prose authors many sentences consist of single clauses or two co-ordinated main clauses. But when authors write complex sentences, two main types are prominent: (1) a narrative sentence in which, after one or more subordinate clauses (or their equivalents, e.g. ablative absolutes or other participial phrases), the sentence is concluded by the main clause (or at least its predicate) and finishes, more often than not, with its main verb; (2) an oratorical period in which words, phrases and clauses are balanced against one another, and where that balance (*concinnitas*) is often marked by rhetorical devices such as antithesis and assonance. As a former orator T. shows his skill in the second type when, as was expected of ancient historians, he puts invented speeches into the mouths of various characters: see, for example, the speech of Cremutius Cordus at 34.2–35.3.[69] But it is in his handling of the narrative or descriptive type of sentence that T.'s individuality is most distinct. Attention will focus here on two major features only.

Ch. 29 begins with the following sentence: 'Tum accusator Cn. Lentulum et Seium Tuberonem nominat, magno pudore Caesaris, cum primores ciuitatis, intimi ipsius amici, Lentulus senectutis extremae, Tubero defecto corpore, tumultus hostilis et turbandae rei publicae accerserentur.' Here the main clause consists of eight initial

or infinitive (as 52.1 *properus*, 57.1 *certus*); the partitive genit. after neuter adjectives (5.2n. *cetera Africae*); the retention of the indic. in subordinate clauses in *or. obl.* (10.2n.); and the use of primary subjunctives for vividness after historic main verbs (2.1n. *si quid*). F.'s long section on 'The syntax and style of Tacitus' (38–74) is still instructive; see also N. P. Miller, *Tacitus: Annals Book I* (1959) 18–36.

[69] The style may loosely be described as neo-Ciceronian. Its clearest differences from Cicero are T.'s greater tendency to use short sentences for emphasis or point, and his studied avoidance of the rhythmical sentence-endings (*clausulae*) favoured by Cicero. (Readers should note that reasons of space have prevented our commenting on T.'s *clausulae* in the Commentary.)

words and is followed by an 'appendix' which is almost three times as long, is introduced by an ablative absolute, gives Tiberius' reaction to the event of the main clause, and is then extended further by an explanatory *cum*-clause. This type of sentence is one of the commonest in T. The appendix is repeatedly expressed by an ablative absolute, which may offer an explanation of, or comment on, the action of the main clause, or may simply add a further fact. The appendix may be very short (as 64.1 'deusto monte Caelio') or of considerable length: the example at 29.1 is of moderate length, but that at 59.3 consists of fifty-five words.[70] The contrast between such sentences and the more conventional narrative type, in which subordinate elements precede and build up to the statement of the main clause, arguably reflects a different way of looking at events and their consequences. When the main clause is completed early in the sentence, emphasis is inevitably thrown on the appended element(s); and since the appendix regularly gives men's motives for acting, or their reactions to events, this type of sentence clearly appealed to T. as the ideal vehicle for the cynical psychology which he so often imputes to his characters.

In the second place, if Cicero's style is characterised by balance and fullness of expression, T.'s sentence construction is notable for its disruption of balance and compression of thought:[71] in effect he carries to extremes features already associated with the style of Sallust (above, p. 7). In particular T.'s habit of deliberately avoiding the expected balance of his sentences is conventionally described by the term *uariatio*, whether it is found in individual words (as 38.4, where *alii* is followed by *multi . . . quidam . . .*) or, more strikingly, in the disposition of

[70] To give some idea of the frequency of this phenomenon in T., here are some further exx. from Book 4 (in each case the first words of the appendix, most often an abl. abs., are given): 2.3 'facili Tiberio', 5.3 'totidem . . . locatis', 9.2 'plerisque additis', 14.1 'Samiis . . . petentibus', 19.3 'silente reo', 29.2 'non occultante Tiberio', 36.3 'comperto', 54.1 'immissis qui . . .', 59.3 'subditis qui . . .', 66.1 'nullo mirante', 71.3 'non Galli amore', 73.1 'soluto . . . obsidio', 74.1 'dissimulante Tiberio'. For further discussion see Martin (2) 221–3, where the notable exx. of 3.3.1 and 14.49.3 are quoted and commented on.

[71] T., like Sallust, was capable of narrative brevity, and ellipse and the omission of non-essentials (such as parts of the verb 'to be') are features of his writing (see the index); but his sentences are perhaps best described as dense in texture, like those of Thucydides (Cic. *De Or.* 2.56, Dion. Hal. *Thuc.* 24).

clauses.[72] Very often, for example, an ablative noun is combined with a causal or purpose clause, as 28.2 'taedio curarum et quia periculum pro exitio habebatur', 48.2 'non spe capiendi sed ut . . . sonorem alterius proelii non acciperet'; alternatively a prepositional phrase can be co-ordinated with such a clause (as 15.3 'ob quam ultionem et quia . . . uindicatum erat'), or the ablative may be followed by an adjective (as 57.1 'specie dedicandi templa . . . sed certus procul urbe degere'). Not infrequently two examples follow each other (as 33.2 'plebe ualida uel cum patres pollerent, noscenda uulgi natura et quibus modis . . . haberetur', where an abl. abs. co-ordinated with a temporal clause is immediately followed by the noun *natura* co-ordinated with an indirect question), or are interwoven (as 8.2, where *nullo metu an ut firmitudinem animi ostentaret* is sandwiched between *per omnes ualetudinis eius dies* and *etiam defuncto necdum sepulto*). In almost all of these cases T. is drawing attention to alternative motives, whether of cause or purpose, and at 57.1 there is the additional contrast between appearance and reality which is basic to his manner of writing.[73]

Such deliberate variation in the construction of his sentences is all of a piece with T.'s avoidance of common or standard terms and his predilection for unusual syntax (above, pp. 20–2): each of these characteristics illustrates the general tendency of his writing to deviate from what may reasonably be called the norm. Although such deviation generally has a serious purpose, as we have seen, there are other cases where it is explicable only by a desire to be different. For example, in the famous passage where he declines to call a spade a spade (1.65.7 'per quae egeritur humus aut exciditur caespes'), it is not immediately apparent why he avoided the word *ligo*, which he had used at *H.* 3.27.2.

Some scholars have argued that T.'s various peculiarities of vocabulary, syntax and sentence structure reach their peak in the

[72] Many exx. (though scarcely all) are noted throughout the Commentary and catalogued in the index under *uariatio*. There is a comprehensive study of the subject by G. Sörbom; for the types discussed here see Martin (1) 91–6.

[73] See below, 1.2n. (*obscurum*), 2.1n. (*praetendebat*), 3.4n. (*specie*). Some other exx. in Book 4 of *uariatio* involving alternative motives are: 9.1 'de reddenda re publica utque . . .', 12.2 'ferox scelerum et quia . . .', 23.2 'non ut . . . sed missis leuibus copiis', 24.2 'terrore nominis Romani et quia . . .', 54.1 'forte an quia . . .', 71.3 'non Galli amore uerum ut . . .' See also below, p. 32 and n. 91.

earlier books of the *Annals* and that his style reverts to the more normal in the later books.[74] More recently, however, it has been shown that this tendency is only partly true, since T. in his later books often selects words or expressions which he had declined to admit in the earlier.[75] His writing represents a constant process of refinement according to his own highly individual terms of reference, and the reader must be constantly on the alert for the deliberate avoidance of the usual and the hackneyed.

Sources

If a modern historian were setting out to write British political history, he would concern himself in the first place with such primary sources as Cabinet papers and *Hansard*. The Roman equivalent to the latter was the *acta senatus*; but though some of T.'s details (such as the motion and counter-proposal, each associated with named individuals, at 20.1–2) suggest that he drew, directly or indirectly, on official sources (4.1n.), it should not be assumed that it was his invariable practice to consult documentary evidence, even where it existed and was available. We have already seen that ancient historiography is quite unlike its modern namesake and that successive republican historians saw their task as improving and expanding on their predecessors (above, pp. 3–8). It is also commonly agreed that ancient historians were generally indifferent to archival material, and there is only one occasion where T. himself says that he has consulted even the *acta* (15.74.3).[76] His apparent familiarity with the idioms of Tiberius' style, whose appearance is intended to provide his utterances with verisimilitude, may well derive from a published collection of the emperor's speeches (8.2n.).

In the Tiberian hexad T. mentions only two sources by name, the elder Pliny (above, p. 9) and the *commentarii* of the younger Agrippina (53.2n.). Each reference is illuminating. In the former case T. uses Pliny to authenticate a detail of the German campaigns of A.D. 15, his

[74] See e.g. 4.1n., 3n., 13.3n., 14.1n.

[75] See in general Goodyear 22–31; detailed studies have been undertaken by Martin (1) (see also 14.1n.) and Adams (1).

[76] Syme (278–86 and *J.R.S.* 72 (1982) 68–82 = *RP* IV 199–222) nevertheless believes that T. is greatly dependent on the *acta*; Martin (2) 200–1 and 206–7 is more sceptical.

narrative of which otherwise derives largely from the accounts of other campaigns of a later date which he had himself already given in his own earlier work, the *Histories*.[77] T.'s resort to such *inuentio* (above, p. 3) on this occasion suggests that he may well have operated similarly on other occasions too (see e.g. pp. 206–7). In the latter case, as T. makes a point of observing, Agrippina provides a detail 'not recorded by historians'. This 'one-upmanship' is entirely typical of ancient historians, who, when referring to their sources, are often motivated by rhetorical considerations such as *aemulatio* with their predecessors. In just the same way T. capitalises on references to nameless *auctores* in order to emphasise an alternative version of events which he seeks to place before his readers (see 10.1n., 57.1n.).

T.'s hostile picture of Tiberius is fundamentally the same as that presented by Suetonius, his younger contemporary (born *c*. 69), and by the Greek historian Dio, consul for the second time in 229.[78] Since there are similarities between Dio and T. (see e.g. 1.1n., 3n.), it is theoretically possible that Dio derived at least part of his material from the *Annals*; but as Suetonius and T., who also share similarities (see e.g. p. 215; 67.1n.), are usually thought to be independent of each other, it is perhaps more likely that all three authors derive their picture of Tiberius from a common literary source which is now lost and whose date and identity are unknown.[79] But while it is interesting to speculate on the extent to which T. may have relied on this source, it should not be thought that the Tacitean portrait is somehow 'second-hand'. Most works of ancient literature are derivative to a greater or lesser extent, and the quality of T.'s narrative, when compared with those of Suetonius and Dio, provides ample evidence that his own contribution to Tiberius' presentation was substantial and unique.

Tacitus and Tiberius

The Tacitean Tiberius, one of the most memorable creations of

[77] See *RICH* 176–9.

[78] For the former see A. Wallace-Hadrill, *Suetonius: the scholar and his Caesars* (1983); for the latter, Syme, App. 36, and F. G. B. Millar, *A study of Cassius Dio* (1964).

[79] Martin (2) 204–5 regards this as 'the simplest theory that will account for the many common elements that exist'; Syme (272–4) is more sceptical.

classical literature, is summed up in the obituary notice at the very end of Book 6 (51.3):

> morum quoque tempora illi diuersa: egregium uita famaque quoad priuatus uel in imperiis sub Augusto fuit [*to A.D. 14*]; occultum ac subdolum fingendis uirtutibus donec Germanicus ac Drusus superfuere [*to 23*]; idem inter bona malaque mixtus incolumi matre [*to 29*]; intestabilis saeuitia sed obtectis libidinibus dum Seianum dilexit timuitue [*to 31*]; postremo in scelera simul ac dedecora prorupit postquam remoto pudore et metu suo tantum ingenio utebatur [*to 37*].

This assessment raises issues which have implications both for the hexad in general and for Book 4 in particular. We shall deal with the general issues first.

In the introduction to his commentary on the *Annals*, F. R. D. Goodyear agreed with the view of many scholars 'that the Greeks and Romans had no clear idea of change and development of character, that the characters found in ancient literature are generally static. Thus, though their *mores* may be revealed to us gradually, their basic characteristics (*indoles*, *ingenium*) are fixed from the start.'[80] Now in the obituary T. presents Tiberius' *mores* or behaviour as deteriorating by stages throughout his life, until the nadir was reached in the final period after Sejanus' death in 31. Since it is only at this point that T. refers to the emperor's *ingenium*, Goodyear inferred, as have other scholars, that in T.'s opinion it was only during the years 31–7 that Tiberius' true character was finally revealed. But since it is implicit in this analysis that in reality Tiberius must always have been as evil as he is said to be in his final years, any evidence to the contrary (such as that displayed during the first years of the reign and summed up at 4.6.2–4) is therefore attributable to pretence and hypocrisy. This attribution explains both the frequency with which *simulatio* and *dissimulatio* are ascribed to Tiberius in the narrative (1.2n.) and the appearance of such phrases as *occultum ac subdolum fingendis uirtutibus* and *obtectis libidinibus* in the obituary. In other words Tiberius' deterioration, as described in the obituary, consists in his gradually revealing more and more of his *ingenium* during the course of time, until at last the truth is laid bare.

[80] G. I 37.

Although the above hypothesis has been generally accepted by scholars,[81] it is not without problems. In the first place it has been shown that the ancients' alleged belief in an unchanging *ingenium* is a considerable over-simplification.[82] In the second place, T. continues to ascribe *dissimulatio* to Tiberius even in the final period of his life (6.50.1), when all question of pretence is supposed to have disappeared.[83] Such inconsistencies have led recently to an alternative interpretation of the obituary, according to which *ingenium* does not here refer to character at all and hence can make no contribution to the question of whether or not Tiberius was 'innately evil'.[84] On this view the deterioration charted in the obituary is restricted to that of Tiberius' behaviour (*mores*) and nothing is implied about Tiberius' 'true character' one way or the other.

Yet if the emperor was not trying constantly to hide his true character during the earlier periods of his life, how are we to explain the *(dis)simulatio* which T. insists on ascribing to him? Scholars such as T. S. Jerome and B. Walker have convincingly demonstrated that T.'s portrait of Tiberius owes much to that of the typical tyrant as described by Xenophon, Plato and Aristotle and especially familiar to Roman readers through its popularity in declamatory literature.[85] The tyrant

[81] In addition to G. 1 37–40 see e.g. Martin (2) 105 and 139–43.

[82] See C. Gill, 'The question of character-development: Plutarch and T.', *C.Q.* 33 (1983) 469ff., esp. 481–7. The two passages where T. himself seems to say that a man's *ingenium* was *not* unchangeable (6.48.2, *H.* 1.50.4) are dismissed by G. as 'intermittent insights of slight importance'.

[83] See Hands, esp. 316–17.

[84] Woodman (2) 197–201, where it is argued that *suo tantum ingenio utebatur* means 'he had only himself to rely on', a reference to Tiberius' isolation after the successive deaths of his partners Germanicus, Drusus, Livia and Sejanus, mentioned earlier in the obituary. For this meaning of *ingenio uti* see *H.* 1.90.2 'in rebus urbanis Galeri Trachali ingenio Othonem uti credebatur'.

[85] Jerome 367ff., Walker 204ff.; also Syme 429. For the Greek authors see 1.2n., 70.2n.; for declamation see Winterbottom, index 3 'tyrants'. Declamation (see *OCD*) provides an excellent guide to early imperial literary taste, which explains our references to it in the Commentary. Jerome 370 and Hands suggested that T. in his portrait of Tiberius exploited the device of Roman lawyers, who, when confronted with a defendant about whom nothing bad was previously known, would argue that hitherto the man 'occultasse sua flagitia' (*Rhet. Herenn.* 2.5, cf. Cic. *Inu.* 2.34). Yet this does not account for charges of *dissimulatio* in such late passages as 6.50.1, already mentioned.

is of course the exact antithesis of the good man or the ideal ruler; and since the latter were expected to lead an open life (Cic. *Off.* 2.44 'nullum obscurum potest nec dictum . . . esse nec factum', Plin. *Pan.* 83.1 'nihil tectum, nihil occultum patitur'), the tyrant will lead a life of hypocrisy and pretence. So in the cases of such tyrannical emperors as Tiberius and Domitian these vices form a natural complement to their equally tyrannical predisposition to suspicion and fear (7.1n., 70.2n.).

It can therefore be argued that the obituary is internally consistent without recourse to the theory of fixed character; but whether its picture is also consistent with that painted at the beginning of Book 4 is another question. The reader of the latter, for example, is unlikely to assume from T.'s reference to sudden deterioration in A.D. 23 that in the obituary further turning-points will be posited in the years 29 and 31 as well. Yet it is unnecessary to conclude that T. is contradicting himself, since in his narrative of 23 he states that the deterioration was then only beginning (4.1.1 *coepit*, 6.1 *initium*). Nevertheless the opening of Book 4 clearly creates a different impression from that given in the obituary, and it is the seeming conflict between the two passages which is symptomatic of the problems raised by the obituary as a whole. The most glaring of these is often said to concern the role of Sejanus.[86]

At 4.1.1 it is stated that Sejanus was responsible for the deterioration of Tiberius' reign in A.D. 23 ('initium et causa penes Aelium Seianum'); in the obituary there is no mention of Sejanus until the years 29 onwards. The first point to note is that the commencement of Sejanus' influence in 23 is itself artificial, since T. has deferred to the opening section of Book 4 several of the earlier manifestations of Sejanus' ambitions which might more properly have been recorded in Book 3.[87] The second point is that the two passages are not factually irreconcilable, since each has a different emphasis:[88] the fact that Tiberius became 'intestabilis saeuitia' under Sejanus' influence in 29–31 does

[86] See Martin (2) 105, 139–42. We make no attempt here to discuss all aspects of the relationship between the obituary and the narrative, for which see again Woodman (2) 201–5.

[87] See 1.1n. (*cuius*), 2.1n. (*una in castra*).

[88] And a different purpose too, according to Woodman (2) 201–2, who also argues (204–5) that in the obituary Sejanus is seen as a stimulating as well as a restraining influence on Tib.

not preclude the possibility that such *saeuitia* had already become operative in the preceding period (e.g. A.D. 26, cf. 4.57.1).

The truth is that, whereas there are few factual contraditions in T.,[89] he frequently manipulates language to create discrepancies between impressions, or between impression and fact, which are designed to lead, or mislead, his readers in a certain direction. So the description of Tiberius at the very start of Book 1 (4.3–5: above, p. 13), where he is credited with *saeuitia*, *ira*, *simulatio* and *secretae libidines* before becoming emperor in A.D. 14, gives an impression which conflicts with the obituary, where the same period is described without qualification as *egregium uita famaque* and where *saeuitia* is not mentioned until the years 29–31. Yet the earlier passage is in reported speech, and T. himself, while leaving the impression with the reader, takes no authorial responsibility for it.

Indeed T.'s portrait of Tiberius consists of a whole series of modifications or adjustments, as if he were photographing his subject from a series of different angles and in different lights: none of the frames, whether in close-up or not, is contradicted by another, but each produces a different effect. Having manipulated our sympathies against the emperor by means of the hostile portrait at the start of Book 1, he modifies that interpretation of the early years in the appreciative summary at the start of Book 4 (6.2–4: see 6.2n.). Having suggested at the start of Book 4 that the deterioration in the reign was sudden and once and for all (1.1), he modifies that impression by presenting a more progressive deterioration in the obituary. And even within the obituary itself his view of the years 14–23, apparently wholly damning ('occultum ac subdolum fingendis uirtutibus'), is implicitly modified by his view of the next period 23–9, which, though presumably worse than its predecessor, nevertheless continued to show elements of good behaviour balancing the bad ('idem inter bona malaque mixtus').

Not without reason has it been said of T.'s narrative in the *Annals* that 'there are many occasions when we have to read him very closely indeed to perceive that he has in fact denied what one thought he had said'.[90] Many of the methods by which T. creates his impressions are

[89] For one example see 68.2n.

[90] Irving Kristol, *Encounter* 6 (May 1956) 86, reviewing the first edition of the Penguin *Annals*. For the technique of 'self-correction' (*reprehensio*) in T. see 57.1n.

familiar and have been thoroughly studied by scholars: for example, his insidious use of rumours and his technique of alternative suggestions.[91] But his general attitude to his subject matter is also enhanced by many of the features which have been mentioned in earlier sections of this Introduction. We have seen that republican historians, apart from such exceptions as Sallust (pp. 1–2, 5–6), responded to their subject matter with patriotic enthusiasm and that the same is likely to have been true of T.'s first-century A.D. predecessors (pp. 8–9). Yet the *Annals* involves a mainly critical appraisal of imperial government in general and of individual emperors in particular. T.'s criticism is underlined by his imitation of Sallust (p. 13), an author seemingly avoided in the first century A.D. precisely because of his association with the kind of indictment of society which T. mirrors so well (p. 9). Indeed by taking to extremes the linguistic and stylistic *uariatio* of Sallust (p. 24) T. emphasises his message that in the early empire society generally was disordered and rotten. A further enhancement is T.'s exploitation of the annalistic format. By using it at all he invites a comparison with Livy (p. 7) and evokes the republican past; but by often avoiding the precise patterns which in Livy were standard, to the extent that in Book 4 only two of the annual units are arranged in the Livian manner (p. 15), he illustrates eloquently that the empire was a different world from the republic.[92]

This highly selective relationship with the historical tradition, on which T. comments in the digression at 32–3 (pp. 169–72), has the effect of reinforcing the critical attitude which he adopts towards the events he relates. That attitude has often been attributed by scholars to T.'s experiences under the tyranny of Domitian (above, p. 10): he is said thereby to have become disillusioned for life and to have projected his disillusionment onto the reigns of the other emperors whom he describes. Yet T.'s own political career was one of unimpeded advancement, as we have seen (p. 10), and indicates that he sought not to oppose the imperial régime in any way but rather to profit from the

[91] In addition to Shatzman see I. S. Ryberg, 'T.'s art of innuendo', *T.A.P.A.* 73 (1942) 383–404; D. Sullivan, 'Innuendo and the "weighted alternative" in T.', *C.J.* 71 (1975/6) 312–26; D. Whitehead, 'T. and the loaded alternative', *Latomus* 38 (1979) 474–95; R. Develin, 'T. and techniques of insidious suggestion', *Antichthon* 17 (1983) 64–95.

[92] Ginsburg 100.

political opportunities which the imperial system offered. Indeed it was the same Domitian who, on T.'s own acknowledgement (*H.* 1.1.3), approved his elevation to the consulship. There is therefore an ambivalence between his own successful career and his authorial attitude towards his subject matter.

Similar ambivalences characterise the narrative itself. Although T. is a merciless critic of emperors such as Tiberius, he nevertheless shows little sympathy for their opponents; criticism of Tiberius for speaking in the senate at 1.74.4–5 does not save the emperor from criticism for staying silent in the senate at 1.77.3; and although T.'s indictment of imperial life is savage, he portrays the republic too as a period of violence and disorder. In other words T.'s attitude towards society and individuals, apart from such rare exceptions as M. Lepidus at 4.20.2 (n.), is predominantly critical, and it is at least arguable that he was temperamentally attracted to the role of Devil's Advocate in his writing. But how far that critical attitude derives not from political conviction but from a compulsive contrariness, of which his love of *uariatio* is simply another manifestation (above, p. 25), remains an unanswered question.

Text

All printed texts of *Annals* 1–6 derive, directly or indirectly, from a single manuscript which was written in Germany in the middle of the ninth century and from which the text of Book 5 was already missing.[93] Early in the sixteenth century, through the intervention of Pope Leo X, the manuscript came to Rome and from it Philippus Beroaldus the Younger printed the first edition of these books of the *Annals* in 1515. Shortly afterwards the manuscript was sent to Florence, city of the Medici, to grace the newly built Laurentian Library, where it is still housed as *Codex Laurentianus Mediceus* 68.1. It is known more briefly as 'the first Medicean' and is abbreviated in the apparatus criticus of modern editions as 'M'.

[93] There is a facsimile of the MS in S. de Vries, *Codices Graeci et Latini photographice depicti* (1902) 7.1; both it and the MSS on which the rest of T.'s work depends are discussed briefly in G. 1 3–4; Martin (2) 236–8; L. D. Reynolds (ed.), *Texts and transmission* (1983) 406–11.

Between M itself and T.'s autograph of the *Annals*, written over seven centuries earlier, it is likely that there was a series of successive handwritten copies, all of which are now lost. Each copying of the text will, inadvertently but inescapably, have introduced errors into it; and the process is cumulative. Hence it has been the task of scholars and editors to try to remove from M the accumulated errors of generations of scribes and to restore, as far as is possible, what T. originally wrote. Many of the errors are simple and obvious, and here it has been easy to restore T.'s words with almost complete certainty. A second class of errors consists of passages where the correct reading is less obvious but where a correction, once suggested, has won general acceptance from subsequent scholars. Many of each of these types of correction were made in the sixteenth century, especially by the notable scholars Beatus Rhenanus and Justus Lipsius,[94] but as a general rule we have not thought it useful for the purposes of the present edition to record either type in our apparatus criticus.[95] There remain certain passages, however, where there is still doubt about either the reading or the interpretation of the text (or both): these we have recorded and, where necessary, discussed in the Commentary.[96]

The division of the *Annals* into numbered chapters goes back no further than an editor at the beginning of the seventeenth century, and the subdivision of each chapter into numbered sections belongs to our own century.[97] But while these divisions are required for reference purposes, they cannot be taken as necessarily representing T.'s own concept of the structure of his narrative. We have therefore reparagraphed the text of Book 4 on a number of occasions where logic or the structure of the narrative seems to require it.

[94] This scholarship is surveyed by G. 1 5–19.

[95] Some exx. of the former type are: 1.1 *ierit* Pichena: *perit* M; 6.4 *acri* Rhenanus: *agri* M; 30.1 *Amorgum* Rhenanus: *amor cum* M; 62.2 *effusius* Lipsius: *effusus* M. Less obvious corrections themselves fall into more than one class: those which are certainly right (e.g. 23.1 *ubi* Lipsius: *sub* M) and those which are still questioned by some scholars (e.g. 28.3 *falso* Ursinus: *falsa* M).

[96] Our recording largely follows the accepted conventions. Angle brackets (⟨ ⟩) indicate the editorial supplement of a word or phrase; square brackets ([ ]) indicate an editorial excision; an *obelus* or 'dagger' (†) indicates an unsolved corruption. '*M marg.*' indicates a reading in the margin of M, '*M corr.*' indicates an alteration (not necessarily a true correction) in the text of M.

[97] See G. 1 11, 17–18 (and n. 3).

CORNELII TACITI
AB EXCESSV DIVI AVGVSTI
LIBER QVARTVS

CORNELII TACITI
AB EXCESSV DIVI AVGVSTI
LIBER QVARTVS

D. 23 C. Asinio C. Antistio consulibus nonus Tiberio annus erat 1
compositae rei publicae, florentis domus (nam Germanici mortem inter prospera ducebat), cum repente turbare fortuna coepit, saeuire ipse aut saeuientibus uires praebere. initium et causa penes Aelium Seianum, cohortibus praetoriis praefectum, cuius de potentia supra memoraui; nunc originem, mores et quo facinore dominationem raptum ierit, expediam.

Genitus Vulsiniis patre Seio Strabone, equite Romano, et 2
prima iuuenta C. Caesarem, diui Augusti nepotem, sectatus, non sine rumore Apicio diuiti et prodigo stuprum ueno dedisse, mox Tiberium uariis artibus deuinxit, adeo ut obscurum aduersum alios sibi uni incautum intectumque efficeret, non tam sollertia (quippe isdem artibus uictus est) quam deum ira
in rem Romanam, cuius pari exitio uiguit ceciditque. corpus illi 3
laborum tolerans, animus audax; sui obtegens, in alios criminator; iuxta adulatio et superbia; palam compositus pudor, intus summa apiscendi libido, eiusque causa modo largitio et luxus, saepius industria ac uigilantia, haud minus noxiae quotiens parando regno finguntur.

Vim praefecturae modicam antea intendit, dispersas per ur- 2
bem cohortes una in castra conducendo ut simul imperia acciperent numeroque et robore et uisu inter se fiducia ipsis, in ceteros metus oreretur. praetendebat lasciuire militem diductum; si quid subitum ingruat, maiore auxilio pariter subueniri; et seuerius acturos, si uallum statuatur procul urbis inlecebris. ut per- 2
fecta sunt castra, inrepere paulatim militares animos adeundo,
appellando; simul centuriones ac tribunos ipse deligere. neque 3
senatorio ambitu abstinebat clientes suos honoribus aut prouinciis ornandi, facili Tiberio atque ita prono ut socium laborum

A.D. 23 non modo in sermonibus sed apud patres et populum
celebraret, colique per theatra et fora effigies eius interque
principia legionum sineret.

Ceterum plena Caesarum domus, iuuenis filius, nepotes **3**
adulti moram cupitis adferebant; et quia ui tot simul corripere
intutum, dolus interualla scelerum poscebat. placuit tamen 2
occultior uia et a Druso incipere, in quem recenti ira ferebatur.
(nam Drusus impatiens aemuli et animo commotior orto forte
iurgio intenderat Seiano manus et contra tendentis os uerberauerat.) igitur cuncta temptanti promptissimum uisum ad 3
uxorem eius Liuiam conuertere, quae soror Germanici, formae
initio aetatis indecorae, mox pulchritudine praecellebat. hanc,
ut amore incensus, adulterio pellexit et, postquam primi flagitii
potitus est (neque femina amissa pudicitia alia abnuerit), ad
coniugii spem, consortium regni et necem mariti impulit. atque 4
illa, cui auunculus Augustus, socer Tiberius, ex Druso liberi,
seque ac maiores et posteros municipali adultero foedabat, ut
pro honestis et praesentibus flagitiosa et incerta exspectaret.
sumitur in conscientiam Eudemus, amicus ac medicus Liuiae,
specie artis frequens secretis. pellit domo Seianus uxorem 5
Apicatam, ex qua tres liberos genuerat, ne paelici suspectaretur.
sed magnitudo facinoris metum, prolationes, diuersa interdum
consilia adferebat.

Interim anni principio Drusus ex Germanici liberis togam **4**
uirilem sumpsit, quaeque fratri eius Neroni decreuerat senatus
repetita. addidit orationem Caesar, multa cum laude filii sui,
quod patria beneuolentia in fratris liberos foret. nam Drusus
(quamquam arduum sit eodem loci potentiam et concordiam
esse) aequus adulescentibus aut certe non aduersus habebatur.

Exin uetus et saepe simulatum proficiscendi in prouincias 2
consilium refertur. multitudinem ueteranorum praetexebat imperator et dilectibus supplendos exercitus: nam uoluntarium
militem deesse ac, si suppeditet, non eadem uirtute ac modestia
agere, quia plerumque inopes ac uagi sponte militiam sumant.
percensuitque cursim numerum legionum et quas prouincias 3

23 tutarentur; quod mihi quoque exsequendum reor, quae tunc
Romana copia in armis, qui socii reges, quanto sit angustius
imperitatum.

Italiam utroque mari duae classes Misenum apud et Rauen- 5
nam, proximumque Galliae litus rostratae naues praesidebant,
quas Actiaca uictoria captas Augustus in oppidum Foroiuliense
miserat ualido cum remige. sed praecipuum robur Rhenum
iuxta, commune in Germanos Gallosque subsidium, octo
legiones erant. Hispaniae recens perdomitae tribus habebantur.
Mauros Iuba rex acceperat donum populi Romani; cetera 2
Africae per duas legiones parique numero Aegyptus, dehinc
initio ab Syriae usque ad flumen Euphraten, quantum ingenti
terrarum sinu ambitur, quattuor legionibus coercita, accolis
Hibero Albanoque et aliis regibus, qui magnitudine nostra
proteguntur aduersum externa imperia. et Thraeciam Rhoeme- 3
talces ac liberi Cotyis, ripamque Danuuii legionum duae in
Pannonia, duae in Moesia attinebant, totidem apud Delmatiam locatis, quae positu regionis a tergo illis, ac si repentinum
auxilium Italia posceret, haud procul accirentur, quamquam
insideret urbem proprius miles, tres urbanae, nouem praetoriae
cohortes, Etruria ferme Vmbriaque delectae aut uetere Latio et
coloniis antiquitus Romanis. at apud idonea prouinciarum 4
sociae triremes alaeque et auxilia cohortium, neque multo secus
in iis uirium; sed persequi incertum fuerit, cum ex usu temporis
huc illuc mearent, gliscerent numero et aliquando minuerentur.

Congruens crediderim recensere ceteras quoque rei publicae 6
partes, quibus modis ad eam diem habitae sint, quoniam
Tiberio mutati in deterius principatus initium ille annus attulit.
iam primum publica negotia et priuatorum maxima apud 2
patres tractabantur, dabaturque primoribus disserere, et in
adulationem lapsos cohibebat ipse; mandabatque honores
nobilitatem maiorum, claritudinem militiae, inlustres domi
artes spectando, ut satis constaret non alios potiores fuisse. sua

4.3 ⟨ut noscatur⟩ quae *Novák*   5.4 fuerit *Lipsius*: fuit *M*

A.D. 23 consulibus, sua praetoribus species, minorum quoque magistratuum exercita potestas; legesque (si maiestatis quaestio
eximeretur) bono in usu. at frumenta et pecuniae uectigales, 3
cetera publicorum fructuum societatibus equitum Romanorum
agitabantur. res suas Caesar spectatissimo cuique, quibusdam
ignotis ex fama mandabat, semelque adsumpti tenebantur prorsus sine modo, cum plerique isdem negotiis insenescerent. plebes 4
acri quidem annona fatigabatur, sed nulla in eo culpa ex principe: quin infecunditati terrarum aut asperis maris obuiam iit,
quantum impendio diligentiaque poterat. et ne prouinciae
nouis oneribus turbarentur utque uetera sine auaritia aut
crudelitate magistratuum tolerarent, prouidebat. corporum
uerbera, ademptiones bonorum aberant. rari per Italiam
Caesaris agri, modesta seruitia, intra paucos libertos domus; ac
si quando cum priuatis disceptaret, forum et ius.

Quae cuncta non quidem comi uia, sed horridus ac plerum- **7**
que formidatus, retinebat tamen, donec morte Drusi uerterentur. nam dum superfuit, mansere, quia Seianus incipiente
adhuc potentia bonis consiliis notescere uolebat et ultor
metuebatur non occultus odii, set crebro querens incolumi filio
adiutorem imperii alium uocari. et quantum superesse ut collega 2
dicatur! primas dominandi spes in arduo; ubi sis ingressus,
adesse studia et ministros. exstructa iam sponte praefecti
castra, datos in manum milites, cerni effigiem eius in moni-
mentis Cn. Pompei, communes illi cum familia Drusorum fore
nepotes. precandam post haec modestiam, ut contentus esset.
neque raro neque apud paucos talia iaciebat, et secreta quoque 3
eius corrupta uxore prodebantur. igitur Seianus maturandum **8**
ratus deligit uenenum, quo paulatim inrepente fortuitus
morbus adsimularetur. id Druso datum per Lygdum spadonem,
ut octo post annos cognitum est.

Ceterum Tiberius per omnes ualetudinis eius dies, nullo metu 2

7.1 odii set *Doederlein*: odiis et *M* 7.2 quantum . . . dicatur! *Watt*: quantum . . . dicatur? *vulgate*

23 an ut firmitudinem animi ostentaret, etiam defuncto necdum sepulto, curiam ingressus est; consulesque sede uulgari per speciem maestitiae sedentis honoris locique admonuit et effusum in lacrimas senatum uicto gemitu, simul oratione continua erexit: non quidem sibi ignarum posse argui quod tam 3
recenti dolore subierit oculos senatus; uix propinquorum adloquia tolerari, uix diem aspici a plerisque lugentium. neque illos imbecillitatis damnandos; se tamen fortiora solacia e complexu rei publicae petiuisse. miseratusque Augustae extremam senectam, rudem adhuc nepotum et uergentem aetatem suam, ut Germanici liberi, unica praesentium malorum leuamenta, inducerentur petiuit. egressi consules firmatos adloquio adules- 4
centulos deductosque ante Caesarem statuunt. quibus adprensis 'patres conscripti, hos' inquit 'orbatos parente tradidi patruo ipsorum precatusque sum, quamquam esset illi propria suboles, ne secus quam suum sanguinem foueret, attolleret, sibique et posteris confirmaret. erepto Druso preces ad uos 5
conuerto disque et patria coram obtestor: Augusti pronepotes, clarissimis maioribus genitos, suscipite, regite, uestram meamque uicem explete. hi uobis, Nero et Druse, parentum loco: ita nati estis ut bona malaque uestra ad rem publicam pertineant.'

Magno ea fletu et mox precationibus faustis audita. ac si **9**
modum orationi posuisset, misericordia sui gloriaque animos audientium impleuerat; ad uana et totiens inrisa reuolutus, de reddenda re publica utque consules seu quis alius regimen susciperent, uero quoque et honesto fidem dempsit.

Memoriae Drusi eadem quae in Germanicum decernuntur, 2
plerisque additis, ut ferme amat posterior adulatio. funus imaginum pompa maxime inlustre fuit, cum origo Iuliae gentis Aeneas omnesque Albanorum reges et conditor urbis Romulus, post Sabina nobilitas, Attus Clausus ceteraeque Claudiorum effigies longo ordine spectarentur.

In tradenda morte Drusi quae plurimis maximaeque fidei **10**

8.4 confirmaret *M*, *Lipsius*: conformaret *M corr.*

A.D. 23 auctoribus memorata sunt rettuli; sed non omiserim eorundem
temporum rumorem, ualidum adeo ut nondum exolescat:
corrupta ad scelus Liuia Seianum Lygdi quoque spadonis 2
animum stupro uinxisse, quod is aetate atque forma carus
domino interque primores ministros erat; deinde, inter conscios
ubi locus ueneficii tempusque composita sint, eo audaciae
prouectum ut uerteret et occulto indicio Drusum ueneni in
patrem arguens moneret Tiberium uitandam potionem, quae
prima ei apud filium epulanti offerretur. ea fraude captum 3
senem, postquam conuiuium inierat, exceptum poculum Druso
tradidisse, atque illo ignaro et iuueniliter hauriente auctam
suspicionem tamquam metu et pudore sibimet inrogaret mortem quam patri struxerat.

Haec uulgo iactata, super id quod nullo auctore certo 11
firmantur, prompte refutaueris. quis enim mediocri prudentia,
nedum Tiberius tantis rebus exercitus, inaudito filio exitium
offerret, idque sua manu et nullo ad paenitendum regressu?
quin potius ministrum ueneni excruciaret, auctorem exquireret,
insita denique etiam in extraneos cunctatione et mora aduersum unicum et nullius ante flagitii compertum uteretur? sed 2
quia Seianus facinorum omnium repertor habebatur, ex nimia
caritate in eum Caesaris et ceterorum in utrumque odio quamuis
fabulosa et immania credebantur, atrociore semper fama erga
dominantium exitus. ordo alioqui sceleris per Apicatam Seiani
proditus, tormentis Eudemi ac Lygdi patefactus est; neque
quisquam scriptor tam infensus extitit ut Tiberio obiectaret,
cum omnia alia conquirerent intenderentque. mihi tradendi 3
arguendique rumoris causa fuit ut claro sub exemplo falsas
auditiones depellerem peteremque ab iis, quorum in manus
cura nostra uenerit, ⟨ne⟩ diuulgata atque incredibilia auide
accepta ueris neque in miraculum corruptis antehabeant.

Ceterum laudante filium pro rostris Tiberio senatus populus- 12

10.2 is *Ernesti*: is Lygdus *M* 10.3 captum *Muretus*: cum *M*: deceptum *Heinsius* 11.1 unicum ⟨filium⟩ *Prammer* 11.3 ⟨ne⟩ *Rhenanus*

23 que habitum ac uoces dolentum simulatione magis quam
libens induebat, domumque Germanici reuirescere occulti
laetabantur. quod principium fauoris et mater Agrippina spem
male tegens perniciem adcelerauere. nam Seianus, ubi uidet 2
mortem Drusi inultam interfectoribus, sine maerore publico
esse, ferox scelerum et quia prima prouenerant, uolutare secum
quonam modo Germanici liberos peruerteret, quorum non
dubia successio. neque spargi uenenum in tres poterat, egregia
custodum fide et pudicitia Agrippinae impenetrabili. igitur 3
contumaciam eius insectari, uetus Augustae odium, recentem
Liuiae conscientiam exagitare ut superbam fecunditate, sub-
nixam popularibus studiis inhiare dominationi apud Caesarem
arguerent. atque haec callidis criminatoribus, inter quos de- 4
legerat Iulium Postumum, per adulterium Mutiliae Priscae
inter intimos auiae et consiliis suis peridoneum, quia Prisca in
animo Augustae ualida anum suapte natura potentiae anxiam
insociabilem nurui efficiebat. Agrippinae quoque proximi in-
liciebantur prauis sermonibus tumidos spiritus perstimulare.

At Tiberius nihil intermissa rerum cura, negotia pro solaciis **13**
accipiens, ius ciuium, preces sociorum tractabat; factaque
auctore eo senatus consulta ut ciuitati Cibyraticae apud Asiam,
Aegiensi apud Achaiam motu terrae labefactis subueniretur
remissione tributi in triennium. et Vibius Serenus pro consule 2
ulterioris Hispaniae de ui publica damnatus ob atrocitatem
morum in insulam Amorgum deportatur. Carsidius Sacerdos,
reus tamquam frumento hostem Tacfarinatem iuuisset, absoluitur, eiusdemque criminis C. Gracchus. hunc comitem exilii 3
admodum infantem pater Sempronius in insulam Cercinam
tulerat. illic adultus inter extorres et liberalium artium nescios,
mox per Africam ac Siciliam mutando sordidas merces sustentabatur. neque tamen effugit magnae fortunae pericula; ac ni
Aelius Lamia et L. Apronius, qui Africam obtinuerant, insontem

12.3 superbam *Muretus*: -iam *M* 12.4 atque *M*: adque *Muretus*
13.2 morum *Lipsius*: temporum *M*

A.D. 23 protexissent, claritudine infausti generis et paternis aduersis
foret abstractus.

Is quoque annus legationes Graecarum ciuitatium habuit, **14**
Samiis Iunonis, Cois Aesculapii delubro uetustum asyli ius ut
firmaretur petentibus. Samii decreto Amphictyonum nitebantur, quis praecipuum fuit rerum omnium iudicium, qua
tempestate Graeci conditis per Asiam urbibus ora maris
potiebantur. neque dispar apud Coos antiquitas, et accedebat 2
meritum ex loco: nam ciues Romanos templo Aesculapii
induxerant, cum iussu regis Mithridatis apud cunctas Asiae
insulas et urbes trucidarentur.

Variis dehinc et saepius inritis praetorum questibus, post- 3
remo Caesar de immodestia histrionum rettulit: multa ab iis in
publicum seditiose, foeda per domos temptari; Oscum quondam ludicrum, leuissimae apud uulgum oblectationis, eo
flagitiorum et uirium uenisse ⟨ut⟩ auctoritate patrum coercen-
dum sit. pulsi tum histriones Italia.

Idem annus alio quoque luctu Caesarem adfecit, alterum ex **15**
geminis Drusi liberis exstinguendo, neque minus morte amici. is
fuit Lucilius Longus, omnium illi tristium laetorumque socius
unusque e senatoribus Rhodii secessus comes. ita, quamquam 2
nouo homini, censorium funus, effigiem apud forum Augusti
publica pecunia patres decreuere, apud quos etiam tum cuncta
tractabantur, adeo ut procurator Asiae Lucilius Capito accusante prouincia causam dixerit, magna cum adseueratione
principis non se ius nisi in seruitia et pecunias familiares dedisse;
quod si uim praetoris usurpasset manibusque militum usus
foret, spreta in eo mandata sua: audirent socios. ita reus cognito
negotio damnatur. ob quam ultionem et quia priore anno in C. 3
Silanum uindicatum erat, decreuere Asiae urbes templum
Tiberio matrique eius ac senatui. et permissum statuere; egitque
Nero grates ea causa patribus atque auo, laetas inter audien-

14.1 qua *Lipsius*: ea qua *M* 14.3 ut *M marg.* 15.1 adfecit *Ritter*: adficit *M*

23 tium adfectiones, qui recenti memoria Germanici illum aspici,
illum audiri rebantur. aderantque iuueni modestia ac forma
principe uiro digna, notis in eum Seiani odiis ob periculum
gratiora.

Sub idem tempus de flamine Diali in locum Serui Malugi- **16**
nensis defuncti legendo, simul roganda noua lege disseruit
Caesar. nam patricios confarreatis parentibus genitos tres simul 2
nominari, ex quis unus legeretur, uetusto more; neque adesse, ut
olim, eam copiam, omissa confarreandi adsuetudine aut inter
paucos retenta (pluresque eius rei causas adferebat, potissimam
penes incuriam uirorum feminarumque); accedere ipsius caerimoniae difficultates, quae consulto uitarentur, et quod exiret e
iure patrio qui id flamonium apisceretur quaeque in manum
flaminis conueniret. ita medendum senatus decreto aut lege, 3
sicut Augustus quaedam ex horrida illa antiquitate ad praesentem usum flexisset. igitur tractatis religionibus placitum in-
stituto flaminum nihil demutari; sed lata lex qua flaminica
Dialis sacrorum causa in potestate uiri, cetera promisco feminarum iure ageret. et filius Maluginensis patri suffectus. utque 4
glisceret dignatio sacerdotum atque ipsis promptior animus
foret ad capessendas caerimonias, decretum Corneliae uirgini,
quae in locum Scantiae capiebatur, sestertii uicies et, quotiens
Augusta theatrum introisset, ut sedes inter Vestalium
consideret.

24 Cornelio Cethego Visellio Varrone consulibus pontifices **17**
eorumque exemplo ceteri sacerdotes cum pro incolumitate
principis uota susciperent, Neronem quoque et Drusum isdem
dis commendauere, non tam caritate iuuenum quam adulatione, quae moribus corruptis proinde anceps si nulla et ubi
nimia est. nam Tiberius, haud umquam domui Germanici 2
mitis, tum uero aequari adulescentes senectae suae inpatienter

16.2 quod *Rhenanus*: quõ *M*: quoniam *vulgate*   17.1 proinde *M*: perinde *Rhenanus*

A.D. 24 indoluit accitosque pontifices percontatus est num id precibus
Agrippinae aut minis tribuissent. et illi quidem, quamquam
abnuerent, modice perstricti (etenim pars magna e propinquis
ipsius aut primores ciuitatis erant); ceterum in senatu oratione
monuit in posterum ne quis mobiles adulescentium animos
praematuris honoribus ad superbiam extolleret. instabat 3
quippe Seianus incusabatque diductam ciuitatem ut ciuili bello:
esse qui se partium Agrippinae uocent ac, ni resistatur, fore
pluris; neque aliud gliscentis discordiae remedium quam si unus
alterue maxime prompti subuerterentur.

Qua causa C. Silium et Titium Sabinum adgreditur. amicitia **18**
Germanici perniciosa utrique, Silio et quod ingentis exercitus
septem per annos moderator partisque apud Germaniam
triumphalibus Sacrouiriani belli uictor, quanto maiore mole
procideret, plus formidinis in alios dispergebatur. credebant 2
plerique auctam offensionem ipsius intemperantia, immodice
iactantis suum militem in obsequio durauisse, cum alii ad
seditiones prolaberentur; neque mansurum Tiberio imperium,
si iis quoque legionibus cupido nouandi fuisset. destrui per haec 3
fortunam suam Caesar imparemque tanto merito rebatur. nam
beneficia eo usque laeta sunt dum uidentur exsolui posse; ubi
multum anteuenere, pro gratia odium redditur.

Erat uxor Silio Sosia Galla, caritate Agrippinae inuisa **19**
principi. hos corripi dilato ad tempus Sabino placitum, immissusque Varro consul, qui paternas inimicitias obtendens odiis
Seiani per dedecus suum gratificabatur. precante reo breuem 2
moram, dum accusator consulatu abiret, aduersatus est Caesar:
solitum quippe magistratibus diem priuatis dicere; nec infrin-
gendum consulis ius, cuius uigiliis niteretur ne quod res publica
detrimentum caperet (proprium id Tiberio fuit scelera nuper
reperta priscis uerbis obtegere). igitur multa adseueratione, 3
quasi aut legibus cum Silio ageretur aut Varro consul aut illud
res publica esset, coguntur patres, silente reo uel, si defensionem
coeptaret, non occultante cuius ira premeretur. conscientia belli 4
Sacrouir diu dissimulatus, uictoria per auaritiam foedata et

24 uxor socia arguebantur. nec dubie repetundarum criminibus
haerebant, sed cuncta quaestione maiestatis exercita, et Silius
imminentem damnationem uoluntario fine praeuertit. saeuitum **20**
tamen in bona, non ut stipendiariis pecuniae redderentur,
quorum nemo repetebat, sed liberalitas Augusti auulsa, computatis singillatim quae fisco petebantur. ea prima Tiberio erga
pecuniam alienam diligentia fuit.

Sosia in exilium pellitur Asinii Galli sententia, qui partem
bonorum publicandam, pars ut liberis relinqueretur censuerat.
contra M. Lepidus quartam accusatoribus secundum necessitu- 2
dinem legis, cetera liberis concessit. (hunc ego Lepidum tempo-
ribus illis grauem et sapientem uirum fuisse comperior. nam
pleraque ab saeuis adulationibus aliorum in melius flexit; neque
tamen temperamenti egebat, cum aequabili auctoritate et gratia
apud Tiberium uiguerit. unde dubitare cogor, fato et sorte 3
nascendi, ut cetera, ita principum inclinatio in hos, offensio in
illos, an sit aliquid in nostris consiliis liceatque inter abruptam
contumaciam et deforme obsequium pergere iter ambitione ac
periculis uacuum.) at Messalinus Cotta, haud minus claris 4
maioribus sed animo diuersus, censuit cauendum senatus
consulto ut quamquam insontes magistratus et culpae alienae
nescii prouincialibus uxorum criminibus proinde quam suis
plecterentur.

Actum dehinc de Calpurnio Pisone, nobili ac feroci uiro. is **21**
namque (ut rettuli) cessurum se urbe ob factiones accusatorum
in senatu clamitauerat et spreta potentia Augustae trahere in
ius Vrgulaniam domoque principis excire ausus erat. quae in
praesens Tiberius ciuiliter habuit; sed in animo reuoluente iras,
etiam si impetus offensionis languerat, memoria ualebat.
Pisonem Q. Veranius secreti sermonis incusauit aduersum 2
maiestatem habiti, adiecitque in domo eius uenenum esse
eumque gladio accinctum introire curiam. quod ut atrocius
uero tramissum; ceterorum, quae multa cumulabantur, receptus est reus neque peractus ob mortem opportunam.

21.2 Pisonem Q. Veranius *Syme*: pisonemque grauius *M*

A.D. 24 Relatum et de Cassio Seuero exule, qui sordidae originis, 3
maleficae uitae sed orandi ualidus, per immodicas inimicitias ut
iudicio iurati senatus Cretam amoueretur effecerat; atque illic
eadem factitando recentia ueteraque odia aduertit, bonisque
exutus, interdicto igni atque aqua, saxo Seripho consenuit.

Per idem tempus Plautius Siluanus praetor incertis causis **22**
Aproniam coniugem in praeceps iecit; tractusque ad Caesarem
ab L. Apronio socero turbata mente respondit tamquam ipse
somno grauis atque eo ignarus, et uxor sponte mortem sumpsisset. non cunctanter Tiberius pergit in domum, uisit 2
cubiculum, in quo reluctantis et impulsae uestigia cernebantur,
refert ad senatum; datisque iudicibus Vrgulania, Siluani auia,
pugionem nepoti misit, quod perinde creditum quasi principis
monitu ob amicitiam Augustae cum Vrgulania. reus frustra 3
temptato ferro uenas praebuit exsoluendas. mox Numantina,
prior uxor eius, accusata iniecisse carminibus et ueneficiis
uecordiam marito, insons iudicatur.

Is demum annus populum Romanum longo aduersum **23**
Numidam Tacfarinatem bello absoluit. nam priores duces, ubi
impetrando triumphalium insigni sufficere res suas crediderant,
hostem omittebant; iamque tres laureatae in urbe statuae, et
adhuc raptabat Africam Tacfarinas, auctus Maurorum auxiliis,
qui, Ptolemaeo Iubae filio iuuenta incurioso, libertos regios et
seruilia imperia bello mutauerant. erat illi praedarum receptor 2
ac socius populandi rex Garamantum, non ut cum exercitu
incederet sed missis leuibus copiis, quae ex longinquo in maius
audiebantur; ipsaque e prouincia ut quis fortunae inops,
moribus turbidus, promptius ruebant, quia Caesar post res a
Blaeso gestas, quasi nullis iam in Africa hostibus, reportari
nonam legionem iusserat, nec pro consule eius anni P. Dolabella
retinere ausus erat, iussa principis magis quam incerta belli
metuens.

Igitur Tacfarinas disperso rumore rem Romanam aliis **24**

21.3 factitando *Woodman*: actitando *M*

24 quoque ab nationibus lacerari eoque paulatim Africa decedere, ac posse reliquos circumueniri si cuncti quibus libertas seruitio potior incubuissent, auget uires positisque castris Thubursicum
oppidum circumsidet. at Dolabella contracto quod erat 2
militum, terrore nominis Romani et quia Numidae peditum aciem ferre nequeunt, primo sui incessu soluit obsidium locorumque opportuna permuniuit; simul principes Musulamiorum defectionem coeptantes securi percutit. dein, quia 3
pluribus aduersum Tacfarinatem expeditionibus cognitum non graui nec uno incursu consectandum hostem uagum, excito cum popularibus rege Ptolemaeo quattuor agmina parat, quae legatis aut tribunis data; et praedatorias manus delecti Maurorum duxere. ipse consultor aderat omnibus.

Nec multo post adfertur Numidas apud castellum semi- **25**
rutum, ab ipsis quondam incensum, cui nomen Auzea, positis mapalibus consedisse, fisos loco quia uastis circum saltibus claudebatur. tum expeditae cohortes alaeque, quam in partem
ducerentur ignarae, cito agmine rapiuntur; simulque coeptus 2
dies et concentu tubarum ac truci clamore aderant semisomnos in barbaros, praepeditis Numidarum equis aut diuersos pastus pererrantibus. ab Romanis confertus pedes, dispositae turmae, cuncta proelio prouisa; hostibus contra omnium nesciis non arma, non ordo, non consilium, sed pecorum modo trahi,
occidi, capi. infensus miles memoria laborum et aduersum 3
eludentis optatae totiens pugnae se quisque ultione et sanguine explebant. differtur per manipulos Tacfarinatem omnes, notum tot proeliis, consectentur: non nisi duce interfecto requiem belli fore. at ille deiectis circum stipatoribus uinctoque iam filio et effusis undique Romanis ruendo in tela captiuitatem haud inulta morte effugit. isque finis armis impositus.

Dolabellae petenti abnuit triumphalia Tiberius, Seiano **26**
tribuens ne Blaesi auunculi eius laus obsolesceret; sed neque Blaesus ideo inlustrior et huic negatus honor gloriam intendit:

24.1 Thubursicum *Nipperdey*: Thubuscum *M*

A.D. 24 quippe minore exercitu insignis captiuos, caedem ducis bellique
confecti famam deportarat. sequebantur et Garamantum legati, 2
raro in urbe uisi, quos Tacfarinate caeso perculsa gens et culpae
conscia ad satis faciendum populo Romano miserat. cognitis
dehinc Ptolemaei per id bellum studiis repetitus ex uetusto more
⟨honos⟩, missusque e senatoribus qui scipionem eburnum,
togam pictam, antiqua patrum munera, daret regemque et
socium atque amicum appellaret.

Eadem aestate mota per Italiam seruilis belli semina fors **27**
oppressit. auctor tumultus T. Curtisius, quondam praetoriae
cohortis miles, primo coetibus clandestinis apud Brundisium et
circumiecta oppida, mox positis propalam libellis ad libertatem
uocabat agrestia per longinquos saltus et ferocia seruitia, cum
uelut munere deum tres biremes adpulere ad usus commean-
tium illo mari. et erat isdem regionibus Cutius Lupus quaestor, 2
cui prouincia uetere ex more calles euenerant: is disposita clas-
siariorum copia coeptantem cum maxime coniurationem dis-
iecit. missusque a Caesare propere Staius tribunus cum ualida
manu ducem ipsum et proximos audacia in urbem traxit iam
trepidam ob multitudinem familiarum, quae gliscebat immensum, minore in dies plebe ingenua.

Isdem consulibus, miseriarum ac saeuitiae exemplum atrox, **28**
reus pater accusator filius (nomen utrique Vibius Serenus) in
senatum inducti sunt. ab exilio retractus inluuieque ac squalore
obsitus et tum catena uinctus peroranti filio ⟨pater⟩ praeparatur. adulescens multis munditiis, alacri uultu structas principi 2
insidias, missos in Galliam concitores belli index idem et testis
dicebat, adnectebatque Caecilium Cornutum praetorium mini-
strauisse pecuniam; qui, taedio curarum et quia periculum pro

26.2 conscia *Lipsius*: nescia *M*: nec culpae nescia *Ryckius*: set culpae nescia *Halm* ⟨honos⟩ *vulgate* (*after Doederlein*): more ọmissusque *M* 27.2 euenerant *Haase*: -at *M* 28.1 peroranti f. ⟨pater⟩ praeparatur *Martin–Woodman*: p. f. praeparatur *M*: p. f. pater; paratur *Memmius*: pater orante f.; praeparatus *Oberlin*: p. f. pater comparatur *Madvig*: p. f. praebebatur *Lenchantin*

24 exitio habebatur, mortem in se festinauit. at contra reus nihil 3
infracto animo obuersus in filium quatere uincla, uocare ultores deos ut sibi quidem redderent exilium ubi procul tali more ageret, filium autem quandoque supplicia sequerentur. adseuerabatque innocentem Cornutum et falso exterritum; idque facile intellectu, si proderentur alii: non enim se caedem principis et res nouas uno socio cogitasse.

Tum accusator Cn. Lentulum et Seium Tuberonem nomi- **29**
nat, magno pudore Caesaris, cum primores ciuitatis, intimi ipsius amici, Lentulus senectutis extremae, Tubero defecto corpore, tumultus hostilis et turbandae rei publicae accerserentur. sed hi quidem statim exempti; in patrem ex seruis
quaesitum, et quaestio aduersa accusatori fuit. qui scelere 2
uecors, simul uulgi rumore territus, robur et saxum aut parricidarum poenas minitantium, cessit urbe. ac retractus Rauenna exsequi accusationem adigitur, non occultante
Tiberio uetus odium aduersum exulem Serenum. nam post 3
damnatum Libonem missis ad Caesarem litteris exprobrauerat suum tantum studium sine fructu fuisse, addideratque quaedam contumacius quam tutum apud aures superbas et offensioni proniores. ea Caesar octo post annos rettulit, medium tempus uarie arguens, etiam si tormenta peruicacia seruorum contra euenissent.

Dictis dein sententiis ut Serenus more maiorum puniretur, **30**
quo molliret inuidiam intercessit. Gallus Asinius Gyaro aut Donusa claudendum ⟨cum⟩ censeret, id quoque aspernatus est, egenam aquae utramque insulam referens dandosque uitae usus
cui uita concederetur. ita Serenus Amorgum reportatur. et 2
quia Cornutus sua manu ceciderat, actum de praemiis accusatorum abolendis, si quis maiestatis postulatus ante perfectum iudicium se ipse uita priuauisset. ibaturque in eam sententiam, ni durius contraque morem suum palam pro accusatoribus Caesar inritas leges, rem publicam in praecipiti

30.1 ⟨cum⟩ *Muretus*

A.D. 24 conquestus esset: subuerterent potius iura quam custodes eorum
amouerent. sic delatores, genus hominum publico exitio reper- 3
tum et ⟨ne⟩ poenis quidem umquam satis coercitum, per
praemia eliciebantur.

His tam adsiduis tamque maestis modica laetitia intericitur, 31
quod C. Cominium equitem Romanum, probrosi in se carminis
conuictum, Caesar precibus fratris qui senator erat concessit.
quo magis mirum habebatur gnarum meliorum, et quae fama 2
clementiam sequeretur, tristiora malle. neque enim socordia
peccabat; nec occultum est quando ex ueritate, quando adum-
brata laetitia facta imperatorum celebrentur. quin ipse, compositus alias et uelut eluctantium uerborum, solutius promptius-
que eloquebatur quotiens subueniret. at P. Suillium, quaes- 3
torem quondam Germanici, cum Italia arceretur conuictus
pecuniam ob rem iudicandam cepisse, amouendum in insulam
censuit, tanta contentione animi ut iure iurando obstringeret e
re publica id esse; quod aspere acceptum ad praesens mox in
laudem uertit regresso Suillio, quem uidit sequens aetas praepot-
entem, uenalem et Claudii principis amicitia diu prospere,
numquam bene usum. eadem poena in Catum Firmium 4
senatorem statuitur, tamquam falsis maiestatis criminibus
sororem petiuisset. Catus (ut rettuli) Libonem inlexerat
insidiis, deinde indicio perculerat. eius operae memor Tiberius,
sed alia praetendens, exilium deprecatus est; quominus senatu
pelleretur non obstitit.

Pleraque eorum quae rettuli quaeque referam parua forsitan 32
et leuia memoratu uideri non nescius sum; set nemo annales
nostros cum scriptura eorum contenderit qui ueteres populi
Romani res composuere. ingentia illi bella, expugnationes
urbium, fusos captosque reges aut, si quando ad interna
praeuerterent, discordias consulum aduersum tribunos,
agrarias frumentariasque leges, plebis et optimatium certamina libero egressu memorabant. nobis in arto et inglorius 2

30.3 ⟨ne⟩ *Bekker*

24 labor: immota quippe aut modice lacessita pax, maestae urbis res, et princeps proferendi imperi incuriosus erat.

Non tamen sine usu fuerit introspicere illa primo aspectu leuia, ex quis magnarum saepe rerum motus oriuntur. nam 33
cunctas nationes et urbes populus aut primores aut singuli regunt. (delecta ex iis et conflata rei publicae forma laudari facilius quam euenire, uel, si euenit, haud diuturna esse potest.)
igitur ut olim, plebe ualida uel cum patres pollerent, noscenda 2
uulgi natura et quibus modis temperanter haberetur, senatusque et optimatium ingenia qui maxime perdidicerant, callidi temporum et sapientes credebantur, sic conuerso statu neque alia rerum ⟨salute⟩ quam si unus imperitet, haec conquiri tradique in rem fuerit, quia pauci prudentia honesta ab deterioribus, utilia ab noxiis discernunt, plures aliorum euentis docentur.

Ceterum ut profutura, ita minimum oblectationis adferunt. 3
nam situs gentium, uarietates proeliorum, clari ducum exitus retinent ac redintegrant legentium animum; nos saeua iussa, continuas accusationes, fallaces amicitias, perniciem innocentium et easdem exitii causas coniungimus, obuia rerum similitudine et satietate.

Tum quod antiquis scriptoribus rarus obtrectator, neque 4
refert cuiusquam Punicas Romanasne acies laetius extuleris; at multorum, qui Tiberio regente poenam uel infamias subiere, posteri manent; utque familiae ipsae iam exstinctae sint, reperies qui ob similitudinem morum aliena malefacta sibi obiectari putent. etiam gloria ac uirtus infensos habet, ut nimis ex propinquo diuersa arguens. sed ⟨ad⟩ inceptum redeo.

25 Cornelio Cosso Asinio Agrippa consulibus Cremutius Cordus 34
postulatur, nouo ac tunc primum audito crimine, quod editis annalibus laudatoque M. Bruto C. Cassium Romanorum

33.1 conflata *Harrison*: consciata *M* 33.2 ⟨salute⟩ *Bringmann*
33.4 Romanasne *Nipperdey*: -ue *M* ⟨ad⟩ *Halm*

A.D. 25 ultimum dixisset. accusabant Satrius Secundus et Pinarius
Natta, Seiani clientes. id perniciabile reo et Caesar truci uultu 2
defensionem accipiens, quam Cremutius, relinquendae uitae
certus, in hunc modum exorsus est: 'uerba mea, patres conscripti, arguuntur: adeo factorum innocens sum. sed neque haec
in principem aut principis parentem, quos lex maiestatis
amplectitur: Brutum et Cassium laudauisse dicor, quorum res
gestas cum plurimi composuerint, nemo sine honore
memorauit.

'Titus Liuius, eloquentiae ac fidei praeclarus in primis, Cn. 3
Pompeium tantis laudibus tulit ut "Pompeianum" eum Augustus appellaret; neque id amicitiae eorum offecit. Scipionem,
Afranium, hunc ipsum Cassium, hunc Brutum nusquam latrones et parricidas (quae nunc uocabula imponuntur), saepe ut
insignis uiros nominat. Asinii Pollionis scripta egregiam eorun- 4
dem memoriam tradunt, Messalla Coruinus imperatorem suum
Cassium praedicabat; et uterque opibus atque honoribus
peruiguere. Marci Ciceronis libro, quo Catonem caelo aequauit, quid aliud dictator Caesar quam rescripta oratione, uelut
apud iudices, respondit?

'Antonii epistulae, Bruti contiones falsa quidem in Augustum 5
probra, sed multa cum acerbitate habent; carmina Bibaculi et
Catulli referta contumeliis Caesarum leguntur; sed ipse diuus
Iulius, ipse diuus Augustus et tulere ista et reliquere, haud facile
dixerim moderatione magis an sapientia: namque spreta exoles-
cunt; si irascare, adgnita uidentur. non attingo Graecos, **35**
quorum non modo libertas, etiam libido impunita; aut si quis
aduertit, dictis dicta ultus est.

'Sed maxime solutum et sine obtrectatore fuit prodere de iis
quos mors odio aut gratiae exemisset. num enim armatis Cassio 2
et Bruto ac Philippenses campos obtinentibus belli ciuilis causa
populum per contiones incendo? an illi quidem septuagesimum

34.3 praeclarus, in primis Cn. Pompeium *Woodman* 34.4 opibus *Acidalius*: opibusque *M*

ante annum perempti, quomodo imaginibus suis noscuntur
(quas ne uictor quidem aboleuit), sic partem memoriae apud
scriptores retinent? suum cuique decus posteritas rependit; nec 3
derunt, si damnatio ingruit, qui non modo Cassii et Bruti sed
etiam mei meminerint.' egressus dein senatu uitam abstinentia 4
finiuit.

Libros per aediles cremandos censuere patres; set manserunt,
occultati et editi. quo magis socordiam eorum inridere libet qui 5
praesenti potentia credunt exstingui posse etiam sequentis aeui
memoriam. nam contra punitis ingeniis gliscit auctoritas, neque
aliud externi reges aut qui eadem saeuitia usi sunt nisi dedecus
sibi atque illis gloriam peperere.

Ceterum postulandis reis tam continuus annus fuit ut **36**
feriarum Latinarum diebus praefectum urbis Drusum, aus-
picandi gratia tribunal ingressum, adierit Calpurnius Saluianus
in Sextum Marium. quod a Caesare palam increpitum causa
exilii Saluiano fuit. obiecta publice Cyzicenis incuria caeri- 2
moniarum diui Augusti, additis uiolentiae criminibus aduersum
ciues Romanos; et amisere libertatem quam bello Mithridatis
meruerant, circumsessi nec minus sua constantia quam praesi-
dio Luculli pulso rege. at Fonteius Capito, qui pro consule 3
Asiam curauerat, absoluitur, comperto ficta in eum crimina per
Vibium Serenum. neque tamen id Sereno noxae fuit, quem
odium publicum tutiorem faciebat. nam ut quis destrictior
accusator, uelut sacrosanctus erat; leues, ignobiles poenis
adficiebantur.

Per idem tempus Hispania ulterior missis ad senatum legatis **37**
orauit ut exemplo Asiae delubrum Tiberio matrique eius
exstrueret. qua occasione Caesar, ualidus alioqui spernendis
honoribus et respondendum ratus iis quorum rumore
arguebatur in ambitionem flexisse, huiusce modi orationem
coepit: 'scio, patres conscripti, constantiam meam a plerisque 2
desideratam, quod Asiae ciuitatibus nuper idem istud peten-

35.4 set *Lipsius*: et *M*

A.D. 25 tibus non sim aduersatus. ergo et prioris silentii defensionem, et quid in futurum statuerim, simul aperiam.

'Cum diuus Augustus sibi atque urbi Romae templum apud 3
Pergamum sisti non prohibuisset, qui omnia facta dictaque eius uice legis obseruem, placitum iam exemplum promptius secutus sum, quia cultui meo ueneratio senatus adiungebatur. ceterum ut semel recepisse ueniam habuerit, ita per omnes prouincias effigie numinum sacrari ambitiosum, superbum; et uanescet Augusti honor, si promiscis adulationibus uulgatur.

'Ego me, patres conscripti, mortalem esse et hominum officia **38**
fungi satisque habere, si locum principem impleam, et uos testor et meminisse posteros uolo; qui satis superque memoriae meae tribuent, ut maioribus meis dignum, rerum uestrarum prouidum, constantem in periculis, offensionum pro utilitate publica non pauidum credant. haec mihi in animis uestris
templa, hae pulcherrimae effigies et mansurae: nam quae saxo 2
struuntur, si iudicium posterorum in odium uertit, pro sepulchris spernuntur. proinde socios ciues et deos et deas ipsas 3
precor, hos ut mihi ad finem usque uitae quietam et intellegentem humani diuinique iuris mentem duint, illos ut, quandoque concessero, cum laude et bonis recordationibus facta atque famam nominis mei prosequantur.'

Perstititque posthac secretis etiam sermonibus aspernari 4
talem sui cultum. quod alii modestiam, multi quia diffideret,
quidam ut degeneris animi interpretabantur: optimos quippe 5
mortalium altissima cupere: sic Herculem et Liberum apud Graecos, Quirinum apud nos deum numero additos; melius Augustum, qui sperauerit; cetera principibus statim adesse; unum insatiabiliter parandum, prosperam sui memoriam: nam contemptu famae contemni uirtutes.

At Seianus nimia fortuna socors et muliebri insuper cupidine **39**
incensus, promissum matrimonium flagitante Liuia, componit ad Caesarem codicillos (moris quippe tum erat quamquam

38.3 deos et deas ipsas *M corr.*: deos et deos ipsos *M*: deos ipsos *Pichena*

. 25 praesentem scripto adire). eius talis forma fuit: beneuolentia 2
patris Augusti et mox plurimis Tiberii iudiciis ita insueuisse ut
spes uotaque sua non prius ad deos quam ad principum aures
conferret. neque fulgorem honorum umquam precatum: excubias ac labores, ut unum e militibus, pro incolumitate
imperatoris malle; ac tamen quod pulcherrimum adeptum, ut
coniunctione Caesaris dignus crederetur. hinc initium spei; et 3
quoniam audiuerit Augustum in conlocanda filia non nihil
etiam de equitibus Romanis consultauisse, ita, si maritus Liuiae
quaereretur, haberet in animo amicum sola necessitudinis
gloria usurum. non enim exuere imposita munia; satis aestimare 4
firmari domum aduersum iniquas Agrippinae offensiones,
idque liberorum causa: nam sibi multum superque uitae fore
quod tali cum principe expleuisset.

Ad ea Tiberius laudata pietate Seiani suisque in eum bene- **40**
ficiis modice percursis, cum tempus tamquam ad integram consultationem petiuisset, adiunxit: ceteris mortalibus in eo stare
consilia, quid sibi conducere putent; principum diuersam esse
sortem, quibus praecipua rerum ad famam derigenda. ideo se 2
non illuc decurrere, quod promptum rescriptu: posse ipsam
Liuiam statuere, nubendum post Drusum an in penatibus
isdem tolerandum haberet; esse illi matrem et auiam, propiora
consilia. simplicius acturum, de inimicitiis primum Agrippinae, 3
quas longe acrius arsuras si matrimonium Liuiae uelut in partes
domum Caesarum distraxisset. sic quoque erumpere aemulat-
ionem feminarum, eaque discordia nepotes suos conuelli; quid si
intendatur certamen tali coniugio?

'Falleris enim, Seiane, si te mansurum in eodem ordine putas, 4
et Liuiam, quae C. Caesari, mox Druso nupta fuerit, ea mente
acturam ut cum equite Romano senescat. ego ut sinam,
credisne passuros qui fratrem eius, qui patrem maioresque
nostros in summis imperiis uidere? uis tu quidem istum intra 5
locum sistere; sed illi magistratus et primores, qui te inuitum
perrumpunt omnibusque de rebus consulunt, excessisse iam
pridem equestre fastigium longeque antisse patris mei amicitias

A.D. 25 non occulti ferunt; perque inuidiam tui me quoque incusant. at 6
enim Augustus filiam suam equiti Romano tradere meditatus
est. mirum hercule si, cum in omnis curas distraheretur
immensumque attolli prouideret quem coniunctione tali super
alios extulisset, C. Proculeium et quosdam in sermonibus habuit
insigni tranquillitate uitae, nullis rei publicae negotiis permixtos! sed si dubitatione Augusti mouemur, quanto ualidius est
quod Marco Agrippae, mox mihi conlocauit! atque ego haec 7
pro amicitia non occultaui; ceterum neque tuis neque Liuiae
destinatis aduersabor. ipse quid intra animum uolutauerim,
quibus adhuc necessitudinibus immiscere te mihi parem,
omittam ad praesens referre; id tantum aperiam: nihil esse tam
excelsum quod non uirtutes istae tuusque in me animus
mereantur; datoque tempore uel in senatu uel in contione non
reticebo.'

Rursum Seianus non iam de matrimonio, sed altius metuens **41**
tacita suspicionum, uulgi rumorem, ingruentem inuidiam de-
precatur; ac ne adsiduos in domum coetus arcendo infringeret
potentiam aut receptando facultatem criminantibus praeberet,
huc flexit ut Tiberium ad uitam procul Roma amoenis locis
degendam impelleret. multa quippe prouidebat: sua in manu 2
aditus litterarumque magna ex parte se arbitrum fore, cum per
milites commearent; mox Caesarem uergente iam senecta
secretoque loci mollitum munia imperii facilius tramissurum; et
minui sibi inuidiam adempta salutantum turba, sublatisque
inanibus ueram potentiam augeri. igitur paulatim negotia 3
urbis, populi adcursus, multitudinem adfluentium increpat,
extollens laudibus quietem et solitudinem, quis abesse taedia et
offensiones ac praecipua rerum maxime agitari.

Ac forte habita per illos dies de Votieno Montano, celebris **42**
ingenii uiro, cognitio cunctantem iam Tiberium perpulit ut
uitandos crederet patrum coetus uocesque, quae plerumque
uerae et graues coram ingerebantur. nam postulato Votieno ob 2

41.1 iam *Muretus*: tam *M*

contumelias in Caesarem dictas, testis Aemilius, e militaribus
uiris, dum studio probandi cuncta refert et, quamquam inter
obstrepentes, magna adseueratione nititur, audiuit Tiberius
probra, quis per occultum lacerabatur, adeoque perculsus est ut
se uel statim uel in cognitione purgaturum clamitaret pre-
cibusque proximorum, adulatione omnium aegre componeret
animum. et Votienus quidem maiestatis poenis adfectus est; 3
Caesar obiectam sibi aduersus reos inclementiam eo peruicacius
amplexus, Aquiliam adulterii delatam cum Vario Ligure,
quamquam Lentulus Gaetulicus consul designatus lege Iulia
damnasset, exilio puniuit Apidiumque Merulam, quod in acta
diui Augusti non iurauerat, albo senatorio erasit.

Auditae dehinc Lacedaemoniorum et Messeniorum lega- **43**
tiones de iure templi Dianae Limnatidis, quod suis a maioribus
suaque in terra dicatum Lacedaemonii firmabant annalium
memoria uatumque carminibus, sed Macedonis Philippi, cum
quo bellassent, armis ademptum ac post C. Caesaris et M.
Antonii sententia redditum. contra Messenii ueterem inter 2
Herculis posteros diuisionem Peloponnesi protulere, suoque regi
Denthaliatem agrum, in quo id delubrum, cessisse; monimenta-
que eius rei sculpta saxis et aere prisco manere. quod si uatum, 3
annalium ad testimonia uocentur, plures sibi ac locupletiores
esse; neque Philippum potentia sed ex uero statuisse: idem regis
Antigoni, idem imperatoris Mummii iudicium; sic Milesios
permisso publice arbitrio, postremo Atidium Geminum praetorem Achaiae decreuisse. ita secundum Messenios datum. et 4
Segestani aedem Veneris montem apud Erycum, uetustate
dilapsam, restaurari postulauere, nota memorantes de origine
eius et laeta Tiberio: suscepit curam libens ut consanguineus.
tunc tractatae Massiliensium preces probatumque P. Rutilii 5
exemplum: namque eum legibus pulsum ciuem sibi Zmyrnaei
addiderant. quo iure Volcacius Moschus exul in Massilienses
receptus bona sua rei publicae eorum ut patriae reliquerat.

43.4 suscepit *M*: suscepitque *Ritter*

A.D. 25 Obiere eo anno uiri nobiles Cn. Lentulus et L. Domitius. **44**
Lentulo super consulatum et triumphalia de Getis gloriae fuerat
bene tolerata paupertas, dein magnae opes innocenter partae et
modeste habitae. Domitium decorauit pater ciuili bello maris 2
potens, donec Antonii partibus, mox Caesaris misceretur. auus
Pharsalica acie pro optumatibus ceciderat. ipse delectus cui
minor Antonia, Octauia genita, in matrimonium daretur, post
exercitu flumen Albim transcendit, longius penetrata Germania
quam quisquam priorum, easque ob res insignia triumphi
adeptus est. obiit et L. Antonius, multa claritudine generis sed 3
improspera: nam patre eius Iullo Antonio ob adulterium Iuliae
morte punito hunc admodum adulescentulum, sororis nepotem,
seposuit Augustus in ciuitatem Massiliensem, ubi specie
studiorum nomen exilii tegeretur. habitus tamen supremis
honor, ossaque tumulo Octauiorum inlata per decretum
senatus.

Isdem consulibus facinus atrox in citeriore Hispania admis- **45**
sum a quodam agresti nationis Termestinae. is praetorem
prouinciae L. Pisonem, pace incuriosum, ex improuiso in itinere
adortus uno uulnere in mortem adfecit; ac pernicitate equi
profugus, postquam saltuosos locos attigerat, dimisso equo per
derupta et auia sequentis frustratus est. neque diu fefellit: nam 2
prenso ductoque per proximos pagos equo, cuius foret cognitum; et repertus cum tormentis edere conscios adigeretur,
uoce magna sermone patrio frustra se interrogari clamitauit:
adsisterent socii ac spectarent; nullam uim tantam doloris fore
ut ueritatem eliceret. idemque cum postero ad quaestionem
retraheretur, eo nisu proripuit se custodibus saxoque caput
adflixit ut statim exanimaretur. sed Piso Termestinorum dolo 3
caesus habetur: quippe pecunias e publico interceptas acrius
quam ut tolerarent barbari cogebat.

45.1 adfecit *M*: adflixit *Hartman* 45.3 quippe *Bezzenberger*: qui *M*

26 Lentulo Gaetulico C. Caluisio consulibus decreta triumphi **46**
insignia Poppaeo Sabino contusis Thraecum gentibus, qui
montium editis inculti atque eo ferocius agitabant. causa motus,
super hominum ingenium, quod pati dilectus et ualidissimum
quemque militiae nostrae dare aspernabantur, ne regibus
quidem parere nisi ex libidine soliti aut, si mitterent auxilia,
suos ductores praeficere nec nisi aduersum accolas belligerare.
ac tum rumor incesserat fore ut disiecti aliisque nationibus 2
permixti diuersas in terras traherentur. sed antequam arma
inciperent, misere legatos amicitiam obsequiumque memoraturos et mansura haec, si nullo nouo onere temptarentur; sin
ut uictis seruitium indiceretur, esse sibi ferrum et iuuentutem et
promptum libertati aut ad mortem animum. simul castella 3
rupibus indita conlatosque illuc parentes et coniuges ostentabant bellumque impeditum, arduum, cruentum minitabantur.

At Sabinus, donec exercitus in unum conduceret, datis **47**
mitibus responsis, postquam Pomponius Labeo e Moesia cum
legione, rex Rhoemetalces cum auxiliis popularium, qui fidem
non mutauerant, uenere, addita praesenti copia ad hostem
pergit, compositum iam per angustias saltuum; quidam audentius apertis in collibus uisebantur, quos dux Romanus acie
suggressus haud aegre pepulit, sanguine barbarorum modico ob
propinqua suffugia. mox castris in loco communitis ualida 2
manu montem occupat angustum et aequali dorso continuum
usque ad proximum castellum, quod magna uis armata aut
incondita tuebatur. simul in ferocissimos, qui ante uallum more
gentis cum carminibus et tripudiis persultabant, mittit delectos
sagittariorum. ii dum eminus grassabantur, crebra et inulta 3
uulnera fecere; propius incedentes eruptione subita turbati sunt
receptique subsidio Sugambrae cohortis, quam Romanus
promptam ad pericula nec minus cantuum et armorum
tumultu trucem haud procul instruxerat.

Translata dehinc castra hostem propter, relictis apud priora **48**

46.1 inculti *Beroaldus*: -u *M*   47.1 postquam *Jac. Gronovius*: quam *M*

A.D. 26 munimenta Thraecibus quos nobis adfuisse memoraui; iisque
permissum uastare, urere, trahere praedas, dum populatio
lucem intra sisteretur noctemque in castris tutam et uigilem
capesserent. id primo seruatum; mox uersi in luxum et raptis
opulenti omittere stationes lasciuia epularum aut somno et uino
procumbere. igitur hostes incuria eorum comperta duo agmina 2
parant, quorum altero populatores inuaderentur, alii castra
Romana adpugnarent, non spe capiendi sed ut clamore, telis
suo quisque periculo intentus sonorem alterius proelii non
acciperet; tenebrae insuper delectae augendam ad formidinem.
sed qui uallum legionum temptabant facile pelluntur; 3
Thraecum auxilia repentino incursu territa, cum pars munitionibus adiacerent, plures extra palarentur, tanto infensius caesi
quanto perfugae et proditores ferre arma ad suum patriaeque
seruitium incusabantur.

Postera die Sabinus exercitum aequo loco ostendit, si barbari **49**
successu noctis alacres proelium auderent. et postquam castello
aut coniunctis tumulis non degrediebantur, obsidium coepit per
praesidia, quae opportune iam muniebat. dein fossam loricam-
que contexens quattuor milia passuum ambitu amplexus est;
tum paulatim, ut aquam pabulumque eriperet, contrahere 2
claustra artaque circumdare; et struebatur agger, unde saxa,
hastae, ignes propinquum iam in hostem iacerentur. sed nihil 3
aeque quam sitis fatigabat, cum ingens multitudo bellatorum,
imbellium uno reliquo fonte uterentur; simulque armenta (ut
mos barbaris) iuxta clausa egestate pabuli exanimari; adiacere
corpora hominum, quos uulnera, quos sitis peremerat; pollui
cuncta sanie, odore, contactu.

Rebusque turbatis malum extremum discordia accessit, his **50**
deditionem, aliis mortem et mutuos inter se ictus parantibus; et
erant qui non inultum exitium sed eruptionem suaderent.
neque ignobiles, quamuis diuersi sententiis, uerum e ducibus 2
Dinis, prouectus senecta et longo usu uim atque clementiam

49.3 simulque *Lipsius*: simul eque *M* 50.2 quamuis *M*: tantum *Madvig*

26 Romanam edoctus, ponenda arma, unum adflictis id remedium disserebat; primusque se cum coniuge et liberis uictori permisit. secuti aetate aut sexu imbecilli et quibus maior uitae quam
gloriae cupido. at iuuentus Tarsam inter et Turesim distra- 3
hebatur: utrique destinatum cum libertate occidere, sed Tarsa properum finem, abrumpendas pariter spes ac metus clamitans dedit exemplum demisso in pectus ferro; nec defuere qui eodem
modo oppeterent. Turesis sua cum manu noctem opperitur, 4
haud nescio duce nostro: igitur firmatae stationes densioribus globis.

Et ingruebat nox nimbo atrox, hostisque clamore turbido, modo per uastum silentium, incertos obsessores effecerat, cum Sabinus circumire, hortari ne ad ambigua sonitus aut simulationem quietis casum insidiantibus aperirent, sed sua quisque
munia seruarent immoti telisque non in falsum iactis. interea 51
barbari cateruis decurrentes nunc in uallum manualia saxa, praeustas sudes, decisa robora iacere, nunc uirgultis et cratibus et corporibus exanimis complere fossas. quidam pontis et scalas ante fabricati inferre propugnaculis eaque prensare, detrahere et aduersum resistentis comminus niti; miles contra deturbare telis, pellere umbonibus, muralia pila, congestas lapidum moles
prouoluere. his partae uictoriae spes et, si cedant, insignitius 2
flagitium, illis extrema iam salus et adsistentes plerisque matres et coniuges earumque lamenta addunt animos. nox aliis in audaciam, aliis ad formidinem opportuna: incerti ictus, uulnera improuisa; suorum atque hostium ignoratio et montis anfractu repercussae uelut a tergo uoces adeo cuncta miscuerant ut quaedam munimenta Romani quasi perrupta omiserint.
neque tamen peruasere hostes nisi admodum pauci; ceteros, 3
deiecto promptissimo quoque aut saucio, adpetente iam luce trusere in summa castelli, ubi tandem coacta deditio. et proxima sponte incolarum recepta; reliquis, quominus ui aut obsidio subigerentur, praematura montis Haemi et saeua hiemps subuenit.

At Romae commota principis domo, ut series futuri in 52

A.D. 26 Agrippinam exitii inciperet, Claudia Pulchra sobrina eius
postulatur accusante Domitio Afro. is recens praetura, modicus
dignationis et quoquo facinore properus clarescere, crimen
impudicitiae, adulterum Furnium, ueneficia in principem et
deuotiones obiectabat. Agrippina semper atrox, tum et periculo 2
propinquae accensa, pergit ad Tiberium ac forte sacrificantem
patri repperit. quo initio inuidiae non eiusdem ait mactare diuo
Augusto uictimas et posteros eius insectari. non in effigies mutas
diuinum spiritum transfusum; se imaginem ueram, caelesti
sanguine ortam; intellegere discrimen, suscipere sordes. frustra
Pulchram praescribi, cui sola exitii causa sit quod Agrippinam
stulte prorsus ad cultum delegerit, oblita Sosiae ob eadem
adflictae. audita haec raram occulti pectoris uocem elicuere, 3
correptamque Graeco uersu admonuit non ideo laedi quia non
regnaret. Pulchra et Furnius damnantur; Afer primoribus 4
oratorum additus, diuulgato ingenio et secuta adseueratione
Caesaris, qua suo iure disertum eum appellauit. mox capessen-
dis accusationibus aut reos tutando prosperiore eloquentiae
quam morum fama fuit, nisi quod aetas extrema multum etiam
eloquentiae dempsit, dum fessa mente retinet silentii
impatientiam.

At Agrippina peruicax irae et morbo corporis implicata, cum **53**
uiseret eam Caesar, profusis diu ac per silentium lacrimis, mox
inuidiam et preces orditur: subueniret solitudini, daret
maritum: habilem adhuc iuuentam sibi, neque aliud probis
quam ex matrimonio solacium; esse in ciuitate *** Germanici
coniugem ac liberos eius recipere dignarentur. sed Caesar, non 2
ignarus quantum ex re publica peteretur, ne tamen offensionis
aut metus manifestus foret, sine responso quamquam instantem
reliquit. (id ego, a scriptoribus annalium non traditum, repperi
in commentariis Agrippinae filiae, quae Neronis principis mater
uitam suam et casus suorum posteris memorauit.)

52.3 correptamque *M*: arreptamque *Woodman* 53.1 *lacuna in M*
53.2 ex re publica *M*: ea re [publica] *Madvig*: ex se [publica] *Wurm*

). 26 Ceterum Seianus maerentem et improuidam altius perculit, **54**
immissis qui per speciem amicitiae monerent paratum ei
uenenum, uitandas soceri epulas. atque illa simulationum
nescia, cum propter discumberet, non uultu aut sermone flecti,
nullos attingere cibos, donec aduertit Tiberius, forte an quia
audiuerat. idque quo acrius experiretur, poma, ut erant
adposita, laudans nurui sua manu tradidit. aucta ex eo suspicio
Agrippinae, et intacta ore seruis tramisit. nec tamen Tiberii 2
uox coram secuta, sed obuersus ad matrem non mirum ait, si
quid seuerius in eam statuisset, a qua ueneficii insimularetur.
inde rumor parari exitium, neque id imperatorem palam
audere, secretum ad perpetrandum quaeri.

Sed Caesar, quo famam auerteret, adesse frequens senatui **55**
legatosque Asiae, ambigentis quanam in ciuitate templum
statueretur, pluris per dies audiuit. undecim urbes certabant,
pari ambitione, uiribus diuersae. neque multum distantia inter
se memorabant de uetustate generis, studio in populum
Romanum per bella Persi et Aristonici aliorumque regum.
uerum Hypaepeni Trallianique Laodicenis ac Magnetibus 2
simul tramissi ut parum ualidi; ne Ilienses quidem, cum
parentem urbis Romae Troiam referrent, nisi antiquitatis gloria
pollebant. paulum addubitatum quod Halicarnasii mille et
ducentos per annos nullo motu terrae nutauisse sedes suas
uiuoque in saxo fundamenta templi adseuerauerant. Perga-
menos (eo ipso nitebantur) aede Augusto ibi sita satis adeptos
creditum; Ephesii Milesiique, hi Apollinis, illi Dianae caerimonia occupauisse ciuitates uisi. ita Sardianos inter Zmyrnaeos- 3
que deliberatum.

Sardiani decretum Etruriae recitauere ut consanguinei: nam
Tyrrhenum Lydumque Atye rege genitos ob multitudinem
diuisisse gentem: Lydum patriis in terris resedisse, Tyrrheno
datum nouas ut conderet sedes; et ducum e nominibus indita
uocabula illis per Asiam, his in Italia; auctamque adhuc

54.1 sua *Rhenanus*: suae *M*

A.D. 26 Lydorum opulentiam missis in Graeciam populis, cui mox a
Pelope nomen. simul litteras imperatorum et icta nobiscum 4
foedera bello Macedonum ubertatemque fluminum suorum,
temperiem caeli ac dites circum terras memorabant.

At Zmyrnaei repetita uetustate (seu Tantalus Ioue ortus illos, **56**
siue Theseus diuina et ipse stirpe, siue una Amazonum
condidisset) transcendere ad ea quis maxime fidebant, in
populum Romanum officiis, missa nauali copia non modo
externa ad bella sed quae in Italia tolerabantur; seque primos
templum urbis Romae statuisse M. Porcio consule, magnis
quidem iam populi Romani rebus, nondum tamen ad summum
elatis, stante adhuc Punica urbe et ualidis per Asiam regibus.
simul L. Sullam testem adferebant, grauissimo in discrimine 2
exercitus ob asperitatem hiemis et penuriam uestis, cum id
Zmyrnam in contionem nuntiatum foret, omnes qui adstabant
detraxisse corpori tegmina nostrisque legionibus misisse. ita 3
rogati sententiam patres Zmyrnaeos praetulere, censuitque
Vibius Marsus ut M. Lepido (cui ea prouincia obuenerat) super
numerum legaretur, qui templi curam susciperet; et quia
Lepidus ipse deligere per modestiam abnuebat, Valerius Naso e
praetoriis sorte missus est.

Inter quae diu meditato prolatoque saepius consilio tandem **57**
Caesar in Campaniam ⟨concessit⟩, specie dedicandi templa
apud Capuam Ioui, apud Nolam Augusto, sed certus procul
urbe degere. (causam abscessus quamquam secutus plurimos
auctorum ad Seiani artes rettuli, quia tamen caede eius patrata
sex postea annos pari secreto coniunxit, plerumque permoueor
num ad ipsum referri uerius sit, saeuitiam ac libidinem, cum
factis promeret, locis occultantem. erant qui crederent in 2
senectute corporis quoque habitum pudori fuisse: quippe illi
praegracilis et incurua proceritas, nudus capillo uertex, ulcerosa
facies ac plerumque medicaminibus interstincta; et Rhodi
secreto uitare coetus, recondere uoluptates insuerat. traditur 3

57.1 ⟨concessit⟩ *Otto*

D. 26 etiam matris impotentia extrusum, quam dominationis sociam
aspernabatur neque depellere poterat, cum dominationem
ipsam donum eius accepisset. nam dubitauerat Augustus Germanicum, sororis nepotem et cunctis laudatum, rei Romanae
imponere; sed precibus uxoris euictus Tiberio Germanicum, sibi
Tiberium adsciuit. idque Augusta exprobrabat, reposcebat.)
profectio arto comitatu fuit: unus senator consulatu functus, **58**
Cocceius Nerua, cui legum peritia; eques Romanus praeter
Seianum ex inlustribus Curtius Atticus; ceteri liberalibus studiis
praediti, ferme Graeci, quorum sermonibus leuaretur. ferebant 2
periti caelestium iis motibus siderum excessisse Roma Tiberium
ut reditus illi negaretur; unde exitii causa multis fuit, properum
finem uitae coniectantibus uulgantibusque: neque enim tam
incredibilem casum prouidebant ut undecim per annos libens
patria careret. mox patuit breue confinium artis et falsi, 3
ueraque quam obscuris tegerentur. nam in urbem non re-
gressurum haud forte dictum; ceterorum nescii egere, cum
propinquo rure aut litore et saepe moenia urbis adsidens
extremam senectam compleuerit. ac forte illis diebus oblatum **59**
Caesari anceps periculum auxit uana rumoris, praebuitque ipsi
materiem cur amicitiae constantiaeque Seiani magis fideret.
uescebantur in uilla, cui uocabulum Speluncae, mare Amun-
clanum inter ⟨et⟩ Fundanos montes, natiuo in specu. eius os
lapsis repente saxis obruit quosdam ministros. hinc metus in 2
omnes et fuga eorum qui conuiuium celebrabant; Seianus genu
utroque et manibus super Caesarem suspensus opposuit sese
incidentibus, atque habitu tali repertus est a militibus qui
subsidio uenerant. maior ex eo et, quamquam exitiosa suaderet,
ut non sui anxius cum fide audiebatur.

Adsimulabatque iudicis partes aduersum Germanici stirpem, 3
subditis qui accusatorum nomina sustinerent maximeque in-
sectarentur Neronem, proximum successioni et, quamquam
modesta iuuenta, plerumque tamen quid in praesentiarum

59.1 ⟨et⟩ *Bezzenberger* 59.2 utroque *Woodman*: uultuque *M*

A.D. 26 conduceret oblitum, dum a libertis et clientibus, apiscendae
potentiae properis, exstimulatur ut erectum et fidentem animi
ostenderet: uelle id populum Romanum, cupere exercitus,
neque ausurum contra Seianum, qui nunc patientiam senis et
segnitiam iuuenis iuxta insultet. haec atque talia audienti nihil 60
quidem prauae cogitationis, sed interdum uoces procedebant
contumaces et inconsultae, quas adpositi custodes exceptas
auctasque cum deferrent neque Neroni defendere daretur,
diuersae insuper sollicitudinum formae oriebantur. nam alius 2
occursum eius uitare, quidam salutatione reddita statim auerti,
plerique inceptum sermonem abrumpere, insistentibus contra
inridentibusque qui Seiano fautores aderant.

Enimuero Tiberius toruus aut falsum renidens uultu: seu
loqueretur seu taceret iuuenis, crimen ex silentio, ex uoce. ne
nox quidem secura, cum uxor uigilias, somnos, suspiria matri
Liuiae atque illa Seiano patefaceret; qui fratrem quoque
Neronis Drusum traxit in partes, spe obiecta principis loci, si
priorem aetate et iam labefactum demouisset. atrox Drusi 3
ingenium super cupidinem potentiae et solita fratribus odia
accendebatur inuidia, quod mater Agrippina promptior Neroni
erat. neque tamen Seianus ita Drusum fouebat ut non in eum
quoque semina futuri exitii meditaretur, gnarus praeferocem et
insidiis magis opportunum.

Fine anni excessere insignes uiri Asinius Agrippa, claris 61
maioribus quam uetustis uitaque non degener, et Q. Haterius,
familia senatoria, eloquentiae quoad uixit celebratae: monimenta ingeni eius haud perinde retinentur. scilicet impetu
magis quam cura uigebat; utque aliorum meditatio et labor in
posterum ualescit, sic Haterii canorum illud et profluens cum
ipso simul exstinctum est.

A.D. 27 M. Licinio L. Calpurnio consulibus ingentium bellorum cladem 62
aequauit malum improuisum; eius initium simul et finis exstitit.
nam coepto apud Fidenam amphitheatro Atilius quidam
libertini generis, quo spectaculum gladiatorum celebraret,

27 neque fundamenta per solidum subdidit neque firmis nexibus
ligneam compagem superstruxit, ut qui non abundantia
pecuniae nec municipali ambitione sed in sordidam mercedem
id negotium quaesiuisset. adfluxere auidi talium, imperitante 2
Tiberio procul uoluptatibus habiti, uirile ac muliebre secus,
omnis aetas, ob propinquitatem loci effusius. unde grauior
pestis fuit, conferta mole, dein conuulsa, dum ruit intus aut in
exteriora effunditur immensamque uim mortalium, spectaculo
intentos aut qui circum adstabant, praeceps trahit atque operit.
et illi quidem, quos principium stragis in mortem adflixerat, ut 3
tali sorte, cruciatum effugere; miserandi magis quos abrupta
parte corporis nondum uita deseruerat, qui per diem uisu, per
noctem ululatibus et gemitu coniuges aut liberos noscebant. iam
ceteri fama exciti, hic fratrem, propinquum ille, alius parentes
lamentari; etiam quorum diuersa de causa amici aut necessarii
aberant, pauere tamen; nequedum comperto quos illa uis
perculisset, latior ex incerto metus. ut coepere dimoueri obruta, **63**
concursus ad exanimos complectentium, osculantium; et saepe
certamen, si confusior facies, sed par forma aut aetas errorem
adgnoscentibus fecerat.

Quinquaginta hominum milia eo casu debilitata uel obtrita
sunt; cautumque in posterum senatus consulto ne quis gladiato-
rium munus ederet, cui minor quadringentorum milium res,
neue amphitheatrum imponeretur nisi solo firmitatis spectatae.
Atilius in exilium actus est. ceterum sub recentem cladem 2
patuere procerum domus, fomenta et medici passim praebiti,
fuitque urbs per illos dies, quamquam maesta facie, ueterum
institutis similis, qui magna post proelia saucios largitione et
cura sustentabant.

Nondum ea clades exoleuerat cum ignis uiolentia urbem **64**
ultra solitum adfecit, deusto monte Caelio; feralemque annum
ferebant et ominibus aduersis susceptum principi consilium
absentiae (qui mos uulgo, fortuita ad culpam trahentes), ni
Caesar obuiam isset tribuendo pecunias ex modo detrimenti.
actaeque ei grates apud senatum ab inlustribus, famaque apud 2

A.D. 27 populum, quia sine ambitione aut proximorum precibus ignotos etiam et ultro accitos munificentia iuuerat. adduntur 3
sententiae ut mons Caelius in posterum Augustus appellaretur,
quando cunctis circum flagrantibus sola Tiberii effigies, sita in
domo Iunii senatoris, inuiolata mansisset: euenisse id olim
Claudiae Quintae, eiusque statuam, uim ignium bis elapsam,
maiores apud aedem matris deum consecrauisse: sanctos ac-
ceptosque numinibus Claudios, et augendam caerimoniam loco
in quo tantum in principem honorem di ostenderint.

Haud fuerit absurdum tradere montem eum antiquitus **65**
Querquetulanum cognomento fuisse, quod talis siluae frequens fecundusque erat, mox Caelium appellitatum a Caele Vibenna, qui dux gentis Etruscae, cum auxilium tulisset, sedem eam acceperat a Tarquinio Prisco, seu quis alius regum dedit (nam scriptores in eo dissentiunt; cetera non ambigua sunt); magnas eas copias per plana etiam ac foro propinqua habitauisse, unde Tuscum uicum e uocabulo aduenarum dictum.

Sed ut studia procerum et largitio principis aduersum **66**
casus solacium tulerant, ita accusatorum maior in dies et
infestior uis sine leuamento grassabatur; corripueratque Varum
Quintilium, diuitem et Caesari propinquum, Domitius Afer,
Claudiae Pulchrae matris eius condemnator, nullo mirante
quod diu egens et parto nuper praemio male usus plura ad
flagitia accingeretur. Publium Dolabellam socium delationis 2
extitisse miraculo erat, quia claris maioribus et Varo conexus
suam ipse nobilitatem, suum sanguinem perditum ibat. restitit
tamen senatus et opperiendum imperatorem censuit, quod
unum urgentium malorum suffugium in tempus erat.

At Caesar dedicatis per Campaniam templis, quamquam **67**
edicto monuisset ne quis quietem eius inrumperet concursusque oppidanorum disposito milite prohiberentur, perosus tamen municipia et colonias omniaque in continenti sita, Capreas se in

65 auxilium tulisset *Lipsius*: auxilium appellatum tauisset *M*: auxilium attulisset *Martin*

. 27 insulam abdidit, trium milium freto ab extremis Surrentini
promunturii diiunctam. solitudinem eius placuisse maxime 2
crediderim, quoniam importuosum circa mare et uix modicis
nauigiis pauca subsidia; neque adpulerit quisquam nisi gnaro
custode. caeli temperies hieme mitis obiectu montis, quo saeua
uentorum arcentur; aestas in fauonium obuersa et aperto
circum pelago peramoena; prospectabatque pulcherrimum
sinum, antequam Vesuuius mons ardescens faciem loci uerteret.
Graecos ea tenuisse Capreasque Telebois habitatas fama tradit;
sed tum Tiberius duodecim uillarum †nominibus et molibus† 3
insederat, quanto intentus olim publicas ad curas, tanto occultior in luxus et malum otium resolutus. manebat quippe suspicionum et credendi temeritas, quam Seianus augere etiam in
urbe suetus acrius turbabat non iam occultis aduersum Agrippinam et Neronem insidiis. quis additus miles nuntios, introitus, 4
aperta, secreta uelut in annales referebat; ultroque struebantur
qui monerent perfugere ad Germaniae exercitus uel celeberrimo fori effigiem diui Augusti amplecti populumque ac senatum auxilio uocare. eaque spreta ab illis, uelut pararent,
obiciebantur.

. 28 Iunio Silano et Silio Nerua consulibus foedum anni principium **68**
incessit tracto in carcerem inlustri equite Romano Titio Sabino
ob amicitiam Germanici: neque enim omiserat coniugem
liberosque eius percolere, sectator domi, comes in publico, post
tot clientes unus eoque apud bonos laudatus et grauis iniquis.
hunc Latinius Latiaris, Porcius Cato, Petilius Rufus, M. Opsius 2
praetura functi adgrediuntur, cupidine consulatus, ad quem
non nisi per Seianum aditus; neque Seiani uoluntas nisi scelere
quaerebatur.

Compositum inter ipsos ut Latiaris, qui modico usu Sabinum
contingebat, strueret dolum, ceteri testes adessent, deinde

67.3 [nominibus et] *Martin*: nomine molibus *or* munitionibus et m. *Watt*: amoenitatibus et m. *Woodman* occultior *M*: occultiores *Weissenborn*

A.D. 28 accusationem inciperent. igitur Latiaris iacere fortuitos primum 3
sermones, mox laudare constantiam, quod non, ut ceteri, florentis domus amicus adflictam deseruisset; simul honora de Germanico Agrippinam miserans disserebat. et postquam Sabinus (ut sunt molles in calamitate mortalium animi) effudit lacrimas, iunxit questus, audentius iam onerat Seianum, saeuitiam, superbiam, spes eius; ne in Tiberium quidem conuicio
abstinet. iique sermones, tamquam uetita miscuissent, speciem 4
artae amicitiae fecere. ac iam ultro Sabinus quaerere Latiarem, uentitare domum, dolores suos quasi ad fidissimum deferre.

Consultant quos memoraui, quonam modo ea plurium **69**
auditu acciperentur: nam loco, in quem coibatur, seruanda solitudinis facies; et si pone fores adsisterent, metus uisus, sonitus aut forte ortae suspicionis erat. tectum inter et laquearia tres senatores haud minus turpi latebra quam detestanda fraude
sese abstrudunt, foraminibus et rimis aurem admouent. interea 2
Latiaris repertum in publico Sabinum, uelut recens cognita narraturus, domum et in cubiculum trahit praeteritaque et instantia, quorum adfatim copia, ac nouos terrores cumulat. eadem ille et diutius, quanto maesta, ubi semel prorupere, difficilius reticentur.

Properata inde accusatio, missisque ad Caesarem litteris 3
ordinem fraudis suumque ipsi dedecus narrauere. non alias magis anxia et pauens ciuitas, ⟨cautissime⟩ agens aduersum proximos: congressus, conloquia, notae ignotaeque aures uitari; etiam muta atque inanima, tectum et parietes circumspectabantur.

Sed Caesar sollemnia incipientis anni kalendis Ianuariis **70**
epistula precatus, uertit in Sabinum, corruptos quosdam libertorum et petitum se arguens, ultionemque haud obscure poscebat. nec mora quin decerneretur; et trahebatur damnatus, quantum obducta ueste et adstrictis faucibus niti poterat,

68.4 fecere *Faernus*: facere *M* 69.1 erat *Rhenanus*: erant *M*
69.3 ⟨cautissime⟩ agens *Martin*: egens *M*: tegens *Lipsius*

). 28 clamitans sic inchoari annum, has Seiano uictimas cadere. quo 2
intendisset oculos, quo uerba acciderent, fuga, uastitas: deseri
itinera, fora. et quidam regrediebantur ostentabantque se
rursum, id ipsum pauentes quod timuissent: quem enim diem 3
uacuum poena, ubi inter sacra et uota, quo tempore uerbis
etiam profanis abstineri mos esset, uincla et laqueus inducantur? non imprudentem Tiberium tantam inuidiam adisse; quaesitum meditatumque, ne quid impedire credatur quominus noui magistratus, quomodo delubra et altaria, sic carcerem recludant.

Secutae insuper litterae grates agentis quod hominem in- 4
fensum rei publicae puniuissent, adiecto trepidam sibi uitam, suspectas inimicorum insidias, nullo nominatim compellato; neque tamen dubitabatur in Neronem et Agrippinam intendi.
(ni mihi destinatum foret suum quaeque in annum referre, aue- **71**
bat animus antire statimque memorare exitus quos Latinius atque Opsius ceterique flagitii eius repertores habuere, non modo postquam C. Caesar rerum potitus est sed incolumi Tiberio, qui scelerum ministros, ut peruerti ab aliis nolebat, ita plerumque satiatus et oblatis in eandem operam recentibus ueteres et praegraues adflixit. uerum has atque alias sontium
poenas in tempore trademus.) tum censuit Asinius Gallus, cuius 2
liberorum Agrippina matertera erat, petendum a principe ut
metus suos senatui fateretur amouerique sineret. nullam aeque 3
Tiberius, ut rebatur, ex uirtutibus suis quam dissimulationem diligebat: eo aegrius accepit recludi quae premeret. sed mitigauit Seianus, non Galli amore uerum ut cunctationes principis opperiretur, gnarus lentum in meditando, ubi prorupisset, tristibus dictis atrocia facta coniungere.

Per idem tempus Iulia mortem obiit, quam neptem Augustus 4
conuictam adulterii damnauerat proieceratque in insulam Trimerum, haud procul Apulis litoribus. illic uiginti annis

70.3 imprudentem *Rhenanus*: prudentem *M* 71.3 opperiretur *Muretus*: aperirentur *M*

A.D. 28 exilium tolerauit Augustae ope sustentata, quae florentes
priuignos cum per occultum subuertisset, misericordiam erga
adflictos palam ostentabat.

Eodem anno Frisii, transrhenanus populus, pacem exuere, **72**
nostra magis auaritia quam obsequii impatientes. tributum iis
Drusus iusserat modicum pro angustia rerum, ut in usus
militares coria boum penderent, non intenta cuiusquam cura,
quae firmitudo, quae mensura, donec Olennius e primipilaribus, regendis Frisiis impositus, terga urorum delegit, quorum
ad formam acciperentur. id, aliis quoque nationibus arduum, 2
apud Germanos difficilius tolerabatur, quis ingentium beluarum feraces saltus, modica domi armenta sunt. ac primo
boues ipsos, mox agros, postremo corpora coniugum aut
liberorum seruitio tradebant. hinc ira et questus et, postquam 3
non subueniebatur, remedium ex bello. rapti qui tributo
aderant milites et patibulo adfixi; Olennius infensos fuga
praeuenit, receptus castello cui nomen Fleuum; et haud
spernenda illic ciuium sociorumque manus litora Oceani
praesidebat.

Quod ubi L. Apronio inferioris Germaniae pro praetore **73**
cognitum, uexilla legionum e superiore prouincia peditumque
et equitum auxiliarium delectos acciuit ac simul utrumque
exercitum Rheno deuectum Frisiis intulit, soluto iam castelli
obsidio et ad sua tutanda degressis rebellibus. igitur proxima
aestuaria aggeribus et pontibus traducendo grauiori agmini
firmat. atque interim repertis uadis alam Canninefatem et quod 2
peditum Germanorum inter nostros merebat circumgredi terga
hostium iubet; qui iam acie compositi pellunt turmas sociales
equitesque legionum subsidio missos. tum tres leues cohortes ac
rursum duae, dein tempore interiecto alarius eques immissus,
satis ualidi, si simul incubuissent; per interuallum aduentantes
neque constantiam addiderant turbatis et pauore fugientium
auferebantur.

72.3 subueniebatur *Rhenanus*: -bat *M* 73.1 castelli *Rhenanus*: -o *M*

28 Cethecio Labeoni legato quintae legionis quod reliquum 3
auxiliorum tradit; atque ille dubia suorum re in anceps tractus
missis nuntiis uim legionum implorabat. prorumpunt quintani
ante alios et acri pugna hoste pulso recipiunt cohortis alasque
fessas uulneribus. neque dux Romanus ultum iit aut corpora
humauit, quamquam multi tribunorum praefectorumque et
insignes centuriones cecidissent. mox compertum a transfugis 4
nongentos Romanorum apud lucum, quem Baduhennae
uocant, pugna in posterum extracta confectos; et aliam quadringentorum manum occupata Cruptorigis quondam stipendiarii uilla, postquam proditio metuebatur, mutuis ictibus
procubuisse.

Clarum inde inter Germanos Frisium nomen, dissimulante **74**
Tiberio damna ne cui bellum permitteret. neque senatus in eo
cura, an imperii extrema dehonestarentur: pauor internus
occupauerat animos, cui remedium adulatione quaerebatur.
ita, quamquam diuersis super rebus consulerentur, aram 2
clementiae, aram amicitiae effigiesque circum Caesaris ac
Seiani censuere; crebrisque precibus efflagitabant, uisendi sui
copiam facerent. non illi tamen in urbem aut propinqua urbi 3
degressi sunt; satis uisum omittere insulam et in proximo
Campaniae aspici. eo uenire patres, eques, magna pars plebis,
anxii erga Seianum, cuius durior congressus atque eo per
ambitum et societate consiliorum parabatur. satis constabat 4
auctam ei adrogantiam foedum illud in propatulo seruitium
spectanti: quippe Romae sueti discursus, et magnitudine urbis
incertum quod quisque ad negotium pergat; ibi campo aut
litore iacentes nullo discrimine noctem ac diem iuxta gratiam
aut fastus ianitorum perpetiebantur, donec id quoque uetitum.
et reuenere in urbem trepidi, quos non sermone, non uisu 5
dignatus erat, quidam male alacres, quibus infaustae amicitiae
grauis exitus imminebat.

73.3 Cethego *Lipsius* 74.3 atque eo *M*: a. [eo] *Doederlein* 74.4 id quoque *Muretus*: idque *M*

A.D. 28 Ceterum Tiberius neptem Agrippinam, Germanico ortam, 75
cum coram Cn. Domitio tradidisset, in urbe celebrari nuptias iussit. in Domitio super uetustatem generis propinquum Caesaribus sanguinem delegerat: nam is auiam Octauiam et per eam Augustum auunculum praeferebat.

COMMENTARY

1–16 The year A.D. 23

Since T. divides his narrative of Tib.'s reign into two halves of three books each, the start of Book 4 is accordingly marked out in various ways as a new beginning (cf. 1.1 *coepit*, *initium et causa*, 6.1 *initium*): see above, p. 14. The narrative of A.D. 23 itself is devoted entirely to home affairs: in this respect it is paralleled only by A.D. 27 in Book 4 and by relatively few other years in *A.* 1–6 as a whole (in general see Ginsburg 53–4, 140–1). This striking divergence from the normal or 'Livian' pattern (above, p. 7; below, p. 143) not only underlines the importance of the year's domestic events but also illustrates the difference between republican historiography and the narrative of Tib.'s reign, on which T. will himself comment later in the book (below, pp. 169–72).

T. divides his account of 23 into four principal sections (1–3, 4–6, 7–12, 13–16), of which the first, significantly recalled at the very end of Book 4 (74–5: above, p. 18), is devoted to the character, achievements and ambitions of the emperor's minister Sejanus.

1–3 Sejanus and a seduction

Though T. begins, as customarily, by using the names of the year's consuls for dating purposes (1.1n.), the earliest events of the year are deferred to the beginning of the second section (4.1n.). This practice, similar to that used in the opening section of the book's final year (68.1–2nn.), has the effect of throwing into relief the present section on Sejanus; and since T. has reserved for this section much information which might otherwise have appeared in Books 1–3 (see e.g. 1.1n. *cuius*), he gives to the emperor's minister a prominence which not only reinforces the bipartite division of the Tiberian hexad but also provides ample and sinister evidence of things to come (see also Ginsburg 24–5). The opening of the section in particular is expressed in powerful and Sallustian language, designed to impose an interpretation of events and individuals on T.'s readers.

1.1 C. Asinio C. Antistio consulibus: the book begins, as do *A.* 2, 5 and 6, with the consular year, expressed by the abl. abs. in T.'s normal way (70% of occasions in *A.* 1–6). Since in the extant books of Livy, all of which deal with republican history, the abl. abs. is used on only about 25% of occasions on which consular reckoning occurs, T.'s preference is significant. While paying lip-service to the republican tradition of consular dating, he employs a construction which logically and syntactically detaches the phrase from the main action of the sentence, thereby underlining the limitation of the consuls' role under the principate and the anachronism of their use for dating purposes (see Ginsburg 11). The point is driven home by the juxtaposed reference to the year of Tib.'s reign (next n.).

C. Asinius Pollio, whose brother was consul in 25 (34.1n.), was son of Asinius Gallus (cos. 8. B.C.: 20.1n.) and grandson of the famous C. Asinius Pollio (cos. 40 B.C.: 34.4nn.); C. Antistius Vetus, whose brother was suffect consul in 28, was son and grandson of the homonymous consuls of 6 and 30 B.C. respectively: the family is praised at Vell. 43.4 (see *AA* 425–6, 428).

nonus Tiberio annus erat: only here does T. use the year of an emperor's reign to express a date (Syme 390 n. 2). As Tib. had succeeded Augustus in August A.D. 14, the ninth year of his reign had already begun in August A.D. 22; but T. heightens the drama of events by deferring his reference to make it coincide with the start of the new (consular) year: see also n. below (*cuius*) and 2.1n. (*una in castra*). For multiple dating used elsewhere to emphasize an important event see esp. Thuc. 2.2.1 (the outbreak of the Peloponnesian War).

compositae 'orderly' or 'peaceful' (*OLD* 8); the word is often contrasted with *turbare* (e.g. Liv. 4.10.6), as here.

rei publicae . . . domus are defining genitives after *annus* (see transl. below) and refer to the public and private aspects of Tib.'s reign: for *domus* used of the extended imperial family see R. P. Saller, *Phoenix* 38 (1984) 345–9.

(**nam . . . ducebat**): the parenthesis illustrates three characteristics of T.'s narrative: (1) the unwarranted attribution of words or thoughts to individuals; (2) the notion of paradox (deaths usually imply mourning); (3) cynicism. The fact that Dio 57.18.6 has a similar observation suggests that both authors are likely to have drawn on the same source and hence that T. has merely sharpened an already hostile tradition. See also 3.2.3 'gnaris omnibus laetam Tiberio Germanici mortem'.

ducere inter ('consider among') is a rare variant for the more usual *ducere pro* or *in*.

cum repente turbare fortuna coepit, saeuire ipse: the indic. is usual in an inverted *cum*-clause which carries the main point of the sentence (*NLS* §237): 'Tib. was in his ninth year of political stability and domestic prosperity when fortune suddenly began to be disruptive and the emperor himself to turn wild/savage' (*turbare* is intrans.: *OLD* 1a, cf. c).

T.'s whole phrase is strikingly modelled on Sallust's description of another famous occasion when Rome's history was thought to have taken a decisive turn for the worse (the destruction of Carthage): *C.* 10.1 'saeuire fortuna ac miscere omnia coepit'. But whereas the deterioration then was caused by the removal of an external fear or *metus hostilis* (Sall. *J.* 41.2: see Earl 13, 41ff.), the deterioration in Tib.'s reign will itself be the cause of domestic fear or *pauor internus* (74.1n.). Note too that T. substitutes *turbare* (a favourite word of his for political confusion) for *miscere*, and pointedly transfers *saeuire* from Sall.'s impersonal *fortuna* to the personal *ipse* (cf. Nero at 15.61.2): hence, while *saeuitia* is one of the standard attributes of tyrants or tyrannical men in Roman oratory and historiography and is often mentioned by T. in connection with Tib. (e.g. 57.1, 1.4.3, 10.7, 53.3, 72.4, 74.2, 3.22.4, 6.6.2, 19.3, 23.2, 51.3, 16.29.2), here there is the additional implication that the emperor is about to take on the characteristics of a perverse and powerful deity.

Although *fortuna* often refers to the unpredictable element in human affairs which was the staple diet of ancient historians (cf. e.g. *H.* 1.4.1, Cic. *De Or.* 2.63, *Fam.* 5.12.4 'fortunaeque uicissitudines' (above, p. 5)), she was also personified and regarded as a goddess in whose honour temples were built (*OCD*). The latter aspect is perhaps more likely to be suggested at dramatic moments such as the present, although we cannot safely infer that T. himself actually believed in her existence (see further 2n. *deum ira*). Note, however, that Sejanus had in his house a statue of Fortuna which turned its back on him just before his fall (Dio 58.7.2–3).

saeuientibus: such men in Book 4 as Visellius Varro (19.1), the younger Vibius Serenus (28.1 'saeuitiae exemplum atrox'), Satrius Secundus and Pinarius Natta (34.1), and the four accusers of Titius Sabinus (68.2).

initium et causa: the same phrase (but in the plur.) is used at significant points in *H.*: 1.51.1 and 2.1.1 (there as object of *fortuna*). The use of two almost synonymous nouns is intended to add emphasis, which here is all the greater since T.'s use of synonyms declines markedly after *A.* 3 (Adams (1) 353).

penes Aelium Seianum: his praenomen was Lucius (Dio 57.19.5). Information on him will be found in *OCD*, Seager, Levick and *AA* 470 (index) and Table XXIII; there is a specialist study by D. Hennig, *L. Aelius Seianus* (1975).

penes, though found in Plaut. and Ter. (only with a pronoun), is non-vulgar, appearing mostly in verse, elevated prose and archaising literature (e.g. Liv. 28.27.11 'causa atque origo omnis furoris penes auctores est').

cohortibus praetoriis praefectum: T. typically avoids the standard *praefectus praetorio*, which he never uses (cf. also 1.7.2, 24.2, *H.* 4.11.3); for this aspect of his style in general see G. 1 342–5 (esp. 344 n. 1); also above, pp. 20–1, 25.

cuius de potentia supra memoraui: at 3.66.3. Sejanus is also described as 'magna apud Tiberium auctoritate' on his appointment as joint praetorian prefect in 14 (1.24.2), and we hear that the senate voted to erect a statue of him in Pompey's theatre in 22 (3.72.3). There are other refs. to him at 1.69.5, 3.16.1, 29.4, 35.2; he is not mentioned in *A.* 2. Because T. divides Tib.'s reign into a better and a worse half, Sejanus, the evil genius of the second half, is given less prominence in *A.* 1–3 than might have been expected (see esp. 2.1n. *una in castra*); clearly, however, his importance is made obvious from the very outset.

potentia is actual power, whether constitutional or not; it is used later of Sejanus at 7.1, 41.2 and 6.8.4, and of his successor as praetorian prefect, Macro, at 6.45.3. 'How strongly Tacitus is drawn to the word needs little documentation' (Syme 413). *supra memoraui* (also at 12.40.2) is a phrase liked by Sallust: one ex. occurs at *C.* 5.7 in the sketch of Catiline on which that of Sejanus is based (below, 3n.).

nunc . . . expediam: 'I will now explain', as *H.* 1.51.1 'nunc initia causasque expediam' (*OLD* 4).

originem, mores: both words refer to standard elements in ancient biographical description: others are *pueritia* or *adulescentia*, *forma*, *ingenium* or *indoles*, and *facta*, each of which (or its near equivalent) occurs in the sketch below. T.'s full-length portrayal of Sejanus not only reflects the importance given to character in historiographical theory (cf. Cic. *De Or.* 2.63: above, p. 2) but is a further indication that Book 4 marks a new beginning (Martin (2) 107): cf. how Sallust's portrayal of Catiline (*C.* 4.5–5.8) and Livy's of Hannibal (21.4.1–10) are placed at the beginning of their respective books.

quo facinore: whereas Cicero used *facinus* predominantly with a pejorative sense, T. follows Sallust in using it both neutrally ('deed') and pejoratively ('crime'). Often the intended meaning can only be inferred from the context, which here suggests 'crime': that is certainly the case at 3.5, where the repetition of the word, answering the question T. asks here, concludes this opening section on Sejanus. Cf. 11.2 (also of Sejanus).

dominationem raptum ierit: *dominatio* = absolute power or 'despotism': see 12.3, 57.3 and 1.1.1 (with G.). The supine in *-um* to express purpose after a verb of motion is rare in Cic. and Caes. but occurs in archaising writers and other historians (*NLS* §152).

1.2 Genitus for the more ordinary *natus* or *ortus* occurs 40 times in T.'s historical works (but only once in the minor works). It is also favoured by Livy and Vell., but avoided by Cic. and Caes. (Adams (2) 125 and n. 25).

Vulsiniis: in Etruria, mod. Bolsena: so 'Seianum Vulsiniensem' at 6.8.3. His date of birth is unknown.

Seio Strabone, equite Romano: L. Seius Strabo is described by Vell. as 'princeps equestris ordinis' (127.3): he was appointed *praefectus Aegypti* in 15, the year after Sejanus had been made praetorian prefect alongside him (1.24.2). See *AA* 300ff. and Table XXIII.

iuuenta is a less common synonym of *iuuentus* but becomes frequent in poetry from Virgil and in prose (esp. historians) from Livy. It is used almost exclusively in the abstract sense, whereas *iuuentus* is also common = *iuuenes*.

C. Caesarem: son of M. Vipsanius Agrippa and Augustus' daughter, Julia. He died in 4 (1.3.3 'mors fato propera uel nouercae Liuiae dolus': see 71.4n.).

non sine rumore: for T.'s attitude to rumours see below, pp. 124, 130, and in general Shatzman. *non sine* is common in all periods and types of language, esp. in Hor. *Odes* and Suet. *Lives* (where it is almost a mannerism); *rumor* + acc. and inf. (*OLD* 3c) recurs at 24.1 and 54.2.

Apicio: M. Gavius Apicius (*OCD*). The surviving cookery book is by a later Apicius.

stuprum is 'illicit sexual intercourse in any form (whether forced or not) or an instance of it' (*OLD* 2a; also Adams (3) 200–1). In T., as in other Latin authors, it is the act of *muliebria pati* (e.g. by Nero), not homosexuality *per se*, which incurs condemnation; to do so for money was regarded as particularly degrading.

ueno dedisse 'had offered for sale'. In the form *ueno* the predicative dative seems confined to T. (also at 13.51.1, 14.15.2); Apuleius has *uenui* thrice. The accus., as in *uenum dare* (sometimes written *uenundare*), is common in historians for the Ciceronian *uendere*: T. has several exx. (e.g. 14.33.2, 16.31.1).

mox 'next' or 'subsequently', picking up *prima iuuenta* above (so too 12.29.1 'prima imperii aetate . . . mox').

deuinxit, adeo ut: sometimes *adeo* qualifies only the preceding word, whether a verb (e.g. 1.3.4 'deuinxerat adeo ut') or an adj. (e.g. 10.1 'ualidum adeo ut', 2.30.1 'uaecordes adeo ut'); sometimes it appears to qualify the whole of a preceding clause (e.g. Cic. *Quint. fr.* 1.2.15 'rem publicam funditus amisimus, adeo ut Cato . . . uix uiuus effugerit'). The present case seems to fall into the latter category. *deuincire* is used by T. only in *A.* and always metaphorically.

obscurum aduersum alios sibi uni incautum intectumque: for the *uariatio* (here chiastic) of prep. ~ dative see *Agr.* 22.4 'comis bonis . . . aduersus malos iniucundus', *H.* 1.35.2 'minitantibus intrepidus, aduersus blandientes incorruptus', both of which also illustrate T.'s fondness for this prep. after adjectives. The form *aduersus* is Ciceronian, that in *-um* archaic and archaising: the predominance of the latter over the former is most marked in *A.* 3–6 (Adams (1) 365). *incautus* + dat. is also at 11.26.2; *uni* = 'alone' (*OLD* 7a), as e.g. 15.1. The metaphorical use of *intectus* is only here in all Latin and seems to derive, appropriately (cf. *uictus est* below), from military combat: it is equivalent to *apertus* (*H.* 2.21.1 'aperti incautique') and the opposite of *tectus* (Cic. *De Or.* 1.32), which is commonly used metaphorically (*OLD* 2b). *intectus* is used literally by T. on several occasions (G. on 2.59.1).

Tib.'s secretiveness, hypocrisy and dissimulation are traits emphasised esp. by Dio (e.g. 57.1.1, 3 'his words indicated the exact opposite of his real purpose') and T. (e.g. 31.2, 60.2, 71.3 'nullam aeque Tiberius, ut rebatur, ex uirtutibus suis quam dissimulationem diligebat', 1.6.1, 11.2, 24.1, 33.2, 3.2.3, 6.1.1, 24.3 'callidum olim et tegendis sceleribus obscurum', 45.3, 50.1 'iam Tiberium corpus, iam uires, nondum dissimulatio deserebat', 51.3 'occultum ac subdolum fingendis uirtutibus', 13.3.2), but also by Suet. (e.g. *Tib.* 24.1, 65.1). See Syme 423, Martin (2) 107–13.

It has generally been thought that T. was led to ascribe these qualities to Tib. because, like other ancient writers, he believed that a man's character was immutable; and since he also believed (so the argument goes) that Tib. had always been as evil as he revealed himself to be in his final years, T. was therefore obliged to account for any contrary evidence (such as that of the years A.D. 14–22, summarised at 6.2–4 below) by saying that Tib. had merely been hiding his vices and feigning virtue. Yet there are objections to this view, and some scholars have argued that T. ascribes duplicity to Tib. because it is a recognised characteristic of the archetypal tyrant (for which see next n. but one and 70.2n.): see briefly above, pp. 28–30; more detail in Woodman (2) 197–201.

T.'s ascription of hypocrisy extends to society as a whole (3.4n. *specie*) and reflects on his function as a historian and on his place in the historiographical tradition, in which earlier examples are Thucydides, whose regular contrasts between allegation (*logos*) and reality (*ergon*) are a feature of his work, and Theopompus, who 'analyses the hidden causes of deeds, the motives of those responsible for them, . . . and reveals all the secrets of *apparent* virtue and *unsuspected* vice' (Dion. Hal. *Ep. Pomp.* 6.7). That T. saw himself as belonging to this tradition is clear from his imitation of Sallust, the 'Roman Thucydides': see above, pp. 5–6 and 13; also below, 32.3 *introspicere*. In general see *RICH* 40–7, 124–8, 167–8, 190 and n. 83.

sollertia = calculated shrewdness. The derivation of the noun from *sollus* (= *totus*) + *ars* (see *OLD* intro. n.) underlines the connection between the two men (next n.).

quippe isdem artibus uictus est: it is typical of the tyrant to eliminate good men and to be surrounded by those like himself (Walker 214): see e.g. Plato, *Rep.* 567B–C, Xen. *Hiero* 5.2, Arist. *Pol.* 1314a4–5; also 7.1n., 11.2n., and W. on Vell. 88.2.

uictus est is more likely to be literal ('was defeated') than metaphorical ('was surpassed'): see Suet. *Tib.* 65.1 'Seianum res nouas molientem . . . astu magis ac dolo . . . subuertit' (and cf. Sall. *J.* 48.1 'se suis artibus temptari animaduortit'). *quippe* often = *nam* (*OLD* 1a, 4b), but the cynicism is typical of T. (cf. 1.58.1): see also 17.3n.

deum ira in rem Romanam: 'A striking and ominous phrase, but no confession of a creed' (Syme 521). As with *fortuna* at 1 above (n.), one should not try to read any deep philosophical or religious meaning into T.'s use of such concepts: they are 'nothing more than devices of style, calculated to enhance his presentation of particular scenes and serving as convenient ways of expressing pathos and indignation' (G. on 1.39.6, where *deum ira* recurs). Cf. also 13.17.1, 14.22.4, 16.16.2 'ira . . . numinum in res Romanas', *H.* 1.3.2, 2.38.2 'eadem illos deum ira, eadem hominum rabies, eaedem scelerum causae in discordiam egere', 4.26.2 'quod in pace fors seu natura, tunc [sc. in bello] fatum et ira dei uocabatur', 84.2. So too in Livy, e.g. 21.25.2 'nec tam ob ueteres in populum Romanum iras quam quod . . . colonias in agrum Gallicum deductas aegre patiebantur', 25.6.6.

The archaising plural *deum*, rare in other prose authors except Livy, is greatly preferred by T. to *deorum*, which he uses only in speeches or virtual speech (Adams (2) 129). *res Romana* is a common equivalent of *res publica* in verse; in prose at e.g. 24.1, 33.2, 1.31.5, Liv. 25.26.11.

cuius pari exitio uiguit ceciditque 'for which his well-being and fall were equally destructive': *exitio* is abl. of attendant circumstances (lit. 'accompanied by whose equal destruction he . . .'; *NLS* §47). *uigere* is similarly contrasted with *occidere* at Cic. *TD* 1.104.

1.3 corpus illi laborum tolerans, animus audax . . . finguntur: this is the closest and most sustained imitation of Sallust in the whole of T. It is worth noting that this passage is peculiarly and exclusively T.'s own, whereas the material on either side (1.1–2 and 2.1) follows very closely the same tradition which appears in Dio 57.19.5–7.

At *C.* 5 Sallust gives a succinct and forceful character sketch of L. Sergius Catilina, whose conspiracy against the state in 63 B.C. was, for Sallust, 'facinus memorabile . . . sceleris atque periculi nouitate' (4.4). In T.'s view Sejanus' *facinus* (1 above) was equally memorable and dangerous to the state: the linguistic imitation of the Sallustian passage is designed to underline the parallelism between the two individuals and events and to suggest that the later period was as intrinsically unstable as the earlier (see Keitel 322–3).

In the following extract from Sallust (5.3–6) exact parallels are indicated by italics, close correspondences by dots:

> *corpus* patiens inediae algoris uigiliae, supra quam cuiquam credibile est. *animus audax* subdolus uarius, cuius rei lubet simulator ac dissimulator; alieni adpetens, *sui* profusus; ardens in cupiditatibus; satis eloquentiae, sapientiae parum. uastus animus immoderata incredibilia nimis alta semper cupiebat. hunc post dominationem L. Sullae *lubido* maxuma inuaserat rei publicae capiundae, neque id quibus modis adsequeretur, dum sibi *regnum pararet*, quicquam pensi habebat.

The parallelism goes beyond the linguistic similarities: the structure of the two passages, inaugurated by the opposition of *corpus* and *animus* (which recurs in the sketch of Sejanus at Vell. 127.3: see W.) and each with a series of antitheses, is also markedly similar. But equally important are the points of difference, which fall into four main categories.

(1) While T.'s *sui obtegens* and *finguntur* are broadly similar to *subdolus* and *dissimulator*, Sall.'s *actual* terms are reserved for Tib. himself, who in these respects is Sejanus' superior (2n. *quippe*): for *subdolus* see 6.51.3 (Tib.'s obituary) and for *dissimulatio* see above, 2n. (*obscurum*); in general Martin (2) 107 and n. 5. (2) Sall.'s antithesis *alieni . . . sui* is transferred from externals (Catiline's handling of money) to T.'s contrast between Sejanus' inner feelings and his behaviour towards others (*sui . . . in alios*, picked up by *palam . . . intus*). (3) Similarly there is in T. an accumulation of contrasting moral qualities expressed by abstract nouns: *adulatio* ~ *superbia*, *pudor* ~ *summa apiscendi libido*, *largitio et luxus* ~ *industria ac uigilantia*. (4) T. is noticeably more compressed than Sall. in that he has only one finite verb in the whole passage (in a subordinate clause).

laborum tolerans: a characteristic of the ideal general, e.g. *Agr.* 18.5, W. on Vell. 79.1 (Agrippa). Sejanus is similarly called 'laboris . . . capacissimum' at Vell. 127.3: see also 39.2n. below. *tolerans* + gen., clearly modelled on Sall.'s *patiens* + gen. above, is used by T. only here and is elsewhere common only in Columella.

audax: a political term: 'in the mouth of upholders of the existing order *audax* carries the connotations of extreme radicalism, irresponsible demagogy, disregard of law, and revolution' (C. Wirszubski, *J.R.S.* 51 (1961) 14). Cicero uses the adj. of Catiline and his supporters, and cf. Titus Vinius at *H.* 1.48.4: '*audax* . . . et, prout animum *intendisset*, prauus aut *industrius*, eadem *ui*' (italics indicate parallels with Sejanus here and at 2.1 below).

obtegens is only here in T. with gen.; he uses the verb of Tib. at 19.2 (n.), 1.76.1 (pres. part. governing an accus.) and 6.51.3 (obituary). See also Cic. *Att.* 1.18.1 'nihil fingam, nihil dissimulem, nihil obtegam'.

criminator is used again in a Sejanus context at 12.4; otherwise it is rare till late Latin. T. uses a whole range of nouns in *-tor* or *-sor* (some of them common, others rare), finding them esp. vivid and expressive (G. on 1.24.2): he is particularly fond of those with discreditable associations (Walker 60). For the typical *uariatio* with the part. *obtegens* cf. 6.38.3 'ostentans et contemptor', 12.4.1 'obtegens . . . prouisor'; the *uariatio* of *sui . . . in alios* is equally typical, e.g. 2.76.3 'sui . . . in Caesares', 14.9.2.

iuxta adulatio et superbia: i.e. servile flattery towards superiors and arrogance towards inferiors (so of Curtius Rufus at 11.21.3 'aduersus superiores tristi adulatione, adrogans minoribus'). Roman writers liked to note the apparently opposite characteristics of a person (see *OLD idem* 10, 13; Hands 313–16): here *iuxta* = 'side by side' or 'alike' (*OLD* 1a, 2) or 'simultaneously' (as if *pariter*).

palam compositus pudor: another correspondence with the sketch of Sejanus in Vell. (127.4 'uultu uitaque tranquillum'), but does *compositus* = 'contrived' or 'composed' (see *OLD*)? The context admits either interpretation, but the latter is perh. preferable since pretence is already implied by *palam* ~ *intus* (seemingly a unique antithesis, although *palam* and *intus* are each contrasted regularly with other adverbs).

summa apiscendi: *summa* is neut. acc. plur. (as 11.26.3 'summa adeptus'), not fem. nom. sing. (as *compositus* might lead one to expect). *apiscor* for *adipiscor* is generally archaic and poetic: T. has it 12 times (all in *A.*) but uses the compound increasingly in the later books. See also below, 3.4n. (*Eudemus*).

saepius industria ac uigilantia: whereas *largitio* and *luxus* generally carry a pejorative connotation, *industria* (e.g. Cic. *Phil.* 13.24, Sall. *J.* 1.3, Liv. 23.14.1, Vell. 43.4) and *uigilantia* (e.g. Cic. *Phil.* 7.20, 8.30, Sall. *C.* 52.29, 54.4, Vell. 79.1) were traditionally predicated of the ideal general or statesman (see also 39.2n.). The qualities are nevertheless capable of misuse, as *haud minus noxiae* (sc. *quam largitio et luxus*) indicates, and it has been argued that their association with republican politicians made them particularly dangerous under the principate (W. on Vell. 88.2).

Note that each pair of nouns is co-ordinated by a different conjunction (*et . . . ac*) without any difference in meaning: such *uariatio* is a conspicuous trait of T.'s work. *modo . . . saepius* illustrates *uariatio* of temporal adverbs, which is common in poetry and in prose from Sallust onwards (e.g. *J.* 45.2 *modo . . . saepe*), although the extra *uariatio* of the comparative *saepius* seems esp. Tacitean (cf. 11.16.2, 14.10.1).

parando regno: dat. of purpse after *finguntur*, as Plaut. *As.* 250 'argento comparando fingere fallaciam'. This use of the dat. gerundive is an archaising feature of which T. is fond (Adams (1) 372–3; see also *NLS* §67 (*Note*) and §207 (4), p. 165).

finguntur underlines, at the end of the account of Sejanus' *indoles*, the fraudulent nature of his apparently good qualities (which probably derive from contemporary propaganda: 39.2n.). At the end of the hexad, however, it is to Tib. himself that T. ascribes the trait of 'pretended virtues' (6.51.3 'occultum ac subdolum fingendis uirtutibus').

2.1 Vim praefecturae: the importance of the post held by Sejanus is clearly shown at 1.7.2, where a prefect of the praetorian guard takes the oath to the new *princeps* after the two consuls but before the senate, soldiers and people. He might also play an important part in securing the succession of a new *princeps*, as did Macro, Sejanus' own successor in the post (6.50.5, Dio 58.28.3–4).

antea qualifies *modicam*.

cohortes: sc. *praetorias*. At this time there were 9 such cohorts (5.3n.), each of 500 men; but hitherto only 3 of them had been stationed in the city, in scattered boarding-house billets (Suet. *Aug.* 49.1, *Tib.* 37.1; Keppie 153–4, Campbell 109–20). Sejanus (below) cleverly applies his arguments both to the 6 cohorts stationed outside the city (*lasciuire . . . subueniri*) and to the 3 within it (*et seuerius . . . inlecebris*).

una in castra conducendo: after the Sallustian insertion of 1.3 above (n.), T. has now reverted to the material which he seems to derive from the same source as Dio (57.19.6). Note, however, that Dio ascribes to A.D. 20 the concentration of the praetorian cohorts into a single camp, an event of which T. has deferred mention until now for dramatic reasons (Syme 286 n. 2): see above, p. 77 and 1.1nn. (*nonus* and *cuius*).

The camp itself was outside the city walls, but built into them, between the Colline and Viminal gates. Note that Latin says *bina castra* but *una* (not *singula*) *castra*. The instrumental use of the abl. gerund (*conducendo*), almost equivalent to a pres. part., is found as early as Terence but is common in both verse and prose only from the Augustan age (*NLS* §205 (d)).

uisu inter se 'by the mutual sight of one another'. The prepositional phrase serves as an adj.: the usage, much favoured by Livy, is here helped by the verbal noun *uisu*.

fiducia ipsis, in ceteros metus: antithesis with chiasmus (i.e. *ab*:*ba* order) and *uariatio* (here of dat. ~ *in* + acc., as 9.2, 12.55.1).

praetendebat: the first of many instances in Book 4 of Sejanus' duplicity, already introduced at 1.2–3 (nn.). The deliberate contrasting of appearance or allegation with reality (which here follows at 2 below: n.) is a fundamental element of T.'s narrative, and he repeatedly uses *praetendo* of a pretext which masks the truth, e.g. 31.4, 2.59.1, 65.4, 3.59.4, 6.18.1, 14.21.1. See further 1.2n. (*obscurum*) above and 3.4n. (*specie*) below.

lasciuire militem diductum 'that discipline suffered when troops were dispersed' (*OLD lasciuio* 3a). The collective sing. *miles* (for *milites*) occurs in prose from Quadrigarius but is common only in Livy, T. and Ammianus; for its use in verse see Austin on *Aen.* 2.20. *diductum* = *qui diductus esset*.

si quid subitum ingruat: after the imperf. tense of the main verb the pres. subj. violates the normal rule of sequence of tenses (for which see *NLS* §§272–83). Such violation is common in Livy but occurs more freely in T. than in any other author (e.g. 7.2, 8.3, 10.3). In many cases the 'violating' subjunctive seems to be used to give a more graphic representation (*repraesentatio*) of the speech from the point of view of the original speaker (*NLS* §284; Handford 156–7). Its effect, accordingly, is not unlike that achieved in Greek by the retention of the indic. of the *or. recta* (instead of the more normal optative) in a clause in *or. obl.* after a historic main verb.

The euphemism of *quid subitum* (also at *G.* 11.1) nicely catches the tone of Sejanus' excuses.

pariter: a remarkable ex. of compression for *si pariter miles subuenisset* and hence also of variation after *si . . . ingruat* above: 'the support would be more effective if the soldiers supported all together'. The pres. infin. instead of the fut. is graphic and avoids the uncommon form with *iri*. For *pariter* see *OLD* 1.

procul urbis inlecebris: *procul*, used + abl. as a preposition, occurs in verse from Ennius but is common in prose only from Livy. Since the word may, but need not, refer to a great distance (*OLD* 2, 1), Sejanus cleverly suggests that the troops now stationed within the city will enjoy a much greater benefit than was in fact the case: the new camp was integral with the city walls (see above). The perilous attractions of city life are a commonplace in classical literature.

2.2 ut perfecta sunt castra '⟨But⟩ after the camp was completed': the adversative asyndeton reveals the reality behind Sejanus' pretexts of 1 above (n.).

inrepere: the historic infin. is used, as often, 'to describe an unfolding scene' (*NLS* §21). T. mostly uses *inrepo* intransitively and metaphorically, of gradual or clandestine insinuation (G. on 1.7.7, 73.1): his only literal use is at 8.1 of poison (analogous to its common use in other authors of the onset of illness). When used + acc., as here, the verb is very rare indeed: it is so used literally first by Phaedrus (*App.* 26.2) and metaphorically by Apuleius (*Met.* 7.1.6 'animum inrepens').

adeundo, appellando: sc. *eos* (= *milites*, understood from *militares* above, where T. has characteristically used an adj. where others would have used *militum*: see G. on 1.3.7). Sejanus' are the standard activities of a general immediately before a battle (e.g. Sall. *C.* 59.5 'circumiens unum quemque nominans appellat'): while he probably did present himself in military terms to his contemporaries (39.2n.), T. ironically hints at the 'battle for the principate' on which he had now embarked (cf. 1.3 'parando regno').

ipse deligere: the pronoun emphasises that Sejanus was thereby exceeding his prerogative; T. much prefers *deligo*, by now an archaism, to the regular *eligo*, which he drops after *A.* 1 (Adams (1) 362).

2.3 neque senatorio ambitu abstinebat . . . ornandi 'nor did he refrain from courting popularity amongst senators by honouring . . .': *senatorio* = *apud senatores*, and the gen. gerund defines *ambitu* (as *H.* 1.19.2). The senators are the second objects of Sejanus' attention after the troops; the third will be the emperor himself (below).

clientes suos honoribus aut prouinciis: *clientes*, normally used of social inferiors, illustrates the paradoxical nature of Tiberian Rome: here they are senators, and their *patronus* merely an *eques* (see R. P. Saller, *Personal patronage under the early empire* (1982) 10, 77–8). Exx. are Iunius Otho, who entered the senate 'Seiani potentia' (3.66.3), and Iunius Blaesus, who as Sejanus' uncle 'atque eo praeualidum' became proconsul of Africa (3.35). See further 34.1, 40.5 and esp. 68.2 (n.).

facili Tiberio atque ita prono ut: T.'s characteristic device of an 'appendix' to the main clause (above, p. 24) is often introduced by an abl. abs., as here, and regularly used for purposes of innuendo. Here the device allows T. to introduce Tib. in a subservient position, while at the same time reserving the climax of the sentence (and of the paragraph) for the result-clause which follows. This syntactical representation of the emperor's paradoxical position is reflected also in T.'s language: *facilis* (*OLD* 9b) and *pronus* (*OLD* 6c) are both used technically of favourable deities, but the latter is also used of humble suppliants (e.g. Juv. 6.49) and thus suggests that the godlike emperor (15.3) is the inferior of his minister. This suggestion has become hard fact by the end of Book 4 (74.2–4nn., cf. also 70.1n.).

socium laborum: Sejanus is similarly called *adiutorem imperii* by Drusus at 7.1 below, *principalium onerum adiutorem* by his contemporary Velleius (127.3), and both 'adviser and assistant' and 'associate in the burdens [sc. of office]' by Dio (57.19.7, 58.4.3). There thus seems little doubt that Tib. regularly referred to Sejanus as his minister and that he probably used the term *adiutor*: if so, T.'s *socium laborum* (already in Cic., e.g. *Balb.* 63) may illustrate his characteristic variation of standard terminology (1.1n. *cohortibus*). The date at which Sejanus began to acquire his 'title' is uncertain. Dio attributes it to 20 after the organisation of the praetorian camp; T. here seems to place it between that moment and the erection of Sejanus' statue in 22 (3.72.3): a point between these two dates therefore seems more likely than 23 itself (as W. on Vell. 127.3).

patres is an archaism for *senatus* (Adams (2) 134–5).

interque principia legionum: after Sejanus' fall Tib. rewarded the Syrian legions 'quod solae nullam Seiani imaginem inter signa coluissent' (Suet. *Tib.* 48.2); for *per theatra* (above) see 1.1n. (*cuius*).

3.1 Ceterum was originally an adverbial accus. ('with regard to the rest') but becomes virtually a conjunction, frequently (from Sallust onwards) with a strong adversative sense ('but', 'but in fact'): see G. on 1.10.1. However, like *sed*, it is also used to mark a resumption (as 12.1) or transition (as 8.2 and perhaps here).

iuuenis filius: Drusus, born 14 or 13 B.C. (3.56.4) and now in his mid-thirties. See Stemma.

nepotes adulti: Nero and Drusus, the two eldest sons of Germanicus (Tib.'s deceased nephew and adopted son), born respectively in A.D. 6 and 7: see further 4.1, 8.3–5, 15.3 and 59.3–60 below. Having both been declared public enemies at Sejanus' earlier instigation, Nero died in 31 (T.'s account, along with almost all Book 5, is lost) and Drusus in 33 (6.23.2). There were also three other male descendants: Germanicus' youngest son, the future emperor Gaius Caligula, born 31 Aug. A.D. 12; and the elder Drusus' twin sons Germanicus and Tiberius Gemellus, born probably in 19 (2.84.1 and G.), the former of whom will die at 15.1 below. See Stemma.

moram . . . adferebant: an expr. found often in Cic. but also elsewhere. *cupitum* (noun), found already in Plaut. *Poen.* 1271 and then in Sall. *H.* 4.47, recurs at 13.13.4.

et quia . . . intutum, dolus . . . poscebat: since Sejanus' intended *scelera* would involve *uis*, and since *uis* embraces such crimes as poisoning (cf. 12.47.1), the contrast is not between *uis* and *dolus* but between *simul corripere* and *interualla scelerum*. The counterpart of *dolus*, and reason for it, is *intutum*: thus the sentence as a whole is virtually chiastic.

corripere = 'destroy', often with the implication of suddenness (*OLD* 4b): see also 19.1n. *intutus* = 'unsafe' is found first in T. (*OLD* 2; G. on 1.38.2).

3.2 placuit tamen occultior uia et a Druso incipere: of these two decisions T. places first that which is more important for the immediate context below (3 *igitur* . . .); the other, which actually explains it, is then co-ordinated with it in apparent defiance of the logical order, instead of being expressed in a subordinate clause (see Austin on *Aen.* 2.353 for this device). Hence *tamen*, initially confusing, contrasts the conventional *dolus* of the previous sentence, anticipated by Sejanus for his *scelera* in general, with the extra subtlety of attacking

Drusus indirectly through his wife: 'But since he decided to begin with Drusus, a still more devious procedure was decided upon.'

The actual making of Sejanus' decision is emphasised by the position of *placuit* and by the change of tense from the earlier imperfects. For the *uariatio* of noun ~ infin. see e.g. 6.32.1; Sörbom 110.

contra tendentis os uerberauerat 'had struck his face as he resisted': *contra tendere* = 'resist', also at 3.10.1, occurs in poetry and from Livy in prose. In Dio 57.22.1 Sejanus is the aggressor, but it is inherently more likely that the son of the *princeps*, esp. as he was 'more than usually quick to anger' (*animo commotior*), should resort to violence. See also 7.1–2 below, and, for another case of Sejanus' revenge, 34.1n.

3.3 igitur is almost always placed first by T. in a sentence but is nearly always placed second by republican authors except Sallust, who uses it in both positions almost equally; Livy prefers it in second place. Here it resumes the main story after the brief parenthesis *nam . . . uerberauerat*: so too at 8.1, 19.2, 24.1, 33.2 and often.

promptissimum uisum: sc. *est*: 'it seemed most practical'. For *promptum est* + inf. see *OLD* 3.

Liuiam: so she is called by T. (ten times) and on inscriptions, but Livilla by Suet. and Dio (see *AA* 170 n. 13): in our commentary she is therefore referred to as Livi(ll)a. She was sister of Germanicus and daughter of Drusus (Tib.'s brother), and thus a first cousin of her husband Drusus (Tib.'s son). See Stemma.

conuertere 'to resort to a specified source of help' (*OLD* 6c, intrans.), as 12.18.1 'ad Eunonem conuertit'.

ut 'as if' (so too 17.3, 46.2 etc.).

adulterio is probably abl. instr., as 1.2.1; conceivably dat. (= *in* or *ad* + accus.), but parallels are lacking.

postquam . . . potitus est 'after he had mastered his first outrage': *potiri* + gen. is mostly archaic (and in the archaising Sallust) except in the phrase *rerum potiri* ('to gain political power', as 71.1), on which T.'s unusual expression seems to be based. *flagitium* is often used of sexual misconduct (*OLD* 4c).

neque femina amissa pudicitia alia abnuerit: the potential perf. subjunc. is commonly used with no observable distinction from the pres. to refer to the present or future (5.4n. *persequi*); but it is also used to refer to the past and to express what was likely to have been the case at the time (as at 67.2): this latter is a form of *repraesentatio* (cf. 2.1n. *si quid*) in narrative (*NLS* §120). We regard *abnuerit* as belonging to the second of these categories, a view which is perhaps supported by the historic tenses *potitus est* and *impulit* on either side of it.

At this point our interpretations diverge. (1) RHM believes that *femina* = '*a* woman': the statement, though clearly intended to be applied to Livi(ll)a, is expressed as a generalisation. Hence: 'and after losing her virtue a woman was not likely to reject other things'. (2) AJW does not believe that T. could have written so counter-factual a generalisation as the statement that a woman, once seduced, was unlikely to reject 'other things', esp. when the *alia* in question include *necem mariti*. Hence *femina* = '*the* woman', referring specifically to Livi(ll)a (as to Agrippina at 12.42.2) and perhaps representing Sejanus' contemptuous view of her. This is therefore one of the occasional cases where *femina* takes its meaning from its context and is used 'to designate an upper-class woman of ill-repute' (J. N. Adams, 'Latin words for "woman" and "wife"', *Glotta* 50 (1972) 236–7 and n. 36).

Either way, T. here alludes to Lucretia's utterance after her rape by Tarquin (Liv. 1.58.7 'quid enim salui est mulieri amissa pudicitia?') in order to point the contrast between then and now: Lucretia saw her rape as a reason for suicide and as an outrage demanding vengeance (which her family promptly exacts by abolishing the monarchy and establishing the republic); Livi(ll)a hopes to capitalise on her adultery to get rid of her husband and establish herself as regent alongside her seducer. The clear echo of Livy (*amissa pudicitia* occurs nowhere else in Latin) illustrates the inversion of the moral order (below, 4n.).

ad coniugii spem . . . necem mariti: the first two phrases are arranged chiastically (*abba*), the second two in parallel (*baba*), which means that the first and third are also chiastic. *consortium regni* is apparently compressed for *spem consortii regni* (cf. 51.2). Note that adultery and poisoning (the method of Drusus' death at 8.1 below) were often associated with each other (3.22.1 'adulteria, uenena', Sen. *Contr.* 6.6, 7.3.6, [Quint.] *Decl.* 319, 354, Quint. 5.11.39 'Catonis iudicio . . . qui nullam adulteram non eandem esse ueneficam dixit').

3.4 auunculus 'great uncle' (as 75 and often: *OLD* 2): her mother

(Antonia *minor*) was the daughter of Augustus' sister Octavia. See Stemma. This tricolon (*auunculus*, *socer*, *liberi*) and the following (*seque . . . posteros*) form an ironic counterpart to the preceding one.

ex Druso liberi: in addition to the twin boys (above, 1n.) there was an older girl, Julia.

seque ac maiores: *-que ac* ('both . . . and'), less common than *-que et* (8.4n.), occurs in verse from Virgil and in prose from Livy: in most cases *-que* is appended to a personal pronoun, as here.

municipali adultero: both words are pejorative: in Roman political invective 'criticisms of social background are a stock theme' and 'charges [of immorality] are conventional' [R. G. M. Nisbet, Cic. *Pis.*, App. 6, pp. 194–5). For *municipalis* see e.g. 62.1, Juv. 8.237 with Courtney's n.; for *adulter*, 13.42.3, Cic. *Pis.* fr. 18 (Nisbet, p. 3), *Cat.* 2.23, Catull. 57.8.

ut pro honestis . . . incerta exspectaret: now, towards the end of the opening section of Book 4, T. gives expression to one of his regular themes, the reversal of moral values (see Walker 241 and n. 3, with numerous other exx.), thus setting the scene for the narrative which follows. Livi(ll)a's conduct was in fact all the more astonishing because she was already married to the heir presumptive. For similar contrasts elsewhere see e.g. 1.2.1, Sall. *C.* 17.6 'incerta pro certis, bellum quam pacem malebant', Vell. 60.2 with W.

sumitur: *adsumo* is a more normal verb for taking into one's confidence (as 13.12.1; *OLD* 8a), but T. regularly prefers simple forms to compound (G. on 1.57.4), as do poets and other writers of stylised prose. Conversely, and typically, T.'s search for *uariatio* leads him to prefer compound to simple when the latter is the more normal (Adams (1) 362–4 (esp. 362 n. 6)). See also above, 1.3n. (*summa apiscendi*).

Eudemus was, as his name suggests, a Greek, like most doctors in the ancient world, and probably a freedman: see in general J. Scarborough, *Roman medicine* (1969) 111. A comparable story is told of Claudius' doctor, Xenophon, said to have murdered the emperor on the instructions of his wife Agrippina (12.67.2). See also Mart. 6.31, [Quint.] *Decl.* 321.

specie artis: T. 'presents Roman society as permeated by lies, living on a basis of elaborate pretences . . . But it is in the political world and at the imperial court that they are most pervasive. It is here that . . . such nouns as *species*, *facies* (in the sense of "false show"), *imago*, *simulatio* are most frequent' (Walker 241 with many exx. in n. 2). See also above, 2.1n. (*praetendebat*) and in general Martin (2) 284 (index *species*).

frequens secretis: the noun is probably dat., and the adj. = 'having regular access to' (cf. *H.* 4.69.3 'frequens contionibus'), on the analogy of its use with *adesse* (55.1 'Caesar . . . adesse frequens senatui').

3.5 pellit domo: a blunt alternative for 'divorce' (*repudiare*): perhaps compare Ov. *Her.* 17.230 'pulsa est Aesonia num minus illa domo?'. The date of Sejanus' action (note again the initial position of the verb) is unknown, but *prolationes* (below) suggests an interval of at least some months between the divorce and Drusus' death.

tres liberos: two sons and a daughter, the latter still a child (*AA* Table xxiii). All three were killed in the aftermath of Sejanus' fall in 31 (5.9.1–2).

ne paelici suspectaretur 'to prevent his mistress from suspecting him' (of duplicity, cf. *ut amore incensus* at 3 above). T. is esp. fond of *suspectare* in this sense; the passive form is particularly rare, being used first here and then in Apuleius (*OLD* 2a). *paelici* is either dat. of agent, which T. employs 'frequently and sometimes audaciously, ignoring restrictions once recognised' (G. on 2.50.3), or dat. of person concerned, as in *alicui suspectus*. The application of the noun to the emperor's daughter-in-law is esp. pejorative.

facinoris: i.e. the murder of Drusus, the *facinus* introduced at 1.1 (n.).

4–6 Senatorial business and the state of the empire

Though the senate's honouring of the young Drusus has dramatic relevance (4.1n.), most of this section consists of a survey which T. introduces by way of reference to a military survey which the emperor himself delivered to the senate in 23 (4.3, cf. a similar device at 3.25.2: 'ea res admonet ut de principiis iuris et quibus modis ad hanc . . . uarietatem legum peruentum sit, altius disseram'). T.'s survey takes the form of a double digression (cf. Vell. 1.14–18), divided into military and political matters (5 and 6): the former is explained as providing a contrast with the military situation of T.'s own day (4.3n.), the latter a contrast with the future deterioration of Tib.'s reign (6.1). Yet since Tib.'s adherence to Augustus' foreign policy (32.2n.) had ensured that the empire had hardly changed since the latter's death, it would have been open to T. to expatiate on the military circumstances of the empire at the start of his narrative of Tib.'s reign, taking as his cue the *libellus* which Augustus had left on his death and which revealed 'quantum ciuium sociorumque in armis, quot classes, regna, prouinciae' (1.11.4). Such a procedure would have provided an almost identical opportunity for a comparison with T.'s own day. That he has chosen instead to place the military survey here, therefore, suggests that his primary (but unexpressed) motivation in ch. 5 was the same as in ch. 6, namely to emphasise still further that A.D. 23 marked a new beginning (cf. also p. 123 below and 57.1n. *quamquam secutus*).

Historians from Herodotus onwards, following Homeric practice, had used catalogues of forces to emphasise the significance of forthcoming events; and surveys comparable to T.'s are used by Sallust to introduce the Catilinarian conspiracy (*C.* 5.9 'instituta maiorum domi militiaeque, quo modo rem publicam habuerint . . . disserere'), by Velleius to introduce the start of the reigns of Augustus (89.2–6) and Tiberius (126.1–5, which is esp. worth comparing with T.'s survey here), by T. himself at the start of *H.* (1.8–11, though the circumstances there are rather different: above, pp. 11–12), and by Dio to introduce the reign of each new emperor (F. G. B. Millar, *A study of Cassius Dio* (1964) 10). Thus, just as T.'s later digression at 32–3 is used to separate one section of Book 4 from another, so here his double survey reinforces the division of the Tiberian hexad into two halves (above, p. 14). In addition, it provides a dramatic pause between Sejanus' plotting in ch. 3 and the murder of Tib.'s son at 7–8.1 – as if translating into narrative terms the *prolationes* of 3.5 above.

4.1 Interim anni principio: though Book 4 began with a statement of the consular year (1.1n.), T.'s narrative has hitherto been devoted to material which both preceded (2.1–3) and, to judge from *Interim*, followed the start of A.D. 23 (by implication, Sejanus' divorce at 3.5). For *anni principio* and variants elsewhere see e.g. 68.1, 3.31.2, 13.34.2.

Drusus: above, 3.1n.; he is distinguished from his namesake, Tib.'s son, by *ex Germanici liberis*. Ginsburg has observed that after Germanicus' death in 19 it is often 'the family and friends of Germanicus which occupy the historian at the year's inception' (26): cf. 17.1, 68.1, 5.1.1, 6.15.1; also below, next n.

quaeque fratri eius Neroni decreuerat senatus repetita: sc. *sunt*. The cross-reference is to 3.29.1. Nero, born in 6, was the natural successor to Tib. after the death of the latter's son later in 23 (8–11 below). Ginsburg notes the dramatic irony in T.'s juxtaposition of the reference to honours with Sejanus' plotting above: 'Drusus, together with his brother Nero, will be the next victims of Sejanus. In advancing Germanicus' children, the senate was merely fattening fresh lambs for the slaughter' (25).

From where did T. derive information about senatorial matters such as this? An official record of senatorial business was kept in the *acta senatus* (5.4.1: see *OCD*). Though the *acta* seem not to have been published since Augustus' day (Suet. *Aug.* 36.1), it is generally assumed that senators themselves had access to them – an assumption which seems to be supported by T.'s single reference to his consultation of them (15.74.3 'reperio in commentariis senatus'). The precision with which T. provides names and motions in senatorial debates is regarded by many scholars (most recently Talbert 326–34 and Syme, *J.R.S.* 72 (1982) 68–82 = *RP* IV 199–222) as proof of his direct dependence on the *acta*.

Information was also available in the *acta diurna*, a 'daily gazette' to which T. refers under A.D. 20 (3.3.2 'non diurna actorum scriptura reperio'). The gazette was widely disseminated (16.22.3 'diurna populi Romani per prouincias, per exercitus curatius leguntur'), and, if identical with the *publica acta* mentioned under 49, easily accessible (12.24.2 'facile cognitu et publicis actis perscriptum'). It is known to have contained senatorial business, and Pliny in a letter to T. takes it for granted that the latter will have read its current issues (*Ep.* 7.33.3, cf. 5.13.8).

Any speculation about T.'s use of such sources, however, must be placed in the context of ancient historians' well known indifference to archival material (see above, pp. 26–7).

patria beneuolentia: abl. of description (*NLS* §83); Drusus had 'inherited' Germanicus' children on the latter's death (8.4 below).

beneuolentia, though rare in Livy, is common in Cicero and thus its occurrence in T. always deserves attention: here it may be intended to give verisimilitude to the emperor's reported speech (see 8.2–3nn).

foret is equivalent to *esset*. Forms of *forem* are twice as popular as those of *essem* in *A.* 1–6 and 11–12 but (with one exception) are dropped entirely in favour of the latter in 13–16. This is one of the most striking instances of T.'s alleged normalisation of style in the later books (Goodyear 22, 24 with refs.).

quamquam arduum sit . . . esse: T.'s *sententia* is integrated into the narrative in a way which is regular in *A.* but less common in his earlier work, where *sententiae* tend to be free-standing and/or used to conclude a passage: see Martin (2) 219–20, Goodyear 26–7.

quamquam + subjunc., where Cic. would have used indic., is quite common in Livy and commoner in T. than the indic. (8:1 in Book 4). Whereas most first-century A.D. writers prefer *quamuis* to *quamquam*, T. generally prefers the latter; only in *A.* 11–16 does he use the two indifferently (Adams (1) 362). Again, while *arduum est* + inf. is common (esp. in Sall., Livy and post-Augustan prose), its use + accus. and inf. seems unexampled elsewhere. *eodem* normally = 'to the same place', but when combined with the partitive gen. *loci* (or *locorum*) it = 'in the same place' and is so used by other authors too. T. seems to have in mind the image of a precariously high and narrow ledge (*arduum, eodem loci*) where a false move by one party would normally endanger the rest.

4.2 saepe simulatum . . . consilium: in fact only twice on T.'s own evidence (1.47.3, 3.47.2–3), although Suet. speaks of it as a frequently declared intention (*Tib.* 38). *refertur* = 'was revived' (as 29.3, 1.26.2); for *simulatum* see 1.2n. (*obscurum*).

multitudinem ueteranorum praetexebat imperator: 'He means that his presence was required to induce the veterans to be content with their reward on dismissal' (F.). This was a long-standing problem: see 1.36.3, 78.3; Campbell 172–3. *imperator* = 'as commander of the armed forces' (cf. 1.7.5).

dilectibus supplendos: the context of a provincial tour suggests that Tib. proposed to rely more on provincial recruits for the legions than had hitherto been customary; and the contrast with *uoluntarium militem* below suggests that *dilectus* implies conscription. For both points see Brunt (1) 241, 414, 636.

modestia 'respect for order, discipline' (*OLD* 2). For the pres. subjunc. *suppeditet* and *sumant* see 2.1n. (*si quid*).

4.3 tutarentur: 'By the late republic the frequentative [for *tueor*] was no longer in use . . . Before T. the only writers of prose who use the frequentative with any freedom are Sallust and, in particular, Livy': Adams (1) 369, who notes that its use almost disappears in *A.* 11–16 (see above, 1n. *foret*). For the typical *uariatio* of noun ~ indir. qu. after *percensuit* see e.g. 31.2, 33.2, 37.2, 58.3; Sörbom 116.

quod mihi quoque exsequendum reor, quae: two interpretations are possible. (1) *quod* is the subject of *exsequendum* (gerundive, sc. *esse*) and serves to introduce the indir. qu. (cf. 40.1 *in eo . . . quid . . . putent*, 74.1): 'Which I think I too should go through, ⟨namely⟩ what . . .'. (2) *quod* is adverbial accus. (cf. Cic. *Phil.* 2.21, Gell. 9.3.5) and *exsequendum* is an impersonal gerundive (again sc. *esse*) with the three indir. questions as its objects: 'In view of which I think I too should go through what . . .' For T.'s primary motivation in writing the survey see above, p. 96; also next n.

reor is elevated and poetic (Cic. *De Or.* 3.153) and in its non-defective forms is preferred by T. to *puto* (Adams (2) 136).

quae tunc Romana copia in armis: *tunc* is used, as often by Livy (Steele 36–8), to contrast present and past conditions (next n.). *copia* (sing.) = 'forces' is uncommon but liked by T. (e.g. 47.1, 56.1; G. on 2.52.2). For *socii reges* see 5.2nn.

T.'s survey begins with the two fleets and then passes to the frontier provinces, starting with Germany and moving in a generally anticlockwise direction until he returns to Rome and its troops (5.3), after which a mention of the auxiliary forces is appended (5.4). The principal emphasis is on the perimeters of the empire, as *angustius* (below) confirms.

angustius imperitatum: sc. *quam nunc* (last n.): T.'s stated (but secondary: above, p. 96) reason for the excursus is to illustrate the expansion of the empire after Tib. and esp. by Trajan (98–117), who is, however, nowhere mentioned in *A.* Britain had become a province in 43, Thrace in 46, Dacia and Arabia Petraea in 106, Armenia in 114; the annexation of Parthia in 116, however, still lay in the future (5.2n.)

imperito (intrans.) is preferred by T. in narrative to *impero* (which he prefers in speeches in *A.*: Adams (2) 135): it is used by historians and other writers of colourful prose from Sall. *J.* onwards and 'retains an archaic and grandiloquent tone' (G. on 1.64.4); the impersonal passive occurs only here in T. and is rare elsewhere.

5.1 utroque mari duae classes 'two fleets, ⟨one⟩ in each sea', i.e. the Tuscan and the Adriatic; the omission of a preposition (here *in*) is typical of T. (again e.g. 27.1 'illo mari'). For the fleets see Starr 13–24.

Misenum apud et Rauennam: in Book 4 a preposition again stands after the first of two co-ordinated nouns at 50.3, 55.3, 59.1 and 69.1; a prep. is placed after a single noun at *Rhenum iuxta* below and 48.1 (twice); a prep. stands between a noun and its dependent genitive at 2 below (*initio ab Syriae*) and 16.4; it stands after two co-ordinated nouns at 8.5 and 55.2. 'Since other prose-writers use anastrophe rather restrictedly, while T., in the *Annals* at least, uses it both often and freely, it must count as a very distinctive feature of his style' (G. on 1.60.3; also on 2.41.1). See also 43.4n. (*Erycum*).

rostratae naues: i.e. warships (*OLD rostratus* 2a).

praesidebant + acc., as 72.3 etc., is a usage in which T. follows Sallust.

Actiaca uictoria: Octavian's victory over Mark Antony off Actium in 31 B.C. concluded the civil war and left him sole ruler of the Roman world.

ualido cum remige: collective singular (mostly poetical and in post-Augustan prose: *OLD* b); *ualido* thus applies to the total unit. Forum Iulii is mod. Fréjus, close to Cannes on the south coast of France.

sed praecipuum robur . . . octo legiones erant: in contrast to T.'s own day, when there were only four. For the strategy (*commune . . . subsidium*) see Luttwak 46–9 and 85 (Table 2.1).

Hispaniae recens perdomitae tribus habebantur: with *tribus* sc. *legionibus*: the case is probably dat. (of agent), as 12.54.2 'cui pars prouinciae habebatur' (see 3.5n. *ne paelici*); but when a (pro)noun is plur., the possibility of (an extended use of the instrumental) abl. cannot be excluded.

Hispaniae is plur. because there were three Spanish provinces (Tarraconensis, Lusitania, Baetica): there were normally three legions in the first of them, but by the end of Nero's reign only one legion (VII Gemina) was left. Though A.D. 23 was more than 40 years since Agrippa's final victory there in 19 B.C., the preceding two centuries of struggle must have made this seem to contemporaries a very short period indeed – which *recens perdomitae* accurately reflects. Cf. Velleius' remarks on the subject at 90.1–4, publ. seven years later in 30; also below, 45.1n.

The adverbial use of *recens* (*OLD recens*[2]) 'enjoys particular favour with historians. T. is predictably partial to it' (G. on 2.21.1).

5.2 acceperat: in 25 B.C. (Dio 53.26.2): see Luttwak 30. For King Juba II see *OCD* 2.

cetera Africae: 'the rest of Africa'; the main verb, shared with the intervening places, is *coercita* below. This use of the genit. after a neuter (substantival) adj., rare in Cicero and Caesar, is found in verse and historical prose and is used by T. very freely indeed: e.g. below 4 *idonea prouinciarum*, 24.2 *locorumque opportuna*, 74.3 *in proximo Campaniae*. 'The genit. is formally partitive, but it is not always easy to decide whether the partitive sense is really present, or whether the two words form a unit which would more normally be expressed by a noun and adjective in agreement' (Austin on *Aen.* 2.332; also on 1.422). In *A.* 4 compare e.g. 74.1 *extrema imperii* ('distant parts of the empire') with 41.1 *tacita suspicionum* ('unspoken suspicions') respectively.

T.'s reference is to the two provinces of Africa proconsularis and Cyrenaica, for which one legion (III Augusta) normally sufficed; but a second (IX Hispana) arrived from Pannonia during the war against Tacfarinas (23.2): it had passed through Rome in 20 (3.9.1). The two Egyptian legions (below) were III Cyrenaica and XXII Deiotariana.

quantum ingenti terrarum sinu ambitur: T.'s precise meaning is difficult to determine. It seems perverse not to interpret *ingenti . . . sinu* as referring to the arc between southern Syria and the (northern) Euphrates which T. has just described (*dehinc initio ab . . . usque ad*), even though its extent (cf. *ingenti*) is very considerably less than that of Africa and Egypt together, which T. has just mentioned. It follows that the *ingens sinus* is coextensive with the area expressed by *quantum . . . ambitur*, and hence that *ambiri* + abl. does not here have its normal meaning of 'be surrounded by' (*OLD* 9a) but the far less usual sense of 'be included within' (*OLD* 10). Hence *terrarum* can be taken equally with *quantum* (which seems to require such qualification) as well as *sinu*. Thus T. means: 'all the land included in the vast sweep of territory between the tip of Syria and the R. Euphrates'. His point is that this huge expanse had only 4 legions in 23 compared with 8 in his own day, a view which *coercita* ('controlled') seems to support.

ingens is much favoured as an elevated synonym of *magnus* by Sallust, Virgil, Livy and T., though it also occurs regularly in some lower genres too.

Hibero Albanoque et aliis regibus: the kingdoms of the first two lay to the W of the Caspian Sea and N of Armenia. Contact with the kings of the Albanians and Iberians began with Pompey, and they are mentioned as seeking Roman friendship in the time of Augustus (*RG* 31.2). From 6.33 (A.D. 35) it is clear that the Iberians could invade Armenia from the north in support of the Romans, and, by control of the Darial Pass (a key mountain route through the Caucasus), could oversee passage south. Their mention here has a particular relevance to the time at which T. was writing *A.* 4 (see further next n.). In the summer of 114, at a meeting at Elegeia in Armenia, Trajan 'apparently installed a new king over Albania and received formal submission both from the Iberians and from the Sarmatian peoples beyond the Caucasus' (A. B. Bosworth, 'Arrian and the Alani', *H.S.C.P.* 81 (1977) 227 with n. 41).

The *alii reges* are likely to be those of minor kingdoms (as indeed *magnitudine* implies), esp. in the Caucasian area; but they will almost certainly include the king of Osroene, Abgar VII, whose guest Trajan was during the winter of 114/15. Other kingdoms mentioned by our late sources (e.g. Festus, *Breu.* 20.2) include those of the Bosphorus and Colchis. See further Magie I 607, II 1465 n. 32.

qui magnitudine nostra proteguntur aduersum externa imperia: a half-truth: as a Roman author T. naturally stresses the protective role of the *imperium Romanum*, but such kings also protected the Roman empire against external threats (see last n.; Luttwak *passim*; D. C. Braund, *Rome and the friendly king* (1984) 91–103).

T.'s reference is primarily to Rome's long-standing enemy, Parthia, for whom *externum imperium* is conventional 'code' (2.56.1; W. on Vell. 101.2). Since the historic present is inappropriate in a survey, esp. one designed to compare the past with the present (4.3nn.), *proteguntur* must be a genuine present tense and the clause must refer to successive kings 'who have been and still are protected' at the time of writing. Hence the passage seems to pre-date A.D. 116, when Parthia's power was eclipsed by Trajan's conquest of the country.

For a century the most important buffer state between Parthia and Rome was Armenia, as T. had indicated at 2.56.1. His failure to mention Armenia by name here may therefore seem surprising, but Syme is probably right to suggest that our passage was written after the annexation of Armenia as a province (*RP* III 1039–40, IV 203–4 (=*J.R.S.* 72 (1982) 70–1)). And since the annexation took place in 114, at the same meeting at Elegeia as mentioned above (last n.; also Magie I 607–8, II 1465–6 n. 33), the passage itself can be dated still more precisely to 115.[1]

5.3 Thraeciam: T. refers to the settlement of 19 (2.67.2): see Magie I 513.

Pannonia . . . Moesia . . . Delmatiam: their respective legions were: VIII Augusta and XV Apollinaris; IV Scythica and V Macedonica; VII and XI (each later called Claudia pia fidelis from 42 onwards). See Wilkes 93–5 and 451. The move from Pannonia to Moesia disrupts T.'s anti-clockwise arrangement; perhaps he regarded the whole of the eastern Danube as a single region, 'Illyricum' (see Wilkes 161).

locatis: VII and XI seem to have been based at Tilurium and Burnum respectively, both of which lay on a network of road communications (Wilkes 97–8).

a tergo illis: sc. *erant*; or possibly supply *accirentur* from below.

si . . . Italia posceret: apart from Rome itself (below), Italy was traditionally ungarrisoned: it was from Dalmatia that Otho had to summon help when he needed it in 69 (*H.* 2.11.1).

tres urbanae . . . cohortes: see Keppie 154, 188–9.

nouem praetoriae: Sejanus later raised their number to 12, Vitellius in 69 to 16 (also doubling their complement): Keppie 187–8

[1] It follows that T. wrote the present passage at least a year later than 2.56.1, which is not inherently improbable. Since Parthia is also described as a great power '*nunc*' at 2.60.4, that passage too is likely to have been written before 116 but (in view of its proximity to 2.56.1) not later than 114. Further, since it is unlikely that in the notorious statement at 2.61.2 ('uentum ad Elephantinen ac Syenen, claustra olim Romani imperii, quod nunc rubrum ad mare patescit') *nunc* refers to a different period from *nunc* at 2.60.4, it seems to follow that *rubrum mare* there is our Red Sea and not, as Syme has argued (768–70, *RP* III 1037–40), the Persian Gulf, which did not become relevant till Trajan's conquest of Parthia in 116 (see G.'s long n.). In that case *nunc* does not allude significantly to a new imperialism but simply provides a contrast with *olim*.

and nn. 19–20. Since these troops now had a city camp (2.1), *insideret* ('occupied'), above, is appropriate for both them and the urban cohorts.

5.4 apud idonea prouinciarum 'at strategic points in the provinces' (above, 2n. *cetera*).

sociae triremes: see Starr, chh. 6–7.

alaeque . . . cohortium: see Keppie 182–6. *auxilia cohortium* (also at *H.* 2.4.4) is a typically Tacitean variation on the regular *cohortes auxiliariae* (1.1n. *cohortibus*).

neque multo secus in iis uirium 'and in them the forces were not very different' (sc. from in the legions). Just as the noun *minus*, originally the neut. of the adj. *minor*, can be used with a partitive gen. and an abl. of comparison (e.g. Liv. pref. 12 'quanto rerum minus'), so here T. uses adjectival *secus* (*OLD secus*[2] A1c) as a noun and follows it (uniquely) with the same construction.

persequi incertum fuerit: the context (esp. *incertum* and *numero*) suggests that *persequi* = 'describe' or 'go through' (*OLD* 8) rather than 'trace' or 'track down' (*OLD* 4). *fuerit*, Lipsius' emendation, makes good sense ('describing them would be unreliable') and is well paralleled at 15.41.1 'numerum inire haud promptum fuerit': the perf. subjunc. is potential and has a future aspect (*NLS* §119). *fuit*, the reading of M, would refer T.'s readers to the time of writing but would involve an awkward ellipse: 'describing them proved unreliable [sc. so I did not do it]': contrast 11.3 below, where *fuit* is clearly correct and there is no ellipse.

gliscerent: a favourite verb of T., used as a choice and colourful variant for *cresco*, which he does not use in *A.* at all. It occurs mainly in verse and historical prose; T. extends its application in various ways, e.g. to number, as here (G. on 1.1.2).

aliquando is to be taken in common (ἀπὸ κοινοῦ) with *gliscerent* as well as *minuerentur*.

6.1 Congruens crediderim recensere: sc. *esse* (*congruens est* + inf. occurs first in T. and Pliny's letters): 'I am inclined to think it is appropriate to review'. The first person use of the perf. subjunc. (last n. but two) is relatively common, esp. in historians (e.g. 10.1 below). *recensere* (*OLD* 2) is used also at Vell. 129.1 for a review of Tib.'s reign; for its use with a following indir. qu. see e.g. Liv. 26.49.9.

quibus modis . . . habitae sint 'how they were handled'. This use of *habeo* = 'handle, manage', of which T. is fond (e.g. 21.1, 33.2), is 'very Sallustian' (G. on 1.54.2): note esp. *C.* 5.9 (above, p. 96). The use of *dies* = *tempus* continues the suggestion of 1.1 (*repente*) that the deterioration in Tib.'s reign was sudden.

This clause anticipates the following survey in 2–4, which itself summarises the events recounted in *A.* 1–3. T. sees the *rei publicae partes* primarily in terms of the class of persons associated with them: 2 senators and magistrates, 3 equestrians, 4 the *plebs*, provincials, and the emperor as *priuatus*. Since this last item involves legal matters which might well have been treated in §2, the dissociation of Tib.'s role as a private citizen from that as *princeps* is striking and constitutes an eloquent tribute to one of his main characteristics (4n.). The rest of T.'s testimony is also approving (note 2 *cohibebat ipse*, *mandabatque*, 3 *mandabat*, 4 *obuiam iit*, *prouidebat*), is supported by other ancient authors, and is accepted by most modern scholars (see below). Its congruence with the narrative of *A.* 1–3, however, is another question. Though Syme has said that Book 3 'presents the ruler in a highly favourable light' (*RP* III 1030), that presentation is only relative to the way in which our sympathies have been manipulated against Tib. from the very start of Book 1.

initium ille annus attulit: *ille annus* looks back to the opening of the book and reaffirms 23 as the turning-point in Tib.'s reign (cf. also 7.1 *uerterentur*); in the obituary at 6.51.3, however, he adds further turning-points in 29 and 31 (see above, pp. 28–30). A single turning-point is also found in Dio, but at the death of Germanicus in 19 (57.13.6).

T. is fond of using *annus* as the subject of a trans. verb, e.g. 15.1, 23.1, 6.45.1; see also 14.1n.

6.2 iam primum 'to begin with' (as 12.68.2, 14.31.1); or possibly 'from the very first' (cf. 1.7.3 'cuncta per consules incipiebat', on Augustus' death in 14).

publica negotia et priuatorum . . . tractabantur: so too Dio 57.7.2 and Suet. *Tib.* 30 'neque tam paruum quicquam neque tam magnum publici priuatique negotii fuit de quo non ad patres conscriptos referretur'. Most of Suet.'s exx. seem to fall under the heading of *publica* (e.g. taxation, public buildings, military appointments), but under *priuatorum negotia* might be included e.g. the recently discovered *senatus consultum* of 19 from Larinum, deterring distinguished men and women from infamous occupations (Sherk 35), or those measures concerning senators in their own capacity as *priuati* (e.g. their property qualifications: 1.75.3–4, 2.37–8, Vell. 129.3 'cum id *senatu auctore* facere potuit'). See esp. Levick 94–5, Talbert 439–40, Brunt (3) *passim*. Suet. interprets Tib.'s practice as evidence of his concern for the senate's *maiestas*, one of the keynotes of the reign (Vell. 126.2 'accessit . . . senatui maiestas') and acknowledged by modern scholars (e.g. Seager 123ff.). See further below, 4n. (*si quando*) and 15.2n.

dabaturque primoribus disserere: two celebrated exx. at 1.74.4 and 77.3 (above, p. 33), but there are others, e.g. 3.60.1 and 3. This is likely to be an area in which Tib. imitated Augustus: see esp. Brunt (3) 443. For impers. *dare* see e.g. 60.1, 3.67.2.

in adulationem lapsos cohibebat ipse: for senatorial *adulatio* see 1.7.1, 8.4, 2.32.2, 3.47.3–4, 57.1, 69.1; Tib.'s reaction at 3.47.4 and 65.3 ('O homines ad seruitutem paratos!'). See Syme 573–4, Brunt (3) 443–4; also M. Vielberg, *Pflichten, Werte, Ideale: eine Untersuchung zu den Wertvorstellungen des Tacitus* (1987) 80–112.

mandabatque honores . . . ut satis constaret non alios potiores fuisse: scholars rightly assume from the context that T. is talking primarily about the consulship, the office for which he uses *honor(es)* as a synonym most often. *mandabat* is a pragmatic recognition of the changes which were introduced into the consular elections in 15, placing them further under imperial control (cf. 1.81.1–2); yet *nobilitatem . . . spectando* indicates that Tib. nevertheless used traditional criteria in assessing candidates for high office: 'under the Republic nobility of birth, military service, distinction in oratory or law, these were the three claims to the consulate' (R. Syme, *The Roman revolution* (1939) 374). The point is continued in the *ut*-clause, which is commonly taken as consecutive ('with the result that there was a general consensus that no others had been better qualified'); taking *ut* as purposive, as AJW prefers, would attest to Tib.'s known determination, inherited from Augustus, to rule by senatorial consent ('in order to produce a general consensus that . . .'). *potior* is almost a technical term for being qualified for office etc. (*OLD* ²3a, cf. 1b).

As the main issue is whether T. is correct in saying that these were the criteria on which Tib.'s consular assessments were based, terminology is important. *nobilitas* was usually applied to men descended from republican consuls (*OCD*), although T. and many modern scholars extend its application also to descendants of those who were consuls between the deaths of Julius Caesar and Augustus (44 B.C.–A.D. 14). A man who attained the consulship without the advantage of *nobilitas* was styled *nouus homo* (*OCD*). During the period in question, A.D. 15–23, the more prestigious post of *consul ordinarius*, the traditional prerogative of the *nobiles*, was occupied by a *nobilis* on 12 out of 13 possible occasions; conversely, all but three of a comparable number of *suffecti* were *noui homines*. Thus T.'s statement that Tib. 'took account of *nobilitas*' is borne out; but whether the same is true of *claritudo militiae* and *inlustres domi artes*, 'the channels of advancement for *novi homines* according to the traditional prescription at Rome' (Syme 580), is more difficult to determine for lack of the appropriate evidence.

The military excellence of the sole 'new' *ordinarius*, L. Pomponius Flaccus (A.D. 17), is assured: he had campaigned with distinction in Moesia in 12 and had probably served with Tib. in Germany or Illyricum earlier (*RP* III 1094). Of the new *suffecti*, C. Vibius Rufus (16) was an orator, frequently cited by the elder Seneca and praised by Asinius Pollio (*RP* III 1087); C. Pomponius Graecinus (16) was praised by Ovid for his *artes* and *militiae labor*, perhaps in Illyricum (*Ex P.* 1.6.7–10; R. Syme, *History in Ovid* (1978) 74–5); C. Vibius Marsus (17) is likely to have had a military record (*RP* III 1353) and must in any case have been impressive in view of his subsequent proconsulship of Africa (26/7–29/30); L. Seius Tubero (18), a relative of Sejanus (29.1n.), had served as a legate under Germanicus (cf. 2.20.1); C. Vibius Rufinus (21 or 22) had probably served under Tib. in 6–9 (*RP* III 1434) and proceeded to the proconsulship of Asia in 36/7. No pre-consular distinction in *militia* or *domi artes* seems to be attested for the remaining *suffecti*, but whether this is due to their own mediocrity or to the vagaries of the historical record is unknown: the merit at least of C. Rubellius Blandus (18) and P. Petronius (19) seems guaranteed, since the former married Drusus Caesar's daughter in 33 and became proconsul of Africa in 35, while the latter held an 'exorbitant tenure' of Asia from 29 to 35 (*RP* III 1354).

The context of T.'s remarks suggests that after 23 Tib. had less regard for the three criteria discussed above but instead allowed his consular appointments to be influenced increasingly by Sejanus. Yet there are no clear signs of such a change. Of the four men who in 28 conspired to ruin a friend of Germanicus through *cupido consulatus*, 'ad quem non nisi per Seianum aditus' (68.2), only M. Porcius Cato was successful – and his suffect consulship came in 36, when Sejanus was dead and earlier friendship with him would have hindered rather than helped advancement.

For general discussion of the consuls under Tib. see Seager 125–9, Levick 96–9, and esp. *RP* III 1350–63 (on those of A.D. 15–19); for Tib.'s characteristic regard for the senate on such issues see esp. Brunt (3) 423–4, 429.

The noun *claritudo* had an archaic flavour and was preferred exclusively by Sall. to its synonym *claritas*, the only form used by Cicero. T. uses each equally in *H.* but greatly prefers *claritudo* in *A.* (31:2): see Syme 716. For *inlustres domi artes* cf. 3.70.3 'bonas domi artes' (of Ateius Capito's fame as a jurist).

sua consulibus . . . species 'the consuls and praetors each enjoyed their appropriate prestige': *OLD suus* 12a (cf. 10a, 11), *species* 4a. (The praetorian elections had been transferred from people to senate, thereby increasing the latter's self-esteem, on Augustus' death in 14: cf. 1.15.1 (and G.); Seager 124, Levick 95–6.)

minorum . . . magistratuum: esp. the quaestorship (which brought with it membership of the senate) and the immediately preceding vigintivirate (see *OCD Vigintisexuiri*).

si maiestatis quaestio eximeretur: these words suggest a reference to the treason court (*quaestio de maiestate*), which is known to have operated under Augustus; but since it is last heard of in 15 (an inference from 1.72.3), scholars generally assume that it became obsolete as the senate, in keeping with its increasing involvement in judicial matters, took over its functions (see Talbert 460ff., esp. 466 and n. 40). If this is correct, and if the present passage is not an argument against it, then *quaestio* here must be non-technical = 'judicial investigation' (*OLD* 3, not 4a) or even 'issue', 'question' (*OLD* 6a). Such a use of words would be typical of T. For *eximo*, *OLD* 3b.

The treason law, which T. regards as the greatest single evil of Tib.'s reign, constitutes the sole element of criticism in his survey of A.D. 14–22. The evidence of T.'s own narrative is as follows: *A.D. 15* cases against Falanius and Rubrius dismissed* (1.73), M. Granius Marcellus

* At the personal insistence or intervention of Tib. (on which see Garnsey 39).

acquitted of *maiestas** but prosecuted for extortion (1.74.6); *16* Libo Drusus anticipated condemnation (probably for *m.*) by suicide (2.27–31), though Tib. swore he would have begged for the man's life (2.31.3); *17* Appuleia Varilla acquitted of *m.** but found guilty of adultery (2.50.2); *20* Cn. Calpurnius Piso anticipated condemnation (probably for *m.*) by suicide (3.10–16), the case against his wife Plancina dismissed* (3.17.4); a charge of *m.* against Aemilia Lepida dropped*, though she was banished on other charges (3.22–3); *21* two knights who falsely accused Magius Caecilianus were punished* (3.37.1); Antistius Vetus charged with *m.** and banished (3.38.2); Clutorius Priscus executed (probably for *m.*) in Tib.'s absence, though the latter insisted on a 10-day stay of execution in future cases (regarded with contempt by T. at 3.51.2); *22* Iunius Silanus banished for *m.* and extortion (3.66–9); Caesius Cordus, though charged with *m.* (3.38.1), banished only for extortion (3.70.1); L. Ennius' case dismissed* (3.70.1).

Thus the general picture is one of initial activity in 15–17, followed by a lull in 18–19 and a resurgence in 20–2 (perhaps corresponding to the periods denoted by the metaphors *inrepserit*, *repressum sit* and *arserit* at 1.73.1). Whether the details largely justify T.'s savage and cynical treatment of the *lex de maiestate* and its operation by Tib. (so G. II 141–50), or whether his interpretation, influenced by Tib.'s later years and by later emperors, is largely contradicted by the 'facts' of his own narrative (so Jerome 330–40, Walker 82–110), are matters of dispute.

For general discussions of the treason trials see Seager 151–62, Levick 182ff.; more technical are Rogers (1) (esp. 6–70); Bauman (1) and (2); Garnsey 19–25, 39.

bono in usu: sc. *erant*. See Levick 180–2. Though *iustitia* was represented on the shield presented to Augustus by senate and people in 27 B.C. (*RG* 34.2), Tib. is the only Julio-Claudian emperor on whose coinage the word appears (in 22): see Sutherland 97–8, Weinstock 247, Wallace-Hadrill. T. is, however, highly sceptical of the word, never using it in *A.* 1–6; contrast Vell. 126.2.

6.3 frumenta 'corn taxes', evidently paid from *ager publicus* in

* At the personal insistence or intervention of Tib. (on which see Garnsey 39).

kind (*frumentum mancipale*) and from private land in cash (*stipendia*): see Rickman 64–5 and 84–5 for the details (complicated and uncertain).

pecuniae uectigales are usu. taken to include *portoria* and *scriptura* (harbour and grazing taxes respectively).

cetera publicorum fructuum presumably refer to minor taxes (e.g. on quarries or mines) paid into the public treasury or *aerarium* (*OCD*). For *cetera* see 5.2n.

societatibus: probably dat. of agent (5.1n. *Hispaniae . . . tribus habebantur*). *societas* (*OLD* 2b) is the technical term for a company of *publicani*, who were responsible for collecting taxes (cf. 13.50.3 'uectigalium societates . . . publicanorum cupidines') and whose managers were usu. *equites* (see *OCD*).

agitabantur 'were managed', as 41.3: see *OLD agito* 13.

res suas Caesar spectatissimo cuique . . . mandabat: *suas* contrasts with *publicorum*, and *cuique* and *quibusdam* with *societatibus*, above. The reference is to the income which entered the imperial treasury or *fiscus* (*OCD*) from the emperor's property and the imperial provinces and which was generally managed by equestrian procurators appointed by the emperor. See Brunt (2) *passim*.

The superl. *spectatissimus*, used only here by T., has a Ciceronian ring, e.g. *Verr*. 3.65 'spectatissimi atque honestissimi uiri'; see also 8.5n.

cum plerique isdem negotiis insenescerent: so with provincial governors it was Tib.'s practice 'continuare imperia ac *plerosque ad finem uitae in isdem* exercitibus aut iurisdictionibus habere' (1.80.1). The verb, used only here in T. and very rare elsewhere, was perh. coined by Hor. *Ep*. 2.2.82; whether *negotiis* is dat. or abl. is uncertain.

6.4 plebes acri . . . annona fatigabatur: *annona* is generally taken = 'price of corn', as elsewhere; but the context (*infecunditati . . . maris*), *acri* (cf. Lucr. 3.65 'acris egestas') and esp. the verb (cf. 49.3 'sitis fatigabat', 1.68.5 'ciborum egestas fatigaret') all suggest that here the meaning is 'corn supply'.

Both here and at 2.87 ('saeuitiam annonae incusante plebe statuit frumento pretium') T. is influenced by Sall. *H*. 2.45 'annonae . . . saeuitia, qua re fatigata plebes'. The archaising *plebes*, preferred to *plebs* by Sall. in *J*. and *H*., is used exclusively by T. in *A*. 1–12; in 13–16, as in Sall. *C*., the two forms are used indifferently. Livy prefers *plebs* to *plebes*.

The importance to the *plebs* of the corn supply, parodied by Juv.

10.81 'panem et circenses', had been recognised by Augustus in 23 B.C., when he eased a shortage with the help of the young Tib. (*RG* 15.1, Vell. 94.3), and again in 22, when he declined the dictatorship but accepted the *cura annonae* (*RG* 5.2), implying that the latter 'could in some sense be regarded as an alternative to the dictatorship' (Rickman 180). In A.D. 14 the importance of the recently appointed *praefectus annonae* is indicated by his swearing loyalty to Tib. immediately after the consuls and along with the praetorian prefect (1.7.2); and in 22 Tib. is made to say: 'hanc, patres conscripti, curam sustinet princeps; haec omissa rem publicam trahet' (3.54.5). See also next n.

quin . . . obuiam iit: as in 19 (2.87, quoted above) and contrasting with his non-intervention in 32, when 'grauitate annonae iuxta seditionem uentum' (6.13.1): see P. Garnsey, *Famine and food supply in the Graeco-Roman world: responses to risk and crisis* (1988) 27–8, 218ff. The verb, like *prouidebat* below, suggests Tib.'s personal concern (also at 64.1); *quin* 'corroborates and amplifies what precedes' (*OLD* 2a); *infecunditas*, fairly uncommon, is perh. Sallustian (*H.* 3.46); for *aspera* + gen. see 5.2n. On transporting grain see in general Rickman 120ff.

impendio diligentiaque echoes Augustus' boast that in 22 B.C. he resolved the crisis 'impensa et cura mea' (*RG* 5.2); but T. typically prefers a rare synonym for the former noun, and a non-technical one for the latter (1.1n., cf. 13.1n.). Vell. praises Tib. for keeping down the price of corn in 14–29 (126.3); on pricing in general see Rickman 143ff.

ne prouinciae nouis oneribus turbarentur: *prouinciae* = 'provincials' (metonymy): see *OLD* 3d. In 15 Achaea and Macedonia complained of heavy taxation and were transferred from senatorial to imperial control, suggesting a reduction in their liabilities (1.76.2 with G.); in 17 tribute was waived for the cities of Asia struck by an earthquake (2.47.2), and reduced for Cappadocia on its annexation as a province (2.56.4). Vell. praises Tib.'s *munificentia* in this regard (126.4).

utque uetera . . . tolerarent, prouidebat: T. contrasts the proverbial lot of provincials (*uetera*), which did not change under Tib. (cf. e.g. 3.54.4, Suet. *Tib.* 32.2), with the behaviour of individual governors. Yet even here the characteristic of Tib.'s early years seems not to be that malpractice, so much a feature of the republic (cf. 1.2.2), entirely disappeared: on the contrary, see e.g. 3.40.3 'continuatione tributorum, grauitate faenoris, saeuitia ac superbia praesidentium'. It was rather the case that more *magistratus* were prosecuted successfully for extortion etc. than at any time during the first century (P. A. Brunt, *Historia* 10 (1961) 224–7). In so far as *prouidebat* suggests measures taken, rather than results achieved, T.'s statement reflects this view; but since *sine auaritia aut crudelitate magistratuum* is explained (chiastically) by the assertion *corporum uerbera, ademptiones bonorum aberant* below (itself chiastic), T.'s praise is in fact more forthcoming than Vell. 126.4 'uindicatae ab iniuriis magistratuum prouinciae'. See in general Seager 170–4, Levick 125ff.

tolerare, as a synonym for *ferre* and *perferre* ('endure', 'bear'), 'belonged to the higher genres of prose' (Adams (2) 133). For Tib.'s *prouidentia* see 38.1n.

rari . . . agri: emperors acquired estates through inheritances from their family, friends or others, and through confiscations. Tib.'s initial policy was indeed restrictive (2.48.2 'neque hereditatem cuiusquam adiit nisi cum amicitia meruisset'), but about to change (20.1 below, Dio 58.16.2). See in general Millar 166–8, 175ff.

modesta 'well behaved' or 'unassuming' (*OLD* 2, 4): contrast 74.4 below.

seruitia = 'slaves' (*OLD* 3b).

intra paucos libertos domus: the comparison is above all with Claudius, whose elevation of such men as Pallas and Narcissus was notorious. See in general Millar 69–83. *intra* = 'without exceeding' or 'within' a limit or restriction (48.1; *OLD* 5); for the common *uariatio* of prepositional phrase ~ adj./part. see e.g. 31.2, 32.2, 34.5, 35.1; Sörbom 92–3.

si quando cum priuatis disceptaret, forum et ius: just as he expected others to act like *priuati* when appropriate (Dio 57.23.5 'in cases of disputes they [imperial procurators such as Capito: below, 15.2n.] must stand trial in the forum according to the laws, on an equal footing with private citizens', under A.D. 23), so Tib. himself was aware of the distinction between his own public and private persona (2.34.3 'hactenus . . . ciuile ratus' (from which T. typically takes the gloss at 21.1 below), 3.12.2 'priuatas inimicitias non ui principis ulciscar'). That he was in general anxious to be seen acting as a *priuatus* or *ciuis* is attested by Vell. 124.2, Suet. *Tib.* 26.1, Dio 57.11.7: see in general A. Wallace-Hadrill, 'Civilis princeps: between citizen and king', *J.R.S.* 72 (1982) 32–48, esp. 39.

For the mood and tense of *disceptaret* see *NLS* §196: 'The subjunctive in generalising clauses containing an idea of repetition, whether introduced by *si* or other conjunctions, becomes common . . . only from Livy onwards. This development is commonest in historical narrative, and the normal tenses are the imperfect and pluperfect.' So again at 32.1 and 60.2. *quando* = 'ever' after *si* (e.g. 32.1; *OLD* 4).

7–12 *Death of Drusus*

This section begins with a paragraph on Drusus' quarrel with Sejanus (7) and ends with another on Sejanus' designs against a future victim, Agrippina (12). In between are two central panels (8–9 and 10–11), in the former of which, though the subject is nominally that of Drusus' death (cf. 10.1 'in tradenda morte Drusi'), the death itself, on 14 September (EJ p. 52 = Sherk 28E), is dismissed obliquely in two sentences (8.1) and T. concentrates instead on Tib.'s speech to the senate (8.2–9.1) and Drusus' funeral (9.2). This treatment allows T. to return to Drusus' death at greater and more insidious length in the second panel, which is presented in the form of an excursus (the funeral of 9.2 being resumed at 12.1).

7.1 Quae cuncta: *cunctus*, an artificial and recherché alternative to *omnis*, is used frequently as a substantive by historians; when used adjectivally, as here, it is more commonly neut. plur. and almost exclusively confined to narrative, also as here. See Adams (2) 129–31.

non quidem . . . sed . . . formidatus: on occasions when Tib.'s behaviour would otherwise seem meritorious (as at 6.2–4 above), T. characteristically depreciates it by the immediate juxtaposition of some other less creditable act or habit (as here and e.g. 66.1, 1.72.1–2): see further Martin (2) 229. Here the depreciation is expressed by forceful language (T. uses *formidare* nowhere else) and by one of his commonest types of *uariatio* (abl. manner ~ adj./part., as 12.1, 14.4.4, *H.* 2.83.1): see Sörbom 89, Martin (1) 92. The metaphorical use of *uia* = 'manner' etc. is common (*OLD* 7a) and applied to Tib. again at 1.54.2 'alia Tiberio morum uia'. For fear see below (*metuebatur*) and 70.2n.

retinebat: the compound verb indicates holding on to something in unpromising or adverse circumstances, as 52.4 and (also of Tib.) 1.75.2 'quam uirtutem diu retinuit, cum ceteras exueret'.

donec . . . uerterentur: the subjunc. after *donec* stating a fact (again at 44.2), where republican Latin has the indic., is common from Livy onwards and slightly more common in T. than the indic. See *NLS* §224, *Note* ii.

nam dum superfuit, mansere: the curious repetition of the thought of *retinebat . . . uerterentur* both emphasises T.'s point and, after the discursive material of chh. 5–6, effects the transition back to the themes of chh. 2–3.

adhuc 'still ⟨only⟩' (*OLD* 1a). For Sejanus' *potentia* see 1.1n. (*cuius*).

notescere is rare in earlier prose (G. on 1.73.3) but occurs several times in *A.* and nowhere else in T. (Syme 731).

ultor: viz. Drusus. The change of subject after *Seianus . . . uolebat* is awkward but explained by the fact that circumstances are still being seen from Sejanus' point of view.

metuebatur non occultus odii: a telling inversion of Accius' proverbial line *oderint dum metuant* (Cic. *Phil.* 1.34, Sen. *Clem.* 1.12.4, Suet. *Cal.* 30.1 etc.): Sejanus, in his efforts at achieving his tyrannical ambitions, experiences the fear to which tyrants are conventionally prone (see 70.2n.). For further similarity between Sejanus and Tib. see 1.2n. (*quippe*) and 11.2n. (*repertor*).

T. greatly prefers the obsolete archaism *metuo* to the normal *timeo* (Adams (2)135). *occultus* + gen. seems peculiar to T.: here it = '(not) concealing his hatred', at 6.36.2 = 'privy to' (*occultos consilii*).

set = *sed* 'with no clear distinction in use' (*OLD*).

incolumi = *uiuo*, as often (*OLD* 1c); but in view of 3.2–5 (above) the dramatic irony of 'safe and sound' (*OLD* 1a) is hard to exclude.

adiutorem imperii: see 2.3n. (*socium*).

7.2 quantum superesse ut collega dicatur! 'how small a step remained ⟨to be taken⟩ before he was called [lit. that he should be called] colleague!' The *or. obl.* is continued with an exclamation (W. S. Watt's suggested punctuation), which, like a rhetorical question in indirect speech, is expressed by the acc. + inf. For *superest* (impers.) + *ut* see *OLD* 6b; for the tense of *dicatur* and *sis ingressus* below see 2.1n. T. reverts to the imperf. subjunc. with *esset* below (n. *ut*).

Sejanus at last became Tib.'s constitutional *collega* in 31, when he was declared *consul ordinarius* alongside the emperor (cf. 5.6.2).

in arduo 'an uphill task' (cf. 12.15.2; *OLD* 2), the metaphor being sustained by *sis ingressus* ('have embarked': see Jocelyn on Enn. *Trag.*

217). For the 'ideal' second person of the perf. subjunc. in a generalising temporal clause see *NLS* §217 (2), *Note* i.

studia 'sympathies' (*OLD* 5a, 6).

exstructa . . . datos . . . cerni: the initial position of the verbs emphasises Drusus' complaints, the grounds of which are repeated from 2.1–3 above (see nn.). *sponte* + gen. (common in T.) is first found in Lucan and Curtius (G. on 2.59.2).

communes . . . nepotes: the expected offspring of the projected marriage (cf. 3.29.4) between Sejanus' daughter, who was still a very young child (3.5n.), and the future emperor Claudius' son, who died soon after the betrothal.

modestiam: a quality claimed by Sejanus himself (cf. 39.2, 40.5) but never attributed to him by T. as an author. The complaints against the mere equestrian by the emperor's son are simultaneously pathetic (*precandam*, sc. *sibi a Seiano*) and bitter (*post haec*).

ut is most easily explained as expanding on *modestiam*; less probably sc. *precandum* from *precandam* above (cf. 33.2n.). Note, however, that T. now reverts to observing the sequence of tenses (*esset*), as he usually does when the dependent subjunc. is that of an indir. command.

7.3 iaciebat: the verb is commonly used by T. of hostile remarks, e.g. *H.* 1.47.1 'conuicia et probra'.

quoque 'even' (*OLD* 4a).

corrupta uxore: without *ab*, as she is viewed merely as an instrument (*NLS* §44): so too 12.4, and cf. also 11.1n.

8.1 igitur Seianus maturandum ratus: *igitur* (3.3n.) resumes the narrative of 7.1 after the self-contained dilation on Drusus' complaints (7.1 *crebro querens* ~ 3 *neque raro . . . talia iaciebat*), which in turn explain why Sejanus has now abandoned the hesitations of 3.1, 5: Drusus' hostility might turn Tib. against his minister.

deligit uenenum: see 11.2n. (*ordo . . . sceleris*).

fortuitus is naturally used of seemingly idiopathic illness: of fever at Suet. *Tib.* 73.2 (contrasting with death by poison) and of spontaneous bleeding at Cels. 2.8.18 (contrasting with blood-letting). Elsewhere T. uses it to contrast natural with enforced death (12.52.2, 16.19.2). For *inrepente* see 2.2n.

Lygdum spadonem: probably Drusus' *praegustator*: cf. the eunuch Halotus, who is similarly credited with poisoning the emperor Claudius (12.66.2).

octo post annos: in 31, after the downfall of Sejanus (Dio 58.11.6): the relevant portion of T.'s narrative is lost. See further below, 11.2n.

8.2 Tiberius per omnes . . . dies: this first part of the sentence lacks a verb, which therefore has to be supplied from the second part (*etiam defuncto* . . .); but whereas the verb in the latter (*curiam ingressus est*) is aoristic and from the context (*consulesque* . . . *erexit*) clearly refers to a single occasion, the verb required in the former must be frequentative (cf. *per omnes* . . . *dies*). Hence *ingrediebatur* (sc. *curiam*) has to be elicited from *ingressus est* and supplied with *Tiberius* . . . *dies*.

ualetudo commonly = ill health (*OLD* 3); for *ceterum* see 3.1n.

nullo metu an ut firmitudinem animi ostentaret: the alternative explanations, typical of T. (above, p. 32), are themselves typically separated by *an* ('or possibly') rather than *aut* (G. on 1.13.6); also typical is the syntactical *uariatio* of abl. noun ~ final clause (also at 48.2, 71.3): in general see Martin (1) 92, (2) 220–3, and above, p. 25.

nullo metu, in view of the contrast with *firmitudinem animi*, seems to be an anticipation of Tib.'s alleged involvement in Drusus' death, which T. mentions but rejects at 10.2–11.3 below. See also 70.2n. *firmitudo animi* is a common phrase at all periods and denotes a quality which the Romans regarded as highly commendable: it is again exhibited (and defended) by Tib. on the death of Germanicus (3.6.2), and cf. 14.49.3 of Thrasea Paetus. *ostento* = 'display publicly', not necessarily with the notion of 'for effect' (though the latter occasionally appears in T., e.g. 46.3, 16.23.2).

sede uulgari: i.e. among the other senators instead of on their normal seat (*sella curulis*) on a raised platform (*tribunal*, cf. 16.30.3). For a similar gesture during the mourning for Augustus see Dio 56.31.1; Talbert 121–2.

per speciem: see 3.4n.

honoris locique 'their place of honour' (hendiadys). The gen. after *admoneo* (also at 1.12.3) is less common than *de* + abl. but is not restricted to a single genre and is esp. favoured by Sall., Livy and Ovid.

simul is usu. taken with *erexit*: 'he reminded the consuls . . . and at the same time, having conquered his own lamentation, he lifted the senate by . . .' Alternatively, *simul* = *et*: '. . . and he lifted the senate by having conquered his own lamentation as well as by . . .'; for this use of *simul* see 29.2n., and, for its joining abl. abs. and instrumental abl., see

11.9.1 (also 3.37.1), *H.* 3.45.2. The notion of Tib.'s setting an example is entirely characteristic.

oratione continua: though described as *continua* (contrasted with *altercatio* at *H.* 4.7.1), the *oratio* is in fact interrupted by the consuls' departure to fetch Germanicus' sons: the interruption is signalled by a sentence of narrative (3 *miseratusque . . . petiuit*), which in turn divides the speech into *or. obl.* (3) and *or. recta* (4–5). The same technique is used for Tib. at 40.1–7 and 3.12.1–7.

Though the amount of dramatic speech in Book 4 is slightly less than T.'s average for the first hexad, the proportion given to Tib. (including almost all that of the first two years' narrative) is increased from *A.* 1–3. Thus while Tib. is 'the most striking character' in *A.* on the basis of his speeches in Books 1–6, the dramatic speech in Book 4 'marks an increasing urgency in the presentation of Tiberius, in the book which sees his withdrawal from Rome' (Miller 5–6 and 9, with appropriate statistics).

Since it was an established convention of Greek and Roman historians to exclude verbatim speeches from their works (except in the case of brief quotations, such as those clearly marked at 14.59.3 and 15.67.2–3), all longer speeches in T. are composed by the author himself. This practice holds good even when the speech actually delivered was publicly available, as was the case with Claudius' speech to the senate in 48, substantial parts of which still survive on an inscription (*ILS* 212; Sherk 55). T.'s version of that speech appears at 11.24, and the co-existence of two versions of the 'same' speech serves as a powerful reminder that the concern of ancient historians, and hence also the expectation of their readers, was rather with plausibility and realism than with accuracy and truth (above, p. 3).

The style of invented speeches would normally differ somewhat, both in vocabulary and sentence structure, from the historian's narrative style, and it is possible that such differences may include verbal or other mannerisms of the historical person for whom the historian invents the speech. Since a convincing case can be made that T. did this in his version not only of Claudius' speech at 11.24 but also of Seneca's at 14.53–4 (see Adams (2) 126–8), the question arises whether he similarly incorporated genuinely Tiberian elements into his own versions of Tib.'s speeches and formal letters to the senate.

It seems certain that T. could and, at least on occasion, did read

Tib.'s utterances. Although too much should not perhaps be made of the brief extract from a Tiberian letter which both he (6.6.1) and Suetonius (*Tib.* 67.1) quote, he sometimes shares phraseology with Velleius in contexts which suggest that each has echoed Tib.'s speeches independently (e.g. *honestam paupertatem* at both 2.48.3 and Vell. 129.3 (see W.)). What is less clear is whether T. consulted speeches in the official *acta senatus* or in a separate collection. Each alternative involves an unproved assumption. While it was technically feasible to make and keep a transcript of everything that was said at senate meetings, there is no evidence that this was normal practice. Yet Talbert (308–34, esp. 326ff. for T.) has argued that the *acta* contained not only the names of individual speakers but also their differing views (see further above, 4.1n. *quaeque*). Similarly, the separate publication of Tib.'s speeches is no more than an inference from Suetonius' statement (*Dom.* 20) that Domitian read nothing apart from Tib.'s *commentarios et acta* (see Syme 285). Yet T.'s actual references to the speeches (1.81.1 'in ipsius orationibus', 2.63.3 'extat oratio', cf. Suet. *Tib.* 28 'extat et sermo eius in senatu') suggest a separate publication rather than anything else (see G.).

With reference to T.'s treatment of Tib.'s speeches, four points may be made. (1) We know a little about the emperor's style both from Suet.'s general remarks (*Tib.* 70.1: see Syme 700) and from the letter which both he and T. quote and which contains several idiolects (e.g. *di . . . deaeque*: see Miller 18). (2) There is some evidence, assembled by Miller, that individual linguistic features occur in the speeches that T. puts into Tib.'s mouth. (3) It is therefore a reasonable hypothesis that at least some of these features (e.g. possibly *deos et deas ipsas* at 38.3 below) are either genuinely Tiberian or intended to recall his manner. On this matter Syme 700–3 and Miller are more positive than Adams (2) 137–8 and G. on 2.38; and see further 37.2–38.3nn. and 40.1–7nn. below. (4) In his version of Claudius' speech T. repeats some of the emperor's main points (see N. P. Miller, *Rh.M.* 99 (1956) 304–15), which makes it likely that, linguistic questions apart, he reproduces the 'main thesis' (to use Thucydides' famous phrase) also of any Tiberian speech which was readily available. Our problem is that we do not know which speeches fall into that category, and hence cannot always be sure even that Tib. actually delivered a speech on the occasions on which T. attributes one to him.

The pervading tone of the present speech is one of 'solemnity' (Syme

701): the emperor's words embody the Roman aristocratic ideal of placing public duty before private interest or emotion.

8.3 non quidem . . . senatus 'Of course it was not unknown to him that the fact of his having endured the senate's gaze . . . could be criticised': i.e. *quod . . . senatus* is the subject of *posse argui*, and *ignarum* is passive (*OLD* 3). For the tense of *subierit* see 2.1n.

Tib. uses the same turn of phrase *non quidem sibi ignara* at 3.69.2 and *nec ignoro* at 3.54.1, although T. himself also favours similar litotes with *ignarus* (e.g. 6.7.5, 32.4, 11.27.1, *H.* 4.84.4). On the other hand, the unparalleled expressions *subire oculos* and *diem aspici* below (analogous to the common *lucem aspicere*, e.g. Cic. *Att.* 3.7.1) are perhaps exx. of the emperor's stylistic *adfectatio* to which Suet. refers (*Tib.* 70.1). The anaphora of *uix* (below) is unparalleled elsewhere in T. or in Cicero's speeches.

imbecillitatis: 'There is in the vocabulary of Tib.'s speeches a marked fondness for abstract nouns of a Ciceronian type' (Miller 14): *imbecillitas* is common in Cic. and recurs in T. only at 15.56.3. See also next n.

e complexu rei publicae: the metaphorical use of *complexus* is also favoured by Cic., who alone has exx. with *patria* and *res publica* (e.g. *Sest.* 53 '⟨e⟩ complexu patriae', *Phil.* 13.9 'res p. . . . suo . . . sinu complexuque recipiet'). Tib. is alluding to the role which actual embraces played in consolatory situations (e.g. *Agr.* 45.4 'satiari uultu complexuque non contigit').

Augustae: the name which Livia, Augustus' widow (and Tib.'s mother), acquired by the terms of her husband's will (1.8.1). Born in 58 B.C., she was now 80; her death in 29 is recorded, along with her obituary, at 5.1.1–4. See also 57.3n. and 71.4n.

rudem 'inexperienced' (*OLD* 3a). The *nepotes* are Nero and Drusus (3.1n.).

uergentem 'declining' (*OLD* 4), as 41.2, 2.43.1, 12.44.4. Born on 16 Nov. 42 B.C., Tib. was now 63.

unica praesentium malorum leuamenta: as might be expected in these tragic circumstances, Tib. resorts to prescriptive cliché: *un(ic)um* is regularly joined with *leuamen(tum)* (e.g. *H.* 2.44.2 and H.), which in turn often governs such words as *mala* (e.g. 1.17.5, 30.3); *praesentia mala* is also a normal combination (e.g. 15.39.3). Apart from *H.* 5.3.2 (an excursus), T. prefers *leuamentum*, found in Cic. and other authors, to *leuamen*, found in Livy and poetry.

8.4 firmatos adloquio: the phrase (cf. also 1.71.3, *H.* 3.36.1) here adds a nice touch of sympathetic verisimilitude, which the diminutive *adulescentulos* maintains. *deductos* = 'escorted' (*OLD* 8b).

quibus adprensis 'taking them by the hand' (cf. *OLD* 1a).

orbatos parente: Germanicus died in 19 (2.72.2).

quamquam esset . . . propria suboles: principally the twins Germanicus and Tiberius Gemellus (3.1n.). *suboles*, mostly archaic and poetic, is one of those words which make a style seem 'grandior atque antiquior' (Cic. *De Or.* 3.153); also elevated is *sanguis* = 'offspring' (*OLD* 10) below. For *quamquam* + subjunc. see 4.1n.

foueret, attolleret: a similar asyndeton recurs immediately below (5 *suscipite*, *regite*): T., says Syme, 'is reproducing a personality, with its characteristic manner' (701), although we cannot know whether this particular mannerism was characteristic of the historical Tib. (above, 2n.). In both cases the asyndeton is followed by a longer parallel clause (next n.). T. greatly favours the metaphorical use of *attollere*: here it = 'to uplift [sc. morally]' (*OLD* 11a) and is similarly coupled with *fouere* at Plin. *Pan.* 44.6.

sibique et posteris confirmaret: although it might be thought that *-que* joins *confirmaret* to the two asyndetic verbs above, an arrangement of which T. is generally fond, there is no co-ordination after *suscipite*, *regite* below and the balance between the two sentences seems intentional (cf. the similar balance at the end of Tib.'s speech at 38.3). We therefore have an ex. of *-que et*, 'the archaic equivalent of Greek τε καί ["both . . . and"] which survives in classical Roman poetry and archaizing prose' (Brink on Hor. *AP* 196). It is common in Sall., Livy and T. but completely avoided by Cic., Caes. and Nepos. Usually *-que* is attached to a personal pronoun, as here and 1.4.1 (see G.), 71.3 (see below), *Agr.* 18.4 (see Ogilvie). See also 5n. below and compare *-que ac* at 3.4n.

confirmaret, apparently the original reading of M, has been changed in the MS to *conformaret*. Which is right? The latter verb is not used elsewhere by T., although an exceptional use could be defended by the context of a Tiberian speech (above, 2n.). On the other hand, T. had written 'quo *sibi* in *posterum* gentem *firmaret*' at *H.* 5.4.1 and 'cunctos *adloquio* et cura *sibique et* proelio *firmabat*' at 1.71.3; and since he has a habit of repeating clusters of words, the repetition of the italicised words here strongly supports *confirmaret*. The choice of the compound form is explained by his having used the simple *firmatos* with *adloquio* immediately above: indeed such repetitions are themselves a feature of T.'s style, e.g. 2.17.5 'nosceretur . . . adgnitum', 15.71.4 'pellitur . . . expulit' (other exx. in Sörbom 42). The meaning is either 'that he should strengthen them for his own sake and that of posterity' or, in the light of 4.1 *arduum . . . esse* above, '. . . should win them over to himself and for the sake of posterity' (the usage of the two datives being the same as that at 1.71.3 quoted (see G.)).

8.5 preces . . . conuerto: since this precise expression is unparalleled, it may be another rendering of a Tiberian idiolect; but cf. 1.11.1 'uersae . . . preces'.

disque et patria coram: since T. commonly couples two longish clauses by *-que* or *et*, but avoids asyndeton in such cases (unless there is anaphora or a strong adversative relationship), it is best to take *-que* here as coupling the two main clauses and not as a further ex. of *-que et* (as at 4 above). For the anastrophe of *coram* see 5.1n.

pronepotes: their mother, Agrippina, was the daughter of Augustus' daughter, Julia, and Agrippa. See Stemma.

clarissimis maioribus: T. is relatively sparing in his use of superlatives, esp. when applied to persons: most of the exx. in *A.* are in speeches (so too *plurimi* at 34.2). See Adams (2) 134 and n. 89; also above, 6.3n. (*res suas*).

suscipite, regite: another hint of Tiberian style (above, 4n.), although asyndeton of two or more imperatives is common in Latin. *suscipere* is technical of a father acknowledging his own new-born child, or of adopting another's child into one's own family (*OLD* 4a).

uicem explete: the noun = 'the place or part filled (in rotation, succession, etc., by a person)' (*OLD* 2a): hence virtually 'duty'. *expleo* = 'discharge (an obligation)' (*OLD* 5b, also a).

9.1 gloriaque '(and) a feeling of pride' (as 1.43.3): i.e. at being chosen for this responsible task.

impleuerat: a pluperf. indic. in the apodosis of a mixed condition (cf. *si . . . posuisset*) is often due to 'sheer rhetorical exaggeration, whereby what might have happened is vividly presented as a fact' (*NLS* §200 (iii)).

totiens: Augustus had thought 'de reddenda re publica' in 30, 29 and 23 B.C. (Suet. *Aug.* 28.1, Dio 52.1.1); and Drusus at some point had written to Tib. 'de cogendo ad restituendam libertatem Augusto'

(Suet. *Tib.* 50.1). Similarly Tib., on succeeding Augustus, had attempted to lessen the imperial burden of the *princeps* (1.11.1, 12.1) and had let it be known that he would not remain in office for ever (Suet. *Tib.* 24.2); he had himself retired to Campania for the year 21/2 (3.31.2), and was currently associating Sejanus in imperial administration (2.3n. *socium*) in much the same way as he had done with his sons Drusus and Germanicus earlier (Strabo 6.4.2). The fact that nothing had changed and that after more than fifty years Rome was still ruled by an emperor no doubt explains T.'s description of these circumstances as *uana et inrisa*; but their frequency (*totiens*) is undeniable. For T.'s habit of depreciating a praiseworthy action by juxtaposition (here marked by the adversative asyndeton after *impleuerat*) see 7.1n.

reuolutus 'relapsing' (*OLD* 4a, rather than 4c).

utque . . . regimen susciperent: there seems to be no precise parallel elsewhere in T. for the *uariatio* of prep. + gerundive ~ clause of indir. command: Sörbom 114–15 quotes only 3.63.4, where the clause is purposive. For T.'s more normal *uariatio* of gerundives ~ indir. commands see 20.1n. *regimen* = 'direction (of government)' (*OLD* 3a) is as old as Enn. *Ann.* 407 Skutsch, regular in epic, and several times in Livy.

quoque 'even' (*OLD* 4a).

9.2 in Germanicum: elliptical for *in memoriam Germanici* (cf. 3.3n.), and *uariatio* after *memoriae Drusi* (2.1n.). An incomplete list of the honours voted to Germanicus is given at 2.83 (see G.); some fragmentary inscriptions (see e.g. Sherk 36) record those given to both him and Drusus but do not enable us to estimate the latter's preferential treatment.

ferme amat 'is accustomed usually ⟨to do⟩': for this use of *amare* (exactly equivalent to the Greek φιλεῖν) see *OLD* 12; for this sense of *ferme*, *OLD* 3a. *ferme* is the archaising form of *fere* and is avoided or used only rarely by Cicero, Caesar and Quint.; Livy has a slight preference for it over *fere*, which T. uses only once in his major works (J. N. Adams, *Antichthon* 8 (1974) 57). For the appended abl. abs. (*plerisque additis* . . .) see 2.3n. (*facili*).

imaginum: the appearance of ancestral busts at funerals provides an excellent illustration of the way in which, in the Roman world, the past habitually impinged on the present. There is a memorable description of the ritual at Polyb. 6.53–4 (see also *OCD imagines*).

origo 'founder' (*OLD* 5a).

Iuliae gentis: Drusus' membership of the *gens Iulia* came via his father Tib., who had been adopted by Augustus: the latter was the grandson of Caesar's sister, Julia, and had himself been adopted posthumously by Caesar in his will.

Aeneas . . . Albanorum reges . . . Romulus: Aeneas' son Ascanius (or Iulus) was the founder and first king of Alba Longa; Romulus' mother, Rhea Silvia, was the daughter of a later Alban king, Numitor. See e.g. Liv. 1.3–4, Virg. *Aen.* 6.760–79.

Sabina nobilitas, Attus Clausus: 'The patrician branch of the *gens Claudia* . . . originated at Regilli, a town of the Sabines. From there it moved to Rome . . ., according to the more usual version of the story, on the advice of Atta [=Att(i)us] Clausus, the head of the family, about five years after the expulsion of the kings [=504 B.C.]' (Suet. *Tib.* 1.1). Naturally much of this story, to which the emperor Claudius alludes in his speech at 11.24.1, is legendary rather than historical and is fraught with problems: see Wiseman 57–65.

10–11 Excursus on the death of Drusus: rumour and refutation

Four key points need to be made. (1) The excursus, which is self-contained (10.1 *rumorem* ~ 11.3 *rumoris*: ring composition), serves as a structural device, somewhat analogous to the digression at 5–6 above (p. 96), to mark the transition from the first stage of Sejanus' plans (the removal of Drusus) to the next (the undermining of the house of Germanicus). (2) T.'s stated reason for the excursus is the enhancement of his historiographical credibility through the rejection of improbabilities and fantasies. This motif is as old as Hecataeus (11.3n.) and indicates that the excursus should not be read, as it often is by modern scholars, as an example of 'source criticism'. Yet T.'s stated reason is no more the whole story here than at 4.3 above (p. 96) or 57.1 below (n.).

(3) The alleged method of Drusus' death is poisoning, a topic whose popularity with writers and readers alike is attested by its regular appearance in the elder Seneca (see Winterbottom II 640 (index); also above, 3.3n. *ad coniugii*) and other works of the first and second centuries A.D. (in general S. F. Bonner, *Education in ancient Rome* (1977) 310–12). Yet if T.'s concern was simply to provide an exciting topic,

why did he not elaborate the 'accepted' version of events which he has already provided at 8.1 above? The fact is that putting a different complexion (*color*) on a series of events was standard procedure in the declamation schools which flourished during the early empire and which delighted their audiences with the clever handling of tricky legal topics (S. F. Bonner, *Roman declamation* (1949) 55–6). There is no doubt that *colores* influenced historiography (Wiseman 7–8, 26), and by producing a different version of Drusus' poisoning T. is responding to a well known enthusiasm of his readers. Indeed since the rumoured version of events contains the extra piquancy of attempted parricide on Drusus' part and the actual murder of his son on Tib.'s part, we must remember that the murder of close relatives was also a favourite topic in the schools (see again Winterbottom II 640 (index 'parricide')). Further, the substitution of the one crime for the other is just the kind of bizarre twist on which declaimers thrived: there is an almost exact parallel in *Declamation* 17 ascribed to Quintilian (below, 11.1n.), and the motif has also left its mark on Suet. *Vit.* 6, where a similar story is told of Vitellius and his son ('ut creditum est'). Moreover, T.'s discussion of the rumour is notable for its personalised tone (10.1 *non omiserim*, 11.1 *refutaueris*, 3 *mihi . . . causa fuit*), its legal language (e.g. nn. on *refutaueris*, *inaudito* and *falsas auditiones* at 11.1 and 3), and above all its rhetorico-legal style (esp. 11.1 *quis . . .?*, *quin potius . . .?*). In other words T., to retain his readers' attention, has handled a typically exciting declamatory *topic* in a typically declamatory *manner*. There is a good parallel for this in Book 9 of Livy, where the author, having denied that there is a place in his work for digressions 'ut . . . legentibus uelut deuerticula amoena . . . quaererem' (17.1), at once provides just such a digression: it deals with the favourite declamatory topic of Alexander the Great and is handled in the same declamatory manner (highly personalised and with many rhetorical questions) as T. uses here (see Steele 42, and W. B. Anderson's edn (1909) 256–8).

(4) The subject of T.'s excursus is a rumour, and rumours are one of his regular devices of insinuation, esp. in the Tiberian books (Shatzman 560–78): thus e.g. at 1.76.4 he presents an unsavoury rumour about Tib. even though he professes to disbelieve it ('non crediderim'). The present case is simply an extended example of the same technique. We must remember that rumours were one of the standard items of evidence (along with witnesses etc.) in a Roman lawcourt (e.g. *Rhet.*

Herenn. 2.9, Quint. 5.1.2). Naturally they could be attacked by lawyers as false or supported as true; but no matter how successful the attack, there might always be the lingering suspicion that a rumour 'is not generally created recklessly and without some foundation' and that there is 'no reason for anybody wholly to invent and fabricate one' (*Rhet. Herenn.* 2.12). The same author referred to *rumor populi*, 'quem ex argumentis natum necesse est esse uerum' (4.53), and this is precisely the convention to which T. appeals elsewhere at 11.27 and *H.* 2.50.2 (see below, 11.3n.). The fact that in the present case he goes out of his way to refute the rumour is neither here nor there: he was doubtless familiar with the rhetorical device of *concessio*, whereby one furthered one's case by pretending to admit evidence which might appear to weaken it (Quint. 9.2.51).

Thus the excursus is a striking example of T. at his most Tacitean. He manages to elevate the tone of his narrative while at the same time pandering to his readers' interests and vilifying Tib. by appearing to defend him.

10.1 plurimis . . . auctoribus: dat. of agent; the *uariatio* of adj. ~ descriptive gen. (also e.g. 21.3) is common in other authors besides T. References to '(very) many writers' are common in T. (e.g. 57.1, *H.* 5.3.1, *Agr.* 10.1) and other Roman historians (e.g. Liv. 21.46.10): modern scholars are usually uncertain how seriously to take them.

eorundem temporum: contemporaneity (e.g. 2.88.1, 5.9.2, 12.67.1, 13.17.2, Liv. 6.12.2), or at least antiquity (e.g. Liv. 2.40.10, 3.47.5), is a natural recommendation for a source. Here the phrase corresponds to *plurimis*, as does *ualidum* to *maximae fidei*. For the perf. subjunc. *omiserim* see 6.1n.; for *adeo* (below) see 1.2n.

10.2 stupro: see 1.2n.

uinxisse: simple form (as 6.45.3) for compound *deuinxisse* (1.2): see 3.4n.

quod . . . erat: 'T., like Sallust and Livy, fairly often retains the indicative in subordinate clauses of indirect speech' (G. on 1.10.2): so *inierat*, *struxerat* below. Hence the clause could as easily be part of the rumour as T.'s own comment. *primores* is adj. (*OLD* 4a).

composita sint: for the tense see 2.1n.

uerteret: sc. *rem* or *consilium*.

occulto indicio . . . moneret Tiberium 'by means of anonymous intelligence he accused Drusus of planning to poison his father and warned Tiberius . . .': i.e. *indicio* (*OLD* 1b) is to be taken with both *arguens* and *moneret*; *ueneni* = *ueneficii* (*OLD* 2b); and *in* + accus. indicates the intended victim (as 2.88.1 'uenenum in Pyrrhum regem').

10.3 fraude captum: whether this or *deceptum* is correct is a nice question. T. prefers *decipere* specifically of deceit (1.10.3 *imagine . . . specie*, 2.46.1, *H.* 3.70.3 *perfidia*) to *capere* (cf. 13.46.2 *forma*, 15.52.1 *amoenitate*), *fraude deceptus* occurs in a whole range of Augustan and post-Augustan authors, both verse and prose (incl. *Aen.* 5.851, Vell., Curt., Val. Flacc. and Suet.), and *de-* could easily have been omitted after 'frau*de*'. Yet *fraude captus* is popular with Livy, who never uses *fraude deceptus*, and T. generally (but not invariably) prefers simple verbs to compound (3.4n.). M's *cum* could have arisen equally easily from either *captum* or *-ceptum*; but perhaps Livy's evidence just tips the balance in favour of *captum*.

postquam . . . inierat: for the indic. see 2n. above. The pluperf. indic. after *postquam*, of which this is the only ex. in *or. obl.* in T. (imperf. at 73.4), 'is sometimes used in the historians . . . where one would normally expect the aorist-perfect' (*NLS* §217 (2) (d)).

tamquam either = 'that', giving the substance of the suspicion (like an accus. + inf.), or 'as if', giving T.'s own explanation of what the suspicion was. There is a comparable case at 22.1.

struxerat: the verb is often used of evil designs etc. (*OLD* 6a) and is favoured by T. for Tib. and informers (Walker 159).

11.1 Haec . . . iactata . . . refutaueris: the verb, which T. uses only here, has a legal flavour (e.g. Cic. *Mil.* 7 'ea mihi esse refutanda quae . . . iactata sunt'; *OLD* 2a). For the generalising second pers. sing. of the perf. subjunc. in a main clause see *NLS* §119; cf. also 7.2n. (*in arduo*).

super id quod 'besides the fact that', an apparently unique collocation for the more normal *praeterquam quod*: T. does not use the latter but likes *super* = 'besides' (*OLD* 7), as 44.1, 46.1, 60.3, 75.

nullo auctore certo firmantur 'are confirmed by no reliable authority' (in fact by no written authority at all, to judge from 2 below: *neque quisquam scriptor . . .*). The omission of *ab* denotes lack of consciousness on the part of any potential author (*NLS* §44 (end)): the case is therefore somewhat different from that at 7.3 (n.).

quis . . . offerret?: here (as at 14.11.2, a not dissimilar context) T.

unusually makes an authorial comment by means of a rhetorical question. The imperf. subjunc. indicates past potential ('would have offered'): *NLS* §121. For *offerre* used of causing or inflicting something unpleasant see *OLD* 6. *inauditus* is a technical term of accused persons (*OLD* 1a).

idque 'and that too', as 39.4 (*OLD is* 7, *-que*[1] 11b).

nullo ad paenitendum regressu: similar expressions elsewhere (e.g. Liv. 24.26.15, 42.13.3, Sen. *Clem.* 1.13.2) indicate a proverbial tone: it is relevant that a connected expression, 'non habent proximorum odia regressum', appears in the very declamation with which the present poisoning has so much in common: [Quint.] *Decl.* 17.12 (p. 312.4). See above, p. 124.

quin potius . . .? 'Would he not rather . . .?': for the tense and mood of the three verbs see on *quis . . . offerret* above. This is the only ex. of *quin* so used in the whole of *A*.

insita . . . cunctatione et mora: Tib. is regularly described in such terms, e.g. 42.1 'cunctantem', 57.1, 71.3 'cunctationes': they contrast with the decisiveness conventionally associated with the ideal general or statesman (71.3n.) and are an aspect of the diffidence and lack of confidence (38.4) which he has displayed from the very start of his reign (1.11.1). Conversely and typically, however, T. can also portray Tib. as forthright (e.g. 1.7.5 'nusquam cunctabundus') and feigning hesitation (1.46.1 'cunctatione ficta') when it suits him.

unicum is used as a noun = 'only son' where *filius* can easily be understood from the context (*OLD* 1b): here the contrast with *extraneos* (*OLD* 1a) and the presence of *filio* above both help. The prepositional *uariatio* of *in* ~ *aduersum* is typical, e.g. 2.56.1, 3.16.3, 46.1, 6.1.2 etc.

nullius ante flagitii compertum: the gen. after *compertus* is found in Livy, T. (e.g. 1.3.4), Apuleius and legal authors. *ante* is used adjectively = 'previous' in the Greek manner, as *Aen.* 1.198 'ante malorum'.

11.2 repertor: 'The language used of Sejanus is often strikingly similar to that habitually used of Tiberius' (Walker 242 n. 1), who is 'callidus et noui iuris repertor' at 2.30.3. Both men used 'the same techniques' (cf. 1.2n.). For nouns in *-tor* see 1.3n.

caritate . . . odio: a perfect chiasmus: abl., *in* + acc., gen. ~ gen., *in* + acc., abl.

fabulosa et immania: the former word denotes items appropriate to *fabula*, i.e. which (like those of myth) are unnatural, implausible or beyond belief: see below, 3n. The latter is regularly used to denote various aspects of the creatures and monsters of myth (see *OLD*). T.'s point is that the world of Tiberian Rome was such that events like these *were* believed (*credebantur*).

atrociore . . exitus: thus there was a rumour that even Augustus, the one emperor in *A.* not to die a violent death, had been murdered (1.5.1: see Shatzman 560–3). We may recall that Claudius' death (by poisoning) was 'commemorated' by Seneca in the *Apocolocyntosis*: the deaths of other *dominantes* may have been given similar treatment in works which are now lost. There was certainly a vogue for 'death-literature' in the early empire (see Plin. *Ep.* 3.10.1, 5.5.3, 8.12.4 with Sherwin-White's nn.).

atrociore . . . fama, a phrase which seems to originate in Sallust (*H.* 1.107, then Liv. 8.20.2), is a typically appended abl. abs. (2.3n.). *erga* = 'in the case of' etc. seems to originate with T. (*OLD* 3), who also extends its other usages (G. on 2.2.3). The use of *dominans* as a noun = *dominus* occurs only once in republican Latin but is slightly more common thereafter: T. restricts it to *H.* and (with the exception of 14.56.3, the only ex. of the singular) *A.* 1–6.

ordo alioqui sceleris: *ordo* = 'the steps or stages (in an action or process)' (*OLD* 9a), as 69.3 'ordinem fraudis', 2.27.1 'eius negotii initium, ordinem, finem curatius disseram'. *alioqui* = 'besides' (*OLD* 2b), a post-republican usage.

Like Suet. (*Tib.* 62.1) and Dio (57.22.1–2) T. records Drusus' poisoning as fact, but many modern scholars have thought otherwise and Syme declared it 'highly suspect' (402 n. 2). (1) Allegations of poisoning were common when a member of the imperial family died prematurely (cf. 1.3.3 Gaius Caesar, 2.73.4 Germanicus), and poisoning often went hand in hand with adultery in the popular mind (3.3n. *ad coniugii*). (2) It is questionable whether, after being divorced from Sejanus (3.5), Apicata would have had direct knowledge of any poisoning. Her story is neither proved nor disproved by her presumed motives for alleging it: viz. revenge on the now dead Livi(ll)a, for whom Sejanus had divorced her, and an attempt at saving her two remaining children from the execution which her eldest son had suffered (see EJ p. 42 = Sherk 28F for the actual sequence of events, rather than Dio 58.11.5–7). (3) The 'corroboration' of the story by

Eudemus and Lygdus is unreliable: they were tortured to extract it and as close associates of Sejanus their fate was already sealed. (4) Two years previously Drusus had had an illness which was thought by some to be terminal (3.49.1) and by many to have been caused by his notoriously intemperate way of life (Dio 57.14.9–10). His death could well have been due to further illness, although the alleged poisoners set out to make their crime resemble illness (8.1).

Apicatam Seiani: sc. *uxorem.*

tormentis Eudemi: the torture of the doctor, probably a freedman (3.4n.), exceeds the normal practice of the late republic, when only slaves were tortured (Crook 274–5).

infensus is greatly preferred by T. to *infestus* (71:30), which most other authors choose overwhelmingly or exclusively. Virgil, however, marginally prefers *infensus* (11:9).

obiectaret: sc. *scelus.*

cum . . . conquirerent intenderentque 'even though they raked up and aimed everything else ⟨at him⟩'. When applied by T. to historiography, the former verb (*OLD* 1c, 2b) is used deprecatingly (as at *H.* 2.50.2, quoted below, 3n.) or apologetically (as at 33.2): compare the simple *quaerere* at Liv. 9.17.1, Vell. 116.5. For the latter verb (*OLD* 7b rather than 5b) see 2.57.2 'intendere uera' (where the unexpressed contrast is with *concealing* the truth).

11.3 arguendique 'and proving it wrong' (*OLD* 5).

claro sub exemplo: the placing of a monosyllabic preposition between adj. and noun is common, though rare with *sub* in prose: elsewhere in T. only at 1.17.5 and 14.48.3 (both *or. obl.*). For the use and meaning of *sub*, denoting a precedent or example, see *OLD* 11b.

falsas auditiones: *auditio* is hearsay, rumour, or hearsay evidence (*OLD* 2), e.g. Cic. *Planc.* 56 'fictis auditionibus'. T.'s point is not that the rumour is false *qua* rumour but that its contents are 'beyond belief' (*incredibilia*, below: see n.).

cura nostra uenerit: *cura* = 'the product of (literary) application' (*OLD* 3b, cf. 8), i.e. T.'s 'work'; *nostra* is an 'authorial plural' (Nisbet–Hubbard on Hor. *Odes* 1.6.5, W. on Vell. 119.1) and hence not unnatural after *mihi* etc. (so too 32.1 'rettuli . . . annales nostros', 71.1 'mihi . . . trademus'). The perf. subjunc. *uenerit*, like the pres. *antehabeant* below, breaks the sequence of tenses after *peterem*: it is as if T. has changed his point of view, *fuit* (above) now signifying 'has been' (not 'was') and being followed by *petam*.

⟨ne⟩ diuulgata atque incredibilia . . . antehabeant 'not to prefer gossip and fantasies, no matter how avidly they are received, to realistic and unromanticised accounts'. *diuulgata* are the rumoured events of 10.2–3, already summed up as *Haec uulgo iactata* at 11.1; *incredibilia* is the gloss which T. puts on them at 11.1–2 and which explains why they should not be preferred to *ueris neque . . . corruptis*.

(1) Rumours and the like, whether true or false, form part of the historical tradition and are thus legitimate material for the historian. Hence the frequency with which Livy introduces material with *fama est* or similar phrases: a good ex. is the story of poisoning at 8.18.1–11, which he would prefer to disbelieve (§2) but nevertheless relates (§3 'sicut proditur tamen res . . . exponenda est'). See Luce 143–50. T.'s attitude was just the same, e.g. at 3.16.1 'neque tamen occulere debui narratum ab iis qui nostram ad iuuentam durauerunt' (see Shatzman 551–60).

(2) The ancients divided narrative into the three categories of *fabula*, *argumentum* and *historia*, of which the first dealt with 'neque ueras neque ueri similes res' (*Rhet. Herenn.* 1.13, cf. Cic. *Inu.* 1.27, Quint. 2.4.2). The usual criterion for *fabula* was what was physically or naturally impossible (F. W. Walbank, *Historia* 9 (1960) 226), and an author would be criticised for including such material in a narrative which belonged to either of the two other categories. Hence ancient scholars often criticise Homer's narrative as *apiston* ('incredible') or Virgil's as *fabulosum* (e.g. Servius on *Aen.* 9.78) or *incredibile* (Servius 'Auctus' on 9.81, cf. Quint. 10.1.28). Similarly Cicero (*Leg.* 1.5) notes that in Herodotus there are countless *fabulae*, although in *historia* most things should have their basis in real life (*ueritas*). To forestall such criticism historians themselves drew attention to the realism of their narrative, often by comparing it with the works of others: e.g. Hecat. fr. 1 'I write what seems to me to be true, for most Greek accounts are laughable in my opinion', Thuc. 1.22.4 'the non-mythical aspect of my work will perhaps seem less entertaining' (sc. in comparison with Herodotus'), Polyb. 2.16.13–15, Sempr. Asell. fr. 2 'id fabulas pueris est narrare, non historias scribere', Dion. Hal. *Ant. Rom.* 1.39.1, 40.6–41.1, Plut. *Thes.* 1.5 etc.; Wiseman 49–51, 158–9.

(3) When the subject-matter of a rumour was itself *fabulosum*, a

historian was faced with a potential conflict between the positive and negative approaches of (1) and (2) above. Usually the conflict was resolved by prefacing the story with an apologetic disclaimer, e.g. Liv. pref. 6 'quae . . . poeticis magis decora fabulis quam incorruptis rerum gestarum monumentis traduntur, ea nec adfirmare nec refellere in animo est' (cf. 5.21.8–9). When faced with the unnatural behaviour of a bird, T.'s attitude was again just the same: 'ut conquirere fabulosa et fictis oblectare legentium animos procul grauitate coepti operis crediderim, ita uulgatis traditisque demere fidem non ausim' (*H.* 2.50.2). Cf. Ovid's play 'non fabula rumor | ille fuit' (*Met.* 10.561–2).

(4) (*a*) At 11.27 T. describes the 'marriage' of Messalina and C. Silius, material which was not intrinsically unnatural but still unlikely: as T. P. Wiseman says, 'the event was implausible but demonstrably true—a paradox with which the historians of the ancient world were ill-equipped to deal' (*History* 66 (1981) 390). T. begins his account by saying only that the matter *seems* more appropriate to *fabula* ('fabulosum uisum iri'), and concludes: 'sed nihil compositum miraculi causa, uerum audita scriptaque senioribus trado'. (*b*) The present case in Book 4 is in many ways analogous: the alleged events (*diuulgata*), though not unnatural, are still unlikely. Yet T. has gone out of his way to portray them in unnatural terms (2 *fabulosa et immania*: see n.): hence he now considers them as belonging to the realm of *fabula* (*incredibilia*), though this no more prevents him from narrating them than it did the story of the truly unnatural bird at *H.* 2.50.2 (above). For his motivation see above, pp. 123–5.

antehabere occurs in Latin only here and at 1.58.3 (see G.): for the tense see on *uenerit* above. For *auide* cf. *H.* 1.4.3 'rumorum auidi'.

ueris neque in miraculum corruptis: *ueris* contrasts with *incredibilia* above; *neque . . . corruptis* alludes by contrast to the distortion of events once they are *diuulgata* by rumour (cf. 3.44.1 'cuncta, ut mos famae, in maius credita'): Livy uses *incorruptus* somewhat similarly (pref. 6, quoted above). There was a recognised genre of 'miracle-' or 'wonder-literature' which flourished in the Hellenistic age and at other times: while it naturally came under the heading of *fabula*, it enjoyed parodying the historian's manner as illustrated by T. here (J. R. Morgan, *CQ* 35 (1985) 475–90). See also 66.2 below.

corrumpere is regularly followed by *in* + accus. (*OLD* 3a), but *in miraculum* looks like a distant echo of Thuc. 1.21.1 *ἀπίστως ἐπὶ τὸ μυθῶδες ἐκνενικηκότα* ('achieved the status of untrustworthy myth').

12.1 Ceterum resumes the narrative from 9.2 after the excursus of 10–11 (see 3.1n.).

laudante ... pro rostris: the set phrase suggests a contrast with the death of Germanicus, of whom it was remarked that he was not *laudatum pro rostris* (3.5.1): see also next n. The platform for public speaking was at this time on the NW side of the Forum.

induebat: though equally metaphorical with both nouns, as often in T. (see G. on 1.69.1), the verb is used differently with each (syllepsis), its combination with *uoces* (*OLD* 3) being bolder than with *habitum* (='attitude' or 'demeanour'). Cf. also 25.3n. The tense, coupled with the pres. part. *laudante* above, conjures up the picture of people actually starting to mourn as Tib. speaks. Again there is a contrast with the genuine mourning for Germanicus (3.1.4, 2.3). For the *uariatio* of abl. noun ~ adj./part. see 7.1n.

occulti contrasts with *induebat*, as *laetabantur* with *dolentum*, above. Again note the *uariatio* of sing. ~ plur. (Sörbom 73).

quod principium fauoris ... male tegens 'This upsurge of goodwill [sc. towards the family of Germanicus], and the fact that the matriarch Agrippina scarcely concealed her ambitions ...' This 'substantival' use of the pres. part. (also at 34.2, 51.2, 67.2) is generally much rarer than that of the perf. (19.4n.): see *NLS* §95. *male* = *uix* or *non* (*OLD* 4–6).

12.2 ubi uidet: the historic present (usu. of verbs of perceiving) in a temporal clause is common only in historians (*NLS* §217 (3)); but an historic infin. in the following main clause, as here (*uolutare*), is quite exceptional.

ferox scelerum echoes the assessment of Rome's enemy Jugurtha by his cousin Adherbal at Sall. *J.* 14.21 'sceleribus suis ferox'. The adj., as often, has the notion of 'exulting in' (cf. *OLD* 4a); but the dependent genitive of an external attribute, evidently on the analogy of its use with personal characteristics (e.g. Ov. *Met.* 8.613 *mentis*), seems unparalleled and is perhaps intended to suggest that Sejanus' criminality was innate.

prouenerant 'had prospered' (*OLD* 6), as often in T. (G. on 1.19.4). For the *uariatio* of adj. ~ causal clause see 2.42.3, 3.63.1.

peruerteret represents a pres. deliberative subjunc. in *or. recta*; an indir. qu. is rare after *uolutare* (*OLD* 4). Sejanus' machinations against Germanicus' family are continued throughout Book 4, e.g. 15.3, 17, 39.4, 54, 59.3–60, 67.3.

spargi uenenum echoes the accusation levelled against Catiline's hoodlums by Cic. *Cat.* 2.23; in both places the verb is simultaneously literal ('sprinkle') and metaphorical ('disseminate'): *OLD* 1a, 6a.

in tres: Gaius, the youngest son, is now added to his two elder brothers (3.1n., 4.1n.).

pudicitia . . . impenetrabili: remarkably, '*penetrare* does not occur in a sexual sense in the Classical period' (Adams (3) 151): the metaphor is of a boundary which cannot be crossed. Agrippina's *pudicitia* contrasts with Livi(ll)a's lack of it (3.3, 1.41.2); the two were also rivals in *fecunditas* (3 below, 2.43.6). Note the chiasmus with *egregia custodum fide* above, both phrases constituting a typically Tacitean abl. abs. (2.3n.).

12.3 contumaciam: so in 19 the dying Germanicus urged his wife: 'exueret ferociam' (2.72.1). See further Walker 63 n. 2.

Augustae is subjective gen.: 'the Augusta's long-standing hatred [sc. of Agrippina]', for which see esp. 1.33.3. For the name Augusta see 8.3n.

conscientiam 'complicity' (*OLD* 1b). *recentem* (see 3.3–5) contrasts with *uetus*.

exagitare 'activated'.

inhiare dominationi: the metaphor, though common (see *OLD*), vividly describes the Tantalus-like action of striving open-mouthed to snatch that which has hitherto proved elusive.

12.4 atque haec callidis criminatoribus: *haec* is probably accus. plur. (sc. *perfecit* or similar, cf. 38.5, 41.1): 'and he carried out these things with cunning accusers ⟨as his instruments⟩'. For the simple abl. see 7.3n.

Iulium Postumum: if this is the homonymous prefect of Egypt in 47, he must have escaped successful prosecution after Sejanus' fall in 31.

Mutiliae Priscae: wife of C. Fufius Geminus (cos. 29): together they committed suicide in 30, perhaps because of their friendship with Livia Augusta (Dio 58.4.5–7).

in animo . . . efficiebat 'influential with the Augusta, she made the old woman, who by her very nature was anxious about her own power, irreconcilable to her grandson's wife'.

tumidos spiritus perstimulare: though the verb seems unexampled elsewhere, the words suggest the goading of a proud animal. *tumidos* (*OLD* 5a) looks back to *superbam* and *contumaciam*; the infin. after *inlicio* is very rare (recurring only at 2.37.1).

13–16 The end of the year

Like Livy and other earlier annalists, T. regularly ends a year's narrative with an account of miscellaneous domestic items, punctuating it by temporal phrases which have no necessary implication for the relative chronology of the events in question: thus 14.1 *Is quoque annus*, 15.1 *Idem annus*, 16.1 *Sub idem tempus*. (The only exceptions to this rule in Book 4 are A.D. 24 and 27.) But whereas certain of the items thus treated are themselves traditional (e.g. natural disasters at 13.1, foreign embassies at 14.1, obituaries at 15.1, religious matters at 16.1–4), T. typically includes events which have no precedents in earlier historiography (e.g. trials at 13.2–3, 15.2). See in general Ginsburg chh. 3 and 5 §II, who however sees the present year differently (110 n. 3).

In the present section T. elaborates some items at unexpected length (e.g. the biographical vignette at 13.3 *hunc . . . sustentabatur*, antiquarian material at 14.1–2 *Samii . . . trucidarentur*, Tib.'s speech at 16.2–3 *nam . . . flexisset*). This treatment increases the reader's suspense over the further ambitions of Sejanus, of which we were given a foretaste at 12.2–4 and of which we are to be reminded at 15.3.

13.1 At Tiberius returns us, after the Sejanus material of 12.2–4, to Tib., who was last mentioned at 12.1 and is now involved in senatorial business (next n.). Cf. 39.1 *At Seianus*.

cura: a regular term for the responsibilities of the *princeps* (in T. note 67.3, 1.11.1, 19.2 (and G.), 3.35.1, 6.4.3): see 6.4n. (*impendio*) above and W. on Vell. 106.3. Examples follow (note esp. *auctore eo*, cf. 3.19.1, 37.1), but T. typically suggests, as do Suet. *Tib*. 52.1 and Dio 57.22.3, that Tib.'s concern was untimely.

Cibyraticae . . . Aegiensi: Cibyra in SW Phrygia gratefully initiated a new civic era and in 30 joined 13 other cities in erecting a colossal statue at Rome (Rogers (2) 15–16, Magie II 1359, G. on 2.47.1–3). Aegium was on the Peloponnesian shore of the Corinthian Gulf. In granting their *preces* (for which see Millar 346) Tib. was continuing his policy of earlier years (6.4n.).

13.2 ulterioris Hispaniae: i.e. the senatorial province of Baetica, where C. Vibius Serenus had been governor *c.* 21/2; on him see further below, 28–30.1.

de ui publica: *uis publica* is 'the arbitrary execution or use of force against Roman citizens' (Seager 171): see 6.4 above. The normal punishment under the *lex Iulia de ui* (8 B.C.) was *interdictio* (Dio 56.27.2), from which *deportatio* differed in forbidding the defendant any choice in his destination: see Garnsey 111–15 for a discussion of the various terms.

ob atrocitatem morum: *atrocitas* is often used of heinous crimes (*OLD* 3); *morum* = 'behaviour', as often in T., e.g. 1.54.2 (quoted 7.1n.), 13.2.1 'seueritate morum', *H.* 4.44.2 'prauitate morum multis exitiosus'. Amorgos is one of the Cyclades.

Carsidius Sacerdos: praetor in 27, disgraced and deported in 37 (6.48.4).

tamquam 'on the grounds that' (*OLD* 7a), as often after verbs of accusing, to which *reus* (sc. *factus*) is equivalent (cf. Val. Max. 5.3.2a). For Tacfarinas see 23.1n.

eiusdemque criminis depends on *absoluitur.*

C. Gracchus: perhaps the *delator* of 6.38.4.

13.3 pater Sempronius: Ti. Sempronius Gracchus, whom T. typically describes by his *nomen* for reasons of *uariatio* (Sörbom 11), had been banished at the turn of the century for adultery with Augustus' daughter Julia and killed in 14 on Tib.'s order (1.53.3–6). Cercina is an island off the E coast of Tunisia.

extorres et liberalium artium nescios: *extorris* is an archaic alternative to the commoner *exul*, appearing in elevated poetry and historical prose. *nescius*, synonymous with *ignarus* (cf. 6.21.1 'litterarum ignarus'), is also archaic and wholly absent from republican prose except in litotes (e.g. *non sum nescius*, cf. 32.1): T.'s usage fluctuates within his works, but the artificial *nescius* is commoner in *A.* 3–5 (Adams (1) 367–8).

ni for *nisi* is much favoured by T. in *H.* and *A.* 1–12 but virtually discarded in *A.* 13–16 (Goodyear 24): see above, 4.1n. (*foret*), 4.3n. (*tutarentur*); below, 14.1n. (*quis*).

Aelius Lamia: consul in A.D. 3, proconsul of Africa in 15/16 or 16/17, governor of Syria from 21/2 to 31/2 (though kept at Rome by Tib.), he died in 33 as *praefectus urbi* and was accorded the distinction of a state funeral (6.27.2, his obituary). His praise by Vell. 116.3 suggests he was supported by Tib. (*AA* 427–8).

L. Apronius: suffect consul in 8, proconsul of Africa 18–21, where (for the second time in his career) he won the *ornamenta triumphalia* fighting Tacfarinas (3.21.1–4); likewise praised by Vell. 116.3. He is mentioned several times in *A.* (e.g. 22.1, 73.1), whereas the no less distinguished Lamia is mentioned only twice (last n.); the latter's governorship of Syria, however, is likely to have been mentioned in Book 5 (*TST* 57 n. 1, *RP* III 1356).

insontem: this synonym of *innocens* became unpopular from the late republic onwards (except in poetry and historical prose) but T. shows an increasing preference for it (Adams (1) 357–8).

claritudine . . . aduersis: causal abl.; the whole phrase forms a chiasmus with *uariatio. infaustus* = 'ill-starred', the ref. being to the second-century B.C. politicians Ti. and Gaius Gracchus, both killed for their supposedly revolutionary ambitions: the evocation of past disaster is typical of T.

foret abstractus 'would have been carried off' (i.e. the same idiom as Engl.), also at *H.* 4.2.3 'aduersis abstractus' (and H.).

14.1 Is . . . annus . . . habuit is a normal expression (e.g. 2.53.1, 13.33.1), found in Caesar and Cicero and common in Livy: see further 6.1n. and above, p. 134. *quoque* perhaps refers back to the previous year, when there had been a similar episode to the following (cf. 3.60–3, on which see Syme 285 n. 4).

Samiis Iunonis, Cois Aesculapii delubro: the temple of Hera/Juno on the island of Samos was ancient and famous (e.g. Hdt. 2.148); Asclepius, patron of healing, was honoured on Cos, birthplace of the 'doctor' Hippocrates. *delubro* is dat. after *firmaretur* (cf. 3.60.1 'uim . . . sibi firmans'; above, 8.4n.).

uetustum asyli ius: asylum (from Greek *a-sylia* = absence of the right of seizure or reprisal) was claimed by many city-states in the Greek world, where piracy and the like were common, and was regularly associated with a particular shrine or temple: see in general e.g. V. Ehrenberg, *The Greek state* (2nd edn, 1969) 105, 195–6; *Cambridge ancient history* (2nd edn, 1984) VII 1.287–90.

petentibus: T. does not say whether the petitions (on which see Millar 346) were granted, but an inscription from Samos honouring the consuls of 23 perhaps expresses gratitude for their success (Magie II

1361 n. 30); and since the inscription records the second consul as C. Stertinius Maximus, who as suffect replaced Antistius Vetus (1.1), the whole episode must belong to the second half of the year (Ginsburg 141).

Amphictyonum: Amphictyonies were religious associations of Greek city-states, usu. with a shrine or temple as the focal point: see *OCD* and Ehrenberg (above) 108–11.

quis praecipuum . . . iudicium: the archaic *quis* is preferred marginally by T. in *A.* 1–12 but *quibus* is more frequent in *H.* and *A.* 13–16: see R. H. Martin, *C.R.* 18 (1968) 144–6; also above, 4.1n. (*foret*), 13.3n. (*ni*). *praecipuus* is used by T. in *A.* for the hackneyed *maximus* (Adams (1) 361).

qua tempestate is regular in T. to introduce antiquarian material (e.g. 2.60.1, 6.34.2, 12.62, *H.* 5.2.1) – appropriately, since the expression itself was recognised as archaic even in Cicero's day (*De Or.* 3.153). This use of *tempestas* = *tempus* is a feature of poetry and historical prose (G. on 1.3.6).

14.2 templo: dat. for the more normal *in* + accus., and *uariatio* after *delubro* at 1.

Mithridatis: the VIth, in 88 B.C. (Vell. 2.18.1–2).

apud 'in' (*OLD* 3), as often in T. (e.g. 15.2, 27.1).

14.3 Variis . . . questibus: abl. abs.: 'Next, after numerous and usually fruitless complaints from the praetors'. The praetors were the presiding magistrates at the chief public games.

rettulit 'brought a motion [*relatio*]', sc. in front of the senate (*OLD* 7): for the practice see Talbert 165–7 and 234–6. *de immodestia histrionum* suggests (but may not actually reflect) the wording of the *relatio*, and that it concentrated on the second of the two aspects mentioned below (next n.).

in publicum seditiose, foeda per domos: Dio is more explicit on the second point (57.21.3 'actors . . . kept debauching women and stirring up trouble'), the former is given more prominence elsewhere (1.54.2 'discordia ex certamine histrionum', 77.2 'actum de ea seditione apud patres', Vell. 126.2 'compressa theatralis seditio', Suet. *Tib.* 37.2 'per discordiam'): the riotous nature of theatrical disturbances, centring on the factions supporting rival actors, posed a threat to public order and hence to stable government (in general A. Cameron, *Circus factions* (1976) 223). Both points are picked up chiastically by *flagitiorum* [3.3n.] *et uirium* below. *in publicum . . . per domos* is itself chiastic, with *uariatio* of prepositions and of adverb ~ substantival adj.

Oscum . . . ludicrum is a synonym for *fabula Atellana* (Cic. *Fam.* 7.1.3), the vulgar farce originally performed in Oscan (hence *quondam*) and associated with the town of Atella (*OCD Atellana*): it thrived on its blend of obscenity and political satire in Tib.'s day (Suet. *Tib.* 45).

leuissimae apud uulgum oblectationis 'the lowest kind of mass entertainment': genit. of description (*NLS* §§84–5), with prepositional phrase instead of the adj. *uulgaris* (2.1n. *uisu*). The more usual accus. *uulgus* is preferred to *-um* by T. in *H.* and *A.* 11–16 but the latter is marginally more frequent in *A.* 1–6 (H. on *H.* 1.36.3). T.'s attitude to the lower classes is consistently superior (Yavetz 141ff.).

eo . . . uenisse ⟨ut⟩ . . . sit: for *eo* (+genit.) *uenire ut* see *OLD eo*[2] 2. *auctoritas* = 'an informal decree of the senate' (*OLD* 4a); see also Talbert 523.

pulsi: as were the leaders of the rival actors' factions (Suet. *Tib.* 37.2; Garnsey 119). The actors themselves were promptly recalled by Gaius (Dio 59.2.5). See further 62.2 below.

15.1 Idem annus . . . adfecit: see 6.1n. and above, p. 134.

alio quoque: i.e. in addition to his grief at Drusus' death.

alterum: i.e. Germanicus (3.1n.). For the *uariatio* of gerund(ive) ~ abl. noun see 1.3.6, 26.2, 3.27.1, 13.31.3, 14.19, 41; Martin (1) 92.

Lucilius Longus: suffect consul in 7; otherwise a political nonentity.

Obituary notices form a large class of T.'s 'end of year' material. Apart from those for members of the imperial family, they begin at 3.30 and, with a very few exceptions (e.g. Julia at 71.4 (n.), L. Piso at 6.10.3), are placed at or near the year's end (see further 61n.). Several cases involve more than one individual, allowing T. to draw comparisons (e.g. 44nn.). See *TST* 79–90, Martin (2) 138–9, Ginsburg 32, 128–30.

tristium laetorumque: the use of neut. plur. adjectives as nouns is commonest where the gender of at least one adj. is clear (e.g. Ov. *F.* 6.463 'miscentur tristia laetis'), but there are exceptions, as here.

Rhodii secessus: 6 B.C.–A.D. 2; below, 57.2. For *unus* see 1.2n. (*obscurum*).

15.2 quamquam without a finite verb is largely post-Ciceronian and frequent in T. (e.g. 20.4, 39.1, 42.2, 59.3, 63.2). For 'new men' see 6.2n. (*mandabatque*).

censorium funus is thought to be equivalent to *publicum funus* (Talbert 370–1 and n. 11); other cases in 21 (3.48.1), 32 (6.11.3 *publico f.*) and 33 (6.27.2 *censorio f.*).

effigiem apud forum Augusti: thus joining the statues of the Roman heroes of old (Suet. *Aug.* 31.5).

etiam tum: T. commonly uses 'temporal innuendo' to suggest surprise that circumstances were not yet as bad as might have been expected or as they later became (e.g. 1.74.5, 3.72.1, 13.18.2); but, as often, his example conflicts with the impression thus created (next n.).

adeo ut procurator Asiae Lucilius Capito . . . causam dixerit: though Asia was a senatorial province, Capito was an equestrian procurator of Tib. (6.3n.): his case thus lay strictly outside the senate's jurisdiction and is therefore a remarkable example of Tib.'s attitude towards the senate (6.2n.): hence *adeo ut* . . . (1.2n.). See Garnsey 30–1, 86, Talbert 467, Brunt (2) 52.

magna cum adseueratione principis: for the emperor's speaking in senatorial debates see Talbert 163ff.; Ginsburg 125 n. 32. The details here (*non se ius . . . mandata sua*) correspond to those in Dio 57.23.4–5 (quoted in part at 6.4n. *si quando*).

familiares applies also to *seruitia* (= *seruos*, cf. 6.4n.).

praetoris: T.'s substitute for *proconsul* (so too 43.3, 45.1), even when, as here and 2.77.1, the position was consular: see Syme 343–4, G. on 1.74.1. Though such avoidance of technical terms is familiar in T. (1.1n. *cohortibus*), the usage had republican precedent and may be employed to recall an age which is long since past.

manibusque 'hands' (as the instruments of violence: *OLD* 8a) is more vivid than 'bands' (*OLD* 22a); for *usus foret* cf. 16.15.2 'manu serui usus'.

audirent: sc. *patres* as subject.

cognito 'having been investigated judicially': a technical verb (*OLD cognosco* 4a).

damnatur: to exile (Dio 57.23.4).

15.3 priore anno . . . uindicatum erat: C. Iunius Silanus, consul in 10, proconsul of Asia in 20–1 and father of the consul of 28

(68.1n.), had been banished in 22 (3.66–9): see *AA* 193, 487 (index), Table XIII. For the impersonal usage see *OLD uindico* 5b; for the *uariatio* of *ob* ~ causal clause see e.g. 1.22.2, 2.42.3, 6.39.3, *H.* 2.4.3; Sörbom 115–16, Martin (1) 93.

templum: see further chh. 55–6 below; Price 258. Cf. also 37.1.

statuere: sc. *templum*. The infin. after *permitto*, exceptional in Cicero, becomes common later (Adams (1) 371).

grates was originally a religious term for thanks to a god but was first used = *gratias* by poets and then (from Curtius) by writers of elevated prose. In *A*. T. greatly prefers it to *gratias*, which he reserves for speeches (Adams (2) 134). For Nero see 4.1n.

laetas inter . . . adfectiones 'to the delighted reactions of his audience'.

recenti . . . Germanici 'with the memory of G. still fresh' (abl. abs.).

illum aspici, illum audiri: the Romans had a remarkable capacity to see one individual in terms of another (J. Griffin, *Latin poets and Roman life* (1985) 188–91) but the resemblance of son to father was obviously evocative (e.g. *Aen.* 4.328–9 'si quis mihi paruulus aula | luderet Aeneas, qui te tamen ore referret' with Pease's n.). The anaphora, relatively rare in *A*., emphasises that Germanicus is 'really present', while both seeing and hearing are mentioned as the principal testificatory senses (e.g. 15.36.3 and again *Aen.* 4.83–4 'illum absens absentem auditque uidetque | . . . genitoris imagine capta'). Germanicus' 'resurrection' is particularly effective after the enthusiasm which greeted the false rumours of the man's survival in 19 (2.82.4–5), and also so soon after the account of Sejanus' plots against his family on Drusus' death (12.2–4).

forma principe uiro digna: the appearance of a leader was expected to match his role: compare Tib. as described by Vell. 94.2 ('uisuque praetulerat principem' with W.) and contrast T.'s own description at 57.2 below. See also 34.2n.

gratiora: though neuter, this refers back to *modestia ac forma* and is explained by *ob periculum*, which itself is explained by *notis . . . odiis*: '⟨qualities⟩ the more welcome because of . . .'

16.1 de flamine Diali: the *flamines* were a group of fifteen priests (*OCD*), each concerned exclusively with the cult of a single god; the priest of Jupiter (*f. Dialis*) was one of the most important. See M. W.

Hoffman Lewis, *The official priests of Rome under the Julio-Claudians* (1955), R. M. Ogilvie, *The Romans and their gods* (1969) 108–9.

There are various likely reasons for T.'s relatively extended treatment of this topic: both he and his readers were interested in antiquarian and religious material (cf. 65n. *Haud fuerit*); he had himself held high priestly office (above, p. 10); the present incumbent had tried unsuccessfully in 22 to be appointed to the proconsulship of Asia (3.58.1–3, 71.2), a position which T. was later to hold himself; and the unpopularity of the priesthood under Tib. provides an ironic link with the narrative of the following year (17.1–2: see Ginsburg 23, 51, cf. 89–90).

Serui Maluginensis: Servius Cornelius Lentulus Maluginensis was suffect consul in 10; his sister was probably the second wife of Sejanus' father (*AA* 297; Table XXIII).

simul = *et* (Adams (1) 359–60).

roganda . . . lege: sc. *de* from above: 'about the approval of a new law' (*OLD rogo* 5b).

16.2 patricios . . . genitos: patricians were members of the most ancient and aristocratic *gentes* of Rome, although Caesar, Augustus and later emperors were empowered to admit new members (*OCD*). *confarreatio*, the oldest and most solemn form of marriage, involved a sacramental meal of *far* ('spelt'); it was exclusive to patricians and obligatory for a major priest, who must also have been the offspring of such a marriage (*OCD*).

tres simul nominari . . . uetusto more: equivalent to *uetustum morem esse tres simul nominari*.

ex quis unus legeretur: *quis* = *quibus* (14.1n.); *legeretur* ('was to be chosen') represents a pres. jussive subjunc. in *or. recta* (*NLS* §§109–10). The choice belonged to the *pontifex maximus* (Tib. himself).

eam copiam: as if *eius copiam*: 'supply *for* it', viz. the production of a short-list of three. Three reasons are then given for the lack of candidates: (1) the rarity of *confarreatio* (*omissa . . . aut . . . retenta*), (2) the difficulties of the priesthood (*accedere . . . uitarentur*), (3) the implications for *patria potestas* (*et quod . . . conueniret*). See next nn. for the details of this interpretation of an exceptionally difficult passage.

pluresque eius rei causas adferebat: T. interrups the *or obl.* for a brief parenthesis where he says that Tib. offered 'various explanations' for *eius rei*, which in our opinion refers to the phrase immediately preceding: *omissa . . . aut . . . retenta* (viz. the rarity of *confarreatio*). Of these various explanations T. adds only 'the most important' (*potissimam*: next n.).

Most modern edd., however, have followed Madvig in extending the parenthesis to *uitarentur*, in which case (*a*) *ipsius caerimoniae* would refer to confarreate marriage, and (*b*) *et* would co-ordinate the abl. abs. *omissa . . . retenta* and *quod* [or *quoniam*] *exiret* . . . as causal expressions exhibiting *uariatio* (24.2n.).

potissimam . . . feminarumque: abbreviated for *quarum potissimam causam esse penes incuriam* etc.: 'of which he said the most important was due to the indifference of men and women'. *penes* (1.1n.) is very rare with non-personal nouns.

accedere ipsius caerimoniae difficultates 'additional considerations were the problems of the priesthood itself . . .' (*OLD accedo* 17): see also next n. In the interpretation offered here, the accus. + inf. is taken to resume the *or. obl.* after the authorial intervention of *pluresque . . . feminarum*; and *caerimoniae difficultates* is taken to refer to the notorious taboos and rituals of the priestly office. These are themselves described as *caerimoniae* by Gellius in his discussion of the *flamen Dialis* (10.15.1 'caerimoniae impositae flamini Diali multae', 18); yet in T. the noun *caerimonia* 'comes almost to stand for the office itself' (F. on 1.62.2 'imperatorem auguratu et uetustissimis caerimoniis praeditum'), as also at 4 below and 1.54.1; see G. on 1.62.2 for the word's wide range of meaning.

et quod exiret e iure patrio qui . . . quaeque . . . conueniret 'and the fact that a man who gained that priesthood, as well as the woman who married him, each left the jurisdiction of their fathers'. *exire* is the appropriate verb for abandoning a legal status (*OLD* 6a), but T. typically avoids the technical *patria potestas*; *conuenire* [*OLD* 1c] *in manum* = 'to marry' (of a wife). The point seems to be that even in the empire *patria potestas* continued to be a powerful legal force in controlling family relationships and property (*OCD*); loss of *patria potestas* over a daughter was evidently regarded as esp. serious, since the subsequent *lex* (below) concerns only the priest's wife. In practice, however, the theoretical restrictions may have been considerably modified, as argued by R. P. Saller (*Continuity and Change* 1 (1986) 7–22), although he makes no reference to our passage. Another recent study is by W. K. Lacey in B. Rawson (ed.), *The family in ancient Rome* (1986) 121–44.

As *accedit* is followed in classical Latin by *quod* and never by *quoniam*, M's *qūo* must be taken as an unusual abbreviation (or scribal error) for *quod*. In T. *accedit* is commonly followed by either a noun or *quod*, though not by both simultaneously; yet the *uariatio* here of *difficultates* ~ *quod* is otherwise typical (cf. 18.1 *amicitia . . . et quod*).

16.3 medendum: medical metaphors are common in political narrative (17.3n.).

senatus decreto aut lege: a *senatus consultum* (for which *decretum* is an alternative) differed from a *lex* in that the latter required ratification by a popular assembly: see *OCD*.

sicut Augustus: the *exemplum* is typical of Tib.: see 37.3n.

horrida often suggests 'unbending' (*OLD* 5) and thus contrasts with *flexisset*. One of Augustus' minor relaxations, concerning the number of nights a *flamen Dialis* might sleep away from his own bed, is mentioned at 3.71.2. See further Gell. 10.15.14 and Ogilvie on Livy 5.52.13.

tractatis religionibus 'after examining the question of impediments': *OLD tracto* 8a (cf. 9), *religio* 3b. Cf. 3.71.2 'de religionibus tractabatur'.

demutari: 'Archaic and very rare', so perhaps a Tiberian idiolect (Syme 702). For a specific request elsewhere from Tib. to the senate see 70.1 (by letter); Ginsburg 124 n. 27.

qua . . . ageret 'whereby the priestess of Jupiter should be under her husband's jurisdiction for ceremonial purposes but should enjoy the ordinary rights of women in all other matters'.

filius: otherwise unknown.

16.4 capiebatur: this technical term for appointing a Vestal virgin (also at 2.86.1) is discussed at Gell. 1.12.

sestertii uicies: 20 × 100,000 sesterces = 2 million s.

sedes inter Vestalium: the privilege was later extended to Caligula's grandmother and sisters and Messalina: 'it seems likely that this was the only way in which prominent women could get a front seat' (E. Rawson, '*Discrimina ordinum*: the *lex Julia Theatralis*', *P.B.S.R.* 55 (1987) 91). For the anastrophe of *inter* see 5.1n.

17–33 The year A.D. 24

T. organises his narrative of 24 on the pattern familiar from Livy: home affairs, foreign affairs, home affairs (Ginsburg 54, 133–4). Yet at the same time he diverges strikingly from Livy, since the domestic 'frame' shows a preoccupation with trials which is quite alien to his great predecessor (18–22, 28–31). This and other differences from republican historiography are commented on by T. himself in the digression with which the year's narrative is concluded (32–3: below, pp. 169–70).

17–22 Home affairs

The first section of domestic narrative exhibits an identical format to the last (below, p. 160): a transitional item (17) is followed by a trial described at length (18–20) and three others described briefly (21–2). In 17 Tib.'s displeasure at the priests for honouring Germanicus' sons both contrasts with his own supportive efforts at 16 above (see Ginsburg 23) and serves to introduce his own and Sejanus' hostility to the house of Germanicus, which forms the background to the central trial (18.1 *amicitia Germanici*, 19.1 *odiis Seiani*). Indeed T. uses his centre-piece to stress the dangers of friendship and hatred (18.3 *pro gratia odium*, 19.1 *caritate . . . inuisa*, *inimicitias*, 3 *ira*, 20.2 *saeuis adulationibus*) and to contrast the perils of excess (18.2 *intemperantia*, *immodice*) with the advantages of moderation (20.3 *temperamenti*). His conclusion that there is a middle way *inter . . . contumaciam et . . . obsequium* (20.3) is anticipated at 17.1 (*adulatione, quae . . . proinde anceps si nulla et ubi nimia est*) and re-emphasised by its antitheses in the later trials (21.1 *feroci*, *iras*, *offensionis*, 3 *immodicas inimicitias*, *odia*).

17.1 consulibus: Ser. Cornelius Cethegus was a political nonentity; the father of L. Visellius Varro had been suffect consul in 12 and *legatus* of lower Germany in 21 (19.1n.). For the abl. abs. see 1.1n.

pro incolumitate principis uota: for this annual custom, which later took place on 3 January, see Weinstock 217–20.

iuuenum: objective gen.: 'affection for the young men' (as 19.1). Since Germanicus' sons had been commended to the senate in the previous year by Tib. himself (8.5), the priests can hardly have expected trouble.

quae . . . anceps si nulla et ubi nimia est 'which in a corrupt society is equally dangerous if it is absent or excessive'; the priests' action was an ex. of the latter. For the *uariatio* of *si* ~ *ubi* see 1.44.5; Sörbom 121; for *proinde* see *OLD* 2c, cf. 1b.

17.2 Agrippinae links up with 12.1 and 4.

illi quidem . . . modice perstricti 'they for their part, despite their denials, were criticised, ⟨but only⟩ lightly'. *quidem* looks forward to *ceterum* below (μέν . . . δέ); for *quamquam* see 4.1n.

ipsius: i.e. Tib.; their identity is unknown.

primores ciuitatis is used regularly by T. for *principes ciu.*: 'he almost certainly took the phrase from Livy, the only earlier writer who uses it' (Adams (2) 140 n. 33).

extolleret 'raise up' (*OLD* 5).

17.3 quippe is preferred in second place marginally in *A.* 2–4 to first, which is its preferred position elsewhere (Adams (1) 366): here it emphasises the verb and suspends the ref. to Sejanus' name, whose machinations against Agrippina are now resumed from 12.4.

ut ciuili bello: ironical in Sejanus' mouth, since he was himself a prime mover in any 'civil war' (e.g. 2.2n. *adeundo*). For *ut* see 3.3n.

qui se . . . uocent 'who called themselves ⟨members⟩ of Ag.'s faction': *partium* (partitive gen.) continues the idea of civil war (*OLD* 16a). For the tense of *uocent* and *resistatur* see 2.1n.

remedium: as at 2.1 above (*procul urbis inlecebris*) Sejanus makes his point all the more effective by presenting the alleged situation in familiar terms. Metaphors of disease are common in Latin and Greek to describe civil or military unrest of various kinds (e.g. *H.* 1.26.1, 3.11.1, Sall. *C.* 10.6 (with Vretska), 36.5; Keitel 320, Fantham 14ff., 218 (index)); correspondingly its cure is expressed by medical metaphors (*remedium*, cf. e.g. 1.9.4, Liv. pref. 9; *RICH* 133–4), arguably anticipated here by *resistatur* (*OLD* 7b) above (as Engl. 'resistance' to a disease).

unus alterue maxime prompti 'one or two of the most active': it was dangerous to be *promptus* in imperial times (1.13.1 'promptum . . . suspectabat' and G., *Agr.* 3.2 'promptissimus quisque saeuitia principis interciderunt'; also above, 1.3n. *saepius*). T. reverts to the normal sequence of tenses with *subuerterentur*.

18.1 C. Silium: C. Silius A. Caecina Largus, consul in 13, commander on the upper Rhine 14–21 (1.31.1), winner of the *ornamenta triumphalia* 15 (1.72.1), victor of Sacrovir 21 (3.46). For his case see Rogers (1) 75–8, Bauman (2) 116–20.

Titium Sabinum: an *eques* whose case is deferred till 28 (19.1; also next n. but one).

adgreditur 'attacked': the verb is commonly used in judicial contexts as a metaphor derived from its use in military contexts (*OLD* 3a–b, e).

amicitia Germanici perniciosa: as at 68.1 'ob amicitiam Germanici', where Sabinus' case is resumed; see also p. 247. The debasement of friendship is a motif of civil unrest (e.g. Thuc. 3.82.6, Sall. *C.* 10.5; Keitel 323) and here shows up Sejanus' allegations of 17.3 as a sham; moreover, since *amicitia* was above all the bond of political and social life in the Roman republic, its perversion is one of T.'s characteristic themes: e.g. 3n., 29.1, 31.3, 33.3, 54.1, 68.3, 74.5 (in general R. Seager, *A.J.A.H.* 2 (1977) 40–50). Other reversals at 3.4n. above.

Silio et quod . . . dispergebatur: sc. *perniciosum* (from above) with *Silio*: 'to Silius was also fatal the fact that, in as much as he was likely to have the greater fall (having been commander . . . and victor . . .), more fear was likely to be disseminated among others'. For the inverted order of expression see 11.21.1. The ellipse of *tanto* (to balance *quanto*) before a comparative is found occasionally in other authors (e.g. Livy) but is common in T. (H. on *H.* 2.78.4, 3.18.2): cf. 69.2. For the conative or inceptive sense of the imperf. indic. see *NLS* §200 (ii); for *procideret* see below.

moderator for *legatus* looks like an ex. of T.'s avoidance of standard terms (1.1n.) but is ironical in Silius' case (cf. also 1.31.3 'quibus Silius moderabatur') because of his alleged lack of *self*-control (2 below).

triumphalibus: since 19 B.C. the award of a full triumph had been restricted to the emperor and his family; others were allowed the *ornamenta triumphalia*, which T. typically (e.g. 23.1, 26.1, 44.1), but not uniquely, expresses by using the adj. as a noun (G. on 1.72.1). The unparalleled adj. *Sacrouirianus* enhances Silius' achievement.

quanto maiore mole procideret: the image is that of a falling building (cf. 15.40.1), appropriate in paraenetic contexts (Hor. *Odes* 2.10.10–11 'celsae grauiore casu | decidunt turres' with Nisbet–Hubbard) and applied to Sejanus himself by Juv. 10.105–7 ('parabat | excelsae turris tabulata, unde altior esset | casus et impulsae praeceps immane ruinae'). *mole* is abl. of 'attendant circumstances' (as *Aen.* 3.656 'uasta se mole mouentem'): *NLS* §47. *procideret* = 'was to fall', a regular but infrequent use of the imperf. subjunc. to express futurity from a past point of view (Handford 84–5).

18.2 suum: emphatic position: '*his* soldiers . . .' (collective sing., cf. 2.1n.). The ref. is to 1.16–52, the mutinies of A.D. 14; see esp. 1.31.3, 40.1.

mansurum: sc. *fuisse* (= *mansisset* in *or. recta*), as fairly often in T.

cupido is preferred in *H.* to *cupiditas*, which in *A.* is entirely avoided; conversely, Cicero and Caesar use *cupiditas* exclusively, which is also preferred by Livy and Vell.; Sall., however, prefers *cupido* (G. on 1.3.6).

nouandi 'of engaging in revolutionary activity' (*OLD nouo* 4b–c).

18.3 destrui . . . fortunam suam 'his position was being undermined'. T. continues to think in terms of building metaphors (see above, 1n., and *durauisse, prolaberentur*); for *fortunam* see 2.71.3 'si me potius quam fortunam meam fouebatis'.

imparemque: sc. *se esse*. T. becomes increasingly fond of omitting *se* in *or. obl.*, and with other tenses of the infin. than the future active, where the omission is common in other authors as well as T. (Adams (1) 370–1).

nam beneficia . . . odium redditur: 'Ever and again the pitiless diagnosis . . condenses into an aphorism, acrid, intense, and unanswerable' (Syme 417) – although the present type of *sententia* is relatively less common in *A.* than in the earlier works (4.1n. *quamquam arduum*). The aphorism is here enhanced by chiasmus and *uariatio* (main clause, temporal clause [*dum*] ~ temporal clause [*ubi*], main clause). For *usque eo* [the more normal order] . . . *dum* see *OLD usque* 4a, *eo*² 3a; *laeta* = 'welcome' (*OLD* 7).

ubi multum anteuenere '⟨but⟩ when(ever) they get far ahead': the verb is archaic and very rare, being used by T. elsewhere only literally (at 1.63.4: see G.); its precise metaphorical use here seems unparalleled. The tense is frequentative (*NLS* §217 (2)).

pro 'instead of'. 'Affection changing to hatred is a thing upon which T. willingly dwells' (K. Wellesley, *C.R.* 12 (1962) 119): see 12.30.2, 14.62.2, 15.67.2, 68.3, *H.* 2.5.2; also above, 1n.

19.1 Agrippinae 'for Agrippina' (17.1n.).

corripi: the verb is regular in T. for the activities of *delatores*, whose violence it suggests (Walker 159, G. on 2.28.3).

placitum: sc. *est*: ironical, as if an official decree of the senate (16.3; *OLD* 5).

immissusque 'was sent in', a similar idiom to Engl. (as of the Marines or SAS): note the 'military' use of the passive (Ogilvie on Liv. 2.26.6).

paternas inimicitias: Silius was given the command against Sacrovir in preference to Varro's father (3.43.3).

19.2 breuem moram, dum . . . abiret: this perhaps suggests that only a short time was to elapse before Varro gave way to one of the suffect consuls half-way through the year (Rogers (1) 77 n. 237).

diem . . . dicere 'to serve a summons' (*OLD dies* 7b).

cuius uigiliis niteretur ne quod res publica detrimentum caperet: the situation recalls 63 B.C., when Cicero, proclaiming his own vigilance (*Cat.* 2.19, 3.3 etc.), persuaded the senate to pass the *senatus consultum ultimum* (1.4): see esp. Sall. *C.* 29.2 'senatus decreuit, darent operam consules ne quid res publica detrimenti caperet' (the ch. ends with the words *consuli ius*). Here, paradoxically, the odious Varro is cast in the role of Cicero, and the unfortunate Silius as Catiline; but also important is the fact that in A.D. 24 ultimate responsibility lay with Tib. (the subject of *niteretur*). See also next n. but one.

proprium 'typical' (*OLD* 4).

scelera nuper reperta priscis uerbis obtegere: the *senatus consultum ultimum* had last been passed in 40 B.C., more than half a century before: hence *priscis uerbis* (defined by Cicero as 'archaisms which because of their antiquity have long passed out of use in everyday speech': *De Or.* 3.153). T.'s attribution of such deceitful practice to Tib. not only illustrates the emperor's characteristic conservatism but also serves to justify the historian's own practice of alleging pretence everywhere (1.2n. *obscurum*, 3.4n. *specie*) and to corroborate the notion of civil unrest (17.3n.), a state of affairs during which words conventionally changed their meanings (Thuc. 3.82.4–8, Isocr. *Antid.* 283–5, cf. *H.* 1.37.4 'quae alii scelera, hic remedia uocat, dum falsis nominibus . . . uocat'). For *nuper* see 34.1n. (*nouo*) and ref. there to Sall. *C.* 4.4.

19.3 igitur multa adseueratione . . . coguntur patres 'So with much earnestness . . .': the picture is more vivid and ironical if *adseueratio* represents the senators' response to Tib.'s speech; *igitur* resumes the story after the brief parenthesis *proprium . . . obtegere* (3.3n.). *coguntur* primarily = 'gathered together', but the notion 'were constrained' is hard to exclude (*OLD* 4a, 12). T.'s irony is maintained by *quasi . . . esset* ('as though it were by due process of law that Silius was being tried, or Varro were a ⟨real⟩ consul or that ⟨state⟩ the republic'): compare 3.66.2 and its ironical *uidelicet*.

coeptaret: though rare elsewhere and mostly poetical, the frequentative form is common in T. (e.g. 24.2, 27.2; but absent from *A.* 13–16): see G. on 1.38.1.

cuius ira premeretur 'by whose anger he was being crushed': the ref. is presumably to Sejanus, to whose role Silius must have alluded obliquely. The appended abl. abs. is typical of T. (2.3n.).

19.4 conscientia belli . . . dissimulatus 'The lengthy cover-up of Sacrovir through complicity in his rebellion'. The substantival use of the perf. part. in the nomin. is strikingly frequent in the earlier books of *A.* (e.g. below *uictoria . . . foedata*, 26.1 *negatus honor*; Adams (1) 371) and much more so than the corresponding use of the present (12.1n.). See *NLS* §95.

nec dubie . . . haerebant: from T.'s statement that the second of the two charges (*repetundae*) was justified, we may infer that he thought the first (*conscientia belli*) *un*justified: that seems borne out by the evidence of 3.41.3 and 47.1 'fide ac uirtute legatos . . . superfuisse'. *criminibus* is probably abl. (G. on 1.65.4, *OLD* 8d).

exercita 'conducted' (*OLD* 8a).

fine 'death': the usage (i.e. without *uitae*) is Augustan and later (*OLD* 10a).

praeuertit 'forestalled' (*OLD* 3a).

20.1 saeuitum tamen in bona . . . petebantur 'His property was nevertheless savaged, not for restitution to the tax-paying provincials (none of whom claimed compensation), but the demands of the imperial treasury were itemised individually, Augustus' generosity to Silius being extorted in the process.' *tamen* suggests that Silius had expected his property to be left alone, as was normally the case with pre-emptive suicides (see 6.29.1; Crook 275–6). *non . . . sed* contrasts the restitution which might have been expected ('*red*derentur', '*re*petebat', ironically picking up 19.4 *repetundarum*) with the strictly unwarranted demands of the *fiscus* (*auulsa*, *petebantur*). The contrast is deployed to introduce the authorial comment *ea prima . . . fuit* below, and is emphasised by the *uariatio* whereby *non ut . . .* is followed not by a second *ut*-clause, as might have been expected, but by *sed* + main clause (very rare: see Sörbom 128). Yet at the same time the contrast is somewhat obscured by the inversion of the logical order of ideas which follow *sed*: we might have expected *liberalitas . . . auulsa* to be subordinate to *computatis . . . petebantur* and expressed accordingly in an abl. abs. (as translated), rather than *vice versa*. For a not dissimilar inversion see 3.2n. (and cf. 18.1); and for the *uariatio* after *non ut* cf. 23.2 below.

Whether *ut* is purposive or consecutive is unclear. For *stipendiarius* see *OLD* 2a; for *fiscus*, 6.3n. (*res suas*).

ea prima Tiberio . . . diligentia fuit: in 20 the proposed seizure of Piso's and Lepida's property had been waived (3.18.1, 23.2, the former on Tib.'s instruction), and in 22 that of Silanus' moderated (3.68.2, with Tib.'s agreement). The use of *diligentia*, a Ciceronian favourite and equivalent to the virtue *cura* (6.4n.), is heavily ironical (for *prima* see 34.1n. *nouo*). See further 6.4n. (*rari*) and G. on 1.75.2. For *erga*, 11.2n.

Asinii Galli: C. Asinius Gallus, son of the consular historian Pollio (34.4n.) and father of the consuls of 23 (1.1n.) and 25 (34.1n.), had been consul in 8 B.C. and proconsul of Asia in 6 B.C.; he married Vipsania after her divorce by Tib. in 12 B.C. Described as *auidus imperii* (1.13.2), he inherited his father's intransigence (1.12.4) and is mentioned by T. more often than any other consular (e.g. 30.1, 71.2–3). He died in custody in 33.

bonorum: Sosia's exclusively. The *uariatio* of gerund(ive) ~ indir. command is typical of T. (1.14.1, 2.36.1, 3.17.4); see also 9.1n. (*utque*).

20.2 M. Lepidus: son of Aemilius Lepidus Paullus, the consul of 34 and censor of 22 B.C., he was consul in A.D. 6, proconsul of Asia in 26 (56.3), and 'the most distinguished senator in the reign of Tiberius' (Syme 526): see *TST* 30–49, *AA* Table IV. T. mentions him almost as often as Gallus, with whom he is again juxtaposed at 1.13.2 ('capax imperii sed aspernans').

quartam: sc. *partem*. The law in question is the *lex Iulia de maiestate*.

hunc ego Lepidum . . . comperior: an authorial statement of unqualified praise is very rare in T. and here emphasised by the unmistakable allusions to Sall. *J.* 45.1 'Metellum . . . magnum *et sapientem uirum fuisse comperior*, tanta *temperantia inter ambitionem* sae̤uiṯiam̤que moderatum' (the last phrase providing further allusions below). Note also *J.* 108.3 'sed *ego comperior* Bocchum . . .' (the deponent form being very rare elsewhere and only here in T.); *sapiens* is used nowhere else of an individual by Sall. or T. (except in an ironical ref. to Seneca in a speech of Nero's at 14.56.2).

pleraque . . . in melius flexit 'many items he steered away from the savage adulations of others for the better', a rather different nuance of the verb from 16.3. The oxymoron of *saeuis adulationibus* implies that men sought to flatter Tib. by advocating *saeuitia* towards his victims.

neque tamen temperamenti egebat, cum aequabili . . . uiguerit: T. continues his allusions to Sall. *J.* 43.1 'fama *tamen aequabili*' and 45.1 (see above); the use of *egere*+gen. is also reminiscent of Sall. (Cic. much prefers abl.). In Lepidus' obituary at 6.27.4 T. praises his *moderatio atque sapientia*: for the importance of this type of figure during the empire, of which L. Piso at 6.10.3 is another (rare) ex. in T., see W. on Vell. 88.2.

T. provides only one ex. of the relationship between Lepidus and Tib.: the latter's encouraging reaction at 3.51.1 to a speech of Lepidus which again contains echoes of Sallust (Syme 354 and n. 9).

20.3 fato et sorte nascendi . . . an sit aliquid in nostris consiliis: T. is no more seriously concerned with fate and astrological determinism here than at 6.22.1–3, but uses these concepts as a convenient foil for the characteristic point that *posse etiam sub malis principibus magnos uiros esse* (*Agr.* 42.2: the whole passage should be compared). For the omission of *utrum* in an alternative indir. qu., as 33.4, 34.5 and 40.2, see *NLS* §182 (4).

inter abruptam contumaciam et deforme obsequium pergere iter . . . uacuum: the phraseology again echoes Sall. *J.* 45.1 (see above), and *pergere iter* (though found occasionally elsewhere) occurs at *J.* 79.5; but T. has transformed the allusions into a sustained metaphor of an unobstructed road (*uacuum*: *OLD* 6a), having a precipitous cliff on one side (*abruptam*: *OLD* 1) and a wasteland on the other (*deforme*: *OLD* 2b). The potential obstacles *ambitione ac periculis* pick up *contumaciam et . . . obsequium* chiastically. For road metaphors applied to a proper way of life see Fantham 70–1.

20.4 Messalinus Cotta: M. Aurelius Cotta Maximus Messalinus was consul in 20 and proconsul of Asia in (?) 35/6. He is scathingly criticised by T. at 5.3.3, 6.5.1, 7.1.

haud minus claris maioribus: sc. *quam Lepidus* (cf. 2n.): Cotta was the younger son of the famous Messalla Corvinus (34.4nn.): *AA* Table IX.

censuit: T. omits to say that the *senatus consultum* was passed (Talbert 439 no. 24), although his interest in questions affecting the wives of senatorial governors is already clear in his long account of a debate at 3.33–4.

quamquam: see 15.2n.

proinde quam 'just as if', used interchangeably by T. for *perinde quam* (H. on *H.* 1.30.3).

plecterentur 'should be punished'. The verb is used only in the passive (*OLD plecto*[2] 2).

21.1 Calpurnio Pisone, nobili: L. Calpurnius Piso (the Augur), consul in 1 B.C. and later proconsul of Asia. His father, Cn. Calpurnius Piso, had been suffect consul in 23 B.C.: hence *nobili* (cf. 6.2n. *mandabatque*). His son is killed at 45.1 below (n.). See *AA* 95–6, 337, 375–7, and Table xxv.

feroci here 'seems to refer to both bold speech and defiant behaviour with regard to the emperor', as often in T. (Traub 255); see also G. on 1.2.1. Like Asinius Gallus (20.1n.), Piso inherited the characteristic from his father (2.43.2).

namque: 'A word of elevated style. In ordinary prose of the late Republic and early Empire it is found only rarely. However, the poets and certain archaizers use it freely' (Adams (2) 142 n. 78). T. uses it throughout *A.* but less often than in *H.* Livy is the first to place it as second word; he is followed by various other authors.

ut rettuli: see 2.34 for both stories.

ob factiones accusatorum: the suggestion that informers on their own formed rival 'parties' is bold but continues the notion of civil disorder (17.3n.).

clamitauerat: T., who likes frequentative verbs, follows Sall. and Vell. in never using *clamo*.

Vrgulaniam: a friend of Livia Augusta (22.2, 2.34.2) and paternal grandmother of Plautius Silvanus below (22.1–2).

quae . . . ciuiliter habuit 'handled these episodes in the manner of an ordinary citizen' (cf. 2.34.3 *ciuile*): see 6.4n. (*si quando*).

sed in animo reuoluente iras . . . ualebat 'but in a mind which brooded on anger, the after-effect remained strong even if the violence of the attack was in remission'. Since *impetus* (*OLD* 3b), *offensio* (*OLD* 3), *languesco* (*OLD* 1, 3b) and *ualeo* (*OLD* 1a) are all used in contexts of (ill-)health, T. suggests that Tib.'s habit of returning to offences seemingly forgotten (e.g. 71.3, 1.7.7 'uerba, uultus in crimen detorquens recondebat'; G. on 1.69.5) is like a chronic illness. For *reuoluente* see Sen. *Ag.* 164 'reuoluit animus'.

21.2 Q. Veranius: father of the consul of 49; see *TST* 54–5.

secreti sermonis: an ominous anticipation of Sabinus' case at 68.3–69.2 below; see also 1.74.3. For the genit. see 2.78.1; *OLD incuso* 2a. Note how T. postpones the participle *habiti* (agreeing with *sermonis*) until after the main verb, a type of hyperbaton of which he is esp. fond (e.g. 47.1) and which he seems to derive from Sallust (who in turn seems to have imitated Thucydides): see J. N. Adams, *P.C.P.S.* 17 (1971) 8–9.

aduersum maiestatem: a most unusual expression: probably sc. *Tiberii.*

ut atrocius uero 'as being more heinous than was credible': *atrox* is often used of serious offences (*OLD* 6b, cf. a; also 13.2n.), while *uerum* (here a noun) regularly involves the notion of credibility (e.g. 1.6.2 'neque . . . credibile erat; propius uero . . .'; *RICH* 87 and n. 68). For poison as a popular theme see p. 123.

tramissum here and at 55.2=*praetermissum* (*OLD* 8).

ceterorum . . . receptus est reus neque peractus 'on the other charges . . . he was listed as a defendant [sc. by the praetor] but not prosecuted': for *recipere* see 2.74.2, 3.70.1; *OLD* 7c; for *perago*, *OLD* 3.

multa: no details are known, but an inscription from Samos, from which the names of Piso and his wife have been erased, suggests 'rapacity in a province' (*AA* 376).

It is less common to have a simple, rather than a superlative, adj. in predicative position in a rel. clause.

mortem opportunam: the notion of being rescued from future horrors by a timely death is common: see Ogilvie on *Agr.* 45.3 or W. on Vell. 66.4.

21.3 Cassio Seuero: one of the principal orators of Augustus' day and famous for his aggression, he had been exiled for *maiestas* in 8 or 12 (1.72.3; Bauman (2) 27–31, *AA* 409–12). His case foreshadows that of Cremutius Cordus below (34.1–2). See also Rogers (1) 79–80, Bauman (1) 259–60.

orandi ualidus: the gen. after *ualidus* seems not to occur before T.; for the *uariatio* of adj. ~ descriptive gen. see 10.1.

iurati: for senatorial oaths see Talbert 261–2.

amoueretur 'should be banished', a 'peculiarly Tacitean' sense (G. on 1.53.4).

eadem factitando: M reads *actitando*, but in the sense of 'keep on doing' this verb does not otherwise occur until very late Latin. *factitare*, on the other hand, has the right nuance (e.g. *H.* 2.10.1 'delationes factitauerat', Cic. *Brut.* 130 'accusationem factitauerit') and again has the same object at 2.59.1 'eadem factitauisse apud Siciliam'.

aduertit: sc. *in se*: 'drew hatred on himself'.

bonisque exutus: an element of *deportatio* (13.2n.; Garnsey 120 and n. 7). The metaphor of stripping is a favourite of T. (Walker 63 n. 2, G. on 1.2.1).

interdicto igni atque aqua: abl. abs. (as 6.30.1) and typical *uariatio* for the normal *aqua et igni alicui interdicere*; for the transitive use of the verb see Suet. *Claud.* 25.5.

saxo Seripho: in cases of apposition involving certain standard nouns (for which T.'s *saxo* is a rare substitute) and a place name, a preposition is normal (e.g. 13.2 'in insulam Amorgum', 71.4 'in insulam Trimerum'); but even in republican prose there are some parallels for its omission. Seriphos is one of the Cyclades.

22.1 Plautius Siluanus: son of the homonymous consul of 2 B.C. and now *praetor urbanus.*

in praeceps 'headlong' (lit. 'into a sheer drop'): *OLD* [2]2a.

tractusque ad Caesarem: in 20 Tib. had been asked to take over the inquiry of a case which had already started and which he immediately referred to the full senate (3.10), but the point here seems to be that an incumbent magistrate like Silvanus could not normally be brought to trial during his period of office (cf. 14.48.2): hence his accuser Apronius, as concerned father of the deceased woman and a distinguished consular too, approached the emperor directly (E. J. Weinrib, *Phoenix* 22 (1968) 48 n. 65; Talbert 481). Nevertheless Tib.'s role as personal inquisitor (2 below) seems odd.

L. Apronio: see 13.3n.

turbata is often used of mental disorder (as 13.3.2, cf. 67.3; *OLD* 5b). Note that this is an authorial comment by T.: the notion of a brainstorm seems supported by *incertis causis* above and by the allegation laid against Silvanus' former wife at 3 below.

tamquam . . . ignarus: sc. *fuisset. tamquam*='that' or 'as if' (see 10.3n.). *eo*='therefore' (*OLD eo*[3] 1a), esp. after *atque* and with *-que.*

sponte mortem sumpsisset: the question 'did she fall or was she pushed?' is said by Quint. to be popular with declaimers (and hence, by implication, with their audiences); he himself spoke in a genuine case involving the same issue (7.2.24). The expression *mortem sumere* seems peculiar to T. (2.66.1, 3.50.2, 14.7.6).

22.2 reluctantis et impulsae: lit. 'of the struggling and propelled woman'.

datisque iudicibus: 'The correct interpretation is uncertain' (Garnsey 26 n. 2). *iudices dare* = 'to appoint judges' in extortion cases where assessment of damages was required (*OLD iudex* 2b), but its application to a case of alleged murder seems unique (Talbert 465 n. 36).

Vrgulania: see 21.1n.

perinde . . . quasi 'just as if' (*OLD perinde* 2b).

22.3 uenas . . . exsoluendas: a Tacitean phrase (11.3.2, 14.64.2, 16.17.5), though he also has several others (e.g. *uenas abrumpere*, 6.29.1 etc.).

praebuit: sc. *seruo* (presumably).

Numantina: Fabia Numantina was daughter of Paullus Fabius Maximus (cos. 11 B.C.), sister of Paullus Fabius Persicus (cos. A.D. 34), and sometime wife of Sex. Appuleius (cos. A.D. 14): see *AA* 418 and Table XXVII.

iniecisse 'induced' (cf. *H.* 3.10.4; *OLD* 8a); *accusari* + infin. is found earlier only in *Rhet. Herenn.* 2.43.

carminibus et ueneficiis 'spells and sorcery': she was accused under the *lex Cornelia de sicariis et ueneficiis* (Garnsey 26 n. 5). Magic of all types was a popular theme in literature (A. M. Tupet, *La Magie dans la poésie latine* (1976)).

marito here = 'ex-husband'.

23–6 Victory over Tacfarinas in Africa

The section is structured to illustrate the reversal of values at Rome. The fighting (24–5) is sandwiched between a flash-back (23.1–2 *nam* . . .), where previous generals are honoured but fail to win the war, and the sequel (26), where Dolabella has won the war but fails to be honoured – because of Sejanus. The reversal is further enhanced because T. imitates Sallust by describing the war in terms of the Jugurthine War, which, despite several generals and abortive victories, was similarly prolonged. Thus T. not only provides his readers with the kind of 'old-fashioned' military narrative whose absence he will lament at 32–3 below (pp. 169–70; also *RP* I 223), but also draws a poignant contrast between past and present: Marius, Jugurtha's eventual victor, was duly awarded a triumph in 104 B.C.[1]

23.1 longo ... bello: the war had begun in 17 (2.52.1) and T. gave progress reports on 20–2 inclusive (3.20–1, 32, 73–4). See esp. *RP* I 218–30.

absoluit 'released'; the metaphor is either judicial or financial (*OLD* 2, 5).

impetrando triumphalium insigni 'for successfully requesting the distinction of the *triumphalia*': for the noun *insigne* see *OLD* 2; for *triumphalia*, 18.1n. *ubi . . . crediderant* (generalising, cf. *NLS* §217 (2) (*c*)) is contemptuous.

omittebant 'discounted', 'forgot about' (*OLD* 6a). See W. on Vell. 82.3 for some other fraudulent victories, incl. Sall. *J.* 98.6 'ipsi duces feroces quia non fugerant, pro uictoribus agere' (of Rome's African enemies).

iamque tres ... et adhuc raptabat ... Tacfarinas: the same idiom as Engl.: 'there were now *three* triumphal statues in the city and Tacfarinas was *still* ravaging Africa'. The statues were those of Furius Camillus (2.52.5), L. Apronius (3.21, but no award mentioned) and Iunius Blaesus (3.72.4).

Ptolemaeo Iubae filio: the son of Juba II (5.2), he had probably succeeded his father only in the preceding year.

incurioso: the adj., common in T. and not infrequent amongst contemporaries, occurs first in Sall. (*H.* 4.36, cf. 2.42).

libertos regios ... mutauerant: as *seruilis* is often applied loosely and disparagingly to ex-slaves (e.g. 13.6.3, 15.54.4), the expression is a hendiadys: 'had exchanged the servile orders of the king's freedmen for fighting'.

23.2 illi praedarum ... populandi 'the receiver of his stolen goods and partner in devastation' (chiastic). The Garamantes, who lived south of the Roman province of Africa, were already helping Tacfarinas in 22 (3.74.2).

[1] For a brilliant modern study of the effects to be achieved by describing one war in terms of another see P. Fussell, *The Great War and modern memory* (1975), esp. ch. 9.

non ut cum exercitu incederet sed . . . 'not ⟨to the extent⟩ that he marched forth with his full army, but . . .': the *uariatio* with the abl. abs. seems unparalleled even for T., but cf. 20.1 (n.).

quae . . . in maius audiebantur 'which were overestimated because of the distance involved', perhaps an echo of Sall. *H.* 2.69 'haec . . . in maius audiuit'.

prouincia: i.e. Africa.

ut quis . . . turbidus: sc. *erat*; *ut quis* for *ut quisque* (which he also uses) is a mannerism confined to T. and commonest in *A.* 1–6. We might also have expected comparative adjs. in the *ut*-clause, corresponding to *promptius*, but such *uariatio* is again very common (e.g. 1.57.1 and G.): cf. the converse (comparative absent from main clause) at 36.3.

ruebant: sc. *ad Tacfarinatem*. A plural verb after *ut quis* is common in T.

Blaeso: Q. Iunius Blaesus (cos. suff. 10) was Sejanus' uncle; see above, 1n., and below, 26.1.

quasi nullis . . . hostibus: *quasi* + abl. abs. is not uncommon in T. (e.g. 15.8.2 'quasi confecto bello') but found in other authors too.

nonam legionem: see 5.2n. (*cetera Africae*).

P. Dolabella: P. Cornelius Dolabella, consul in 10 and governor of Dalmatia 14–20 (Wilkes 82), was noted (3.47.3, 69.1) for the excessive *adulatio* which Tib. detested (17.1); see also 66.2.

incerta belli is Livian (30.2.6, 39.54.7). See also 5.2n. (*cetera*).

24.1 Igitur takes up the story after the flash-back which began at *nam priores* (1). See also 3.3n.

lacerari 'was being torn to pieces': since the verb, together with *decedere* (*OLD* 1a), *circumueniri* (*OLD* 1a) and *incubuissent* (*OLD* 5a) below, can be used of animals, there is perhaps a sustained metaphor from hunting.

eoque: see 22.1n. (*tamquam . . . ignarus*).

quibus libertas seruitio potior: T.'s barbarians regularly utter calls for freedom (e.g. 1.59.6): here they deploy the language of the seditious Aemilius Lepidus at Sall. *H.* 1.55.26 'potiorque uisa est periculosa libertas quieto seruitio'.

incubuissent 'pressed their attack' (as 73.2; see also above); = fut. perf. in *or. recta*.

Thubursicum: *c.* 45 miles S of Hippo Regius: see *RP* 1 218–21.

oppidum circumsidet: both words are of course common, but since the section contains several echoes of Sall. *J.* 20–1, cf. 21.2 'oppidum circumsedit'.

24.2 terrore nominis Romani et quia . . . nequeunt: the *uariatio* of abl. (abs.) ~ causal clause is quite common in T., e.g. 28.2; Sörbom 115, Martin (1) 92; above, p. 25. Elsewhere T. writes *Romanum nomen* in that order, as other authors mostly do; the present order is regular in Sall. and preferred by Livy.

primo sui incessu: the arrival of a new general was always potentially significant (e.g. Thuc. 7.42.3): here the genit. of the pronoun (instead of the adj. *suo*) emphasises Dolabella's decisiveness and suggests a contrast with the abortive operations of others (23.1–2).

obsidium is overwhelmingly preferred by T. in *A.* 1–6 to *obsidio*, which is marginally preferred in 13–16. See also 73.1n.

locorumque opportuna: as Liv. 30.12.10 'opportuna moenium'; see also 5.2n.

Musulamiorum: a sub-division of the Gaetuli, to the south of Mauretania and Numidia (*RP* I 220). Despite being nominally ruled by Tacfarinas, some of them evidently acknowledged allegiance to Rome.

securi percutit: 'A Republican and consecrated term' (Syme 725, cf. Cic. *Pis.* 84; *OLD percutio* 2b). For similar punishments see G. R. Watson, *The Roman soldier* (1969) 119–21.

24.3 excito: i.e. to help Dolabella, after the indifference of 23.1 above.

legatis is evidently imprecise for the singular: after the withdrawal of Legio IX, only one legion – and hence only one *legatus legionis* – remained.

praedatorias manus: the same phrase occurs in Sall. *J.* 20.7, where it is used of Jugurtha's tactics *against* Rome's allies in the same general area of Africa.

ipse consultor aderat omnibus: *ipse* used of a commander (e.g. *Agr.* 20.2, Sall. *J.* 100.4 (twice, of Marius)), his omnipresence (e.g. *Agr.* 37.4, Sall. *J.* 100.3 'apud omnes adesse' (of Marius again), Vell. 85.2) and his advice (e.g. Sall. *J.* 85.47 'egomet . . . consultor . . . adero' (Marius' speech): the noun is Sallustian) are all commonplaces of battle narrative and serve to underline Dolabella's Marius-like excellence and to make his later mistreatment all the more unjust (26.1).

25.1 adfertur '⟨news⟩ was brought' (*OLD* 14b).

semirutum: though found in Livy and elsewhere, the adj. was perhaps a Sallustian coinage (*H.* 2.64).

Auzea: 'This is presumably the fort Auzia (Aumale) in Mauretania, over 200 miles to the west of Thubursicu' (*RP* 1 221 n. 5).

mapalibus: cf. Sall. *J.* 18.8 'aedificia Numidarum agrestium, quae mapalia illi uocant' (also 46.5).

25.2 et . . . ac: the former joins *coeptus* and *aderant*, the latter *concentu* and *clamore* (where note the assonance, alliteration and chiasmus).

aderant semisomnos in barbaros: though such attacks are commonplace in battle narratives, in this Sallustian section cf. *J.* 21.2 'semisomnos . . . fugant funduntque'; the verb *adesse* is abnormally frequent in *J.* (e.g. 50.4), though nowhere coupled with *in.*

cuncta . . . prouisa: *omnia prouidere* is a phrase favoured by Sall., e.g. *C.* 60.4 (and Vretska), *J.* 49.2 (Jugurtha's speech), 100.3 (of Marius).

non . . . non . . . non: triple anaphora of *non* occurs only once in Sall., in a dissimilar context (*C.* 7.5), but cf. *J.* 99.2 'neque fugere neque arma capere neque omnino facere aut prouidere quicquam poterant' (of the Mauri and Gaetuli).

pecorum modo: the comparison seems to originate in Latin with Sall. *C.* 58.21, *H.* 4.67: see W. on Vell. 119.2.

trahi, occidi, capi: so Sall. *J.* 101.11 'sequi, fugere, occidi, capi' (Marius' victory over Jugurtha's troops). T.'s tricolon balances the triple anaphora above.

25.3 memoria laborum et . . pugnae 'with the memory of their sufferings and of the battle so often desired against elusive ⟨enemies⟩'. *memoria laborum* etc. is a commonplace of battle narratives (esp. in pre-battle exhortations), and barbarians are often elusive (so Tacfarinas again at 2.52.3, 3.74.1).

explebant: a slight syllepsis, since the verb, though equally metaphorical with both nouns, is used differently with each (*sanguine* being = *caede* by metonymy).

differtur '⟨the word⟩ was spread through the units that they should all . . .' (*OLD* 3a).

non nisi: such phraseology is found + abl. abs. from Plautus onwards. Again at 67.2.

deiectis 'struck down' or 'dislodged' (*OLD* 7a, 8a).

isque finis armis impositus rounds off the strictly military narrative which began at 23.1 'is demum . . . bello absoluit'. Tacfarinas' defeat was not followed by a lasting peace (*RP* I 224), but *armis* (dat.) nicely suggests a reference to 'fighting' in general and thus prepares us for the digression at the end of the year (below, pp. 169–70).

26.1 triumphalia is to be taken in common (ἀπὸ κοινοῦ) with *petenti*, which contrasts ironically with *impetrando* at 23.1 above, and *abnuit*. See also 18.1n.

Seiano tribuens: when Tib. awarded the *triumphalia* to Blaesus in the first place, 'dare id se dixit honori Seiani, cuius ille auunculus erat' (3.72.4).

intendit 'intensified' (*OLD* 5a). For the substantival *negatus* see 19.4n.

minore exercitu: viz. Africa's original Legio III Augusta, the other having been withdrawn (23.2).

caedem ducis: compressed for *famam caedis ducis* (see also 3.3n.).

deportarat 'had brought home' (*OLD* 2a).

26.2 Ptolemaei . . . studiis: cf. 24.3.

repetitus 'was revived' (*OLD* 3).

antiqua patrum munera: 'The gift of the trappings of a *triumphator* to foreign kings . . . became regular . . . by an early date in the second century B.C. at the latest' (E. Rawson, *J.R.S.* 65 (1975) 155, with exx.). The contrast with Dolabella's treatment is striking.

27–31 *Home affairs*

The third section of the year's narrative displays the same tripartite structure as its predecessors, and, like the first of them (above, p. 144), consists of a transitional item (27: see 1n.) followed by a trial described at length (28–30) and three others described briefly (31). An extra dimension is added to the central trial by its protagonists, who are father and son. Such violations of *pietas* figure prominently in that index of popular intellectual taste, the *Controuersiae* of the elder Seneca; and parricide, to which the case is expressly compared at 29.2, was particularly relished (above, p. 124). But at the same time the case intensifies the perversion of *amicitia* which was depicted in the corresponding domestic section at the start of the year (p. 144) and thus illustrates both the *saeuitia* of the age (28.1) and the breakdown of society (cf. 18.1n. *amicitia*) in a particularly acute and symbolic form. See also Keitel 324.

27.1 aestate 'season' in two senses. It is still the 'campaigning season' (*OLD* 1c), since this was a second war, again aimed at *libertas* (below; cf. 24.1n.), but on the domestic front. Yet it is also the season at which seeds are scattered (Plin. *NH* 19.106 'aestate . . . semen emittunt'), since these are the metaphorical terms T. uses to describe the outbreak (*mota . . . semina*, cf. Stat. *Theb.* 4.212 'semina mouit'). *oppressit* = 'choked' or 'stifled' (as Colum. 5.6.18 'uitis . . . incremento opprimetur'). For the related metaphor *spargere bellum* see 3.21.4 (of Tacfarinas), *Agr.* 38.2 (and Ogilvie).

apud Brundisium: in the famous slave war of 73–71 B.C. Spartacus had similarly attracted his greatest support in the extreme south of Italy.

positis: simple for *propositis*, as 1.7.3 (where G. remarks that it is hard to parallel outside T.).

agrestia presumably agrees with *seruitia* (6.4n.) in hyperbaton.

cum uelut munere deum . . . illo mari explains *fors* above. *uelut* is in keeping with T.'s usual scepticism (1.2n. *deum ira*). For ships as subject of the verb see *OLD appello*[1] 4b; the indic. is normal in the inverted *cum*-construction (*NLS* §237). *ad usus* = 'to meet the needs'; *illo mari* = the Adriatic, the ships being based at Ravenna (5.1n.).

27.2 cui prouincia . . . calles euenerant 'to whom the *calles* had fallen as his responsibility': *calles* is short for *siluae callesque* (Suet. *Iul.* 19.2), 'public pasturelands in Italy allotted yearly to a magistrate' (*OLD* 2b).

coeptantem cum maxime 'just when it was beginning' (*OLD cum*[2] 13b).

familiarum 'household slaves'. For the varying attitudes taken towards such slaves see the case described at 14.42–5; I. Kajanto, *Arctos* 6 (1969) 48–60.

gliscebat immensum echoes Sall. *H.* 3.56 'immensum aucto mari et uento gliscente'. *immensum* is adverbial, as 40.6.

plebe ingenua 'the free-born population' (as 16.13.2). While there are no statistics to prove T.'s contention that the number of slaves was growing as that of the free-born declined, it would be in keeping with a general trend (see e.g. Brunt (1) 131).

28.1 miseriarum ac saeuitiae exemplum atrox: one of the functions of classical historiography was exemplary, and aimed at the moral improvement of readers (33.2n.). Usually this function is made explicit only in a preface (e.g. Liv. pref. 10 'exempli documenta'), but sometimes the actual word *exemplum* is used in narrative as well (as here and e.g. *H.* 3.51.2). This development may be due to the influence of *exempla* in forensic and epideictic oratory, which culminated in the collection of historical *exempla* made by Valerius Maximus in the 30s A.D.

An *exemplum* was more effective if dramatically presented, and the case here well illustrates historiographical *mimēsis* (imitation) or *enargeia* (vividness), whereby a historian 'turns his readers into spectators, as it were, and reproduces in their minds the feelings . . . which were experienced by those who actually viewed the events' (Plut. *Mor.* 347A). Hence the vivid details of dress, expression, movement, and reported speech (1–3). And since these same details evoke the reader's indignation against the prosecutor, and a corresponding pity for the defendant, we must remember that *indignatio* and *misericordia* were standard ploys of the forensic orator (e.g. Cic. *Inu.* 1.100–5 (note esp. 103 on acts of cruelty towards parents) and 106–9 respectively). See further n. below (*ab exilio*).

The words *miseriarum . . . atrox* are in apposition to the main sentence, something of which T. is esp. fond (G. on 1.27.1). *miseriarum* applies to the elder Serenus, *saeuitiae* to his son.

Vibius Serenus: for the elder and his exile see 13.2n.; the younger, a specialist 'in lodging rash and groundless accusations' (Garnsey 38), reappears at 36.3. See also Bauman (2) 114–15.

ab exilio retractus . . . praeparatur: scholars have been troubled both by the absence from M of an expressed subject, corresponding to *adulescens* below, and by the possible meaning of *praeparatur*. Madvig proposed to solve both difficulties simultaneously by reading *pater comparatur* ('was matched against'); Halm coupled Madvig's suggestion with those of some earlier editors to read *pater oranti filio comparatur*. Yet *praeparatur* seems intended to combine incongruously with the participles *retractus*, *obsitus* and *uinctus* in order to provide an ironic comparison with the over-elaborate preparations of the younger Serenus below (*multis munditiis* etc.): his father's circumstances represented the very opposite of preparation (for such deliberate incongruity between participle(s) and main verb see E. Laughton, *The participle in Cicero* (1964) 9). And *perorare* is used by T. elsewhere of delivering as well as merely concluding a speech (e.g. 2.30.1 and G.). We therefore think it preferable to supply *pater* before either *peroranti* or *praeparatur*. The noun, esp. if abbreviated, might have been omitted before the prefixes of either word, esp. if the prefixes were themselves abbreviated: this is indeed the case with *peroranti* in M, but the alternative proposal produces the extra effectiveness of a juxtaposition with *filio* (cf. *H.* 3.25.2 'filius patrem interfecit', 2.1.3). Hence: 'dragged back from exile, and covered with dirt and filth, and in addition bound with a chain, the father was prepared for his son's harangue'.

It was standard practice for orators, if they wished to rouse the pity of their audience, 'producere ipsos, qui periclitentur, squalidos atque deformes' (Quint. 6.1.30, cf. suppliant legates at Liv. 29.16.6 'obsiti squalore'): thus the picture of Serenus *père*, to which the archaic *inluuies* adds emphasis, suggests that his son's attack is misconceived from the start. Subsequently the latter's own appearance in court is miscalculated (2nn.), his accusation against Lentulus and Tubero misfires (29.1), and he himself ends up experiencing similar treatment to that which had been meted out to his father (29.2 'retractus . . . adigitur'). T.'s narrative of the whole episode thus constitutes a typical example of sustained cynicism at the younger Serenus' expense.

28.2 adulescens multis munditiis: an orator's dress was important; but it should be 'splendidus et uirilis' (Quint. 11.3.137), whereas *munditiae* risked suspicion of effeminacy (3.30.2). Details of dress are also characteristic in dramatic historians such as Duris (B. L. Ullman, *T.A.P.A.* 73 (1942) 39). The word *adulescens* is similarly derogatory (Ogilvie on Liv. 2.56.10).

alacri uultu: an orator's appearance was also important, and 'dominatur . . . maxime uultus' (Quint. 11.3.72); *oculi asperi* were sometimes appropriate (ibid. 75), but not if the defendant was one's own father.

index idem et testis 'simultaneously informer and witness' (as 15.55.3).

adnectebatque 'and he added', but possibly with the notion of deception which the simple verb contains (*OLD necto* 9a).

taedio . . . et quia . . . habebatur: for the *uariatio* see 24.2n.

28.3 quatere . . . uocare: the historic infinitives, their initial position, and the alliteration of *u-* all emphasise the drama: for the scene cf. Plin. *Ep.* 7.27.5 'manibus catenas gerebat quatiebatque' (of a ghost). *redderent exilium* is intentionally pathetic.

ubi procul tali more ageret 'where he could live far removed from such behaviour': *agere* is intrans. (*OLD* 35); *more* is heavily ironical in view of *atrocitatem morum* applied to the elder Serenus himself at 13.2. For *procul* (prep.) see 2.1n.

si proderentur alii expresses defiance: the father is confident either that no one can be produced or (as happens, cf. 29.1) that the *alii* whom his son will produce are highly improbable conspirators.

uno socio: probably abl. abs.: 'with ⟨only⟩ one person as his accomplice' (*NLS* §50, not 46 (ii)). As is sometimes the case with Latin, 'only' must be added to the Engl. rendering to bring out the full sense (see Kenney on Lucr. 3.144).

29.1 Cn. Lentulum: Syme has argued (*AA* 284–99, esp. 292–4) that all T.'s references to a Cn. (Cornelius) Lentulus are not to the consul of 18 B.C. but to his namesake 'the Augur', the consul of 14 B.C., who was now in his 70s or early 80s and died in 25 (44.1).

Seium Tuberonem: suffect consul in 18 and half-brother, or son of a half-brother, of Sejanus: *AA* 300–12 (esp. 307) and Table XXIII; Levick, Table D. The appended abl. abs. (*magno pudore Caesaris*) adds a new and typically cynical element: above, p. 24.

senectutis . . . corpore: for this type of *uariatio* see e.g. 61, 5.1.1; Sörbom 77. For that of *tumultus* ~ *turbandae* below see e.g. 11.26.2; Sörbom 112.

exempti: sc. *crimini* or *periculo* (the latter a common combination in T.).

29.2 scelere uecors: the notion that (consciousness of) crime leads to madness (also at 1.39.2 'conscientia uecordes', *H.* 2.35.5 'scelere . . . uecordes'; W. on Vell. 91.3) is standard tragic psychology.

simul . . . rumore territus: *simul* = *et*. This use of *simul* to join single words or, as here, small groups of words is rare in earlier prose and verse but common in T., who, however, has it more frequently in *A.* 11–16 than in *A.* 1–6 (Adams (1) 359–60).

uulgi . . . minitantium: an extension of the common usage whereby a collective noun is followed by a plural *finite* verb (e.g. *H.* 5.13.2 'uulgus . . . mutabantur'): cf. 62.2. In *H.* and *A.* T. overwhelmingly prefers the frequentative *minitor* to *minor* (24:4), the latter being preferred by Cicero (22:39 in speeches).

robur: the *Tullianum* (*OCD*) or state prison (by metonymy).

saxum: sc. *Tarpeium*, from which murderers and traitors were hurled (*OCD*).

parricidarum poenas: they were scourged, sewn in a sack (along with a cock, a dog, a viper and an ape) and thrown into the sea (*OCD parricidium*).

retractus . . . exsequi accusationem adigitur: a dramatic reversal of fortune (*peripeteia*): see above, 28.1n. (*ab exilio retractus*).

29.3 damnatum Libonem: for the case of M. Scribonius Libo in 16 see 2.27–32.

litteris: an archaism preferred to *epistula* by Livy and Curtius as well as T., who increasingly prefers it as his writing develops (Adams (1) 357): cf. also 69.3, 70.4.

sine fructu fuisse: the three other accusers of Libo (cf. 2.30.1) had been awarded praetorships *extra ordinem* (2.32.1), but Serenus must either have been praetor designate or already held the office by this date, as he was proconsul of Spain *c.* 22. Hence his complaint is likely to have been that he lacked comparable recognition.

tutum: sc. *est* or *erat*.

aures cannot literally be 'proud and too inclined to take offence', but the noun is often used with adjs. indicating an attitude of mind (e.g. 1.31.5; *OLD* 2c).

rettulit 'revived', as 4.2.

medium . . . arguens 'criticising the intervening period too in various ways.'

etiam si . . . contra euenissent 'even though the torture [in the *quaestio seruorum* at 1 above] had turned out negatively through the slaves' steadfastness': the loyalty of slaves under torture was a popular topic, appearing in the 'blurb' at *H.* 1.3.1 and in Valerius Maximus' collection of *exempla* (e.g. 6.8.1). For the legal background see Crook 274–5.

30.1 more maiorum: evidently being scourged to death (Suet. *Nero* 49.2).

quo = *ut*: the usage is archaic and quite rare unless a comparative adj. or adv. is present, but liked by Sallust and increasingly preferred by T. as his writing develops (e.g. 55.1): Adams (1) 356.

Gallus Asinius: see 20.1n. Inversion of names, as here, is found in other authors but is a mannerism of T. (G. on 1.8.3).

Gyaro aut Donusa: the former is one of the Cyclades, the latter a small island E of Naxos.

dandosque uitae usus cui uita concederetur 'and that the necessities of life should be provided for one whose life was being spared': polyptoton, i.e. the repetition of a word in a different case (cf. Quint. 9.3.37), recurs in another reported utterance of Tib. at 1.73.4 and may be intended to suggest his manner. For a similar intervention by Tib. in 22 see 3.69.5.

reportatur: it seems from Dio 58.8.3 that Serenus was an enemy of Sejanus, of which T. gives no hint, and that he was pardoned by Tib. in 31.

30.2 actum de praemiis . . . abolendis, si quis . . . priuauisset: this proposal, had it been carried, would have formalised the existing convention (on which Silius had unsuccessfully relied, cf. 20.1n.) and deprived accusers of their entitlement to a quarter of a condemned man's property under the present law (20.2).

ibaturque: the imperfect indic. in the apodosis of a mixed condition (cf. *ni . . . conquestus esset*) 'is often used of a movement attempted or begun but not finished' (*NLS* §200 (ii)): cf. 64.1. *in sententiam ire* is a technical expression of senatorial procedure (*OLD eo*[1] 16).

inritas . . . in praecipiti: sc. *fore*. For Tib.'s earlier participation in senatorial debates see e.g. 2.33.4, 38.1–3, 3.64.4 (Ginsburg 124 n. 27).

subuerterent potius iura quam custodes . . . amouerent: both language and thought look authentic (cf. 2.36.3 *subuerti leges* in a speech of Tib.); *custodes* used of *delatores* is not necessarily pejorative (cf. 3.28.3): such people were inevitable in the Roman legal system.

30.3 genus hominum publico exitio repertum 'a breed of men designed for the extinction of their fellows'. The language is apocalyptic, as if describing a primeval race (cf. the frequency in Lucr. 5 of *reperire* (*OLD* 6) and of such phrases as *hominum genus*) whose behaviour is worse than that ascribed to the worst of wild beasts, which proverbially refrain from attacking their own species (see e.g. Mayor or Courtney on Juv. 15.159, Tarrant on Sen. *Ag.* 738ff.). Cf. also 11.2 *repertor* (n.), 19.2 *scelera nuper reperta*. *exitio* is dat. of purpose.

31.1 His . . . intericitur 'Amidst these events, so unremitting and so depressing, there was a brief but pleasurable interval': *adsiduis* is more justified than *continuus* at 36.1 (n.), but the anaphora of *tam* is without parallel in *H.* or *A.* and is esp. emphatic. *adsiduis* and *maestis* both prepare us for the digression at 32–3 below (p. 170).

qui senator erat is evidently inserted to distinguish him from his brother, the *eques*: such differentiation of rank is a Tacitean mannerism (G. on 1.75.2; Talbert 249 n. 10).

31.2 et quae fama clementiam sequeretur: *clementia* was one of the special virtues of Tib.'s reign, partnering *moderatio* (38.4n.) on the coinage of (?) 22/3 and recognised by the erection of an *ara clementiae* in 28: see Rogers (2) 35–59, Weinstock 241, Levick 87–8, Wallace-Hadrill 310–11, 320–1, 323. However, another of Tib.'s virtues was *iustitia* (6.2n., cf. 1.72.3 'exercendas leges esse'), and it was inevitable both that the two should sometimes conflict and that the conflict would damage the *fama* which Tib. so keenly desired (38.1–3, 40.1). T.'s handling of this conflict is here typical, since *meliorum* assumes that the exercise of *clementia* was morally preferable on every occasion, which cannot be the case in a society regulated by laws and punishments. Similarly his attitude to Tib.'s *clementia*: L. Piso's praise of *clementia principis* at 3.68.2 is qualified at 3.69.5 where the authorial *prudens moderandi* is counterbalanced by *propria ira* (cf. 3.22.2 'irae et clementiae signa'); cf. also 42.3 below (*inclementiam*) and 6.14.2 ('obliuione magis quam clementia'). Also Syme 387.

Though the context here relates to *clementia* specifically, T.'s aphorism *gnarum meliorum . . . tristiora malle* would also serve as a more general epitaph on the *princeps*. It was the 'tragedy of Tiberius' that he knew well enough the paths to popularity but could not bring himself to follow them (e.g. 1.76.5 'tristitia ingenii'): see Yavetz 103–13.

For the *uariatio* of noun (here in genit.) ~ indir. qu. see 4.3n. (*tutarentur*) and Liv. 38.12.6 'gnarum locorum hominumque et cuius interesset frangi Gallorum opes'.

neque enim . . . nec . . . celebrentur provides an authorial comment on the two elements (*meliorum* ~ *neque . . . peccabat*, and *fama* ~ *celebrentur*) by which contemporary opinion was perplexed (*mirum habebatur*). Thus: 'for it was not *socordia* that made him do wrong; nor is there any mystery about when an emperor's actions are applauded genuinely and when with simulated pleasure.' *socordia* is usu. physical = 'lethargy' (*OLD* a) and in this meaning is a favourite noun of Sallust; but it can also be intellectual = 'stupidity' (as 35.5), a meaning evidently associated with the elder Cato (*OLD* b). Here the latter seems predominant, perh. = 'carelessness': Tib.'s actions were deliberate and intended.

For an indir. qu. + *occultum est* (also at 11.28.1) see Sall. *J.* 24.5; for the *uariatio* of prepositional phrase ~ adj./part. see 6.4n. (*intra*).

quin 'In fact' or 'What is more' (6.4n.).

uelut eluctantium uerborum 'a man whose words almost struggled to get out': gen. of description (*NLS* §§84–5); for the *uariatio* with *compositus* (1.3n.) see 10.1n. (*plurimis*). Tib.'s speech is characterised elsewhere: 52.3, 70.1, 1.11.2 'suspensa semper et obscura uerba', 33.2 'sermone, uultu adrogantibus et obscuris', 13.3.2 'artem . . . callebat qua uerba expenderet, tum ualidus sensibus aut consulto ambiguus'. The unusualness of Tib.'s speaking out is here underlined by *eloquebatur*, used elsewhere in *A.* only at 3.65.3, again of Tib.

For the subjunc. *subueniret* see 6.4n. (*si quando*).

31.3 P. Suillium: P. Suillius Rufus, half-brother of the general Corbulo and of Caligula's wife Caesonia, was quaestor in (?) 15 and recalled from banishment after Tib.'s death, becoming suffect consul in (?) 41. See *RP* II 806–8, *AA* 182; also below.

cum Italia arceretur: only a proposal, as *censuit* below makes clear.

amouendum in insulam: see 13.2n. (*de ui publica*) and 21.3n.

obstringeret: the omission of a direct object (here *se*, as 1.14.4) is most unusual; for senatorial oaths see 21.3n. (and 1.74.4 for one from Tib.); for the authentic wording *e re publica* see Talbert 261 and n. 2.

uertit: intransitive (*OLD* 21a).

quem uidit sequens aetas . . . numquam bene usum: though such expressions as *uidit aetas* are common in Latin, T. 'generally eschews anticipatory notices' (*RP* II 807): for another ex. in the Tiberian books see 6.32.4 (L. Vitellius). Suillius was a vigorous prosecutor under Claudius (11.1–6) but again banished, to the Balearic Islands, under Nero (13.42–3, where the charge of being *uenalis* is repeated).

31.4 Catum Firmium: an *agent provocateur* and one of those rewarded in the case of Libo Drusus (2.27.2 (hence *ut rettuli*); above, 29.3n.). For the inversion of names see 30.1n.

tamquam . . . sororem petiuisset: this case thus looks back to that of the Vibii Sereni (28–30) as a violation of *pietas*. For *tamquam* see 13.2n.

inlexerat . . . perculerat 'had lured into [lit. with] a trap, then destroyed with the evidence': the former verb is a favourite of T. (esp. in *A*. 1–6) but almost entirely absent from Cicero, in whom the latter verb is common.

alia praetendens 'putting forward other considerations as his excuse' (see 2.1n.). Each of the three cases in this ch. has involved intervention by Tib., the first of laudable *clementia*, the second of severity which later proved justified, and the third of reprehensible leniency.

quominus senatu pelleretur non obstitit: for withdrawal of senatorial status, and the emperor's role therein, see 42.3; Talbert 27–9.

32–3 Digression on Tacitus' historiography of Tiberius

Ancient historians often used digressions to separate one section of their narrative from another, and T. uses the present digression, which is clearly signalled as such (33.4n.), to separate his accounts of the years 24 and 25. However, by concluding with the dangers attendant on praising virtue and on free speech (33.4) T. prepares us for the opening episode of the following year (34–5): see e.g. Ginsburg 49.

Whereas most ancient historians went out of their way to claim superiority over their predecessors (32.1n.), T. argues in the digression that his work must seem to compare *un*favourably with those of republican historians. The comparison is repeated several times on various grounds, the most prominent being that the content of his narrative is allegedly unimportant and unexciting compared with that recommended for historiography by Cicero (above, pp. 2–5). To emphasise his point T. reverses many of the claims which historians traditionally made in their prefaces and which he himself had deployed at length in the preface to his own earlier work, the *Histories* (e.g. *H.* 1.2.1 *opus adgredior . . . atrox proeliis* ~ 32.2 *immota . . . pax*). At the same time, however, various parallels with that earlier preface (e.g. *H.* 1.2.3 *ob uirtutes . . . exitium* ~ 33.3 *perniciem innocentium et . . . exitii causas*) suggest that T. is now tracing on the domestic front a disintegration of the moral order which is comparable with that accompanying civil war.

Since T. makes these points arise naturally out of the immediately preceding narrative (e.g. 32.2 *maestae urbis res*, 33.3 *continuas accusationes* ~ 31.1 *His tam adsiduis tamque maestis*), he inevitably implies that his argument is particularly appropriate to the narrative of Tib.'s latter years and hence that his account of these years is qualitatively different from that of the earlier years. This suggestion in its turn reinforces the division of the reign itself into two halves, which was emphasised at 1.1 above. Further, since digressions were traditionally regarded as a device for entertaining one's readers (Cic. *Brut.* 322) and as being particularly at home in historiography (e.g. Plin. *Ep.* 2.5.5), T. shows conscious irony in using the vehicle of a *digression* precisely to *deny* that his work contains the pleasurable elements which historiography was expected to contain. See further *RICH* 180–5.

T.'s argument is carefully articulated by the repetition and contrast of words and ideas. Just as his narrative of the year's events has been divided into three sections (p. 143), each of which is itself divided into three (pp. 144, 155, 160), so also the digression is arranged on a triadic structure: there are three sets of three examples in 32.1–2, three constitutions in 33.1–2, three further examples in 33.3, and three objections to Tiberian historiography in 33.4. The deliberate nature of the argument lends added persuasion to a message which was designed to shock his readers.

32.1 parua . . . et leuia memoratu: historians conventionally claimed to record the greatest and most memorable events (e.g. Hdt. pref., Thuc. 1.1.1, Polyb. 1.2.1, Cic. *De Or.* 2.63 'in rebus magnis memoriaque dignis', Sall. *C.* 4.2 'memoria digna', *J.* 5.1 'magnum', Liv. 21.1.1, Dion. Hal. *Ant. Rom.* 1.1.2–3, 3–6). Here T. gives the impression of doing the exact opposite. For *memoratu* cf. *digna memoratu* at *H.* 2.24.1, *Agr.* 1.2, and *haud magna memoratu* at Liv. 38.29.3; for *leuis* + abl. supine cf. Liv. 27.15.9 'leue dictu'.

set nemo annales nostros . . . contenderit 'but let no one compare . . .': this meaning of *contendo* is common (*OLD* 9), but the perf. subjunc. to express a prohibition is rare (*NLS* §129). For the authorial plural *nostros* after *rettuli . . . referam* above see 11.2n. (*cura nostra*). *annales* is often used = simply '(annalistic) history', e.g. 34.1, 43.3, 53.2, Liv. 43.13.2 'meos annales'.

Historians regularly claimed to rival and improve on their predecessors (e.g. 1.1.2–3, *H.* 1.1.1–3, Hecataeus fr. 1, Thuc. 1.20.3, Cato, *Orig.* fr. 77, Sempr. Asell. fr. 1, Asin. Pollio fr. 4, Liv. pref. 2). Here T. affects to decline such *aemulatio*.

ueteres is transferred (by enallage) to *res* from *populi*, to which it strictly belongs: cf. 1.1.2 'ueteris populi Romani prospera uel aduersa'.

ingentia illi bella . . . captosque reges: war and battle had been standard topics of historiography since Herodotus (pref.), who derived his image of the genre from Homer's *Iliad*: cf. e.g. Thuc. 1.1.1–2, 23.1–3, Cic. *Or.* 66 '(historia) in qua . . . saepe . . . pugna describitur', Tac. *H.* 1.2.1. Other standard topics were the besieging of cities (e.g. *H.* 1.2.2 'haustae aut obrutae urbes'; G. M. Paul, '*Urbs capta:* sketch of an ancient literary motif', *Phoenix* 36 (1982) 144–55) and the fate of famous men (e.g. 33.3 below (n.), Cic. *Fam.* 5.12.5). Once again T. dissociates his work from the norm; but see further below, 58.3n. (*adsidens*) and 62.1n. (*ingentium bellorum*).

ad . . . praeuerterent 'turned their attention to' (usu. deponent: *OLD* 5); for the subjunc. see 6.4n. (*si quando*).

discordias consulum . . . optimatium certamina: T. adopts three different ways of describing the series of crises (many of them similar in nature) which characterised the later republic. A tribune of the people would seek to win popular support, and a reputation for himself as a *popularis*, by proposing either agrarian or corn legislation (the former aimed at the redistribution of land in Italy and the provinces, the latter at the provision of cheap or free corn in Rome). Such proposals inevitably conflicted with the interests of the conservative aristocracy (*optimates*), from whose ranks the consuls were almost exclusively drawn and who sought to preserve the status quo. Well known exx. are the tribunates of Ti. Sempronius Gracchus (133) and his brother Gaius (123, 122), L. Appuleius Saturninus (103, 100), P. Servilius Rullus (63) and P. Clodius Pulcher (58). Exx. of the historians of such crises are the optimate L. Cornelius Sisenna (praetor in 78) and the *popularis* C. Licinius Macer (praetor in 68): only scraps of their works survive. T.'s belief that these crises were exciting may seem strange to us, but Livy's work, in which early Roman history is often presented in a late-republican guise, suggests that they exercised a continuing fascination at Rome.

libero egressu 'with unrestricted elaboration'. *libero* suggests freedom to choose between domestic and foreign affairs (either because both were available or because the historians themselves were unconstrained); it also reinforces the contrast between *egressu* and *in arto* (below), and anticipates the theme of free speech at 33.4 below. The precise metaphorical use of *egressus* is most unusual.

32.2 nobis contrasts with *illi* above (adversative asyndeton).

in arto et inglorius labor: historians were expected to seek *gloria* (e.g. Sall. *C.* 1.3, cf. Liv. pref. 3) and to have their eye on posterity (35.3, 3.65.1, *H.* 1.1.1, Lucian, *Hist. conscr.* 61, 63): T. here denies that he can do so since (*quippe*) many of the events themselves lack *gloria* – and exceptions are dangerous (33.4). His words recall Virg. *G.* 4.6 'in tenui labor; at tenuis non gloria', his typical *uariatio* of prep. ~ adj. (6.4n.) being emphasised by the assonance of *in . . . in-*.

princeps proferendi imperi incuriosus: T. made the same point about Augustus (1.3.6), who passed on to Tib. his *consilium coercendi intra terminos imperii* (1.11.4): see Seager 162–74, Levick 125–47.

Non . . . sine usu fuerit introspicere 'it will not prove [lit. have been] futile to investigate': *non sine usu* is a Tacitean variation on the more common *ex/in usu* (*esse*); *introspicere* is commonly used of investigating behaviour etc. (*OLD* 3), which turns out, by implication, to be the context here (cf. 33.2).

illa primo aspectu leuia: these words, which pick up *leuia . . . uideri* at 1 above, round off T.'s first argument and remind readers that despite the unattractiveness of his material, its unimportance is only apparent – a point which leads neatly into his second argument at 33.1–2 below. See also next n.

ex quis magnarum saepe rerum motus oriuntur: T. completes the transition to his second argument by means of a commonplace (cf. e.g. Thuc. 2.3.6, Arist. *Pol.* 1303b17–18, Caes. *C.* 3.68.1, 70.2, Liv. 25.18.3, 27.9.1, Plin. *Ep.* 1.20.12). For *quis* see 14.1n.

33.1 nam cunctas . . . regunt: this generalisation is illustrated below by *ut . . . sic . . .* (n.).

conflata rei publicae forma laudari . . . potest: T. alludes to Cic. *Rep.* 1.53–4: among various linguistic similarities note esp. 'formam rei publicae maxime laudant . . .; probo anteponoque singulis illud quod conflatum fuerit ex omnibus'. The allusion confirms E. Harrison's emendation *conflata* (*C.R.* 37 (1923) 22), a favourite verb of Cic. and used nowhere else by T. The usual change to *consociata* gives an unacceptable meaning to that verb (see *OLD* 2). *rei p. forma* is common = 'system/form of government' (*OLD forma* 6b).

One should not conclude from this parenthesis that T. himself idealised the so-called 'mixed constitution', of which there is a famous discussion at Polyb. 6.3–10 (see Walbank's nn.).

33.2 igitur resumes the argument of *nam . . . regunt* after the brief parenthesis *delecta . . . potest*.

ut . . . sic . . . are used to separate earlier (*olim*) democratic (*plebe . . . uulgi* ~ 1 *populus*) and oligarchic (*patres . . . senatusque et optimatium* ~ 1 *primores*) constitutions from the present (*conuerso statu . . .*) autocracy (*unus* ~ 1 *singuli*), and hence also the republic from the empire.

For the *uariatio* of abl. abs. ~ temporal clause (here with *cum*) see e.g. 71.1, 1.25.2, 2.33.2, 6.51.3.

quibus modis temperanter haberetur: indir. qu. after *noscendum erat*, which has to be understood from *noscenda* (sc. *erat*) above; for the *uariatio* with a noun (here nomin., *natura*) see 4.3n. (*tutarentur*). The use of *habeo* is clearly analogous to that at 6.1 (n.), although the meaning 'maintain' is perhaps more appropriate here.

conuerso statu: either 'now that the *status* has changed' or 'when the *status* changed': it is not clear whether T.'s switch from the preceding historic sequence (*credebantur* etc.) to the following primary sequence (*imperitet*, *fuerit* etc.) occurs here, or with *neque alia . . . salute*, or with *si . . . imperitet* itself. There is a clearer case of such a switch at 11.3 (n.).

status, used by republican writers to describe the political state of affairs, had subsequently been exploited by Augustus to suggest the continuity of his régime with the republic (W. on Vell. 131.1). T.'s reference to 'change' (also at 1.4.1) is thus pointed.

neque alia rerum ⟨salute⟩ quam si unus imperitet: such forms of expression are very common in T. (e.g. 17.3 'neque aliud gliscentis discordiae remedium quam si unus alterue . . .', 1.6.3 'ut non aliter ratio constet quam si uni reddatur', 9.4 'non aliud discordantis patriae remedium fuisse quam ⟨ut⟩ ab uno regeretur'), and *remedio* would be a possible supplement after *rerum* were it not for the fem. *alia*. Bringmann's *salute*, however, has a comparable meaning (and is coordinated with *status* at *H.* 4.85.2).

The *si*-clause is of the substantival type which follows such words as *solus* or *unus* (to which *neque alia . . . quam* is equivalent) and explains what a preceding noun consists of (e.g. 14.6.1 'solum insidiarum remedium esse putauit si non intellegerentur'). Since the clause here is not intended to describe the present form of constitution but rather prescribes a formula for the indispensable optimum, the verb is subjunctive. In such cases *si* is virtually interchangeable with *ut* (see the exx. quoted above, and cf. 13.25.4 'non aliud remedium repertum est quam ut histriones Italia pellerentur'). The meaning therefore is: 'and there being no other salvation for the state than if one man should rule'.

haec . . . in rem fuerit 'it will prove [lit. have been] of advantage that these things are investigated and recorded': for the acc. + inf. after *in rem est*, rather than the normal infin. (*OLD res* 13b), see Liv. 44.19.3. T.'s sentence picks up 32.2 'non tamen sine usu fuerit introspicere', from which it is clear that *illa primo aspectu leuia* there ~ *haec* here.

plures aliorum euentis docentur: historiography is didactic, and therefore useful, because it provides examples of behaviour for readers to 'imitate or avoid' (Liv. pref. 10, cf. 28.1n.). T.'s point is that since the constitution has remained unchanged since Tib.'s day, the events of the latter's reign are relevant to his readers. Elsewhere T. reminds his readers that they in turn may be scrutinised by some future Tacitus (3.65.1). Both these types of usefulness seem to be combined at Diod. 1.2.8. See too next n.

33.3 ut profutura, ita minimum oblectationis adferunt: the fut. part. is used almost like an adj. = 'advantageous'; *ut . . . ita* = 'although . . . nevertheless' (*OLD ut* 5b). As well as being useful (last n.), historiography was also supposed to provide pleasure (Duris fr. 1, Cic. *Or.* 37, *De Or.* 2.59, *Fam.* 5.12.4–5 (above, p. 5), Vitr. 5 pref. 1, Plin. *Ep.* 5.8.4). Ideally the genre should exhibit both aspects (Cic. *Fin.* 5.51 'esse utilitatem in historia, non modo uoluptatem', cf. Hor. *AP* 343); and while at 32.2–33.2 T. defended his work on grounds of utility, his return here to the subject of 32.1 suggests a preoccupation with its alleged lack of pleasurable elements.

situs gentium: geographical (and ethnographical) material is the first of three standard elements by which T. illustrates the pleasurability of normal historiography: cf. e.g. Cic. *Or.* 66 '(historia) in qua . . . regio saepe . . . describitur', *De Or.* 2.63 (above, pp. 2, 6, 12, 18), Sall. *H.* 3.61–80, Tac. *H.* 5.2–10, Lucian, *Hist. conscr.* 19; *situs* is the technical term for alluding to such material, e.g. Sall. *J.* 17.1, Hor. *Ep.* 2.1.250–9, Liv. *per.* 103–4, Vell. 96.3, Tac. *Agr.* 10.1. See also below, p. 242.

uarietates proeliorum: for battle as a standard element see 32.1n.; for the importance of suspense in historical narrative see Cic. *Fam.* 5.12.4–5 (above, p. 5).

clari ducum exitus: for the third element see e.g. Cic. *Fam.* 5.12.5, *Brut.* 43, *Diu.* 2.22. Cf. also *H.* 1.3.1.

retinent: the verb is almost technical for holding the attention (*OLD* 2b).

fallaces amicitias: see 18.1n. (*amicitia*).

obuia . . . satietate 'being faced with a glut of monotonous material' (almost hendiadys): the adj. suggests both that the author is presented with little choice of material and that the reader will find it an obstacle to his enjoyment; the two nouns sum up the numerous words for similarity earlier in the sentence and contrast with *uarietates* and *redintegrant* above.

33.4 Tum quod 'Then ⟨there is the fact⟩ that . . .': T. now turns to his third argument (33.3 being simply a repetition of 32.1) and provides further exx. of the difficulty of writing Tiberian historiography.

neque refert cuiusquam . . . extuleris: the impers. verb is here followed by a genit. (as often) and indir. qu. (*OLD* 1c); *utrum* is omitted in the first half of the qu. (20.3n. *fato*), the second half of which is introduced by *-ne* (*OLD* 5c).

posteri manent: and so are able to object to one's treatment of their ancestors, on grounds of either faint praise or excessive criticism (Plin. *Ep.* 5.8.13).

utque 'and even if' (as 40.4: see *OLD* 35).

reperies qui . . . putent 'you will find ⟨those⟩ who, on account of their own similar behaviour, think that the crimes of others are being imputed to themselves' (the subjunc. is generic, as if *qui* had been preceded by *sunt*, not *reperies*). Readers were evidently alive to hidden meanings, innuendo or – to use the technical term – *emphasis* (*Rhet. Herenn.* 4.67, Quint. 8.3.83 etc.).

gloria ac uirtus infensos habet: praise of the excellence of others invited the disbelief of readers (Sall. *C.* 3.2 (note *uirtute atque gloria*)) or even their hostility (34.1, Thuc. 2.35.2). Here T., by omitting explicit mention of the author's role, suggests also his favourite theme of the reversal of moral order (*Agr.* 1.4 'tam saeua et infesta uirtutibus tempora', 41.1 'infensus uirtutibus princeps'; Walker 81, W. on Vell. 88.2 (§5)).

ut . . . arguens 'as exposing/indicting their opposites from too close at hand'. The comparison is with the heroism (implied in *extuleris* above) of the Punic Wars, which, unlike more recent examples, is too far distant to produce significant comparisons with contemporary criminality. *ut* combines the ideas of comparison (as if *uelut*) and cause, as 59.2.

sed ⟨ad⟩ inceptum redeo: the same or similar words are regularly used to signal the end of digressions, e.g. Sall. *J.* 4.9 'nunc ad inceptum redeo', 42.5, Vell. 68.5 and W.

34–45 The year A.D. 25

The pattern of this year's narrative, in which a short section on foreign affairs follows a much longer sequence of domestic events, is highly unusual, having no parallel in the Tiberian or Neronian books; yet this emphasis follows on naturally after the preceding digression (above, pp. 169–70). The narrative comprises five sections, of which the first (34–6) reveals further the machinations of Sejanus (but see 34.1n.) and continues the series of trials with which the previous year ended. Since the second section (37–8) contrastingly shows Tib. himself in a favourable light (below, pp. 186–7), the reader is invited to speculate on the nature of the relationship between the two men which was stressed at the start of the book (1.1). That speculation is satisfied in the central section (39–41), where Sejanus and Tib. exchange correspondence. The exchange results in foregrounding Tib.'s retirement from Rome, a dramatic move from which T. diverts our attention by the miscellaneous items of the penultimate section (42–4). The final chapter (45) on rebellion in Spain provides a transition to the following year (below, p. 204).

34–6 Cremutius Cordus and other trials

The highlight of this section is the famous trial of Cremutius Cordus, who has little historical significance beyond the present episode but is the only historian in the whole of classical historiography to play so active a role or deliver a speech. T.'s unique presentation of a fellow historian in the context of his historiography is thus memorable and suggestive. The man's speech has won many admirers, who, in the light of T.'s comments on two contemporary historians at *Agr.* 2.1–2, see it as T.'s own impressive and dignified defence of free speech or historiography or both.[1]

34.1 Cornelio Cosso Asinio Agrippa: the former 'is only a date' (*AA* 298); his father was consul in 1 B.C. and his brother in 26 (46.1n.). M. Asinius Agrippa, a grandson of Asinius Pollio (4n.), died in 26 (61); his brother had been consul in 23 (1.1n.).

postulatur: for various views on the legal aspects of the case see Rogers (1) 86–7, Bauman (1) 268–71, (2) 31 n. 42, 99–103; also Seager 194–5, Levick 193–4. The case was heard in the senate: for such material at the start of a year see also 68–70.3, where *clientes* of Sejanus are again involved (Ginsburg 27–8).

nouo ac tunc primum audito crimine: it is probably true that no one previously had been charged with having written a history (*editis annalibus*). The elder Seneca describes the burning of T. Labienus' books in similar terms (*Contr.* 10 pref. 5 'res noua et inuisitata supplicium de studiis sumi'), but apparently ascribes the responsibility to his oratory rather than to his history (4–8). In any case Cordus' speech and most of our other evidence (Dio 57.24.2–3, Suet. *Tib.* 61.3, but not Sen. *Marc.* 1.3–4, 22.4–8) mention his praise of Brutus and Cassius as the nub of the charge, which was certainly novel (below, 2n.). T. himself, by emphasising novelty (*nouo*) but suggesting that other similar cases would follow (*tunc primum*, cf. 20.1 *ea prima . . . diligentia*), both implements rhetorical theory (*Rhet. Herenn.* 1.7 'attentos [sc. lectores] habebimus si . . . de rebus . . . nouis', cf. Sall. *C.* 4.4 'sceleris atque periculi nouitate') and evokes the venerable *archē kakōn* ('start of disasters') motif (e.g. Hom. *Il.* 5.62–3, *Od.* 8.81.2, Thuc. 2.12.3, Virg. *Aen.* 4.169–70 etc.). Cf. also 1.72.3, 2.27.1.

annalibus: the history (32.1n.), of which only one fragment survives (Sen. *Suas.* 6.19), evidently covered the civil wars and Augustus.

[1] For a full and perceptive analysis of the episode see H. Cancik-Lindemaier and H. Cancik, *Der altsprachliche Unterricht* 29 (1986) 4.16–35, who also draw some telling parallels with Orwell's *Nineteen eighty-four*.

accusabant . . . Seiani clientes: both elements are emphasised by their position in the sentence. Sejanus had been smarting from a caustic remark of Cordus' three years earlier (Sen. *Marc.* 22.4), but both he and Tib. are conspicuous by their absence from Cordus' speech, where the verbs are studiedly passive (2 *uerba . . . arguuntur*, *dicor*). See also 2.3n. (*clientes*).

34.2 id perniciabile reo et Caesar . . . accipiens 'that was fatal for the defendant, as was Tiberius' receiving his defence with a pitiless expression': for the pres. part. see 12.1n. (also similar *uariatio* with a (pro)noun).

The ideal ruler was supposed to look with benevolence on his people (e.g. Hor. *Odes* 4.5.6–7 'uultus ubi tuus | adfulsit populo'), but T. regards Tib.'s as the *uultus instantis tyranni* (*Odes* 3.3.3). It was also standard rhetorical practice to influence an audience by unflattering descriptions of the accused (Quint. 9.2.40–1; Jerome 373–4): hence other descriptions of Tib. in T. at 60.2 'toruus aut falsum renidens uultu', 1.12.3, 33.2, 2.28.2, 29.2, 3.3.1, 15.2, 44.4, 67.2, 6.50.1. The emperor was 'adducto fere uultu', according to Suetonius (*Tib.* 68.3), whose description 'provides the most striking example of an emperor whose physical merits and defects correspond from a physiognomical point of view to the virtues and vices of his character' (E. C. Evans, *H.S.C.P.* 46 (1935) 68). See also 15.3n., 57.2n. For T.'s other refs. to Tib.'s attendance at trials see Ginsburg 125 n. 31.

in hunc modum is one of T.'s commonest expressions for introducing *or. recta* in *A.*, but has no intrinsic implications for genuineness or otherwise (for which see 8.2n.). The present speech 'is all Tacitus' (Syme 337 n. 10).

The speech has four paragraphs. (1) Cordus gives two reasons why the *lex maiestatis* is inapplicable to his case (next two nn.). (2) He cites three precise precedents and a transitional one (3–4). (3) Other precedents which are less immediately relevant to his own predicament but closer to the 'case law' of the *lex m.* (next n. but one) (5–35.1 *ultus est*). (4) He denies that he wrote *belli ciuilis causa* (35.1–3).

uerba . . . arguuntur . . . factorum innocens: by contrast at 1.72.2 T. himself describes the convention which obtained until the very last years of Augustus: 'facta arguebantur, dicta impune erant'. G. notes: 'These famous words are broadly true . . . The exceptions are early, few, and debatable.'

sed neque haec . . . laudauisse dicor: with *haec* sc. *composui* or even *fuerunt*; both logic and word-order indicate that *neque* = *ne . . . quidem* (*OLD* 2b).

Cordus' defence here rests on two points. (1) The *lex maiestatis*, under which his treatment of Brutus and Cassius was alleged to fall, did not extend beyond Tib. as emperor or (cf. 2.50.2) Augustus, under whom Cordus' history was written and by whom it had even been heard (Dio, Suet. cited, 1n.). The validity of this defence is supported by 1.72.3, where Aug.'s extension of the law to cover other individuals is said by T. to be sharp practice ('primus Aug. cognitionem de famosis libellis *specie* legis eius [sc. maiestatis] tractauit'). (2) The *lex maiestatis*, in so far as it concerned the written word, had previously been confined to criticism or libel (cf. 31.1, 1.72.3, Sen. *Contr.* 10 pref. 4–8, Dio 57.22.8). (The same is also true of the spoken word.) Cordus' work, however, was not critical but encomiastic (*laudauisse dicor*). He thus seeks to apply the age-old dichotomy between encomium (*laus*) and censure (*uituperatio*) which permeated all ancient society and its literature and runs as a refrain through his speech (concluding with *odio aut gratiae* at 35.1). The only remaining question was whether Cordus, by praising, had intended criticism, since the two were recognised to be two sides of the same coin; and this question he answers in his final paragraph (35.2n.).

34.3 eloquentiae ac fidei: the great historian Livy (64 B.C.–A.D. 17) was proverbially *eloquens* (*Agr.* 10.3, Quint. 10.1.101); *fides* here = the impartial assessment of character (as Plin. *Ep.* 5.8.14), in which Livy excelled (Sen. *Suas.* 6.22). The gen. after *praeclarus* seems unparalleled.

in primis is usually (and by RHM) taken with *praeclarus* (cf. *Agr.* 9.1, Cic. *Sen.* 39 'magni in primis et praeclari uiri', Plin. *Ep.* 5.8.1), but AJW thinks that despite Plin. *NH* 22.119 its juxtaposition with the superlative adj. '*prae*clarus' is odd and that it more naturally accompanies *Cn. Pompeium* as 'introducing the leading member of a group' and 'as the first item in a series' (*OLD imprimis* 1b, 2).

"Pompeianum": Livy doubtless did praise Pompey, whom early-imperial writers tended to glorify as a heroic soldier-citizen whose death had been a tragedy, while at the same time they criticised the *Pompeiani* who under his banner had resisted Caesar and Octavian (P. Grenade, *R.E.A.* 52 (1950) 57–61). But since the evidence also suggests that Livy supported Augustus wholeheartedly (*RICH* 136–9), it seems that Cordus has chosen to take literally a joking suggestion by Aug. that admiration for Pompey meant sympathy for his supporters too (*Pompeianus* being capable of either interpretation).

Scipionem, Afranium: Q. Caecilius Metellus Pius Scipio, consul with Pompey in 52 B.C. and an enemy of Caesar; L. Afranius, consul in 60 and another Pompeian. See *OCD* for both men.

Cassium . . . Brutum: this is the first of three occasions on which Cordus uses this order of their names as opposed to the order at 2 above, where he is represented as quoting the charge-sheet. But whether this is due to T.'s own 'hostility to convention' (Syme 557 n. 7) is uncertain, since the precedence of Cassius is common in some other ancient sources (see E. Rawson in *PP* 102ff.; also on the liberators' posthumous fame).

latrones et parricidas: two regular terms of abuse in Roman oratory, yet each has a special point here: Brutus and Cassius had been notoriously brutal, e.g. on Rhodes and in Lycia in 42 B.C.; and Julius Caesar, whom they helped to assassinate, was *parens patriae* (Weinstock 200ff.). See also Bauman (2) 219 and n. 183.

uocabula imponuntur: Cordus anticipates the charge that he has tried to stir up civil war, to which explicit reference is made at 35.2 below, and turns the tables on his accusers by saying that it is others who are guilty of that offence, since it is they who are responsible for changing names (for the point of which see 19.2n. *scelera*). See also 35.5n. (*externi*). *imponere* makes his charge all the more sinister (*OLD* 14b).

34.4 Asinii Pollionis: the great republican remained hostile to Augustus throughout his life (76 B.C.–A.D. 4) and wrote a history of the years 60 to (perhaps) 31/30 B.C. in which that hostility was probably evident (*RICH* 127–8). His grandson as consul no doubt listened to Cordus' speech.

memoriam tradunt: a Livian expression (8.10.8, 9.41.4).

Messalla Coruinus: another great republican (64 B.C.–A.D. 8), he fought for Brutus and Cassius at Philippi but later joined and enthusiastically supported Augustus: see *AA* 72, 200–26, 502 (index); Table IX. Also next n. Little is known of his history.

opibus atque honoribus: the former applies more to Pollio, whose *honores* came relatively early (consul in 40, *triumphator* 39 or 38) but whose foreign campaigning brought him immense wealth (which he used to build a public library at Rome). The latter applies more to Corvinus, who was consul with Augustus in 31, *triumphator* in 27, *praefectus urbi* (very briefly), augur, *frater Arualis*, and (from 11 B.C.) *curator aquarum*. He was also patron of a literary circle which included the poet Tibullus.

peruiguere: the verb appears to be unique in classical Latin.

quo Catonem caelo aequauit: after his suicide at Utica in 46 B.C., M. Porcius Cato was rapidly idealised and became the subject of several panegyrics, incl. one each from Cicero and Brutus (M. Gelzer, *Caesar* (1969) 301–4). Hints of superhumanity were appropriate in panegyric and esp. applicable to Cato, 'dis quam hominibus propior' (Vell. 35.2): hence T.'s expression here (cf. *Aen.* 11.125 'quibus caelo te laudibus aequem?', addressed to Aeneas).

dictator: not pejorative but factual: sc. 'though' or 'when'. Caesar became dictator in 46 B.C.

rescripta oratione: the *Anticato* which Caesar produced in 45 (Gelzer [above] 302–3). *rescribo* is technical for a judicial or literary response (*OLD* 3): see esp. Suet. *Aug.* 85.1 'multa . . . prosa oratione composuit, ex quibus nonnulla in coetu familiarium . . . recitauit, sicut rescripta Bruto de Catone, quae uolumina cum (iam senior) ex magna parte legisset, fatigatus Tiberio tradidit perlegenda.'

respondit is here used with both accus. (*quid aliud*) and instrumental abl. (*oratione*): the former includes the possibility of a nonverbal response.

34.5 Antonii epistulae: traces are preserved in, e.g., Suet. *Aug.* 7.1, 16.2, 63.2, 69.2; see M. P. Charlesworth, *C.Q.* 27 (1933) 172–7. Hardly any traces of Brutus' speeches, and none of his *contiones*, have been preserved.

referta contumeliis Caesarum: Catullus attacked Julius in poems 29, 54, 57, 93; M. Furius Bibaculus, his contemporary, probably wrote a mock-epic on the Gallic wars (I. M. LeM. DuQuesnay, *Poetry and politics in the age of Augustus* (ed. Woodman and West, 1984) 54–5), but there seems no independent evidence that he attacked Octavian too.

dixerim: for the subjunc. see 6.1n. (*congruens*); *utrum* is omitted in the following indir. qu. (20.3n. *fato*).

moderatione is designed to appeal to Tib.: it was one of his special virtues (38.4n.).

si irascare: for the 'ideal' second pers. sing. of the pres. subjunc. in generalising conditional clauses see *NLS* §195; the clause illustrates *uariatio* with *spreta* (=*si spernas*) above, as e.g. *H.* 4.18.4; Sörbom 119.

35.1 non attingo Graecos is not strictly a *praeteritio* (the rhetorical device whereby one mentions items by denying their mention); Cordus means only that he will not offer individual examples.

libertas . . . libido: the former = 'free speech', a typically Athenian notion (C. Wirszubski, *Libertas as a political idea at Rome* (1950) 7, 13); the latter = *licentia*, a rare sense found also at 1.72.3 'libidine qua uiros feminasque . . . diffamauerat' (perh. also 5.4.3), Cic. *De Or.* 3.4 'libidinem tuam libertas mea refutabit'.

Antithesis of contrasting alliterative words, as here, is rare in T.'s narrative but not unusual in speeches; the same is true of polyptoton (*dictis dicta* below). See Adams (2) 124 and nn. 14, 16. For the omission of *sed* in *non modo . . . etiam* cf. 3.19.2.

aduertit 'took punitive action' (*OLD* 8), a simple for compound *animaduertere* which is probably peculiar to T. and commonest in *A.* 1–6 (G. on 2.32.3).

solutum 'exempt' (sc. from punishment): *OLD* 10b. For the *uariatio* with *sine obtrectatore* see 6.4n.

quos mors . . . exemisset: *odio* and *gratiae* refer chiastically to the precedents of the two preceding paragraphs (34.5–35.1, 34.3–4). In one sense the dead were of course less liable to rouse passions than the living (this is the very platform on which the *A.* is based: 1.1.3 'sine ira et studio, quorum causas procul habeo', cf. *H.* 1.1.2–3); yet at 33.4 (nn.) T. has just pointed out that things are hardly so straightforward. *exemisset* is generic subjunc. (*NLS* §155).

35.2 num enim . . . belli ciuilis causa populum . . . incendo?: the usual interpretation of this question is: 'For surely it is not the case that I am inflaming the people in support of civil war by public speeches at the very moment when C. and B. are holding the field in full armour at Philippi?' In other words Cordus is making the point that times have changed and C. and B. are no longer alive, a point which follows on from *mors* above and is picked up by *perempti* below; and since it is an obvious fact that C. and B. are no longer at Philippi,

Cordus hopes that the corollary will be equally obvious, viz. that in writing his history he is not inciting people to civil war.

AJW, however, believes that the abl. abs. refers to the subject-matter of Cordus' history, the writing of which constituted the precise charge against him: 'For surely it is not the case that, just because C. and B. hold the field in full armour at Philippi [sc. in my history], I am inflaming the people by public speeches with civil war as my motive?' Following on from the reference to *gratia* above, Cordus is saying that a sympathetic account of the liberators' battle is in no way the same as a public incitement to civil war. By omitting all reference to his role as an author, a device T. had adopted in his own person at 33.4 (n. *gloria*), Cordus represents as *actually* taking place that which in his history is merely *described.* He thus uses the same technique to refer to the immediacy (*enargeia*) of his historical narrative as Horace had used to praise that of Pollio's (*Odes* 2.1.17–19 with Nisbet–Hubbard). This not only prepares the way for Cordus' second question (below) but also seeks to exculpate his work on the grounds that it exhibits a quality at which all ancient historians aimed (see 28.1n.) and which therefore implies nothing about his personal motive (*causa*).

Yet Cordus' argument, on either of these interpretations, is flawed and (we may suspect) disingenuous. For T. has just been careful to remind us that readers were alive to double meanings in works of history (33.4n. *reperies*); and they were also accustomed to seeing one individual in terms of another (15.3n. *illum aspici*). It would not have been difficult to interpret Cordus' narrative as criticism of the principate and a call to arms.

an illi quidem . . . retinent? 'Or is it rather the case that they for their part, who have actually been dead for seventy years, as naturally preserve at least part of their memory in the works of historians as they are made familiar by their statues – which not even Augustus destroyed?' In AJW's opinion (see last n.) this second question has three functions: it transfers attention from the author (*causa . . . incendo*) to his subject ('illi *quidem*'); it points out that despite the immediacy of Cordus' narrative the liberators are long since dead (*perempti*); and it capitalises on the well known analogy between historiography and the visual arts, to which the first question above had alluded, to argue that the former deserves the same treatment as the latter.

Despite its dazzling compression, however, Cordus' argument is once again flawed. His precise rendering of the date recalls the unique and (given T.'s annalistic format) strictly redundant manner in which the funeral of Junia, Cassius' wife and Brutus' half-sister, is dated at the end of Book 3: 'sexagesimo quarto post Philippensem aciem anno' (76.1). T. concludes both that episode and the book with a memorable but ambivalent sentence: 'praefulgebant Cassius atque Brutus eo ipso quod effigies eorum non uisebantur' (2). For while *praefulgebant* supports Cordus' concluding remark (3 'etiam mei meminerint'), the fact that it was still too dangerous to allow their *imagines* to be displayed publicly undermines the validity of the analogy on which his present argument is based.

35.3 posteritas: esp. applicable in the case of an historian (32.2n. *in arto*).

si . . . ingruit: the pres. tense, unusual in a future condition (except in colloquial Latin), conveys the imminent likelihood of the *damnatio* (e.g. Sall. *C.* 58.9 'si uincimus, omnia nobis tuta erunt'): T. makes Cordus accept, appropriately in the light of his arguments (above, 2nn.), that the outcome of the trial is a foregone conclusion.

35.4 Libros . . . cremandos: a talionic punishment (cf. 2 *incendo*) to be exacted by the aediles, who had also burned Labienus' books at the end of Augustus' reign (Dio 56.27.1). The fire is kept burning metaphorically by *exstingui* below (5).

occultati et editi: the former by his daughter Marcia and others (Dio 57.24.4), the latter with the express permission of Gaius (Suet. *Gaius* 16.1). Quint. 10.1.104 refers to expurgated editions.

35.5 socordiam 'stupidity' (31.2n.).

ingeniis 'men of genius' (*OLD* 5b): the dat., as often, is a cross between possessive and 'of advantage' (sometimes called 'sympathetic': *NLS* p. 46).

externi reges aut qui eadem saeuitia usi sunt: T. will later describe Tib. himself in language appropriate to an alien autocrat (58.2–3nn.), while Sejanus has embarked on a battle for the principate (2.2n. *adeundo*) with the co-operation of *saeuientes* (cf. 1.1) such as Secundus and Natta (34.1). Thus whoever is responsible for setting light to 'civil war', it is certainly not Cordus (2 above).

dedecus . . . gloriam: the chiasmus emphasises each noun.

36.1 postulandis reis tam continuus annus fuit ut 'the year was so unbroken with the prosecution of defendants that . . .'; Rogers however notes that 'fewer are recorded in this year than in any of the preceding or any of several others' ((1) 86). T.'s disingenuous generalisation is typical. The use of the (modal?) abl. gerundive seems paralleled only at 11.5.1, though its origin can perhaps be seen in e.g. Liv. 3.65.4 'insectandis patribus tribunatum gessit'.

feriarum Latinarum: this, the most famous of the movable holidays (*fer. conceptiuae*), was held on several consecutive days in the second quarter of each year (Scullard 39, 111–15; Ginsburg 134).

praefectum urbis: a temporary appointment (not to be confused with the permanent one established by Augustus with the same name), held often by young men of rank (such as Germanicus' son here) while the consuls and other magistrates were honouring Jupiter Latiaris outside Rome on the Alban Mount.

adierit may seem initially to suggest ritual participation, as often (*OLD* 9); its true meaning here, 'accost for a purpose indicated or implied by the context' (*OLD* 4), is typically deferred till the end of the sentence (*in Sex. Marium*): Salvianus is an accuser. See also below, 3n. (*sacrosanctus*). The grounds of the accusation are unknown, but Marius was later accused of incest with his daughter and killed (6.19.1).

36.2 publice: i.e. not a private prosecution like Salvianus' (cf. 43.3). 'The communal charge is a phenomenon not fully understood' (Bauman (2) 81 n. 70).

quam bello Mithridatis meruerant: since the Third Macedonian War was *c.* 74–72 B.C. (*MRR* II 106–8), how do T.'s statement and its counterpart at Suet. *Tib.* 37.3 square with the inference of modern scholars from App. *Syr.* 12.45 that Cyzicus, a town on Propontis, had been a *ciuitas libera* since the establishment of Asia as a province in the late second cent. B.C.? Either T. and Suet. have made a mistake, or *meruerant* = 'deserved' or 'earned' rather than 'won'. Note T.'s typical substitution (also at 55.4) of a genit. for the more normal adj. (here *Mithridatico*): see G. on 1.3.7.

nec: the connective element of the word joins the nomin. *circumsessi* with the abl. abs. *pulso rege* (41.2n. *secretoque*), its negative element goes with *minus . . . quam*: 'after being besieged and having beaten off the king by their own endurance no less than with the help of Lucullus' force'. For the episode see App. *Mithr.* 75–6.

36.3 Fonteius Capito: consul in 12 with Germanicus, he was proconsul of Asia probably in 23/4 (*AA* 237–8). Rogers (1) 89 assumes that the charges were extortion and treason, the latter no doubt likely with Vibius Serenus as prosecutor (cf. 28.2); or Capito may simply have been accused of failing to prevent the *incuria Cyzicenorum.*

comperto 'it having been established that . . .': for such abl. abs. of impersonal verbs see *NLS* §93 *Note* (2); *comperto* occurs in Sall., Liv. and often in T.

noxae: predic. dat., as 3.13.1 (*OLD* 4a, *NLS* §68).

destrictior: lit. 'more unsheathed', as of a sword; the metaphorical use must = 'sharp', 'ready', 'dangerous' *uel sim.* (see *OLD destringo* 4), contrasting with perhaps *leues* below and with *obsequens* ('obliging') at Val. Max. 8.2.2. For *ut quis* see 23.2n.

sacrosanctus: this word, unique in T., points the irony of 1 above: whereas Salvianus was exiled for having violated formal ritual with his attempted prosecution, successful accusers were themselves almost technically inviolable (like tribunes: for discussion of the term and its implications see Weinstock 220–1).

leues, ignobiles 'ineffectual ⟨and⟩ undistinguished people': asyndeton of this type is much commoner in *A.* 1–12 than 13–16 (Adams (1) 355).

37–8 Tiberius and the imperial cult

Though the ostensible theme of this section has already been anticipated at 36.2 (*caerimoniarum diui Augusti*), a deeper and more significant link is provided by the notion of *memoria*. Cordus' defence of free speech arose from his decision to commemorate the dead (cf. 34.4 *memoriam*, 35.2 *memoriae*, 3 *posteritas*); and his prediction that as a result he himself would be remembered (35.3 *meminerint*) was fulfilled by T. at the emperor's expense (35.5 *memoriam*, *auctoritas*, *dedecus sibi atque illis gloriam*). It is therefore with some irony that here in the very next section T. allows Tib. a speech in which he responds to ruler cult by expressing concern for the preservation of his own memory (38.1 *meminisse*, *memoriae meae*, 2 *mansurae*, 3 *cum laude et bonis recordationibus*, *famam*).

Yet the suggestive juxtaposition of these episodes cannot disguise the nobility of the emperor's sentiments. Nor is it intended to, since T. follows the speech with a coda (38.4–5 and nn.) where he attributes to contemporary public opinion a point-by-point rejection of Tib.'s words which manifestly fails to hit its target and from which Tib. emerges with his reputation enhanced. Such manipulation of his readers' sympathies, first in one direction and then in another, is typical of T. and especially of his treatment of an emperor for whom he cannot conceal his reluctant admiration.

37.1 Hispania ulterior: see 13.2n. For 'the precedent of Asia' below see 15.3.

ualidus alioqui spernendis honoribus: though the adj. can be used with dat. gerundive of purpose (e.g. Liv. 25.36.9), here and at 3.10.2 the case seems rather to be abl. ('strong in rejecting honours'). *alioqui* here = 'at other times', 'as a general rule' (*OLD* 1b). For Tib.'s well known attitude to divine honours see Seager 144–8, Levick 139–40.

in ambitionem flexisse: when used of a change of attitude, *flectere* (intrans.) 'seems peculiar to T. (and Amm. 28.1.57)': G. on 1.13.5.

huiusce modi orationem: though the speech is T.'s own creation, it may contain traces of the emperor's own vocabulary: see nn. below and in general 8.2n.

37.2 constantiam ... desideratam 'that many people have looked for [sc. and not found] a consistent policy from me', i.e. in contrast with *flexisse* above. *desidero* occurs nowhere else in *A.* and may recall Tib.'s language (Syme 701, Miller 16–17). The *uariatio* of *defensionem* ~ *quid ... statuerim* (below) is, however, typical of T. (4.3n. *tutarentur*).

37.3 templum apud Pergamum: 29 B.C. (Dio 51.20.7): see Price 178, 182, 252 (and coin illustration at plate 2b).

qui ... uice legis obseruem: the subjunc. is causal (*NLS* §156) but the position of the clause before the main verb, and hence before the unexpressed antecedent of *qui*, is unusual. *uice* + genit. recurs in a Tiberian context at 6.21.3 and perhaps recalls the emperor's manner (Miller 16–17); conversely *facta dictaque* seems thoroughly Tacitean, recurring in a similar context at *Agr.* 46.3 'ut omnia facta dictaque eius secum reuoluant'. *obseruem* keeps alive the legal flavour (*OLD* 4a).

For Tib.'s devotion to Augustus and his precepts see 1.77.3 'neque fas Tiberio infringere dicta eius'; Seager 174–7, Levick 223–4, Brunt (3) *passim*, esp. 425 and n. 7.

placitum iam: it was 'already pleasing' to Tib. because it had been adopted earlier by Augustus; Tib. followed the precedent *promptius* because *ueneratio senatus* was involved besides himself (15.3). Concern for the senate is authentic Tib. (6.2n.).

ut . . . ueniam habuerit 'although a single acceptance [sc. of cult] will prove to be pardonable': for the expression see Hor. *Ep.* 2.1.169–70 'habet comoedia . . . ueniae minus' (Cic. *Mil.* 84 'habiturus esset impunitatem'). *ut* . . . *ita* = 'although . . . nevertheless', as 33.3 (n.).

effigie numinum: probably compressed for 'the kind of statue that divinities normally have'.

ambitiosum refutes the charge of *ambitio* levelled at 1 above.

uanescet: the simple form of *euanescere* is favoured in verse from the Augustan age and in prose in post-Augustan writers.

38.1 Ego me . . . mortalem esse . . . satisque habere . . . testor: Tib.'s protest (cf. also 3.6.3) is remarkable when we consider (1) the regularity with which other emperors accepted divine cult, (2) the appearance of the emperor's head on the obverse of coins, which 'was one of the numerous signs that he occupied a place of ambiguity between humanity and divinity' (Wallace-Hadrill 315), (3) the ease with which divinity was traditionally associated with great men of all types (e.g. Cic. *Rep.* 6.26 (the elder Scipio to Africanus in a dream) 'tu uero . . . sic habeto non esse te mortalem . . . deum te igitur scito esse', a passage which T. may well be recalling (see below, and 33.1n. *conflata*); also 34.4n. *quo Catonem* and 74.2n. *crebrisque*).

officia: the accus. after *fungi* is an archaism (*OLD* 1a) which recurs in a Tiberian directive at 3.2.1 and may be intended to recall the emperor's style (Miller 16), but, as usual, we cannot be certain (Syme 284). The repetition of *satis* also recurs in Tiberian utterances at 2.26.2 and 3.69.4; see further below, 39.4n.

ut = *si*: the usage seems unique in T. and very rare elsewhere, although scholars compare Cic. *Amic.* 52.

maioribus meis dignum: this is the first of four qualities for which Tib. wishes to be remembered. The context (cf. esp. *saxo*, *sepulchris* below) suggests that he is issuing his own epitaph, a genre in which it had long been conventional to claim rivalry with one's ancestors (see E. H. Warmington, *Remains of old Latin* (Loeb, 1940) IV no. 5.6 'facile facteis superases gloriam maiorum', 10.5–6 'facta patris petiei. | maiorum optenui laudem'; cf. also *Agr.* 46.3 'sic patris, sic mariti memoriam uenerari et . . . figuram animi . . . complectantur').

Yet the listing of *four* qualities suggests that Tib. is here proposing his personal 'virtues'. Greek philosophers had traditionally spoken of a canon of four (or sometimes five) cardinal virtues (bravery, temperance, justice and wisdom); and a series of four virtues, but with considerable variation as appropriate, was regularly claimed by great men or attributed to them by others (Weinstock 228–59, Wallace-Hadrill 300–7). Thus Augustus was presented with a shield, testifying to his *uirtus*, *clementia*, *iustitia* and *pietas* (*RG* 34.2).

Now it is clear from *Agr.* 46.2–3 (for which see further above and 37.3n.; below, 2n.) that *pietas* was an important element in *aemulatio maiorum*: 'admiratione te potius et laudibus et . . . *similitudine colamus*: is uerus honos, *ea* coniunctissimi cuiusque *pietas*'. Hence Tib. is here represented as claiming *pietas*, a virtue publicised on the coinage of 22/3 and intended to recall *inter alia* his devotion to his adoptive father Augustus (M. Grant, *Roman anniversary issues* (1950) 36). For *pietas* in a similar context cf. also Cic. *Rep.* 6.16, a work already recalled in Tib.'s speech (see above).

rerum uestrarum prouidum: *prouidentia* was one of the cardinal virtues of Tib.'s reign, appearing in altar dedications, on coins, and throughout the literary sources (see Rogers (2) 20–34, esp. 27–8, Levick 90, W. on Vell. 115.5).

constantem in periculis: *constantia* is primarily a military virtue (e.g. Curt. 5.7.1 'illam in subeundis periculis constantiam', of Alexander) but often applied to the political sphere, as here. T.'s attribution of this claim to the emperor is notable, since the quality was arguably not a feature of the historical Tib. (Levick 91) and was claimed as an official virtue only on the coinage of Claudius (Sutherland 129, 131, Wallace-Hadrill 321).

offensionum . . . non pauidum: *non pauidum* suggests that *offensionum* is passive, 'not afraid of being attacked' (cf. 3.54.6 'graues et plerumque iniquas [sc. offensiones] pro re publica suscipiam', in a speech of Tib.). The emperor is referring to one of the recognised aspects of *fortitudo*, viz. *patientia* (e.g. Cic. *Inu.* 2.163, cf. *Part. Or.* 77, *Rhet. Herenn.* 3.5).

38.2 haec mihi in animis uestris templa, hae . . . effigies . . . mansurae: the demonstratives *haec* and *hae* refer back to the four unexpressed abstract qualities lying behind Tib.'s words at 1 above (see nn.) and identify them with physical structures (*templa, effigies*). The identification, emphasised and made more vivid by the anaphora, is conceptually and linguistically bolder than passages (1) where the permanence of abstract qualities is contrasted with the impermanence of physical objects (e.g. *Agr.* 46.3–4 'simulacra uultus imbecilla ac mortalia sunt, forma mentis aeterna . . . : quidquid ex Agricola amauimus . . . manet *mansurum*que est *in animis hominum*'); (2) where physical objects are used as metaphors for works of literature, which, though able to confer immortality, are themselves also physical (e.g. Cic. *Arch.* 30 'consiliorum relinquere ac uirtutum nostrarum effigiem . . ., summis ingeniis expressam', Virg. *G.* 3.13 'templum de marmore ponam'); (3) where physical and abstract are linked by means of a genitive (e.g. Isoc. *Nic.* 36 'Desire to leave as a memorial images of your excellence rather than of your body', Cic. *TD* 3.3 'nullam eminentem effigiem uirtutis', *Off.* 3.69).[1] These differences suggest the originality of T.'s expression, which is nevertheless facilitated (1) by the characteristic trait of Roman religion whereby abstract qualities are turned into divine personifications (Wallace-Hadrill 314, cf. 319–33), (2) by a common use of the figure metonymy whereby the name of a divinity stands for his or her temple or statue, e.g. Virg. *Aen.* 3.275 'formidatus nautis aperitur Apollo' (='the temple of A.'), Tibull. 2.5.27 'lacte madens illic suberat Pan' (='the statue of P.'): see further Smith on Tibull. 2.5.22. Hence the abstract *prouidentia*, for example, to be elicited from *rerum uestrarum prouidum* at 1 above, will have suggested Providentia to Tib.'s audience, which in turn will have evoked her physical temple or statue. Yet although it is this association of ideas on which the emperor has relied for his metaphorical identification of abstract with physical, his point in making the identification is precisely to reject the usual implications of that association in his own particular case. Physical temples and statues are the very last things he wants.

quae saxo struuntur . . . pro sepulchris spernuntur: 'Observe the alliteration' (Syme 701); the assonance of the verbs also gives point to the *sententia*. In its literal sense *struere* is preferred by T. to *exstruere* in

[1] Different again are passages where a statue, though metaphorical, is of a physical person (e.g. Cic. *Phil.* 9.12, Dio 52.35.3 'It is golden and silver statues of yourself which you should not allow to be made, but others ⟨of yourself⟩ which by benefactions you should construct *in the souls of men* and which will not tarnish or perish').

A. 1–6; in 11–16 he, like Caesar and Cicero, prefers the compound (Adams (1) 363–4). *pro* = 'like' (*OLD* 9c): the neglect of gravestones was proverbial.

in odium uertit: Tib. is made attractively to forget that memory is subject to the same processes of hatred as gravestones; T. himself, however, characteristically does not forget (cf. 6.2.1 'atroces sententiae dicebantur in effigies quoque *ac memoriam* eius [sc. Liuiae]'). *uertit* is again intrans., as 31.3 (n.).

38.3 deos et deas ipsas: since gods and goddesses are coupled elsewhere in a Tiberian utterance (6.6.1 'di . . . deaeque': see Miller 18), this corrected reading of M may well be right: *ipsas* suggests 'real' goddesses in contrast to such personified abstractions as Providentia above (1). *hos*, below, embraces both fem. and masc., as often (e.g. Varro, *RR* 1.1.5 'inuocabo . . . Iouem et Tellurem: itaque quod ii parentes magni dicuntur . . .').

usque would more normally precede *ad* (*OLD* intro. n. and 3a). The complete phrase is balanced (and varied) by *quandoque concessero* below; similar balance characterises the remainder of the sentence.

intellegentem . . . iuris mentem duint: the second (cf. 1n.) archaism of the speech (*duint* for *dent*: *OLD do* intro. n.) perhaps recalls the emperor's style (Syme 700, Miller 16), though cf. Cic. *Cat.* 1.22 'mentem . . . duint'. For Tib.'s knowledge of law, both human and divine, see Levick 89, 253 n. 33.

intellegens + genit. goes back at least to Cic. (*OLD* 2): so too *sciens*, used with similar phraseology at 3.70.3 and 6.26.1; see also 33.2 'callidi temporum'.

concessero: used without *uitā* also at 13.30.2 and perhaps 2.71.1 (see G.): evidently a Tacitean peculiarity.

38.4 alli . . . multi . . . quidam . . . interpretabantur: typical of T. are (1) the *uariatio* of pronoun and adj. (e.g. 60.2 *alius . . . quidam . . . plerique*; Sörbom 32–3), which here is extended by the three different constructions after the verb, and (2) the imputing to unnamed persons of alternative explanations, the last of which is often (but not always) the most hostile (e.g. 1.76.4, 80.2: see above, p. 32). Note too that the nameless spokesmen each deploy successively less sympathetic *colores* on the same alleged characteristic of Tib.: just as *diffidentia* is the more reprehensible aspect of *modestia* (cf. Quint. 9.2.72), so *metus*, which lies behind *degeneris animi*, is of *diffidentia* (cf. *H.* 1.72.2,

Plin. *Ep*. 5.1.7). Both the application of *colores* and the 'variations on a theme' are also typical of T. (see respectively above, p. 124, and below, 60.2).

modestiam: the quality (also at 1.11.1, 3.56.2, 5.2.1) is closely related to *moderatio*, which Tib. made his own 'peculiar and distinctive virtue' (Rogers (2) 88). He publicised it on the coinage and in official correspondence: see EJ 102 (*b*) = Sherk 31, the emperor's letter to the people of Gythium in which he expresses views on ruler cult almost identical to those in his speech here. It has left its mark throughout the literary sources and is perhaps the one imperial virtue which T. disparages only rarely. See Rogers (2) 60–88, Syme 416, 754, Levick 89, 253 n. 29; G. on 1.8.5, W. on Vell. 122.1.

quia diffideret 'on the grounds that he lacked confidence' (sc. that he was equal to such an honour: cf. Suet. *Tib*. 67.2): see 11.1n. (*insita*) for this characteristic.

ut degeneris animi 'as ⟨a sign⟩ of degeneracy', in comparison with Augustus (cf. *melius Augustum* below) and hence an implied rejection of *maioribus meis dignum* at 1 above (the first in a series of such rejections: above, pp. 186–7). The allusion to *Aen*. 4.13 'degeneres animos *timor* arguit' (see Pease) suggests that in this third and final explanation of his behaviour Tib. is being accused of the same *metus comparationis* with Augustus as earlier at 1.76.4.

38.5 optimos quippe mortalium: since Tib. was the first to be known as *optimus princeps* (Vell. 126.5, Val. Max. 2 pref., and on inscriptions), the sarcasm is palpable.

altissima cupere: an attempted rejection of Tib.'s argument that his acceptance of further cult would be *ambitiosum*, *superbum* (37.3); but T. undermines its validity by echoing Sall. *C*. 5.5 'nimis alta semper cupiebat', where the revolutionary Catiline is described.

deum: see 1.2n.

additos is almost technical in contexts such as these (*OLD* 9, Nisbet–Hubbard on Hor. *Odes* 2.19.13 of Bacchus).

melius Augustum: sc. *fecisse* or *egisse* (see G. on 1.43.1 'melius et amantius ille qui gladium offerebat').

sperauerit: for the tense see 2.1n.

insatiabiliter: this uncommon word, used by T. only here, is used by Lucretius in a memorable and exaggerated parody (3.907 with Kenney's n.): to reject Tib.'s claims at 1 above (*satisque habere*, *satis* *superque*) his opponents are thus made to choose a word whose tone again undermines their contention (see Syme 727).

prosperam sui memoriam: as if this had not been the keynote of the emperor's speech (above, p. 186). Cf. also 6.46.2 'illi non perinde curae gratia praesentium quam in posteros ambitio'.

contemptu famae contemni uirtutes: the charge of moral reversal (3.4n.), emphasised by its final position (Walker 57 n. 1) and the *figura etymologica*, wilfully distorts Tib.'s views: he had in fact expressed a deep desire that his virtues should be recognised by contemporaries and remembered by posterity (1–3 above).

39–41 Sejanus and Tiberius

This section occupies the structural centre of the year's narrative and very nearly the mathematical centre of Book 4 as a whole (above, pp. 16–17). Ancient authors often placed in a central position those matters to which they wished to give an extra significance, and this exchange of letters between the two protagonists is the pivot on which the plot of the book hinges. Alarmed by Tib.'s response to his request for Livi(ll)a's hand, Sejanus determines to persuade the emperor to leave Rome; and it is the success of his persuasion which leads in the following year to his own supremacy for half a decade (57.1).

The letter is a time-honoured device in classical historiography (e.g. Thuc. 1.137.4, 7.11–15), and an exchange of letters (e.g. Arr. 2.14) is comparable to the device of matching speeches. Whether the present letters are any more genuine than most speeches it is impossible to say for certain: although Sejanus' portrayal of himself is paralleled in the contemporary work of Velleius, and Tib.'s letter perhaps displays some linguistic verisimilitude (see nn. below), Syme is rightly sceptical of their authenticity (404, 702). Like speeches, letters in the ancient world fell into certain categories: there were public and private types, each divided into further classifications such as that which recommended individuals for political advancement and is exemplified by Cicero, *Ad Familiares* 13. By making Sejanus write a letter recommending his own *self*-advancement, T. has capitalised on generic convention to underline Sejanus' ambition; and whereas most letters of recommendation were public documents, Sejanus' is seemingly private and thus has the extra dimension of appearing revelatory. For its part Tib.'s letter provides a masterly example of sustained dramatic irony, since it invites comparison with another letter from the emperor which in 31 would end Sejanus' years of supremacy and seal his immediate fate (40.7n.).

39.1 nimia fortuna . . . cupidine incensus: two key elements in tragic drama. It was proverbial that too much success leads to danger, which wise men therefore sought to prevent (e.g. Camillus after the capture of Veii at Liv. 5.21.14–15 (*nimia sua fortuna*): see Ogilvie). *socors* here = 'dulled', 'careless', 'insensitive' (cf. 31.2n.). Though expressions such as *cupidine incensus* are normally used of a person's own emotion, here the point (expanded by *promissum . . . flagitante Liuia*) seems to be that Sejanus was roused by *Livi(ll)a*'s desire: for *muliebris* = 'a/the woman's' see *OLD* 1a–b. The adj. can of course also = 'for the woman' (*OLD* 3), but such a meaning here would not square with Sejanus' pretended affection at 3.3 above ('*ut* amore incensus').

promissum: at 3.3.

(moris quippe tum erat . . . scripto adire): why does T. comment on a practice which had begun with Caesar, continued thereafter, and remained absolutely normal in his own day (Millar 240ff., 537ff.)? *quamquam praesentem* suggests a contrast with Tib.'s later absence from Rome (57.1), when communication by letter was perforce abnormally frequent: his inaccessibility in 26–37, dreamed of by Sejanus at the end of this section (41.2), is foreshadowed here in 25 (*tum*) at its beginning.

moris (*OLD* 3b) is possessive gen.; for *quamquam* see 15.2n.

39.2 eius: as if *epistula* (*uel sim.*) had preceded.

patris Augusti: a most appropriate form of *captatio beneuolentiae* in Tib.'s case (cf. 37.3n.) and redeployed at 3 below; cf. 40.6 (*at enim*).

iudiciis 'marks or instances of esteem' (*OLD* 10a).

neque fulgorem honorum umquam precatum: so too Vell. 127.4 'nihil sibi uindicantem'. The obvious analogy is Augustus' great minister Maecenas, who never sought political advancement but remained an *eques* throughout his life.

excubias ac labores, ut unum e militibus, . . . malle: Sejanus' actual position (2.3n. *socium*) was such that he could not claim realistically to be only a common soldier: hence *ut*, nicely ambiguous ('as' or 'as if'). The insincerity of his words is underlined by the fact that, when he is praised by Tib. for *labor uigilantiaque* (3.72.3) or by Vell. as *laboris . . . capacissimum* and *animo exsomnem* (127.3–4), these phrases reflect Sejanus' own attempts to present himself as the ideal general (1.3nn. *laborum*, *saepius*, cf. 2.2n. *adeundo*), perhaps deriving this element of his image from Augustus' other great minister, the soldier Agrippa, an archetypal man of *labor* (Syme 402–3). The motif 'one of the men' is part of this conventional picture (W. on Vell. 85.5, 114.1–3).

quod pulcherrimum: sc. *esset*. Either the clause is object of *adeptum* and explained by *ut . . . crederetur* (as printed) or it is parenthetical and *adeptum* introduces *ut . . .* (see *OLD adipiscor* 2b).

Sejanus' daughter had been betrothed to Claudius' son Drusus in 20 (7.2n.).

39.3 audiuerit is disingenuous, since Augustus' deliberations about Julia were presumably well known (Suet. *Aug*. 63.2). For the tense see 2.1n.

in conlocanda filia 'in ⟨the matter of⟩ giving his daughter in marriage' (*OLD colloco* 9a).

haberet = pres. jussive subjunc. in *or. recta*.

sola necessitudinis gloria usurum 'who would enjoy only the glory of the relationship'.

39.4 non enim exuere imposita munia: litotes (understatement by means of the negativing of an opposite, cf. *Rhet. Herenn*. 4.50, Donatus on Ter. *Hec*. 775) and, in the light of 41.2 below, heavily ironical: relief from his responsibilities is the very last thing Sejanus wants.

satis: sc. *fore* or *esse* (cf. 6.37.4): 'he reckoned it would be sufficient . . .' The sense is: 'I want nothing more than that Livi(ll)a's house should be protected'; *idque* [11.1n. *nullo*] *liberorum causa* diverts attention from Livi(ll)a herself. *aestimare* (*OLD* 7a) = *existimare*, simple for compound.

multum superque: taken with *satis* above, the phraseology resembles that in Tib.'s speech at 38.1 (*satis, satis superque*: see n.): Sejanus addresses the emperor 'in his own language'. *sibi* contrasts with *domum* above, and *expleuisset* = fut. perf. in *or. recta*: 'for himself ⟨the amount⟩ of life which he lived along with such a *princeps* would be more than enough'.

40.1 pietate Seiani: dramatic irony: the reader knows that Sejanus' request has nothing to do with *pietas*.

tamquam ad integram consultationem 'as though for a full deliberation'. The phrase is ironical: T. makes Tib. reply using similar terms to those in which he had been approached (39.3 *consultauisse*) and suggesting that despite the length and tone of the present letter a considered response was yet to come. No wonder Sejanus reacts the way he does (41.1).

ceteris mortalibus . . . putent 'other people's plans depended on what they thought was self-interest': the use of *stare* is regular, though more normally followed by the simple abl. (*OLD* 21a); for a pronoun expanded by an indir. qu. see 74.1 and 4.3n. (*quod*). For the tense of *putent* see 2.1n. *mortales* for *homines* is an archaism popular with historians (Gell. 13.29) but smacks of the authentic Tib. (cf. 38.1).

praecipua rerum ad famam derigenda: *famam* again looks authentic (38.1–3: above, p. 186), but see also 31.2n. *derigo* + *ad* = 'to regulate in the light of' (*uel sim.*): *OLD dirigo* 6c. For *praecipua rerum* see 41.3 below.

40.2 illuc . . . quod promptum rescriptu: *illuc* acts as antecedent to *quod* . . .; *rescriptu* governs the accus. + inf. *posse . . . propiora consilia*. *rescribere* is the technical term for an imperial response (*OLD* 2a), but its supine form seems unparalleled.

nubendum . . . an . . . tolerandum haberet 'whether she should marry after / in the light of Drusus' death or continue in the same household': *habeo* + gerund(ive), exactly like Engl. 'I have (to do something)', is a post-republican prose usage (*OLD* 17a) which T. exploits esp. in *D.*; for the omission of *utrum* see 20.3n. After *Drusum* sc. *mortuum*, as 1.16.3 'post Augustum': such brachylogy with *post* is common in T. and other authors, and in some cases 'a causal sense may be detected' (G. on 1.68.5 with exx.), as perhaps here (see further *OLD post* 4). The absolute use of *tolerare* (as if *uitam* were understood) is most unusual (*OLD* 2b).

matrem et auiam: the former is Drusus' widow Antonia *minor*, younger daughter of Mark Antony and Octavia (sister of Augustus); the latter is Livia Augusta.

40.3 simplicius 'more directly' (sc. than that): the reference is primarily to the content of Tib.'s reply (cf. 7 *haec . . . non occultaui*), but T. doubtless intends us to recall the complications which usually accompanied the emperor's speech (31.2n.).

quas . . . arsuras: sc. *esse*: the clause has been attracted into the acc. and inf. construction, as often happens when the relative pronoun is used instead of *et* + a demonstrative pronoun (here *eas*): see *NLS* §230 (6) and *Note*, §289.

distraxisset: =fut. perf. in *or. recta*.

sic quoque 'even as things were', a reference to 12.3 (n.); for *quoque* see *OLD* 4a.

nepotes suos must refer to the sons of Tib.'s adopted son Germanicus (3.1n.), as well as to his own surviving grandson Ti. Gemellus (still a child).

conuelli is vivid for *conuulsum iri* (2.1n.).

quid si intendatur certamen tali coniugio?: the verb = 'intensify' (*OLD* 5a); for the tense see 2.1n. The question ironically recalls *Aen.* 4.47–8 'quam tu urbem, soror, hanc cernes, quae surgere regna | coniugio tali', where Anna successfully persuades Dido to forget her dead husband Sychaeus and contemplate a marriage to Aeneas which, while allegedly enhancing her own power, would have meant disaster for the future of Rome.

40.4 Falleris enim, Seiane: 'Notably effective is the exordium in reported discourse, breaking by intensity of the emotion into appeal and argumentation' (Syme 317); see also 8.2n.

C. Caesari: son of Augustus' daughter Julia; he died in A.D. 4.

ut cum equite Romano senescat: more dramatic irony (cf. 39.1 *flagitante*).

ego ut sinam 'even if . . .' or 'even supposing . . .', as 33.4 (n.).

fratrem . . . patrem: Germanicus and the elder Drusus respectively.

40.5 qui te inuitum . . . consulunt: more details in Dio 57.21.4 (A.D. 23). In view of the situation described at 2.3 above (nn.), Tib.'s remark is dramatically ironic; compare also the scenes depicted at the very end of Book 4 (74.3–4nn.). The metaphorical use of *perrumpo* recurs in T. only in a Tiberian context at 3.15.2 and may thus suggest a Tiberian idiolect (Miller 16). Cf. the siege tactics which Horace ironically recommends to a pest wanting access to Maecenas (*S.* 1.9.54–6).

excessisse iam pridem equestre fastigium: Sejanus' immense power and relatively humble status were two sides of the same coin and explain the two areas of his unpopularity which Vell. tries to counter in chh. 127 and 128 respectively (see W.).

amicitias may, but need not, be concrete = 'friends' (*OLD* 2b). The reference is pointedly (cf. 39.2n.) to such men as Maecenas.

40.6 at enim 'But you say that . . .' (*OLD at*[1] 4b): cf. 39.3 above.

mirum hercule si, cum . . . permixtos!: the sentence is an ironic exclamation, implying its opposite: 'What a surprise that, when he turned his mind to all the items of concern and foresaw no limit to the elevation of whomsoever he raised up by such a marriage, it was C. Proculeius and others like him whom he discussed . . .!' For *distraho* see *OLD* 8 (esp. Liv. 22.7.10); *immensum* is probably adverbial (as 27.2), *attolli* is vivid for the (defective) fut. pass. infin. (2.1n.), and *extulisset* = fut. perf. in *or. recta.*

Proculeius was a favourite of Augustus (see further Nisbet–Hubbard on Hor. *Odes* 2.2.5). *tranquillitas*, otherwise unexampled in *A.* and *H.*, may be intended to recall Tib.'s apparent liking for Ciceronian abstract nouns (Miller 14–15); but the *uariatio* of abl. of quality ~ part./adj. is typical of T. (e.g. 1.24.3, 3.65.1; Sörbom 90).

sed si dubitatione Augusti mouemur: Tib. turns Sejanus' trump *exemplum* on its head. *dubitatio*, another Ciceronian abstract noun, recurs thrice in *A.*, twice in Tiberian contexts (1.7.7, 3.41.3): Miller 14.

quanto ualidius est quod 'how much more telling is the fact that . . .'. In 21 B.C. Julia married Agrippa, who died in 12 B.C., whereupon she married Tib. in the following year.

40.7 non occultaui picks up *simplicius acturum* (3) and rounds off this section of the argument; but T. doubtless intends his readers also to recall Tib.'s habitual secretiveness (1.2n.). See also next n.

ceterum neque . . . aduersabor: this announcement 'comes as a distinct surprise after such telling arguments against the marriage' (Seager 198), but it well illustrates Tib.'s *suspensa semper et obscura uerba* (1.11.2), the avoidance of which he has just professed (*non occultaui*). After the lengthy dissuasion of 3–6 above, however, Sejanus knows he has little choice in the matter.

quibus . . . parem 'by what further bonds I am contemplating linking you to myself'. Dio under 31 refers to Sejanus as 'betrothed' (58.7.5), Suet. describes him as *spe adfinitatis . . . deceptum* (*Tib.* 65.1), and after his death he is called Tib.'s *gener* (5.6.2, 6.8.3). Whether this means that Sejanus' request for Livi(ll)a was eventually successful, or whether he gained her daughter Julia or some other lady, is uncertain (*AA* 170–1).

excelsum is perhaps another Tiberian idiolect, recurring in *A.* only at 3.53.3 (a speech of Tib.): Miller 16.

uel in senatu uel in contione non reticebo: i.e. a continuation of the process which had already started (cf. 2.3 'apud patres et populum'); but these closing words 'are intended (there can hardly be a doubt) to foreshadow what happened in the Senate when the *verbosa et grandis epistula* was read out on October 18 of the year 31, conveying the doom of Aelius Seianus' (*AA* 170, cf. Juv. 10.71, Suet. *Tib.* 65.1). Similar foreshadowing at 70.1 (n. *sollemnia*).

41.1 Rursum Seianus non iam de matrimonio: sc. *agit* (*uel sim.*), as 38.5 (n.): 'In reply Sejanus no longer argued about the marriage'. See *OLD ago* 40a; for *rursum*, *OLD* 4.

tacita . . . inuidiam: the tricolon nicely suggests a note of desperation in Sejanus' protestations; see also 3n. For *tacita* + genit. see 5.2n. (*cetera*).

procul is a preposition here, as 2.1 (n.).

amoenis: the conventional adj. for attractive locations (*OLD* 1a–b): see further 3n.

41.2 secretoque loci mollitum is Sejanus' private interpretation of the *quies et solitudo* he will urge on Tib. at 3 below: he hopes that the countryside will work its enervating effects even on one as *durus* as the emperor (30.2, 1.54.2 [opp. *molliter*], 3.52.1).

uariatio involving the co-ordination of part./adj. with an abl. abs. (instead of another part. or word of similar type) is common in T., esp. in the later books of *A.*: e.g. 36.2 'circumsessi nec . . . pulso rege', 50.4 'immoti telisque . . . iactis', 12.45.1, 66.1 'admotus . . . et dolo intellecto', 16.21.1 'infensus et accedentibus causis'; Sörbom 91, Martin (1) 94–5. Here *uergente . . . senecta secretoque . . . mollitum* probably falls into this category.

minui . . . augeri: vivid pres. for fut. (2.1n.): the contrast is emphasised by the chiasmus. For Sejanus' earlier *potentia* see 1.1n. (*cuius*), 7.1.

41.3 negotia . . . solitudinem: Sejanus resorts to the conventional arguments in favour of country life, which he handles from the standard oratorical viewpoints of blame and praise (*increpat*, *extollens*); the former involves another tricolon (see above, 1n.).

quis abesse . . . offensiones ac praecipua rerum . . . agitari: *quis* (14.1n.) is either dat. or abl. (of separation) with *abesse*; with *agitari* it is abl. of place 'where', or understand *ubi*. For the infin. in the rel. clause see 40.3n. (*quas*); for *agito*, 6.3n. Sejanus' language is again shrewd (cf. 2.1nn. *cohortes*, *procul*, 17.3n. *remedium*): he echoes the concern for *praecipua rerum*, and the disdain for *offensiones inanes et inritas*, which Tib. himself evinced at 40.1 and 3.54.6 respectively.

42-4 The end of the year

The penultimate section of the year's narrative follows a generally similar pattern to that of the final section of A.D. 23 (13–16: above, p. 134): a transition is made from Sejanus via the person of Tib. to three categories of senatorial business (42 three trials, 43 three foreign embassies, 44 three obituaries). Here, however, the sequence of thought has an additional aspect. Tib.'s involvement with the senate is presented (42.1) as a motive for his leaving Rome, which he has just been urged by Sejanus to do and which he eventually does towards the end of the following year (57).

42.1 per illos dies: such temporal phrases (also at 43.1 *dehinc*, 44.1 *eo anno*, cf. 45.1 *Isdem consulibus*) are common at the end of a year (above, p. 134): none of them provides any hint of absolute dating within the year, and only *dehinc* a relative date.

Votieno Montano: a noted orator from Narbonese Gaul, who is mentioned often by the elder Seneca. For his case see Bauman (2) 120–1.

cognitio 'judicial inquiry' (*OLD* 3).

cunctantem: see 11.1n. (*insita . . . cunctatione*).

uocesque, quae . . . ingerebantur: as the verb is commonly used of insults etc. (e.g. 1.39.4 *contumelias*; *OLD* 2b), *uoces* must = 'words' or 'talk' (*OLD* 7). Whether *plerumque* = 'for the most part' (with *uerae*) or '(very) often' (with *ingerebantur*) is unclear. *coram* (adv.) = 'in his presence'.

42.2 e militaribus uiris: sc. *unus* (see G. on 2.60.3). Aemilius was perhaps a tribune of the praetorian cohort who is mentioned on an inscription (G. on 2.11.1).

quamquam without a finite verb is common in T. (15.2n.); for its use with a prepositional phrase cf. 12.56.3, 15.44.5.

quis: see 14.1n.

purgaturum 'would clear his name' (used absolutely, unless *probra* is to be understood from earlier in the sentence): *OLD* 8e, d, cf. 7.

42.3 maiestatis poenis: he was apparently exiled to the Balearic Islands, where he died in (?) 27.

obiectam sibi ... amplexus 'embracing all the more stubbornly the mercilessness towards defendants with which he was charged'. A double paradox: not only is Tib. himself both defendant and judge, but *inclementia* overturns the *clementia* which he advertised so carefully (31.2n.).

Vario Ligure: possibly the son of a praetorian prefect under Augustus. For the importance attached to adultery cases in Tib.'s reign see Garnsey 22–3.

Lentulus Gaetulicus consul designatus: see 46.1n. He had probably been elected no earlier than October, but 'there was no regular timetable for consular elections during the Julio-Claudian period' (Talbert 204).

lege Iulia damnasset: the *lex* prescribed banishment without further penalty; *exilio* (below) implies also loss of property (cf. 21.3). For the subjunc. see 4.1n. (*quamquam*).

in acta diui Augusti non iurauerat: such an oath had been regular on 1 Jan. each year (Talbert 201): like Claudius, Tib. did not permit swearing *in acta sua* (1.72.1 and G.). In 66 Thrasea Paetus faced a similar charge (16.22.1).

albo senatorio: 'The list of members of the senate in order of seniority, publicly displayed, and updated each year' (Talbert 523). For expulsion see 31.4n.

43.1 Auditae ... legationes: though Greece (Achaea) had been transferred to the emperor's jurisdiction in 15 (1.76.2), the deputations are heard in the senate as if it were still a senatorial province.

iure templi 'right of ⟨control of⟩ the temple'. Limnae is on the slopes of Mt Taygetus, on the borders of Laconia and Messenia.

Philippi: the father of Alexander the Great had moved into the Peloponnese after the decisive battle of Chaeronea in 338 B.C.

43.2 inter Herculis posteros diuisionem: Temenus, Cresphontes and the sons of Aristodemus took possession of Argos, Messenia and Laconia respectively.

protulere 'adduced [sc. as supporting evidence]' (*OLD* 5), here followed by both noun and acc. + inf.; though the latter construction with *proferre* seems hard to parallel, such *uariatio* is very common in T. (e.g. 46.2, 2.79.3, 6.25.2; Sörbom 110–11).

Denthaliatem: the Denthalioi inhabited the disputed border area between the Spartans and Messenians.

cessisse 'had become the property of, had passed into the possession of' (*OLD* 15a).

aere prisco 'their original bronze'.

43.3 **quod si uatum, annalium ad testimonia uocentur** 'But if they were being challenged on the basis of [lit. to] testimony from poets, histories . . .': both word-order and asyndeton are emphatic and dismissive. For *uocare* in this sense see *OLD* 5; for the tense, 2.1n.

locupletiores 'more reliable' (*OLD* 4).

Antigoni . . . Mummii: Antigonus III of Macedonia occupied Sparta in 222 B.C.; L. Mummius was in charge of Greece after the fall of Corinth in 146.

permisso publice arbitrio 'having been entrusted collectively with the arbitration' (in 135 B.C.). For *publice* see 36.2.

praetorem: see 15.2n.; he was probably praetorian proconsul.

datum: sc. *ius templi* (or perhaps *iudicium*: 'judgement was given in favour of . . .').

43.4 **Erycum:** probably an alternative to the noun *Eryx* (so *OLD*), in which case the placing of the preposition between two nouns in apposition resembles that at e.g. 2.60.1 (where G. remarks that the usage seems restricted to *A.* and is 'recently borrowed from the poets'). Alternatively the word may be an adj. formed from *Eryx*, in which case the anastrophe is analogous to that at e.g. 15.18.2 'portu in ipso'. See also 5.1n.

uetustate dilapsam, being an expression found often in inscriptions, suggests the wording of the official request.

ut consanguineus: in A.D. 4 Tib. had been adopted into the *gens Iulia*, traditionally descended from Venus via her son Aeneas, who allegedly founded her temple on Mt Eryx (*Aen.* 5.759). According to Suet. *Claud.* 25.5 the actual rebuilding belongs to Claudius' reign.

43.5 **P. Rutilii:** P. Rutilius Rufus, consul in 105 B.C., was exiled in 93 or 92 after a notoriously unjust condemnation for extortion.

ciuem sibi . . . addiderant 'had made him a fellow-citizen'.

in Massilienses: evidently elliptical for *in ciuitatem Massiliensium*: 'having been admitted to Massilian citizenship by virtue of this precedent'. Moschus, an orator from Pergamum who figures in the works of the elder Seneca, had been exiled to Marseilles after being condemned on a charge of poisoning.

44.1 Obiere . . . uiri nobiles: for obituaries see 15.1n.; for *nobilitas*, 6.2n. (*mandabatque*). These two aristocratic generals, 'victorious beyond the great rivers, echo back to a more expansive epoch, evoking nostalgia and pointing the contrast with the deep peace of Tiberius' reign' (*TST* 86). For Lentulus see also 29.1n.

super . . . triumphalia: *super* = 'in addition to' (*OLD* 7); Lentulus' *triumphalia* (18.1n.) had been won on the lower Danube *c.* 9 B.C. (*RP* III 879–80).

gloriae: predic. dat. (*NLS* §68 (i)): 'Lentulus . . . had had to his credit'. T.'s description of him here recalls what was said on his first introduction at 1.27.1 'ante alios aetate et gloria belli' (Syme 750).

44.2 Domitium: L. Domitius Ahenobarbus (consul 16 B.C.) was legate successively in Illyricum and Germany, and had been proconsul of Africa (13/12 B.C.). He was grandfather of the emperor Nero (75n.). See Suet. *Nero* 1–5 for the family history; also *AA* 483 (index) and Table VIII.

pater: Cn. Domitius Ahenobarbus (cos. 32 B.C.). He commanded a fleet in the Adriatic against the triumvirs in the late 40s (hence *maris potens*).

donec . . . misceretur: Gnaeus transferred his allegiance to Mark Antony in 40 and to Octavian just before Actium in 31. For the subjunc. after *donec* see 7.1n.

auus: L. Domitius Ahenobarbus (cos. 54 B.C.). The decisive battle of Pharsalus, where Caesar defeated Pompey, was 9 Aug. 48 B.C.

minor Antonia: in fact *maior*: she was the elder daughter of Octavia (Augustus' sister) and Mark Antony. See Stemma.

transcendit: the verb is not often used of crossing rivers (*OLD* 1b). The date was *c.* 2 B.C. (*RP* III 1100, 1102–3).

quam quisquam priorum: sc. *eam penetrauerat* from *penetrata Germania* above.

insignia triumphi: another of T.'s variations on *ornamenta triumphalia* (18.1n.).

44.3 obiit et L. Antonius: this is the only occasion on which T. provides three obituaries, and one of only three occasions where the recipient had not been consul (*TST* 80). Yet Antonius' life in exile offered a striking contrast with the active careers of Lentulus and Domitius, whose noble birth he equalled (*multa claritudine generis*): indeed Antonius' mother (Marcella *maior*) was half-sister to Domitius' wife Antonia *maior*, who was therefore his aunt (see Stemma); and his father (Iullus Antonius) was son of Mark Antony (Antonia's father) by the latter's third wife, Fulvia.

Iullo Antonio: the second son of Mark Antony (last n.), he was spared by Octavian and became consul in 10 B.C. After his adultery with Augustus' daughter Julia he committed suicide in 2 B.C. (Vell. 100.4). See *RP* II 912–36.

sororis nepotem: sc. *suae* (=*Augusti*): 'grandson of his ⟨own⟩ sister'. L. Antonius' mother, Marcella *maior* (above), was the daughter of Augustus' sister Octavia by her first marriage to C. Claudius Marcellus (cos. 50 B.C.). See Stemma.

ubi . . . tegeretur 'where the stigma of exile could be disguised by the appearance of scholarship' (Marseilles being a 'university town', cf. *Agr.* 4.2); the subjunc. expresses purpose. T.'s cynical suggestion of a formal exile is anticipated by *seposuit* (above), which he often uses = 'banish' (*OLD* 2b).

tumulo Octauiorum: though Syme (*AA* 118) assumes that this is Augustus' mausoleum, for which T. has a variety of expressions (3.4.1 'tumulus Augusti', 9.2 't. Caesarum', 16.6.2 't. Iuliorum'), *Octauiorum* seems rather to denote the tomb of Antonius' grandmother's family, the Octavii. The senate's role in the burial is unclear but perhaps illustrates Tib.'s general policy of involving them in matters which strictly could have been dealt with by himself alone. The *uariatio* of *per decretum* for the normal abl. seems Sallustian (*C.* 51.36), and thus anticipates the Sallustian colouring of the next section (see below).

45 Death in Spain

Hitherto the narrative of 25 has been devoted entirely to domestic matters, as if confirming T.'s remarks at 32–3 above (pp. 169–70). Yet the year ends with an account of an incident in Spain which is marked by colourful language and has an analogue in Sallust (cf. also above, pp. 155–6). The account is essentially transitional: it both continues the obituary theme of ch. 44 and anticipates the insurrection in Thrace to which T. will devote the first six chh. of the following year (Syme 310).

45.1 citeriore Hispania: i.e. Hispania Tarraconensis.

Termestinae: their main town was Termes, near Numantia.

praetorem prouinciae: 'Not a consular but a legate of praetorian rank, acting governor when L. Arruntius was detained at Rome' (*AA* 377). See also 15.2n. (*praetoris*).

L. Pisonem: Syme (*RP* III 1227, *AA* 377–8) infers from Sall. *C.* 19, a passage in which Cn. Piso (quaestor 65 B.C.) meets a similar death (see below) and to which T. eventually alludes at 3 below (n.), that L. Piso must be a descendant of his and hence son of the L. Piso mentioned at 21.1–2 above (n.).

pace incuriosum: it is typical of T. to see a drawback in the pacification of Spain which others welcomed (5.1n.). *incuriosus* (23.1n.) combines the notions of 'careless' and 'unsuspecting' (*OLD* b–c).

in itinere: so too his great-grandfather 'iter faciens occisus est' (Sall. *C.* 19.3).

uulnere ... adfecit is a common phrase (e.g. 2.5.3); here, uniquely, it is expanded by *in mortem* expressing the consequence of the action, as 62.3 'in mortem adflixerat', 15.2.2 'in exitium suum abrumpunt'; *OLD in* 20. The passage at 62.3 has been used to support the emendation *adflixit* here; but *adfligo* seems mostly used of dashing with or against stones or masonry (as *saxoque caput adflixit* at 2 below), which is clearly not the case here.

saltuosos locos echoes *saltuosa loca* at Sall. *J.* 38.1, 54.3. For the pluperf. after *postquam* see 10.3n.

45.2 neque: adversative (*OLD* 5).

clamitauit: 'The assassin duly exhibits Spanish defiance when put to torture' (Syme 729, comparing Liv. 21.2.6).

postero: sc. *die* (as 73.4).

saxoque caput adflixit ut statim exanimaretur: this type of suicide is a commonplace in classical literature (W. on Vell. 120.6). See also 15.57.2 (self-strangulation).

45.3 Termestinorum dolo: i.e. there was a collective responsibility for his death. A participle + *haberi* (= *existimari*) recurs only at 12.15.2 and Sall. *H.* 4.42.

e publico: sc. *Termestinorum*: 'embezzled from the public purse of the T.' (i.e. by their own people).

acrius quam ut tolerarent barbari: in the manner of the learned poets of the Augustan age T. defers till the very end the allusion which provides the clue to the passage on which his section has been based

(Sall. *C.* 19.4 'imperia eius iniusta, superba, crudelia barbaros nequiuisse pati').

cogebat is probably conative: 'attempted to collect'.

46–61 The year A.D. 26

T. divides his narrative of the year into foreign and domestic events (46–51, 52–61), one of his commonest arrangements (Ginsburg 54, 136–40) but without parallel in Book 4. If we except the final ch. of obituaries as a special case (61n. *Fine anni*), T. has placed at the start and end of his narrative the two most dramatic items of the year, on this occasion reserving his central sections for events of relatively less immediate importance (52–4) or minimal interest (55–6). The single most significant event of the year, Tib.'s departure from Rome, is held back till 57.1–59.3, thereby maintaining the suspense which T. initiated at 42.1 (above, p. 200); but artistic considerations are even more clearly evident in his placing of the Thracian campaign at the very start, since no detriment to that suspense would have been caused if he had placed it where he himself says it belongs, viz. the second half of the year (cf. 51.3 *hiemps*; Ginsburg 19, 138). One reason for this striking dislocation is therefore likely to be the tastes of his readers (below).

46–51 War in Thrace

From the official record of the award to Poppaeus Sabinus, the victorious general, T. will have known that there was a war in Thrace in this year; but it is difficult to believe that he knew as many details of the campaign as are presented here. In fact almost every detail, as many of the following notes are intended to make clear, can be paralleled in the accounts of other battles at other times given by Sallust (esp. that with the Isaurians in 76/75 B.C. at *H.* 2.87, cf. Syme 729), Caesar (esp. the battle of Alesia in 52 B.C. at *G.* 7.69–90), Livy and T. himself. Naturally these similarities do not prove that T.'s account is not historically true: there are likely to be recurring elements of time, terrain and climatic conditions in many military engagements and hence in their description. But the ancients' literary approach to historiography, and their practice of emulating and borrowing from earlier works (including their own), are fundamental considerations which indicate that battle narratives should rather be seen in terms of conventional realism. Indeed the absence of geographical reference from the present account (only *montis Haemi* at 51.3), together with the placing of the narrative after the official notice of Sabinus' victory (46.1n.), suggest that T. used the latter as a 'peg' on which to hang a set-piece *descriptio pugnae*. On this topic in general see above, pp. 2–4, N. Horsfall, *G. & R.* 32 (1985) 197–208 (also below, 47.1n.), *RICH* 22–8, 83–94, 176–9.

Such *descriptiones* were aimed primarily at the entertainment of readers, and T. has intensified his account by means of vivid language (e.g. 50.4 *nimbo*) and such rhetorical devices as anaphora (49.3 *quos . . . quos*, 51.1 *nunc . . . nunc*), asyndeton (cf. G. on 1.33.2) and historic infinitives (e.g. 49.3, 50.4–51.1), and chiasmus (e.g. 46.1 *pati . . . dare*, 48.1 *omittere . . . procumbere*). The only missing element is a speech in *oratio recta*, for which the indirect discourse of 50.1–3 must suffice. While the finished product, coming early in the second half of the Tiberian hexad, rivals the dramatic military narrative of Book 1, its appearance is surprising so soon after T. has lamented the *absence* of such exciting material at 32–3 above (pp. 169–70). Yet such paradoxes are quintessentially Tacitean, and the elaboration of upheavals on the imperial frontiers (46.1 *motus*) provides the background to the no less significant upheavals on the domestic front later on (52.1n.).

46.1 consulibus: Cn. Cornelius Lentulus Gaetulicus, brother of the consul of 25 (34.1n.) and son of the consul of 1 B.C., was legate of Upper Germany 29–39 and then killed for his part in a plot against Gaius. His daughter was betrothed to a son of Sejanus, his own friendship with whom he defended in a letter to Tib. (6.30.2–4). See *AA* 481 (index). His sister is thought to have been married to the other consul, C. Calvisius Sabinus, son of the consul of 4 B.C. and later legate of Pannonia (*AA* 298 n. 120).

Poppaeo Sabino: consul in 9 and 'the exemplary *nouus homo*' who governed Moesia for 24 years (*AA* 178); he was grandfather of Poppaea, Nero's mistress and wife.

contusis Thraecum gentibus: the context (*decreta . . . insignia*, cf. 18.1n.), the abl. abs. (often used for commemorative legends on coins), and even *contusis* (originally poetical but cf. e.g. *H.* 4.28.3 (and H.),

Liv. 40.52.6 'classis regis Antiochi . . . fusa, contusa fugataque est') combine to suggest the atmosphere of an official report.

montium editis: the same expression occurs at 12.56.2, Curt. 6.6.25; in general see 5.2n. (*cetera*).

inculti atque eo ferocius agitabant 'lived a barbarian and hence all the more savage life'. M reads *incultu*, but though the noun is Sallustian (*C.* 55.4, *J.* 2.4), its meaning there is different from that required here (see *OLD*). The adj. *incultus* is even more popular with Sall. (e.g. *C.* 2.8, *J.* 18.1 (of Africans)); and for an adj. + intrans. *agitare* = 'live' (*OLD* 12b; a favourite usage of Sall.) see *J.* 74.1 and in T. again at 1.50.1, 11.21.1. For *ferocius agitare* cf. *C.* 23.3; *ferocia* is often attributed to barbarians (e.g. *Agr.* 11.4, Vell. 106.2; Traub 252). For *eo* see 22.1n.; for the *uariatio* of adj. ~ adv. see Sörbom 96–7.

motus 'revolt' (*OLD* 9b).

super hominum ingenium 'in addition to the people's character': disparaging references to the *ingenium* of barbarians are conventional (e.g. *H.* 4.13.2).

dilectus 'conscription' (Brunt (1) 637).

aspernabantur: *aspernari* + infin. occurs only here in classical prose and is very rare in verse.

ex libidine: though found elsewhere, the phrase occurs five times in Sallust. For the typical unruliness of barbarians cf. e.g. *H.* 4.67.2 'cuncta ex libidine agere' (and H.), *G.* 7.1 'nec regibus infinita ac libera potestas', Caes. *G.* 4.1.9 'nihil omnino contra uoluntatem faciunt'.

ductores is more common in poetry than prose; *belligerare* is 'a mild archaism' (G. on 2.5.2): each contributes to the outlandishness of the barbarian leaders.

46.2 ac tum introduces another *causa motus* (*OLD tum* 9).

rumor incesserat: the expression is otherwise uncommon, but liked by T. (G. on 1.5.1).

disiecti 'dispersed'.

antequam . . . inciperent: for the subjunc. where no notion of purpose is involved see *NLS* §§225, 228 (b).

memoraturos: the fut. part. to express purpose, though found earlier, is common only from Livy onwards (*NLS* §92 (d)). The part. is here followed by both direct object(s) and acc. + inf. (sc. *esse* with *mansura*), a typically Tacitean *uariatio* (43.2n. *protulere*).

temptarentur: here = 'to be tried ⟨beyond endurance⟩' (cf. *OLD* 10c). (*noua*) *onera* is a conventional complaint (6.4, 1.76.2, 2.42.5 etc.).

ut uictis 'as if they were a conquered people'. The antithesis between freedom and slavery is conventional (24.1n.); similarly, troublesome barbarians are often 'youthful' (*iuuentutem*, e.g. Vell. 107.1–2, 114.4) and 'ready to die' (*promptum . . . ad mortem*, as 50.1 below): that some of them will eventually decide to surrender (50.1–2) is not yet envisaged. For the *uariatio* of dat. ~ *ad* + acc. see e.g. 14.38.3, 2.6.3, 37.4.

46.3 castella rupibus indita: the picture is again conventional (cf. Hor. *Ep.* 2.1.252–3 'arces | montibus impositas').

parentes et coniuges ostentabant: this inversion of the conventional *teichoskopia* (where women look down on their fighting menfolk) is itself used for a reversal at 51.2 below (n.). *ostento* = 'show for effect' (8.2n).

arduum: a bitter pun in view of *rupibus indita*, and realistic.

47.1 donec . . . conduceret: here the subjunc. is clearly purposive: 'until he could amalgamate his armies into one' (cf. 7.1n.). Sabinus' 'conciliatory replies' seem borrowed from Liv. 8.21.3 'mitius responsum'.

Pomponius Labeo: having governed Moesia for 8 years, he committed suicide in 34 (6.29.1, Dio 58.24.3). The legion was either IV Scythica or V Macedonica (5.3n.).

Rhoemetalces: King of Thrace since 19 (5.3n.).

qui fidem non mutauerant refers to 46.1–3 above, but barbarians were conventionally treacherous (W. on Vell. 118.1).

addita praesenti copia 'with the addition of his existing force' (i.e. to those of Labeo and the king); for *praesens* see *OLD* 8; for sing. *copia*, 4.3n.

compositum 'deployed' (*OLD* 6).

per angustias saltuum: a typical enemy trick (e.g. 1.63.1); see also N. Horsfall, *P.B.S.R.* 50 (1982) 45–52.

uisebantur 'showed themselves' (*OLD* 2b).

suggressus is liked by T., perhaps because of its use at Sall. *H.* 4.83 (G. on 2.12.1).

47.2 in loco communitis 'fortified on the spot / where he was' (as 1.63.5, 13.41.1; *OLD locus* 4b).

montem . . . angustum et aequali dorso continuum . . .

castellum: lit. 'a mountain which was narrow and stretched in a level ridge up to the nearest fort' (i.e. a narrow plateau): realistic but conventional detail (e.g. Caes. *G.* 7.44.3 'dorsum . . . eius iugi prope aequum, sed hunc locum . . . angustum', Liv. 44.4.4 'iugum montis in angustum dorsum cuneatum').

magna uis armata aut incondita 'a large force, partly armed and partly scratch'.

more gentis refers not to *ante uallum* but to *carminibus . . . persultabant*, all three elements of which are conventional of foreign tribes (e.g. of the Germans at *H.* 5.15.1 *persultabant*, 2 *cantu*, 17.3 *tripudiisque*). See also 49.3n. (*iuxta*).

47.3 dum eminus grassabantur 'for as long as they were moving forward at a distance'.

eruptione subita turbati: a conventional development: *H.* 3.26.3 4.30.1, Liv. 37.5.6, 38.29.2. *recepti*, below, = 'rescued'.

nec minus . . . trucem: sc. 'than the Thracians themselves'. The Sugambri, defeated by the Romans in 12 B.C., were notoriously fierce (Hor. *Odes* 4.2.34 'feroces', 4.14.51 'caede gaudentes'; G. on 2.26.3).

48.1 hostem propter: for the anastrophe of the preposition see 5.1n.

priora munimenta . . . memoraui: cf. 47.2 and 1 respectively.

dum populatio lucem intra sisteretur 'provided that their plundering was kept within daylight hours' (6.4n. *intra*, and see again 5.1n. for the anastrophe); for the verb see *OLD* 6d.

uigilem: when used of things, the adj. is usually restricted to poetry (*OLD* 1b).

uersi in luxum . . . procumbere: the various clements in this description are all conventional, e.g. 1.50.4, *Agr.* 5.1, Liv. 4.34.4, Virg. *Aen.* 9.236.

48.2 populatores is more common in elevated poetry than in prose (except Livy).

adpugnarent: the verb is peculiar to T. and probably coined by him (G. 2.81.1).

sed ut . . . non acciperet 'so that in the din of battle, with each man concentrating on the danger to himself, he would not catch the sound of the other engagement': *clamore*, *telis* are causal abl., *suo . . . periculo* dat. after *intentus*. In final clauses *ut . . . non* is used for *ne* when *non* negatives a particular word (here *acciperet*): see *NLS* §139 *Note*. For the *uariatio* with *spe* see 8.2n.

tenebrae . . . delectae . . . formidinem: another typically barbarian ploy, e.g. *G.* 43.4 'atras ad proelia noctes legunt ipsaque formidine atque umbra feralis exercitus terrorem inferunt'. The placing of *ad* between gerundive and noun 'is only an occasional quirk: in T., as elsewhere, it usually precedes' (G. on 1.64.5).

48.3 cum pars munitionibus adiacerent: more conventional detail (e.g. 1.65.1 'cum . . . adiacerent uallo').

plures extra palarentur: compare e.g. Sall. *J.* 44.5 'uti quoique lubebat, ab signis aberat . . . et palantes agros uastare' (this passage echoed at 49.3 below); but similar situations are commonly described in Livy too.

perfugae et proditores: the alliteration conveys the hatred of the accusers (cf. Cic. *Rosc. Am.* 117 'initio proditor . . . deinde perfuga'). For the absence of a comparative after *quanto* (to balance *infensius*) see 23.2n. (*ut quis*).

ferre . . . incusabantur: an infin. after passive *incusari* (also at 6.3.3) seems exclusive to T. *ad . . . seruitium* = 'for the enslavement of themselves and their country' (*OLD ad* 46).

49.1 si 'to see if', a usage often found in battle narrative (e.g. 15.13.1 'si . . . hostem in proelium eliceret').

barbari successu noctis alacres: cf. 1.64.3 'Germani ob prospera indefessi', *H.* 3.77.4 'secundis ferox', 5.15.2, Sall. *H.* 4.76 'ut in secunda re . . . acres', *J.* 94.4, Front. *Strat.* 2.5.36 'alacres successibus uictoriarum'.

praesidia 'redoubts'.

fossam . . . amplexus est 'he built a connecting trench-and-parapet system, covering four miles in circumference'.

49.2 contrahere claustra artaque circumdare 'he drew in the cordon so as to surround [lit. and surrounded] a narrow area': *claustra* refers to the trench-and-parapet system mentioned above (as 12.31.4; *OLD* 5b). The process described is that whereby a circumvallation of 4 miles in length (above) was gradually reduced to a point from which they could build an *agger* overlooking the enemy (below).

struebatur agger: another standard development (e.g. *H.* 3.20.3), though the compound *exstruere* is more common (38.2n.); for *saxa, hastae, ignes* cf. e.g. 2.81.2 'hastas, saxa et faces ingerere'.

49.3 nihil aeque quam sitis fatigabat: from *H.* 5.3.2 'sed nihil aeque quam inopia aquae fatigabat' (and H. for many variations), cf. *H.* 2.39.2 'penuria aquae fatigarentur'.

imbellium: i.e. women and children.

iuxta: i.e. alongside the men, women and children. Such phrases as *ut mos barbaris* are a feature of ethnographical contexts, e.g. 47.2, *Agr.* 33.1 'ut barbaris moris', Vell. 107.1 'ut illis mos est'.

egestate pabuli: from Sall. *J.* 44.4 (see above, 48.3n.), where *odor* also occurs (see below).

sanie: the discharge from wounds or corpses (*OLD*).

50.1 his deditionem . . . eruptionem suaderent: the three possibilities of *deditio*, suicide and *eruptio* (the first two of which are governed by *parantibus*, the last by a verb of saying, *suaderent*) are each associated in turn with a leading representative in 2–4 below (the first two of whom speak, while the last simply acts). The general picture is again conventional (e.g. Caes. *G.* 7.77.2 'ac uariis dictis sententiis, quarum pars deditionem, pars . . . eruptionem censebat'); for barbarian suicides see 3n. below.

50.2 neque ignobiles, quamuis diuersi sententiis, uerum e ducibus Dinis . . . ponenda arma . . . disserebat: if the text is right, which is not certain, a verb (e.g. *disserebant*) has to be supplied with *neque ignobiles*: 'and it was not the *ignobiles*, although they had different views, but one of the leaders, Dinis, who spoke openly for laying down arms . . . and was the first to give himself up to the victors'. There is a comparable ellipse of a verb at 8.2 (n. *Tiberius*). Disagreement amongst barbarians is another conventional motif (e.g. 1.68.1 'diuersis ducum sententiis', *H.* 4.76.1 'apud Germanos diuersis sententiis certabatur', Caes. *G.* 7.77.2 quoted above).

prouectus senecta et . . . uim . . . Romanam edoctus: advisory elders are a conventional feature of battle narratives from Homer onwards; here T. recalls both Sall. *H.* 2.87 'illi quibus aetas imbellior et uetustate uis Romanorum multum cognita erat' and Liv. 6.32.7 'longa societate militiam Romanam edoctae'. For the internal accus. after the passive of verbs of teaching see *NLS* §§14, 16 (iii).

aetate aut sexu imbecilli: repeated from 1.56.3 'quod imbecillum aetate ac sexu'. For the anastrophe of *inter* see 5.1n.

50.3 properum finem, abrumpendas . . . clamitans: it is not clear whether *properum finem* is *or. obl.* (sc. e.g. *petendum esse*, balancing *abrumpendas*) or direct speech (sc. e.g. *petamus*); a third possibility is to supply e.g. *suadens*, understood from *clamitans* (by zeugma) and balancing it.

nec defuere qui . . . oppeterent: collective suicide by barbarians is a conventional motif, e.g. 3.46.4 (*mutuis ictibus*: see 1 above), Sall. *J.* 76.6, Liv. 21.14.1, 28.22.5–23.2. The intrans. use of *oppetere* appears to be almost exclusively poetical before T. (G. on 2.24.2).

50.4 **firmatae stationes:** another conventional development (Liv. 4.27.7, 5.43.2 etc.).

nimbo atrox: *atrox* is commonly used of storms (*OLD* 1b), but to heighten the drama T. here uniquely prefers the more poetical *nimbus* to *imber*, which he uses 18 times. A *locus classicus* for fighting in rain is Thuc. 2.4.2.

uastum silentium: a Livian phrase (10.34.6) used also at *H.* 3.12.2, *Agr.* 38.2; but since *uastus* is also used regularly of an extent of territory, we are meant also to imagine the eerie silence stretching across (*per*) no man's land, broken only by the incessant rain. For the omission of *modo* with *clamore turbido* see *OLD* 6b.

cum . . . circumire, hortari: Sall. and Livy had earlier used the historic infin. in the inverted *cum*-construction, but T. uses it more regularly for vividness (G. on 2.31.1). See also 51.1n. For *circumire* see 2.2n. (*adeundo*).

ad 'at' or 'in response to' (*OLD* 33a). For *ambigua sonitus* see 5.2n. (*cetera*).

casum 'opportunity', probably a Sallustian meaning (*J.* 25.9, 56.4; *OLD* 7). The substantival use of the part. of *insidiari*, first in Sall. *J.* 113.5 and Caes. *G.* 8.19.3, becomes standard from Livy onwards.

sed . . . seruarent: sc. *ut*. For the *uariatio* of part. ~ abl. abs. see 41.2n. (*secretoque*).

51.1 **manualia saxa, praeustas sudes, decisa robora iacere:** so too Sall. *H.* 2.87 'saxa, pila, sudes iacere'; *manualis* had been used by the archaising republican historian Sisenna (fr. 23 'm. lapides'), and *praeustae sudes* ('fire-hardened stakes') by Caes. *G.* 5.40.6 (see also below) and Virg. *Aen.* 7.524. *decisa robora* are 'hewn boughs'. *iacere* is the first of nine successive historic infinitives, the second highest number in T. (*Agr.* 38.1 has 10) and reminiscent of the battle narratives of *H.* The anaphora of *nunc*, only here in T. and originally poetical, was introduced into prose by Livy.

complere fossas is a common phrase in Caesar and Livy: for the various fillers see e.g. *G.* 3.18.8 (*uirgultis*), 7.79.4 (*cratibus*), Liv. 26.6.2 (*corporibus*).

eaque: the *propugnacula*. *prensare* is 'a mild poeticism [which] gained no general acceptance in early imperial prose' (G. on 1.68.2).

miles: sc. *Romanus*. *deturbare* and *comminus* (above) are both common in military narrative but note esp. the latter at Caes. *G*. 7.86.5 and both at Sall. *H*. 2.87.

muralia pila are also used at Caes. *G*. 5.40.6 (see above) and 7.82.1. Here we must understand a verb such as *uibrare* from *prouoluere* (by zeugma).

51.2 his: i.e. the Romans.

The general meaning of *his . . . flagitium* is clear, but the details have evoked almost as many interpretations as there are interpreters. There is a clear contrast between victory (*uictoriae*) and defeat (*si cedant*); and since *flagitium* is the consequence of defeat, it is quite likely (though not inevitable) that *spes* is therefore the consequence of victory. In other words *partae uictoriae* is not an objective genit. = 'hope of victory gained', which is good English in the sense 'hope of victory soon to be gained' but is not readily paralleled in Latin; rather it is subjective or possessive genit. = 'hope from victory gained' (lit. 'a gained victory's hope'), i.e. the hope of *praeda* or *spolia* in the aftermath of victory. If so, the motif is the same as 14.36.2 'parta uictoria cuncta ipsis cessura' and esp. *H*. 1.57.2 'parta uictoria magnae spes'.

The verb with both *spes* and *flagitium* is likely to be *addunt animos* below, and on this interpretation the Latin means: 'The one side was encouraged by the hope(s) consequent upon victory gained and by the still more notable disgrace of defeat, the other side by . . .' But we recognise that other interpretations are possible. For the vivid pres. subjunc. *cadant* see 2.1n.

extrema iam salus et adsistentes . . . coniuges: the first element is compressed for the more normal *extrema spes salutis* (cf. 3.3n. *ad coniugii*); in the second the participle is substantival (see 12.1n. *quod.*). The presence of women at battles is a commonplace of barbarians (e.g. 14.34.2, *H*. 4.18.2–3, *Agr*. 32.2, *G*. 7.2, 8.1), but T. intends us to be aware of the dramatic reversal between their confident display at 46.3 and their *lamenta* here.

nox . . . opportuna is again Livian (7.35.10).

aliis . . . aliis: apparently Thracians and Romans respectively, to judge from the rest of the sentence.

suorum atque hostium ignoratio 'the inability [sc. of the

Romans] to recognise either themselves or the enemy': a *locus classicus* for this motif is Thuc. 7.44.2ff.

montis anfractu repercussae 'echoing back from the mountain amphitheatre [lit. curvature]'.

51.3 deiecto: see 25.3n.

adpetente . . . luce: perhaps from Caes. *G.* 7.82.2, but cf. also Liv. 10.20.9 etc.

coacta deditio: again from Sall. *H.* 2.87.

proxima . . . recepta 'neighbouring ⟨areas⟩ were received [sc. in surrender] on the initiative of their inhabitants', as 13.39.5 'alia sponte incolarum in deditionem ueniebant'.

52–4 Agrippina and Tiberius

This section, a companion piece to 39–41 above (see p. 15), comprises three brief encounters between Tib. and Agrippina, two of which are also juxtaposed by Suetonius (*Tib.* 53.1), the other derived uniquely by T. from the memoirs of Agrippina's daughter (53.2). Each incident is trivial in itself and anecdotal in nature; but all three illustrate and typify the events which Sejanus has been setting in train since 23 (12.2–4, cf. 17.2–3). In addition, Agrippina's pathetic request for a husband (53.1) contrasts with Sejanus' confident request for a wife the previous year (39), although each is characteristically rejected by Tib. (cf. 53.2n.). Similarly Sejanus' false suggestion that Tib. intended to poison his daughter-in-law (54.1) is the counterpart of the false rumour at 10.2–3 that he manœuvred Tib. into poisoning his son (above, pp. 123–4).

52.1 At Romae commota principis domo: *At Romae* is common in T. to express a transition from foreign to domestic affairs, but here *commota* perhaps indicates a similarity between the two spheres of activity: both were earthquake-like upheavals (cf. 46.1 *motus*). For another such link see 27.1n.

To which domestic events does *commota . . . domo* refer? Most scholars mention 12.2–4, some including also the death of Drusus at 8.1ff.; but it is more natural to think of 39–41, the scene which instigated Tib.'s decision to leave Rome (cf. 42.1) and to which the present section is the companion piece (above).

ut . . . inciperet 'in order that the process of future destruction intended for Agrippina should begin': the genit. might have been expected after *exitii* (as *H.* 2.60.2), but *in* + accus. is used either to denote an intended victim (10.2n.) or under the influence of its occasional use with *esse* (as 6.22.1). The case at 60.3 is easier because of *meditaretur*.

The clause is to be taken with the main sentence *Claudia . . . postulatur*, although *inciperet* seems odd of a chain of events which has already begun at 12.2–4; T. must envisage a qualitative difference between the preliminary moves there and the more ominous developments here (*exitii*).

Claudia Pulchra: daughter of Augustus' niece Marcella *minor* and M. Valerius Messalla Appianus (cos. 12 B.C.), and hence second cousin (*sobrina*) of Agrippina, the granddaughter of Augustus. She was the widow of the unfortunate general Quintilius Varus. See Stemma; *AA* 147–9, 327 and Tables III, VI, VII. See Bauman (1) 234–5 for the case.

Domitio Afro: Cn. Domitius Afer, praetor in the previous year (Syme 589), prosecuted Claudia Pulchra's son in the following year (66.1), became an outstanding orator (see 4 below) and suffect consul in 39. He died in 59 (14.19).

recens praetura: abl. of separation; elsewhere 'T.'s use of *recens* with the abl. is highly idiosyncratic and also rather various' (G. on 1.41.3).

modicus dignationis 'moderate in reputation' (*OLD modicus* 6; G. on 2.73.2).

properus clarescere: an infin. after *properus* seems unparalleled.

deuotiones 'curses' (*OLD* 2). Furnius is otherwise unknown.

52.2 atrox: at 12.22.1 the younger Agrippina is 'atrox *odii*'; perhaps hatred is here being implied as a characteristic of her mother too.

quo initio inuidiae 'with this to provoke [lit. as provocation of] her indignation'; for the meaning of *inuidia* see e.g. 53.1, 3.67.4; *OLD* 1a.

non eiusdem: sc. *esse*: 'the same man had no business to . . .' (lit. 'it was not ⟨the business⟩ of the same man to . . .'); *NLS* §72 (1) (iii).

non in effigies mutas diuinum spiritum transfusum: though *diuinus* is regularly used of emperors (2.87 and G.) or of those with divine connections (e.g. Liv. 5.43.8), Ag. here underlines her relationship with the deified Augustus (3.4.2 'solum Augusti sanguinem') by resorting to the language of popular Pythagoreanism (*transfusum*), which believed in the transmigration of souls (see esp. *Aen.* 6.713ff.).

imaginem ueram: for family likenesses see 15.3n. *esse* is probably to be understood both here and with *ortam* below (for the omission of *se* with the subsequent infinitives see 18.3n. *imparemque*); alternatively, put a comma after *ortam*: 'she, who was the true likeness, sprung from divine stock, appreciated . . .'

intellegere . . . sordes 'she appreciated the danger [sc. to herself] and was adopting dark clothes [sc. like a suppliant]': for *suscipere* (probably with a future sense, cf. 2.1n.) see *OLD* 6a; for *sordes*, *OLD* 2a.

frustra Pulchram praescribi 'it was to no purpose that Pulchra's name was the heading [sc. on the charge sheet]': *OLD praescribo* 1a.

causa sit: for the tense of *sit* see 2.1n.

quod Agrippinam . . . ad cultum delegerit 'that she had chosen to devote herself to Ag.' (lit. 'chosen Ag. for devotion'). The proper name not only avoids the ambiguity of *se* but capitalises on the various effects (pathos, arrogance) of self-reference (for which see G. Williams, *Tradition and originality in Roman poetry* (1968) 462–3). For *cultus* see *OLD* 10a; for the tense of *delegerit* see 2.1n.

Sosiae: cf. 19.1 'Sosia . . . caritate Agrippinae inuisa principi'.

52.3 raram . . . uocem elicuere 'extracted a rare response': the possessive genit. *occulti pectoris* (rather than *a* + abl., as Lucr. 3.57–8) underlines Tib.'s characteristic secretiveness (1.2n.). For Tib.'s speech in general see 31.2n.; for *elicio* see 45.2; *OLD* 3.

correptamque has been interpreted variously by scholars: (1) 'having been rebuked' (*OLD* 6), but this seems tautologous with *admonuit*; (2) 'having been grasped', but though the action squares with Suetonius' account of the incident (*Tib.* 53.1 'Agrippinam . . . manu apprehendit'), *corripio* is normally used only of more violent grasping or seizing (*OLD* 1). It is therefore possible that we should read *arreptamque*, i.e. 'taken by the hand' (cf. *OLD* 1).

Tib. liked Greek *sententiae* (3.65.3; Suet. *Tib.* 70–1); the origin of this one is unknown.

damnantur: the sentence is unknown.

52.4 diuulgato ingenio 'now that his talent was common knowledge'.

nisi quod . . . dum . . . retinet silentii impatientiam 'except that his last years greatly impaired his eloquence too, in as much as he retained a horror of silence despite his mental exhaustion'. For quasi-causal *dum* see G. on 1.23.5; for *retinere* see 7.1n.

53.1 peruicax . . . implicata: the former is not used + genit. before T.; *implico*, commonly used of disease (*OLD* 8a), occurs nowhere else in T. For Ag.'s character see 12.3n.

uiseret is often used of visiting the sick (*OLD* 3b); such visits were a habit of Tib. (Dio 57.11.7, Vell. 114.1 and W.), as of Augustus (Millar 112): for the ethical background see J. C. Yardley, *Phoenix* 27 (1973) 285–6.

habilem . . . iuuentam: the truth of each element is somewhat belied by *peruicax irae et morbo corporis implicata* above, illustrating the pathetic desperation of Ag.'s request.

esse in ciuitate *:** at this point there is gap of a third of a line in M. While the simple insertion of ⟨*qui*⟩ after *ciuitate* would restore complete sense, the length of the gap suggests that more than a single word may be missing.

53.2 non ignarus quantum ex re publica peteretur: while Tib.'s own solitariness and marital history can hardly have made him naturally sympathetic to Agrippina's pleas, the expression of his reaction here is difficult. (1) RHM and others understand *ab Agrippina* with *peteretur*: 'knowing how much was being demanded of the state [sc. by Ag.]', i.e. although she had put her request in personal terms (*daret maritum* etc.), Tib. realised that it had political implications and reacted accordingly. This theme has already surfaced in his reply to Sejanus' similar request above (40.2ff.). (2) AJW prefers to take *peteretur* non-personally (*OLD* 13): 'knowing how much was called for on the part of/in the interests of the state', i.e. Tib. expected others to subordinate their personal inclinations to the national interest in the same way as he himself had done since becoming emperor reluctantly. This theme too is typical of Tib. (e.g. 13.1) and is found in his reply to Sejanus; here it is given ironical point by the emperor's imminent withdrawal from his own responsibilities later this same year (57.1). For *ex* = 'on the part of' see 6.4 'nulla . . . culpa ex principe'; for *ex re publica* = 'in the interests of the state' see Gell. 6.3.47, 11.9.1 (*e re p.* is more normal).

ne tamen . . . foret: *tamen* contrasts with the refusal of Agrippina's prayers which is implicit in *non ignarus . . . peteretur* on either interpretation above. Most scholars take *offensionis* passively ('to avoid appearing resentful', cf. *OLD* 6b), on the analogy of e.g. 3.64.2 'dissimulata offensione' (cf. 2.42.3, 4.29.3); but since Tib. did not in fact give expression to his refusal (*sine responso . . . reliquit*), AJW prefers to take it actively (*OLD* 6a) and to see Tib. as observing the proprieties of his visit despite his bluntness on other occasions (52.3). This would also allow *manifestus* to have what appears to be its primary meaning (*OLD* 1): hence 'lest he should be caught out in giving offence or being afraid'. Either way, both fear (here of the revival of Germanicus' house if Ag. should remarry) and the desire to conceal it are typical of Tib.: see respectively 70.2n., 1.2n.

manifestus + genit. is Sallustian (G. on 2.85.3).

quamquam instantem 'despite her insistence' (15.2n.).

commentariis Agrippinae: the eldest daughter of Germanicus and Ag. was born in 15 and murdered by her son Nero in 59 (14.3.3–8.5). T.'s reference to her memoirs, for which he and the elder Pliny are our only evidence, well illustrates the spirit of rivalry in which ancient historians cite their predecessors or sources (*a scriptoribus . . . non traditum*): see above, p. 27. T. was presumably attracted to the work by its antagonism towards the various emperors whom Agrippina had known. For *annalium* see 32.1n.

casus suorum: the deaths, between 31 and 33, of her mother and brothers (Nero and Drusus), for all of which Tib. was in some degree responsible.

54.1 Ceterum continues the main story (*maerentem . . .*) after the brief parenthesis on Agrippina's *commentarii*: see 3.1n.

immissis: see 19.1n.

amicitiae: see 18.1n.

simulationum nescia 'unable to put on an act'; or just possibly 'unaware of ⟨Sejanus'⟩ deceptions' (for which see 1.2–3nn.).

propter: adverbial ('nearby').

non uultu aut sermone flecti: it is not clear whether the nouns are abl. of respect ('did not change in expression or conversation') or instrumental ('was not distracted by anyone's glance or conversation').

aduertit 'noticed' (*OLD* 6a), a much commoner meaning of the simple form than that at 35.1 (n.).

audiuerat 'had been told' (*OLD* 8b); the *uariatio* of causal abl. ~ causal clause (24.2n.) is here effected by *an* (8.2n.), as e.g. 13.12.2.

idque: i.e. the fact that she *nullos attingere cibos*.

ut erant adposita 'exactly as they had been served'.

nurui: the noun, like *soceri* above, emphasises how unnatural are the results of Sejanus' intrigues.

54.2 coram is adverbial (as 42.1): here = 'in her presence'/'directly [sc. to her]'.

matrem: Livia Augusta, whose hatred of Ag. (12.3) made her an obvious confidante.

non mirum: sc. *fore*; *statuisset* = fut. perf. in *or. recta.*

a qua . . . insimularetur 'by whom he was being accused of poisoning'. Sejanus' deception is paying off.

secretum . . . quaeri 'privacy was being sought for its perpetration'. *secretum* = 'conditions in which no witnesses are present' (*OLD* 3a); this is the only occurrence of the 'recherché compound' *perpetrare* in *A.* 1–6, though it is more common in 11–16 (Adams (1) 364).

55–6 Senatorial business

This section is the sequel to the senate's decision of three years earlier to allow a *templum Tiberio matrique eius* in Asia (15.3).

55.1 quo: see 30.1n.

famam is the rumour just mentioned.

statueretur = pres. jussive subjunc. in *or. recta.*

neque . . . memorabant 'their arguments scarcely differed one from another', a comment borne out by T.'s presentation, esp. of the cases of Sardis and Smyrna (note e.g. *simul* at both 3 below and 56.2).

studio: sc. *de* from above.

bella Persi et Aristonici: respectively 171–168 and 131–129 B.C. *Persi* is the archaic genit. of *Perseus* (king of Macedonia); for Aristonicus see *OCD* 1.

aliorumque regum: including Mithridates VI (14.2).

55.2 simul: preposition (*OLD* 12c) in anastrophe (5.1n.): 'along with'. Hypaepa is in Lydia, Tralles in Caria, Laodicea in Phrygia, Magnesia on the borders of Caria and Lydia (though there is a homonym in Lydia itself).

tramissi: see 21.2n.

parum ualidi refers more strictly to their arguments (as 40.6) than to the people themselves (a form of hypallage: see *OLD* 7b, cf. a.).

referrent 'although they referred to Troy as the parent of...' (*OLD* 18).

paulum addubitatum quod 'they paused for a time over the fact that...': Asia was notorious for its earthquakes (13.1).

uiuoque in saxo: sc. *fore*. The phrase originated with Virg. *Aen.* 1.167 and became popular with Ovid, but this is perhaps the only ex. in prose (J. C. Plumpe, *Traditio* 1 (1943) 6). See *OLD uiuus* 4a.

eo ipso nitebantur 'they were relying on this very fact', viz. *aede Augusto ibi sita*.

caerimonia ... uisi 'seemed to have occupied their own cities fully with the worship of...': Lourdes is an obvious modern ex. of what is meant.

55.3 inter: for the anastrophe see again 5.1n.

resedisse 'had remained as a settler' (*OLD* 2a).

uocabula illis ... his: respectively Lydia and Etruria (for which *Tyrrhenia* is an alternative, e.g. Ov. *Met.* 14.452).

55.4 bello Macedonum: that with Perseus (1n.); for the *uariatio* of genit. noun instead of the more normal *Macedonico* see 36.2n.

ubertatemque ... terras: it is tempting to understand *ubertatem* as alluding to the Pactolus, the principal river of Sardis and proverbially rich with gold; but since this would anticipate the point of *dites ... terras*, an allusion to the mineral resources which enabled Sardis to invent coinage, perhaps *ubertatem* rather suggests inexhaustible flow (so *OLD* 2). The latter, along with a friendly climate and mineral wealth, comprise standard elements in the praise of cities (Menand. rhet. 3.344ff.): see Thomas 3, 11–12 (on *temperies*), 15–16, 44–5. *circum* is an adv. used adjectively, as 2.24.1 (see G.).

56.1 repetita 'having traced back' (sc. to its origins): *OLD* 7a.

seu ... condidisset: virtual *or. obl.* after *repetita uetustate*. *illos* are the *Zmyrnaei*; had T. written *se*, readers might initially have thought that the pronoun referred to *Tantalus*.

una Amazonum: the eponymous Smyrna.

transcendere 'proceeded' (*OLD* 5a).

officiis: in apposition to *quis* (14.1n.).

copia: see 4.3n.

externa ... in Italia: respectively against Antiochus in 191–188 and the Social War of 91–88 B.C. Before *quae* we must understand *ad ea*.

M. Porcio consule: Cato 'the Censor' was consul in 195 B.C.

quidem . . . tamen combines flattery with self-praise, neatly and chiastically (*magnis . . . iam* ~ *nondum . . . ad summum elatis*).

stante . . . Punica urbe: the verb is often used of cities (*OLD* 15), but T. is recalling Sall. *H.* 1.11 'stante Carthagine', typically substituting an adj. for the more normal noun in apposition.

56.2 adferebant 'they adduced L. Sulla as evidence that . . .' (*OLD* 13a).

ob . . . uestis explains *grauissimo in discrimine* (the First Mithridatic War in 85 B.C.: see *MRR* II 58).

adstabant: for the mood see 10.2n. (*quod*).

56.3 rogati sententiam: for the internal accus. in this technical expression see *NLS* §16 (ii).

Vibius Marsus: suffect consul in 17, proconsul of Africa 27–30, accused of *maiestas* in 37 (6.47.2), legate of Syria *c.* 42: a 'remarkable survivor' (*RP* III 1554 (index)).

M. Lepido: for him and his characteristic *modestia* (below) see 20.2n.

ea prouincia = Asia.

qui templi curam susciperet: purposive; the antecedent is unexpressed. For the temple itself see Price 185, 258 (no. 45).

Valerius Naso: a gentleman from Verona (*RP* II 716).

57–60 Tiberius' departure from Rome exploited by Sejanus

Tib.'s departure from Rome, the most important event of the year and one of the most decisive of his whole reign, is emphasised by both the excursus on its motivation (57.1–3) and the foreshadowing occasioned by astrological predictions (58.2–3). Yet the highlight of the section, significantly, is the exploitation of this event by Sejanus (59.3–60.3), who is brilliantly presented as a master puppeteer, manipulating henchman and victim alike (59.3–60.2). Indeed Tib.'s departure seems almost forgotten (60.2n. *Enimuero*), until T. returns to it towards the end of the narrative of the following year (67.1n.).

57.1 Inter quae suggests, if taken literally, that Tib. left Rome while the senatorial debate of 55–6 was still in progress and thus underlines his alleged motive for attending the debate in the first place (55.1 'quo famam auerteret').

diu meditato prolatoque saepius consilio is confirmed by 3.31.2 under A.D. 21 ('Tiberius . . . in Campaniam concessit, longam et continuam absentiam paulatim meditans') but hardly squares with the reference (below) to Sejanus, whose alleged influence in the matter was mentioned only in the preceding year (41). For Tib.'s procrastination see 11.1n.

in Campaniam ⟨concessit⟩, specie dedicandi templa: the omission of a verb of motion seems out of place in elevated historical narrative, and it would be strange if T. avoided explicit mention of one of the cardinal events of the reign. We cannot know what verb has dropped out, but *concessit* is more likely than most (see last n.).

Tib.'s departure is resumed at 58.1 below, effectively isolating the intervening sentences as an extended parenthesis; but this does not mean that they are a later insertion or represent T.'s second thoughts (so Syme 695–6): see further below. The dedicating of temples is resumed at 67.1 (n).

apud Nolam Augusto: the emperor had died there on 19 August A.D. 14 (1.5.3, 9.1).

certus procul urbe degere: as Sejanus had planned (41.1). *certus* + inf. occurs only in poetry before T. (*OLD* 10a); for intrans. *degere* see *OLD* 2a; for *procul* (prep.) see 2.1n.

quamquam secutus . . . rettuli: although this clause implies that hitherto T.'s *primary* explanation was the influence of Sejanus, any such inference is precluded by *diu . . . consilio* above (n.). In fact the clause is an elaborate rhetorical foil, analogous to that which begins the excursus on Drusus' death (10.1 'quae plurimis . . . auctoribus memorata sunt rettuli; sed . . .': see n.) and similarly designed to give greater emphasis to the alternative explanation of events which follows. There, however, the primary and alternative explanations are mutually exclusive, which is not the case here (see below). For other occasions where T.'s stated and real explanations differ see 4.3n. (*angustius*) and pp. 96 and 123 above.

sex . . . annos . . . coniunxit: A.D. 31–7. For the verb see *OLD* 6.

plerumque permoueor num . . . uerius sit 'I have often been moved ⟨to consider⟩ whether it might be more probable for it to be ascribed to the man himself': the use of *permoueo* is unparalleled (cf. *OLD* 2 rather than 3b), but *num* makes the meaning clear; somewhat analogous are Cic. *Diu.* 1.35 'nec adducar totam Etruriam delirare' and Ov. *F.* 5.73–4 'sua maiores tribuisse uocabula Maio | tangor'. The passage has been explained convincingly by T. J. Luce (*PP* 154–5) in terms of the familiar rhetorical device of 'self-correction' or *reprehensio*, more common in T. than usually allowed (above, p. 31). Luce rightly notes that this second explanation does not exclude the earlier one but rather complements it: there is thus a contrast with the excursus at 10–11, where the alternative explanation was discounted as *not* being *uerum* (cf. 11.3).

saeuitiam ac libidinem: cf. Tib.'s obituary at 6.51.3 'intestabilis saeuitia sed obtectis libidinibus' (of the years 29–31); cf. also 6.1.1 'scelerum et libidinum' (A.D. 32), and above, 1.1n. (*cum repente*).

57.2 erant qui crederent . . . pudori fuisse: scholars have been puzzled by the relationship of this sentence both to its immediate predecessor and to *et Rhodi . . . insuerat* below. Two interpretations will be offered here, although it is common to both of them that *quoque* signals a close relationship between the present sentence and the preceding one: those people denoted by *erant qui crederent* accepted the view that Tib. withdrew from Rome to hide his vices, but believed that he felt his *physical appearance too* to be a source of shame. The grounds both for that belief and for the emperor's shame are given in *quippe . . . interstincta.*

At this point our interpretations diverge. (1) RHM believes that *et Rhodi . . . insuerat* ('and indeed in the privacy of Rhodes he had become accustomed to . . .') is a comment on T.'s own view that *ad ipsum referri uerius sit . . . locis occultantem.* The intervening sentences *erant qui crederent . . . interstincta* are to be regarded as parenthetical, indicating a sub-division of those who basically accepted T.'s own view but gave the additional reason of Tib.'s shame at his appearance. This interpretation, already advanced by M. R. Comber (*Rh.M.* 119 (1976) 181–4), assumes the same logical relationship achieved by the drastic remedy of transposing *et Rhodi . . . insuerat* to follow *locis occultantem* (J. P. V. D. Balsdon, *C.R.* 61 (1947) 44–5, and earlier by H. Cron in 1874).

(2) AJW believes that, just as *corporis quoque habitum pudori fuisse* looks back to *saeuitiam ac libidinem . . . locis occultantem* in the previous sentence, so *in senectute* looks forward to *Rhodi secreto* (referring to Tib.'s younger days) below, the intervening sentence *quippe . . . interstincta* being parenthetical. The sentence preceding this parenthesis is concessive, as if *quidem* (μέν) followed *erant*, and acts as a foil for *et*

Rhodi . . . insuerat, where T. rejects as irrelevant the notion of physical shame in order to reaffirm his own earlier explanation by means of a parallel from Tib.'s life on Rhodes. Hence: 'It is true there were those who believed that in his old age his physical appearance too had been a source of shame (for . . .); and yet in the privacy of Rhodes he had been accustomed to avoid crowds and conceal his pleasures.' This use of *et* = *et tamen* is common in T., e.g. 2.86.2; G. on 1.13.2.

praegracilis et incurua proceritas: the first adj. is 'exceedingly rare' (Syme 343 n. 5) and probably unique; compare the more flattering but prosaic Suet. *Tib.* 68.1 'fuit (Tiberius) . . . statura quae iustam excederet'.

nudus capillo uertex: 'Bald men were common enough at Rome. Only one of them will be admitted to the dignified pages of the senatorial annalist, and the word *caluus* is eschewed: instead, a poetical periphrasis alludes to the denuded summit of a Roman emperor' (Syme 343). More likely, perhaps, T. shares a technique with Juvenal, in whose satires 'the dignified is employed to intensify the squalid' (N. Rudd, *Themes in Roman satire* (1986) 109). T. is consciously manipulating the notion that the appearance of a ruler was supposed to match his role (15.3n.)

ulcerosa facies ac . . . medicaminibus interstincta: the part. = 'blotchy'; *medicamina* are either salves or cosmetics (*OLD* 2a, 3), the latter perhaps more appropriate to the inveterate dissembler. Compare Suet. *Tib.* 68.2 'facie honesta, in qua tamen crebri et subiti tumores'.

Rhodi secreto: Tib.'s retirement on Rhodes was 6 B.C.–A.D. 2. *secreto* (54.2n.) is here followed by a genit. (as 41.2).

57.3 impotentia: 'Represented by T. as a prominent characteristic of Livia' (G. on 1.4.5, cf. 5.1.3); the same reason for Tib.'s departure is given by Suet. *Tib.* 51.1 and Dio 57.12.6 (the latter providing a graphic account of Livia's power and authority): see also 71.4n.

neque 'but . . . not' (*OLD* 5).

dubitauerat . . . imponere 'had been considering . . . appointing' (*OLD dubito* 4).

nepotem: by Octavia's second marriage (in 40 B.C. to Mark Antony).

euictus: see 12.25.2 (a similar situation) and *OLD* 4a.

sibi . . . adsciuit 'adopted' (*OLD ascisco* 1c), from which *coniunxit per* *adoptionem* (*uel sim.*) must be understood with *Tiberio Germanicum* (zeugma). Both adoptions took place in A.D. 4 (1.3.3, 5): see Seager 37.

reposcebat 'demanded constant repayments on' (a financial metaphor).

58.1 arto comitatu: abl. of accompaniment (*NLS* §§43 (5), 46).

Cocceius Nerua: suffect consul in 21 or 22, *curator aquarum* from 24, and grandfather of the emperor Nerva. He starved himself to death on Capri in 33 (6.26.1–2). See *AA* 221–5.

ex inlustribus: for *ex* see 42.2n.; for *inlustribus* see 68.1n.

Curtius Atticus: later to be eliminated by Sejanus (6.10.2).

ferme: sc. *omnes*.

leuaretur: the verb = 'cheer', 'regale', 'refresh', 'divert', as Ov. *Tr.* 1.8.17–18 'quid fuit . . . sodalem | . . . adloquiis . . . leuare tuis' and earlier in Cicero.

58.2 caelestium 'astronomy' (*OLD* 4c): hence *periti c.* = 'astrologers'. Since Tib. himself seems to have taken astrology seriously (see Levick 18, 167–8, 217, 231 n. 37; G. on 2.27.2), T.'s reference takes on an extra significance.

patria careret: i.e. lived in exile, an allusion to the alienation between Tib. and his fellow citizens which T. will stress increasingly from now on. *patria carere*, favoured by Cicero and used of his own exile (e.g. *Sest.* 49, 145, *Att.* 3.26), suggests a contrast between him and Tib.: the former was a reluctant exile and wrote as if the constitutional government shared his exile with him (e.g. *Red. Sen.* 34; Fantham 123), but Tib.'s exile was self-imposed and welcomed (*libens*, cf. 6.15.3 'ambiens patriam et declinans').

58.3 mox patuit . . . tegerentur 'subsequently there was disclosed the narrow dividing-line between science and error, and in what mysteries reality was shrouded'. For the *uariatio* of noun ~ indir. qu. see 4.3n.

ceterorum nescii egere 'as regards everything else they acted in ignorance' (*OLD ago* 36; lit. 'ignorant of everything else'): i.e. although the astrologers' prediction was correct (*haud forte dictum*), they had not foreseen how nearly they would be wrong (*cum* . . .).

adsidens: lit. 'sitting near', but the extended sense of 'besieging' (as 6.43.1 'adsidendo castellum') is impossible to exclude (*OLD* 1–2): Tib. will, as it were, return regularly from exile (above, 2n.) to lay siege to the walls of the very city from which he was supposed to govern. The metaphor is developed at 6.1.2 (treatment is meted out *uelut in captos*), 19.2 (where *iacuit immensa strages . . . dispersi aut aggerati* resembles the aftermath of a military operation, cf. 1.61.2), 39.2 ('Tiberius . . . urbem iuxta . . . quasi aspiciens undantem per domos sanguinem aut manus carnificum'), and has as its consequence the suggestion that Tib. is waging civil war against fellow Romans (Keitel 307, 317ff.). At the same time, therefore, T. provides for his readers metaphorically the *expugnatio urbis* for whose absence from his narrative he expressed regret at 32.1 (n.): see *RICH* 186–90.

59.1 ac forte: though these words commonly introduce a new episode in T., here they have a different function (cf. 42.1); they continue the story of 58.1–2 (cf. *illis diebus*) and hence refer to a time earlier than that of 58.3 (cf. *saepe*, *extremam senectam compleuerit*). Yet 58.3 and the present passage are nevertheless complementary. At 58.3 T. observed that the astrologers, though predicting aright ('*haud forte* dictum'), were very nearly wrong ('ceterorum nescii'); here he notes that the rumours of Tib.'s death which followed those predictions (58.2 'multis . . . properum finem uitae . . . uulgantibusque'), though wrong ('ac *forte*', '*uana* rumoris'), were very nearly right ('anceps periculum auxit': next n.).

anceps periculum: in so far as it affected Tib. himself (*oblatum Caesari*), the danger was *anceps* because it could have gone either way (cf. *OLD* 7–8); the fact that he escaped ought to have dispelled the *uana rumoris* of his impending death, but since he very nearly died the episode in fact had the opposite effect (*auxit*) and hence was *anceps* also in the sense that it was capable of two interpretations (*OLD* 9).

amicitiae constantiaeque . . . magis fideret: the second was a virtue which T. would appreciate (38.1n.); *amicitia* was the foundation on which his relationship with Sejanus was based, and officially celebrated as such two years later (74.2n.). The inherent irony of the situation is spelled out by T. at 2 below (*quamquam exitiosa . . . cum fide audiebatur*).

Speluncae: mod. Sperlonga on the Golfo di Terracina and 65 miles S of Rome. The natural grotto (*natiuo . . . specu*), in which the *triclinium* was fashionably situated, gave its name to the *uilla*, which was further up the hill. The grotto was distinguished by four groups of sculpture representing scenes from the life of Odysseus, who as another master of deceit perhaps appealed to Tib.: they may even have been erected there at the emperor's request after his year-long visit to Campania in 21. See A. F. Stewart, *J.R.S.* 67 (1977) 76–90, with plates IX–XII.

mare . . . montes 'between the sea off Amyclae and the hills of Fundi'; for the position of *inter* see 5.1n.

59.2 genu utroque et manibus . . . suspensus: M reads *uultuque*, which, unlike the two instrumental ablatives by which it is surrounded, would be abl. of respect: either Sejanus had his face suspended over that of Tib. or *suspensus* is literal with *genu* and *manibus* but metaphorical with *uultu* ('with anxiety written all over his face'). Neither of these interpretations seems to us at all likely, and, rather than resort to the drastic remedy of excising *uultuque*, we suggest emending to *utroque*. Though T. elsewhere places this adj. before the noun, the proposed order is otherwise acceptable (Plin. *NH* 11.250 'in ipsa genus utriusque commissura').

incidentibus: sc. *saxis*: 'the avalanche'.

maior 'more influential' (*OLD magnus* 12a, *maior* 6a); sc. *erat* or *fiebat*.

quamquam . . . suaderet: for the subjunc. see 4.1n.

ut: see 33.4n. (*ut . . . arguens*).

59.3 Adsimulabatque iudicis partes: Sejanus is seen as the kind of actor-manager/producer that was common in the ancient world: a theatrical metaphor (*OLD assimulo* 2, *pars* 9a) which recurs throughout the paragraph. The cynicism (continued in *subditis* . . . below) is typical after the emphasis on Sejanus' *fides* at 1–2 above.

qui accusatorum nomina sustinerent 'to assume the characters of accusers' (*OLD nomen* 15a, *sustineo* 5b). Sejanus, though the real accuser, has pre-empted the role of impartial judge, so his henchmen adopt the role of accusers in his stead.

quamquam modesta iuuenta: abl. of description (*NLS* §§43 (6), 83): for his *modestia* see 15.3; for *quamquam* see 15.2n.

conduceret 'was appropriate' (*OLD* 6b).

apiscendae potentiae: evidently genit., cf. 12.66.1 'oblatae occasionis propera'.

erectum et fidentem animi: sc. *se* after *ostenderet*. *fidens animi* occurs first at *Aen.* 2.61; since *erectus animus* (-*o*) is common (*OLD erectus* 2a), the genit. of reference (*NLS* §73 (6)) is perhaps extended also to *erectus* in the interests of *uariatio*. The arguments are those of any king-maker, e.g. Liv. 1.41.3 '"erige te..."'.

uelle ... exercitus: these arguments recall those addressed by the army to Nero's father Germanicus (1.35.3, cf. 7.6, 33.2), whom he strikingly resembled (15.3n.): such recollections are of course standard in hortatory speeches.

segnitiam is the interpretation placed upon Nero's *modestia* (above) by the *liberti et clientes*, and is underlined by *iuxta* (adverbial, like *contra* above): a young man should not be as capable of dismissal as an old man. *insulto* + accus. = 'mock at' is perhaps modelled on Sall. *H.* 2.23; for the tense see 2.1n.

60.1 nihil ... cogitationis: sc. *erat*.

contumaces: like his mother (12.3), but *procedebant* (*OLD* 5c) and *inconsultae* underline his lack of intention (*cogitatio*).

quas = *et eas* (as 40.3).

exceptas auctasque: the former = 'noted down', 'seized on', or 'intercepted' (*OLD* 6, 14a–b); the latter = 'embellished', 'exaggerated' (*OLD* 11b).

diuersae ... sollicitudinum formae 'various *scenes* of paranoia': the notion of visibility is basic to *forma* (see *OLD*) and this is an appeal to the reader's visual sense (cf. 28.1n.) which is maintained by vivid historic infinitives in three of the following four scenes (as *Agr.* 37.3 'tum uero ... grande et atrox spectaculum: sequi, uulnerare, capere ...', cf. also *H.* 3.28, *Aen.* 2.369 'plurima mortis imago'). Yet since *forma* is also used regularly to indicate appearance as opposed to reality, T. at the same time underlines the fact that the scenes were (so to speak) stage-managed (cf. 59.3n.) by Sejanus' *fautores*, who constituted ironic and appreciative spectators (see below). For Livy's use of spectators etc. for visual enhancement see J. B. Solodow, *T.A.P.A.* 109 (1979) 257–8 nn. 15–16.

60.2 alius ... quidam ... plerique: typical of T. are both the *uariatio* and the representation of different aspects of similar occasions (see 38.4n.).

insistentibus 'standing firm', as Cic. *Phil.* 12.8 (*OLD* 4a); or perhaps 'egging on' (*OLD* 7a).

Seiano fautores aderant: *Seiano* is possessive dat. with *fautores*, as often after nouns derived from verbs which themselves take a dat. (e.g. 6.37.3 'Tiberio ... auxiliator'). *fautor* can be a theatrical as well as a political supporter (*OLD* 2, 3), and *adesse* = 'to be present as a spectator or auditor' (*OLD* 5).

Enimuero is here best taken as adversative (see G. on 2.64.3): 'Tib., on the other hand . . .'. Scholars generally have made the natural assumption that the events of this paragraph belong to Rome, in which case some further chronological displacement seems evident since Tib. departed from Rome at 57.1 above (Ginsburg 138). Seager, however, assumes that Tib. was accompanied by Nero as far as Campania (204 n. 1).

toruus aut falsum renidens uultu continues the graphic writing of the previous paragraph (28.1–2nn.; also 34.2n.). *falsum* is an internal accus. (*NLS* §13, p. 10), as e.g. Hor. *Odes* 3.27.67, Petr. 127.1.

seu loqueretur seu taceret . . ., crimen: cf. Sen. *Contr.* 6.8 'Varius Geminus apud Caesarem dixit: "Caesar, qui apud te audent dicere, magnitudinem tuam ignorant; qui non audent, humanitatem."' For the subjunc. see 6.4n. (*si quando*).

uxor: he had married Julia, daughter of Tib.'s son Drusus, in 20 (3.29.3). According to Lucr. 5.1158–60 'se multi per somnia saepe loquentes | . . . protraxe ferantur | et celata alte in medium et peccata dedisse'.

in partes: sc. *suas*: 'to his own faction' (17.3n.).

spe obiecta: Sejanus sees Drusus as a wild dog needing to be bribed with food (Sen. *Const. Sap.* 14.2 'illum . . . tamquam canem acrem obiecto cibo leniet'; *OLD obicio* 1a, cf. 3b): so too *praeferocem* and *insidiis* at 3 below are also applicable to animals.

loci, si . . . labefactum demouisset: Sejanus invites Drusus to demolish an older and allegedly unstable building which is occupying a desirable site (for the metaphor cf. Cic. *Phil.* 4.13 'uirtus . . . quae numquam . . . labefactari potest, numquam demoueri loco'; and see Fantham 130). The subjunc. = fut. perf. in *or. recta.*

60.3 atrox . . . ingenium . . . accendebatur is a Livian expression (3.11.9). *super* = 'in addition to' (*OLD* 7). For *cupido potentiae* cf. *H.* 2.38.1 'uetus ac iam pridem insita mortalibus potentiae cupido'; *solita fratribus odia* reverses, as elsewhere (e.g. Sall. *J.* 10.5), the proverb of brotherly love: fraternal enmity is a microcosm of civil war (e.g. *H.* 3.51.1–2).

semina is a very common metaphor for destruction etc. (exx. in *OLD* 7); *meditari*, below, = 'plot' (cf. *OLD* 3a).

61 The end of the year

61 Fine anni excessere . . .: 'There is no hope of extracting anything precise from such words. Indeed I suspect T. sometimes writes *fine anni* only because the items he places under this rubric ended the year's record in his source . . . That so many distinguished men should happen to die as the year closed strains coincidence. Winter is wont to kill off the elderly, but does so indifferently in January and February as well as December' (G. on 2.41.1). For obituaries in general see 15.1n.

quam: sc. *magis*: Asinius Agrippa, consul in 25 (34.1), was grandson of Asinius Pollio (34.4nn.) and Marcus Agrippa, both *noui homines*.

degener 'inferior to his ancestors' (*OLD* 2): cf. 38.4.

Q. Haterius: suffect consul in 5 B.C. and a subsequent source of embarrassment (1.13.4–6, 3.57.2), he had married a daughter of M. Agrippa and hence by marriage was a brother-in-law of Tib. and related to Asinius Agrippa above (see 44.2–3 for another obituary of relatives). Having been born *c.* 63 B.C., he was now almost 90. See *AA* 145–6, 485 (index).

quoad uixit: explained by what follows. The *uariatio* of abl. ~ gen. is typical (29.1n.).

monimenta . . . haud perinde retinentur: *monimentum* is regularly used of literary output (*OLD* 5a), but its connotations of permanency and immortality endeared it esp. to the poets of the late republic and early empire (e.g. Catull. 95.9, Hor. *Odes* 3.30.1): see further below. *haud perinde* is often used elliptically by T. (G. on 2.88.3), with the precise ellipse depending on context: here perhaps sc. 'as when he was alive' or 'as might have been expected'. *retinere* is appropriate to both literal and metaphorical *monimenta* (*OLD* 7b, 9, 11, 12).

impetu magis quam cura uigebat is the kind of lapidary contrast common in literary verdicts (e.g. Ov. *Am.* 1.15.14 'ingenio non ualet, arte ualet') and appropriate to an obituary. *impetus* is used of Haterius also at Sen. *Contr.* 4 pref. 9 and refers to his famous 'flow' or lack of control (see below); for its use of water, rivers etc. see *OLD* 1. *cura* is an equivalent to *labor* (below), used rarely except by Ovid, who uses it often; like *labor* it generated the metonymy 'work (of literature)', which T. uses of *A.* at 11.3 (n.). *uigere* is often used of literary survival (*OLD* 3b).

meditatio et labor: the two virtues are those promulgated by the followers of Callimachus in the late republic and early empire. *labor* (Callimachus' *πόνος*) is used first by Lucr. and esp. by Horace and produced the metonymy 'work (of poetry)': see Brink on *Ep.* 2.1.224–5. *meditatio* suggests the *uigiliae* (*OLD* 4b: Callimachus' *ἀγρυπνίη*) which was often associated with it (e.g. Hor. *AP* 291 'limae labor et mora' and Brink; also on 269). Immortality (*in posterum*) was also important to the same group of poets (e.g. Catull. 1.10, Hor. *Odes* 3.30). For all these ideas and expressions see e.g. N. B. Crowther, *Mnem.* 31 (1978) 33–44. Though such terminology had long since been applied to historiography by Catullus (1.5–6: see F. Cairns, *Mnem.* 22 (1969) 153–4), we may presume that it had also become commonplace to express literary approbation in general. Under the guise of a rhetorical foil for his dispraise of Haterius (*utque aliorum* ...), T. is also providing a 'testimony to his own quality' (Syme 624 n. 3).

ualescit: the verb occurs nine times in T. and always metaphorically; it 'is generally rare and earlier attested perhaps only at Lucr. 1.942, 4.17' (G. on 2.39.4).

canorum illud et profluens echoes Cicero's appreciation of the orator Carbo at *De Or.* 3.28 'profluens quiddam habuit ... et canorum' (Syme 324, 727) but is transformed into dispraise by the change in literary values accompanying the neoteric revolution, which had intervened with the poets of Catullus' generation. *canorus* now suggests 'empty sound' (Hor. *AP* 322 'uersus inopes rerum nugaeque canorae' and Brink); and *profluens* recalls another of Seneca's verdicts on Haterius (*Contr.* 4 pref. 11 'multa erant quae reprehenderes ..., cum torrentis modo magnus quidem sed turbidus flueret'), which in turn echoes Horace's Callimachean critique of Lucilius (*S.* 1.4.11 'cum flueret lutulentus, erat quod tollere uelles').

62–7 The year A.D. 27

This year's narrative, the shortest of the book, resembles that of A.D. 23 in being devoted exclusively to domestic affairs (above, p. 77). T. opens with two disasters which occupy two-thirds of the whole (62–5). The first, at Fidenae, is man-made and described at length in metaphorical terms of the *expugnationes urbium* for which T. at 32.1 said he had no opportunity (62.1n.); he concludes by referring briefly to precautionary measures for the future (63.1 *in posterum*) and to the generosity which was displayed in the aftermath by leading men and which compared with that of antiquity (63.2). The second disaster, at Rome, is natural and scarcely described at all: instead T. concentrates on the generosity of the emperor (64.1–2), which, by way of a proposal for the latter's commemoration in the future (64.3 *in posterum*), in turn leads into an antiquarian excursus (64.3–65). T. thus follows a similar sequence of ideas to that in the first disaster, while avoiding the same scale of treatment.

The last third of the narrative is taken up with an accusation (66) and Tib.'s withdrawal to Capri (67). Since this arrangement mirrors, in reverse order, the two penultimate episodes of the previous year (57.1–59.2 Tib. departs to Campania, 59.3–60 a series of accusations), it brings both an extended passage of narrative and a momentous period of the emperor's life to a simultaneous conclusion. See below, 67.1n.; more detail in Woodman (1) 152–4.

62–3 Disaster at Fidenae

62.1 consulibus: M. Licinius Crassus Frugi, son of the consul of 14, achieved military distinction and suffered execution under Claudius: see *AA* 488 (index). L. Calpurnius Piso (his original praenomen was Gaius, cf. 3.17.4) was later *praefectus urbi* under Tib. and possibly governor of Dalmatia: see *AA* 379, 477 (index).

ingentium bellorum cladem aequauit: at 32.1 T. specifically denied that Tib.'s reign offered the chance to describe *ingentia bella*, the staple diet of republican historians. Hence the present *malum improuisum* (the same expression is used of a violent fire at 13.57.3) is explicitly compared with a military event at both the start and end of the episode (63.2 *magna post proelia*), where also, in the light of its aftermath, it is itself elevated to the status of a *clades* (63.2, 64.1). The military analogy is sustained throughout, and, since the *malum* involves the destruction of a building, the closest parallels are with the besieging of a city, the popular topic (32.1n.) for which Quint. offers detailed instructions at 8.3.67–70 (see further below). *aequare* = 'to match' in terms of both similarity and scale (cf. *OLD* 6, 10–11).

initium simul et finis exstitit 'it was over almost as soon as it had started': comparable expressions are used to report military success in battle (e.g. 3.47.1 'ortum patratumque bellum', Liv. 44.32.5 'bellum prius perpetratum quam coeptum Romae auditum est'). For *simul* see *OLD* 8b.

apud Fidenam: *apud* = 'near' (*OLD* 1a) rather than 'at': cf. *propinquitatem* at 2 below. The town was 5 miles N of Rome on the Via Salaria; it is more usu. plural, Fidenae.

libertini generis is perh. added through aristocratic prejudice (cf. also 2.85.4).

per solidum 'on [lit. through ⟨and onto⟩] solid ground': cf. Vitruv. 1.5.1 'fundamenta . . . fodiantur ad solidum et in solido'. Elsewhere, when it suits him, T. avoids the technicalities of building (13.31.1).

in sordidam mercedem: purposive (*OLD in* 21a); for similar *uariatio* of prep. phrase ~ causal abl. see e.g. 15.44.5; Sörbom 85. The upper classes were not themselves averse to profit (provided it was large enough) but claimed to be motivated by the desire for social and political distinction rather than by profit alone: hence *sordidam*.

negotium 'contract'.

62.2 procul uoluptatibus habiti: the juxtaposition with *imperitante Tiberio* suggests that Tib., notoriously averse to public spectacles (14.3, 1.76.3–4, Suet. *Tib.* 47), imposed his aversion on the people while at the same time enjoying himself privately (57.1 *libidinem*, 2 *uoluptates*, 59.2 *conuiuium celebrabant*); and while Tib. escaped with his life when his banquet was suddenly and violently interrupted (59.1 'repente . . . obruit'), his subjects in the amphitheatre were less fortunate when it suddenly (1 *improuisum*) and violently (*ruit* etc. below) collapsed. For *procul* (prep.) see 2.1n.

uirile ac muliebre secus: an adverbial accus. phrase, found esp. in historians in passages of drama and pathos (see *OLD secus*[1] b), and here used, like the nomin. *omnis aetas*, in apposition to *auidi*: 'fans . . . ⟨of⟩ both the male and female sex, ⟨of⟩ every age'.

effusius 'in greater numbers' (*OLD* 3b). The adverb modifies *adfluxere* above: the hyperbaton and the *uariatio* of constr. (last n.) both contribute to the effect of the crowd scene.

pestis 'destruction', 'death-toll' (*OLD* 1), as at 2.47.1 (a nocturnal earthquake).

conferta mole, dein conuulsa 'since the building was packed [sc. with spectators] before it collapsed': the whole sentence *unde* . . . *conuulsa* is expanded by *dum* . . . *operit* (see 52.4n.). Collapsing buildings are of course *de rigueur* in siege descriptions (Quint. 8.3.68 'ruentium tectorum').

immensamque uim mortalium: each word contributes to the pathos: *immensam* combines conventional exaggeration ('beyond number', e.g. Thuc. 3.87.3, 5.74.3; in general, C. R. Rubincam, *A.J.A.H.* 4 (1979) 77–95) with horror (mutilation prevented accurate counting, cf. 63.1); *uim* is more evocative than e.g. *multitudinem* (see Pease on Virg. *Aen.* 4.132); and *mortalium*, effectively juxtaposed, underlines the precariousness of life (cf. 40.1, 68.3). Compare Suet.'s prosaic statement on the same disaster: 'supra xx hominum milia . . . perierant' (*Tib.* 40).

intentos: such plurals are esp. common after collective nouns like *uis*; so too *qui* . . . *adstabant.* See 29.2n.

praeceps is adverbial (as 6.17.3) and is used for the more normal *in praeceps* (as 22.1).

62.3 ut tali sorte qualifies *cruciatum effugere* below and is restrictive ('as far as one can in such a situation').

miserandi magis: sc. *erant.* By actually referring to pity T. intensifies the emotional tone.

ululatibus et gemitu coniuges aut liberos noscebant: 'wives or children' is more specific than *muliebre secus, omnis aetas* at 2 above and thus more pathetic; their cries are conventional in the aftermath of disasters such as the fire at Rome in 64 (15.38.4 'lamenta pauentium feminarum') or sieges (Quint. 8.3.68 'infantium feminarumque ploratus') or the eruption of Mt Vesuvius in 79 (Plin. *Ep.* 6.20.14 'audires ululatus feminarum, infantum quiritatus, clamores uirorum; alii parentes, alii liberos, alii coniuges uocibus requirebant, uocibus noscitabant; hi suum casum, illi suorum miserabantur'). *noscebant* = 'kept on recognising' or 'tried to recognise'.

hic . . . ille, alius . . .: the *uariatio*, a feature of post-battle descriptions etc. (e.g. 15.38.6 'quidam . . . alii', Sall. *C.* 61.8 'alii, pars . . . fuere item qui . . .', Plin. cited above), is here combined with (double) chiasmus (see Sörbom 131).

comperto: see 36.3n.

latior ex incerto metus: again conventional, e.g. *H.* 4.33.3 'latiorem . . . terrorem' (more exx. in H.), Liv. 9.24.8 'nox . . . omnia ex incerto maiora territis ostentat'.

63.1 coepere dimoueri obruta: note that where earlier authors mostly use passive *coeptus sum* with a passive infin., T. always uses the active *coepi*.

concursus: sufficiently conventional in military narrative to be parodied by Hor. *S.* 1.9.78 'undique concursus' (E. Fraenkel, *Horace* (1957) 118).

et saepe certamen, si . . . fecerat 'and there was often a quarrel in cases where a face beyond recognition, but corresponding stature or age, had led to errors of identification': *fecerat* is to be taken in common with *facies*, *forma* and *aetas*; *par* means that the *forma* or *aetas* of any given corpse corresponded with the *forma* or *aetas* of more than one individual during life. Questions of mistaken identity are a staple ingredient of drama and must also have figured prominently in actual and declamatory legal cases (cf. [Quint.] *Decl.* 388 (p. 437.28 Ritter = p. 286.18–19 Winterbottom) 'quomodo autem potuit confusa facie agnosci? aetas, inquit, conueniebat; . . . statura').

debilitata uel obtrita 'maimed or crushed to death / killed', as Plin. *Ep.* 8.17.5 'multi eiusmodi casibus debilitati, obruti, obtriti' (of flooding).

cautumque . . . ne . . .: a legal expression (as 2.85.1; *OLD* 7a–b).

minor . . . res: elliptical for *minor res quam res quadr. milium* (gen. of description, with which *quam* is commonly omitted: *OLD minor*[2] 1a, 3a). The sum is the same as the minimum capital qualification for equestrian status.

firmitatis: apart from *H.* 2.34.2 and *D.* 23.3, T. elsewhere prefers *firmitudo*.

63.2 sub 'in response to' (*OLD* 24b).

procerum: the noun, used by T. mostly in *A.*, is elevated in tone.

fomenta: similar *noblesse oblige* from Agrippina at 1.69.1; for doctors see 3.4n.

quamquam: see 15.2n.

maesta facie directs attention to the contrast with the happy *spectaculum* which the victims had but recently been watching (62.1, 2; also above, 60.1n. *diuersae*); and the adj. intensifies the melancholy from which the city had already been suffering (32.2).

ueterum institutis: the very early republic (Liv. 2.47.12 'saucios milites curandos diuidit patribus': 480 B.C.). T.'s phrase, a variation on the commoner (and Ciceronian) *maiorum instituta* (at e.g. 2.2.3), involves a slight ellipse: '⟨the practices of⟩ the city at that time were like those of our ancestors'.

64–5 Disaster at Rome

64.1 cum . . . adfecit 'when a violent fire did unprecedented damage to the city' (*uiolentia* is probably nomin.: cf. 15.38.1, quoted below). Rome was highly susceptible to fire (6.45.1, 15.43.1), but *ultra solitum* (*OLD solitus* 2b) is the kind of magnifying expression of which historians are fond (69.3n.): so too at 15.38.1 'omnibus quae huic urbi per uiolentiam ignium acciderunt grauior'.

deusto monte Caelio: the perf. part. is to be understood in a present sense, of the circumstances accompanying the main verb: so too e.g. 1.65.3, 77.1, 6.45.1 'deusta parte circi'.

ferebant: a mixed condition (cf. *ni . . . isset* below). Here the imperf. indic. (30.2n.) seems to suggest the ellipse 'they were saying ⟨and would have continued to say⟩, had not . . .': the year clearly *had* been 'death-bringing' (*OLD feralis* 2, cf. 3a–b; G. on 2.31.2).

qui mos uulgo 'as is the way with the common people': for this parenthetic use of *qui* see *OLD* 12a.

trahentes: for *trahere* = 'ascribe', 'interpret' see *OLD* 20b. The antithesis *fortuita* ~ *culpam* is a (legal) commonplace (W. on Vell. 118.4).

ex modo detrimenti 'in proportion to the extent of the damage(s)' (*pro modo* is much commoner). For Tib.'s response, typical of the first half of his reign (6.4 *obuiam iit*), see 2n. below.

64.2 famaque: probably sc. *ei* (from above) and *erat*: 'he had a good reputation amongst the people'.

sine ambitione aut proximorum precibus 'without lobbying ⟨from anyone⟩ or the intervention of relatives': explained (almost chiastically) by *ignotos . . . accitos*, 'he had helped even people who were ⟨hitherto⟩ unknown or whom he had sought out for himself'.

ultro accitos: *ultro* with a passive verb indicates spontaneity on the part of the agent (here Tib.): *OLD* 5b.

munificentia: one of Tib.'s 'virtues': see 1.46.2, 2.26.1, 6.45.1 (also after a fire), Vell. 126.4 'fortuita . . . ciuium . . . principis munificentia uindicat' (and W.), 130.2 'qua liberalitate . . . tum proxime incenso monte Caelio omnis ordinis hominum iacturae patrimonio succurrit suo!' See Levick 218.

64.3 quando 'since', + subjunc. in *or. obl.*, as 6.6.2; see *OLD quando* 3. The senator is otherwise unknown.

id: i.e. remaining intact. *euenisse* indicates that the *or. obl.* is still in force.

eiusque statuam . . . maiores . . . consecrauisse: in 191 B.C., to commemorate the part she had played in rescuing the ship which brought the statue of the *mater deum*, Cybele (see *OCD*, Powell on Cic. *Sen.* 45), to Rome in 204 B.C. (Liv. 29.14.12). Since the consecration of the statue *preceded* its two escapes from fire in 111 B.C. and A.D. 3 (Val. Max. 1.8.11), the past tense of *elapsam* is (somewhat oddly) relative to the senatorial debate of A.D. 27 and not to that denoted by the main verb *consecrauisse*. For *deum* see 1.2n.

augendam caerimoniam loco 'they should enhance the sanctity of the place in which . . .'. The language (also at 3.61.2 'auctam . . . caerimoniam templo') here has extra point in alluding to and explaining the proposed name *Augustus*, which, in addition to its religious and supernatural connotations, was derived from *augeo* (Suet. *Aug.* 7.2 'loca quoque religiosa . . . augusta dicantur ab auctu'). There is no evidence that the proposal was ever implemented. For *caerimonia* see *OLD* 1 and G. on 1.62.2.

ostenderint: for the tense see 2.1n.

65 Haud fuerit absurdum tradere is the kind of apologetic formula often used to introduce digressions or digressive material: cf. 6.28.1 (on the phoenix) 'de quibus congruunt et plura ambigua sed cognitu non absurda promere libet' (cf. 3.55.1 'causas eius mutationis [sc. in luxury] quaerere libet',[1] with which contrast 13.29.1 'uarie habita ac saepe mutata eius rei forma'), 12.24.1 (on the pomerium) 'uarie uulgata; sed . . . noscere haud absurdum reor', *H.* 4.48.1 (a retrospect) 'si pauca repetiero . . . non absurda', Vell. 38.1 (on the provinces) 'haud absurdum uidetur propositi operis regulae paucis percurrere'. Sometimes, as at 4.3 and 3.25.2, the digression is made to arise naturally from the narrative (above, p. 95); sometimes there is no introductory formula or statement at all, as at 11.14.1 (on the alphabet). Similarly digressions are often concluded formulaically

[1] Cf. Liv. 9.17.2 'ut quaerere libeat' (on Alexander the Great).

(33.4n.); here the narrative is instead resumed by linking phraseology at 66.1 (n.). For the perf. subjunc. *fuerit* ('it would not be . . .') see 5.4n. (*persequi*).

The present digression is not relevant to the main narrative of the year, which otherwise, however, would be even shorter (p. 232); but antiquarianism in general flourished in the early second century A.D., and antiquarian digressions of various sorts had always been popular with historians (T.'s other three are mentioned above). The type illustrated here is aetiological and involves the etymology of proper names: these were traditional matters of intellectual curiosity (see e.g. F. Cairns, *Tibullus* (1979) 90–9) and were naturally at home in historiography (E. Gabba, *J.R.S.* 71 (1981) 60–1). In general see E. Hahn, *Die Exkurse in den Annalen des Tacitus* (1933).

Scholars have debated the source(s) of T.'s information. It is clear (see below) that he owes something to the speech which Claudius, himself an antiquarian, delivered to the senate in 48 on the subject of citizenship. That T. had personal knowledge of that speech, itself derived in part from Liv. 4.3–5, is clear from the fact that his version of it at 11.24 reproduces several of the main points of the original (which has been preserved: *ILS* 212): see 8.2n. But whether T. here under A.D. 27 borrowed from it at first hand (so Syme 286, 709–10), or whether he used an intermediary such as Claudius' contemporary Aufidius Bassus (above, p. 9; see G. B. Townend, *Rh.M.* 105 (1962) 364–5), is incapable of proof.

Querquetulanum: 'The name of various places and deities associated with oak-woods' (*OLD*).

cognomento: this noun, which T. prefers overwhelmingly to the standard and 'Ciceronian' *cognomen* (25:1, cf. G. on 1.23.5), is used, like *uocabulum* below, as a variation for *nomen*.

siluae frequens fecundusque: the very rare genit. after *frequens* (*OLD* 2) is facilitated by the co-ordination of *fecundus*, with which the genit. is more common (several exx. in T.).

appellitatum occurs only here in T. and, apart from the archaisers Gellius and Apuleius, elsewhere only in Claudius' speech (see above): col. 1, lines 21–2 'montem Caelium occupauit et a duce suo Caelio ita appellitatus' (the ending is clearly wrong: edd. read *appellitauit*). It is, however, clear that T.'s version of events, while close to Claudius', is not identical: in Claudius it is Servius Tullius who occupies the hill and names it after his leader Caelius Vivenna; in T. it is Caeles Vibenna himself who is given the hill by Tarquinius Priscus and from whom it subsequently derives its name. Varro had made Vibenna a friend of Romulus (*LL* 5.46); the hill was associated with Ancus Martius by Cic. (*Rep.* 2.33) and with Tullus Hostilius by Livy (1.30.1). See *OCD* Vibenna.

auxilium tulisset: Lipsius' emendation is supported by the same phrase at 3.41.2 (and cf. *solacium tulerant* at 66.1 below), although *attulisset* would perhaps explain better the corrupt reading of M. The intrusive *appellatum* was presumably a scribal gloss on, or correction of, *appellitatum*.

nam scriptores in eo dissentiunt: the scholarly manner suits an antiquarian digression: see again Claudius' speech, lines 16–17 'nam et hoc inter auctores discrepat'. For *ambigua* (below) and the like see the refs. quoted on *Haud fuerit* above. Livy opens his history with the converse: 1.1.1 'Iam primum omnium satis constat', 6 'duplex inde fama est'.

aduenarum: used by T. only here and at 11.24.4, in his version of Claudius' speech (in the original of which, however, the word does not appear). *e(x)* is regular in etymologies (*OLD* 14d).

66 Quintilius Varus accused

66.1 Sed: resumptive (as 70.1): similarly *studia procerum* and *largitio principis* link with the main narratives of 63.2 and 64.1–2 respectively. See further next n.

ut . . . aduersum casus solacium tulerant: the two episodes above, in which the upper classes and Tib. have been shown in a favourable light, are depicted in quasi-medical terms (cf. Cels. 6.7.3 'commune . . . auxilium aduersum omnium aurium casus'; *OLD casus* 9b) and characteristically (see Martin (2) 229) act as a foil (*ut . . . ita*, cf. 33.3n.) for the unpleasant *accusatorum . . . uis* below, which is also seen in similar terms (next n.).

maior in dies et infestior uis sine leuamento grassabatur: *uis* ('violent attack of disease, misfortune': *OLD* 9b) and *grassari* ('run riot, rage, etc., esp. of diseases, conditions': *OLD* 4) define the metaphorical terms of the sentence: they are sustained by *infestior*, to which T. normally prefers *infensus* (11.2n.) but which is often used of things inimical to health (*OLD* 4a), and *leuamentum* (*OLD* 2); even *in dies* corroborates the tone of a medical bulletin (Vell. 123.1 'ingrauescente in dies ualetudine'). See also next n. There is no independent evidence to confirm or refute T.'s sinister generalisation, and he himself provides only one example to illustrate it (see 36.1n.; also 15.2nn. *etiam tum* and *adeo ut*).

corripueratque is often used of *delatores* (19.1n.; *OLD* 1e) but here may continue the metaphor above (*OLD* 5a).

Varum Quintilium: son of P. Quintilius Varus, the Roman commander in the German disaster of A.D. 9; he had been engaged to a daughter of Germanicus (see *AA* 149, 315, 327). The relationship with Tib. (*propinquum* below) was through his mother, Claudia Pulchra (52.1n.). For the inversion of names see 30.1n.

Domitius Afer ... condemnator: see 52.1. *condemnator*, which does not recur till late Latin, well illustrates T.'s fondness for nouns in *-tor* (1.3n. *criminator*).

plura ... accingeretur 'was girding himself for further outrages': for the metaphor see *H.* 4.79.1; *OLD* 3a. The subjunc. is due to virtual *or. obl.* after *nullo mirante*.

66.2 Publium Dolabellam: see 23–6 above (23.2n.).

miraculo: predic. dat. (*NLS* §68), here foll. by acc. + inf. (see *OLD* 2a) and contrasting with *nullo mirante* above: Dolabella's readiness to attack a relative (*Varo conexus*) is a further illustration of the state of society (see 28.1n. and p. 161) and by normal standards would qualify as material for the frankly incredible 'wonder-literature' which T. rejects at 11.3 (nn.).

claris maioribus: his grandfather was consul in 44 B.C.: hence *suam ... nobilitatem* (6.2n.) below.

et Varo conexus: they were cousins (Dolabella's mother is thought to have been Varus' aunt: *AA* 98, 316 and Table XXVI): hence *suum sanguinem* (75n.) below. For the *uariatio* with the abl. descr. above see 40.6n.

suam ... suum: the anaphora emphasises the incredulity of contemporary observers.

perditum: for the supine see 1.1n.

opperiendum reminds us of Tib.'s continuing absence (67.1 below); T. does not say whether the trial was ever resumed.

67 Tiberius' withdrawal to Capri

The key feature of this section is that T. equips his account of Capri with the kind of full-scale ethnographical description which was normally reserved for foreign countries and in which references to physical geography (1–2 *trium milium . . . subsidia*), climate (2 *caeli temperies . . . peramoena*), original inhabitants (2 *Graecos . . . tradit*) and present organisation (3 *sed tum Tiberius . . .*) were all conventional (see Thomas 1ff., 126–30). By thus describing Capri as a foreign country, which it was not, T. not only emphasises still further (cf. 58.2n.) the emperor's alienation from his subjects (Thomas 128) but also provides in metonymical terms the kind of *situs gentium* for which at 33.3 he said he had no opportunity (*RICH* 190).

67.1 At Caesar both contrasts with the immediately preceding episode (he might have been expected to take an interest in his *propinquus*) and returns us at last to the sequence of events which began at 57.1 (where *in Campaniam ⟨concessit⟩*, *specie dedicandi templa* ~ *dedicatis per Campaniam templis* here). The account of these same events in Suet. *Tib*. 39–41 is in many respects so close as to suggest a common source; but whereas T. places the disasters at Fidenae and Rome before Tib. reaches Capri, Suet. makes Tib. leave Capri in response to the Fidenae disaster (that at Rome is not mentioned). There is no way of telling which version is correct; but whereas Suet.'s is perhaps more natural, T.'s emphasises the finality of the withdrawal, thereby adding to its significance. See Woodman (1) 150ff., esp. 150–2.

ne quis quietem eius inrumperet: *suam* might have been expected; but though such exchanges of pronouns are fairly common (cf. 56.1n.), here *eius* may suggest the impersonal officialese of a document (so W. Pfitzner, mentioned by K.). For *inrumpo* = 'break in upon', 'interrupt (an activity)' see *OLD* 3b; for *quamquam* + subjunc., above, 4.1n.

tamen indicates that Tib. experienced a spontaneous tedium in addition to that induced by milling crowds (*quamquam . . .* above). 'In T. and elsewhere *municipia et coloniae* (and vice versa) is frequently used to designate the Italian towns generally' (G. on 1.79.1).

Capreas would normally follow *in insulam* (as 13.2, 71.4), but cf. *H.* 4.32.1 'Geldubam in castra'.

trium milium . . . diiunctam: T.'s readers 'would hardly have required the information that this island is three miles off the Campanian coast, opposite Surrentum. The detail, however, is demanded by the genre' (Thomas 126–7).

67.2 solitudinem . . . maxime: Tib.'s desire for *solitudo* (both the condition and the place) and *quies* (1 above) was played upon by Sejanus two years earlier (41.3).

crediderim: for the subjunc. see 6.1n.

importuosum circa mare: a characteristic detail of foreign descriptions (e.g. 12.20.1) and ethnography (Thomas 127 and n. 13): see esp. Sall. *J.* 17.5 'mare saeuom, importuosum' (Africa). *circa* is adjectival ('the surrounding sea'), like *circum* at 55.4 (n.): the former word becomes a common alternative for the latter from the Augustan age (in prose esp. in Livy).

uix modicis . . . subsidia: a similar detail appears in T.'s description of Britain (*Agr.* 10.5 'mare pigrum et graue remigantibus'). For *subsidium* = 'refuge', 'haven' see 5.8.1; *OLD* 5 (rare).

neque adpulerit quisquam nisi gnaro custode: for the verb used absolutely or intrans., of persons, see *OLD appello*[1] 4a; the perf. subjunc. is used for *repraesentatio* (see 3.3n. *neque femina*). For the abl. abs. see 25.3n.

caeli temperies: 'precisely the . . . ethnographical formula expressing the ideal climate' (Thomas 127): T. puts it into the mouth of others at 55.4 above (n.) and uses it to sustain his ethnographical framework here.

mitis obiectu montis: for *mitis* of climate etc. see *OLD* 7a (cf. b); *obiectus* is commonly found in topographical contexts (*OLD* 1b).

saeua uentorum: see 5.2n. (*cetera Africae*).

aestas 'the island in summer': the very bold metonymy is facilitated by *obuersa*, the appropriate word for facing a prevailing wind (Ov. *F.* 5.381 'Pelion Haemoniae mons est obuersus in austros').

pelago: i.e. πέλαγος, the open sea; an elevated and mostly poetical word, used by T. at *H.* 5.6.2 in his ethnography of Judaea.

peramoena: a unique intensification (G. on 1.7.4) of the standard *amoenus* (41.1n.) and chosen to evoke the so-called *locus amoenus* or 'idyllic location' (see Hor. *Ep.* 1.16.15; Nisbet–Hubbard on Hor. *Odes* 2.3, Brink on Hor. *AP* 17).

prospectabatque 'and it [sc. the island] looked out on . . .' (*OLD* 3).

antequam . . .uerteret: *Vesuuius . . . ardescens* refers primarily to the great eruption of 79; for the substantival use of the pres. part. see 12.1n.; for the subjunc. after *antequam* see 46.2n. *faciem loci* (also at 14.10.2) = 'the landscape' (*OLD facies* 2a).

Graecos ea tenuisse . . . fama tradit: 'The diction and style of this statement are an essential part of the tradition . . . his sole intention is to provide the passage with ethnographical status' (Thomas 127). *tenere* (*OLD* 8) is regularly used in ethnographical contexts (ibid. 105 n. 15); *ea* = 'those parts' or simply 'the island'; *Telebois* is dat. of agent (they originally inhabited the islands off Acarnania). Such phraseology as *fama tradit*, which both appeals to tradition and absolves the author from any personal responsibility for its correctness, is often used by poets (see e.g. Austin on *Aen.* 6.14) and historians when dealing with mythological matter or very early 'history': it is therefore esp. common in ethnographical contexts apropos of founders or first settlers. See e.g. *H.* 2.3.1 'conditorem templi . . . uetus memoria . . .; fama recentior tradit . . .' (digression on the temple of Venus at Paphos), 4.84.3 'maior hinc fama tradidit' (digression on Serapis), Sall. *J.* 17.7 'sed qui mortales initio Africam habuerint . . . quamquam ab ea fama, quae plerosque obtinet, diuorsum est . . .' (ethnographical digression). See also G. on 2.60.1.

67.3 sed tum Tiberius . . . insederat: Tib. is now the island's latest settler, but this account of how his settlement was organised (above, p. 242) is highly uncertain. M reads *nominibus et molibus*, which scholars have interpreted in two different ways. (1) Sc. *ea* (from above) or *insulam* with *insederat*, which presumably derives from *insido* (though in the (plu)perf. is indistinguishable from *insideo*) and takes the accus. elsewhere in T. (e.g. *G.* 43.2 'saltus et uertices montium insederunt', *H.* 5.2.1 'nouissima Libyae insedisse'). On this view *nominibus* and *molibus* are abl. and constitute a hendiadys: 'but now Tib. had settled there in twelve huge and individually named villas' (lit. 'in the names and edifices of . . .'). In support of this view is adduced Suet. *Tib.* 65.2, in which it is said that Tib. once spent nine months in a *Villa Ionis* but which scholars conventionally emend to *Iouis*, inferring from the joint evidence of both passages that there were twelve villas, each named after one of the twelve great gods of Rome. Yet the evidence of Suet. is not strictly admissible since its emendation is not independent of T.; and in any case we do not believe that such a hendiadys is possible. (2)

Take *nominibus* and *molibus* as dat. with *insederat*, since the verb (with the same qualification as mentioned above) is certainly followed by the dat. at Virg. *Aen.* 6.708 and elsewhere (*OLD insido* 1b) and in T. probably at 12.64.1 'fastigio ... insedit' (though Nipperdey emended to *fastigium*). On this view T. is referring to the villas 'of former owners, now absorbed into his own grounds' (F.) and means: 'had taken up his position on the names and ruins of twelve villas'. Yet we do not believe that *nominibus insido* is possible Latin.

In our view the text is corrupt, but the extent and nature of the corruption are difficult to determine. (1) RHM suggests that *nominibus* is a corruption of *moenibus* and that *moenibus et molibus* arose from a marginal gloss *moenibus uel molibus*. Of course one cannot now tell from this hypothetical formulation whether the true reading should be *moenibus* or *molibus*. While *moenia* can be used of the walls of sumptuous private houses (e.g. *H.* 5.11.3 with H.'s parallels), T.'s use of *moles* + genit. elsewhere (13.31.1 'molem amphitheatri') perhaps suggests that *molibus* is correct and hence that the corrupt *nominibus et* should be deleted. (2) W. S. Watt has suggested either that *nominibus et* is a corruption of *nomine* caused by anticipation of the ending of *molibus* ('in twelve edifices which were villas only in name', i.e. really something much grander) or that *nominibus* is a corruption of *munitionibus* ('in the defensive edifices of...', hendiadys). In the former case the use of *nomen* is idiomatic (*OLD* 15), and the remains of Tib.'s establishment on Capri are certainly very extensive (J. H. D'Arms, *Romans on the Bay of Naples* (1970) 88–9 with plates 2–3); but the word-order is awkward. The latter receives some support from Plin. *NH* 3.82 'Tiberi principis arce nobiles Capreae' and would sustain the military imagery of the earlier narrative (58.3n.). (3) AJW suggests that *nominibus* may be a corruption of *amoenitatibus*, producing another hendiadys: 'in the attractive edifices of...' The noun provides a good introduction to *luxus et malum otium* at the end of the sentence, the *uariatio* after the compound *peramoenus* above is typical of T. (Sörbom 65), and for the expression cf. 14.52.2 'hortorum quoque amoenitate et uillarum magnificentia quasi principem supergrederetur', 15.52.1 'cuius (uillae) amoenitate captus Caesar', *H.* 2.87.1 'uillarumque amoenitates' (and H.'s parallels for the plural form). Yet since none of these proposals carries complete conviction, it has been decided simply to indicate that the text is corrupt.

intentus: for the absence of a comparative after *quanto* (to balance *tanto occultior* below) see 23.2n.

curas: see 13.1n.

tanto occultior . . . resolutus: although the statement forms 'a savage contrast' with the idyllic description of the island (Syme 349), it is in keeping with ethnographical convention, according to which 'the ideal and balanced environment . . . breeds a race lacking in fortitude and with a low moral worth' (Thomas 129). *occultior*, used adverbially (as 12.1, 40.5), contrasts thematically with *publicas*; there is a more formal contrast between *resolutus* and *intentus*; and the two clauses together are virtually chiastic.

quam: object of both *augere* and *turbabat*: Tib.'s existing inability to distinguish between those he could trust and those he could not (above) represented a mental confusion which Sejanus sought to aggravate (cf. *turbata mente* at 22.1). Some editors, however, understand *eum* with *turbabat*.

67.4 quis: dat. plur.; see 14.1n.

miles: collective sing. (2.1n.).

nuntios, introitus 'messages, visitors'.

uelut in annales referebat: the precise significance of these words is unclear, but the context suggests an implication that the soldiers recorded minutiae as though they were matters of great historical importance: see Sempr. Asell. fr. 1 'annales libri . . . id est quasi qui diarium scribunt'. For *refero* = 'record', 'note down', 'enter' see *OLD* 8a.

ultroque struebantur qui monerent perfugere 'and in addition people were arranged to warn them to take refuge . . .' *struo* is not normally used of people (*OLD* 6b), but cf. 11.12.1 'strueret crimina et accusatores'; *ultro* here = 'in addition to everything else' (*OLD* 3a); *qui* is purposive; and the infin. after *moneo*, rare in earlier prose, is common in poetry and post-Augustan prose (*NLS* p. 104 *Note*).

celeberrimo fori 'in the throng of the forum', a choice variant on the more normal *in foro celeberrimo* (e.g. Cic. *Verr.* 2.2.133): cf. Apul. *Apol.* 16 'in propatulo et celebri' (*OLD celeber* 1a); for the genit. see 5.2n.

auxilio: predic. dat. (*NLS* §68), first extended to *uocare* by Virg. *Aen.* 5.686; again in T. at 12.45.1.

spreta: concessive: 'although rejected by them'.

uelut 'as though'; its use + subjunc. is first in Nepos, then often in Livy (*OLD* 5a).

obiciebantur: Suet. says that these charges were falsely brought against Agrippina on the occasion of her banishment to Pandateria in 29 (*Tib.* 53.2): see Bauman (2) 85–92 for discussion.

68–75 The year A.D. 28

If readers of Book 4 have believed that T. surpasses himself with the narrative of each successive year, they will not be disappointed by the final year of all. The narrative is organised on the same 'Livian' pattern as A.D. 24 (home affairs, foreign affairs, home affairs); but on this occasion the divergence from Livy is not restricted to the domestic 'frame' (above, p. 144) but extends also to the central section (72–3), for which T., with a characteristic *Schadenfreude* (see Syme 528–31), has selected a Roman military defeat. Nevertheless it is the two domestic sections in which his genius for dramatic narrative is above all revealed (68–71, 74–5). It will become clear that these sections, by resuming some of the principal themes of the preceding half-decade (above all *amicitia*, by which they are themselves linked), together bring the book as a whole to a fitting conclusion. Yet at the same time, by ending on notes of ill omen, T. carries the reader forward to the later stages of the Tiberian hexad and beyond (74.4n., 75n.).

68–71 Home affairs

The main theme is *amicitia Germanici* (68.1), which also figured prominently in the first section of A.D. 24 (17–22: cf. 18.1 *amicitia Germanici*; and above, p. 144); and the victim is Titius Sabinus, whose case Sejanus had cynically deferred in that same year (19.1). 'No episode in Tacitus', says Walker (105), 'is more effective emotionally . . . At the end of a series of more or less detailed episodes comes one which in its vividness and horror distils the emotional content of all the others.'

Sabinus had been a genuine friend of Germanicus and his family (68.1 *amicitiam*, *sectator*, *comes*, *unus* (*cliens*), 3 *amicus*); but now, in events which are the counterpart of Nero's treatment in 26 (59.3–60.2) and mark a deterioration of behaviour since 24 (cf. 71.1n., also 70.3n.), he is lured by the *dolus* (68.2) of an *agent provocateur* into a false and fatal friendship (68.4 *speciem artae amicitiae, quasi ad fidissimum*). The high point of the drama is a scene familiar from any spy novel (69.1–2): Sabinus is trapped into revealing his 'treachery' in the presence of witnesses, for whom T. expresses his contempt by ridicule (69.2n.). Then, in a scene which foreshadows Sejanus' own fall (70.1nn.), Sabinus is condemned, and Rome, as was the intention with Silius' trial in 24 (18.1), is gripped by a collective fear (69.3 *anxia et pauens ciuitas*, 70.2 *id ipsum pauentes quod timuissent*). Urban society disintegrates as the streets and meeting-places are deserted (69.3n., 70.2n.): the wasteland, which *adulatio* was in danger of producing in 24 (20.3n.), has been brought about by *pauor*.

68.1 consulibus: C. Appius Iunius Silanus, son of the consul of 10 (15.3n.), was later accused of *maiestas* in 32 (6.9.3), became governor of Hispania Tarraconensis, and was killed shortly after marrying Domitia Lepida, mother-in-law of the emperor Claudius (Dio 60.14.3–4). See *AA* 487 (index). About P. Silius Nerva little is otherwise known.

foedum anni principium incessit: since these words are equally applicable to a weather-report (*OLD foedus*[1] 2a, *incedo* 6a 'to arise', 'come on'), the effect of the appended abl. abs. (above, p. 24) is maximised (*tracto in carcerem* . . .); much less suspenseful are 16.13.1 'tot facinoribus foedum annum etiam dii tempestatibus et morbis insigniuere', Liv. 8.18.1 'foedus insequens annus seu intemperie caeli seu humana fraude fuit'. The date was 1 January (70.1); see further Ginsburg 24.

inlustri: as opposed to e.g. *modico* (1.73.1 and G.), but the precise reference of these and other similar descriptions of *equites* is unclear (Brunt (2) 62 n. 139). There is, however, a contrast with *foedum*, as e.g. 15.32 *fin.* For Sabinus' case see also Bauman (2) 121–2; for imprisonment see Garnsey 148.

neque enim omiserat . . . percolere: the pluperfect tense indicates that reference is being made to an earlier period than *anni principium*; *adgrediuntur* below is subsequent in time to *omiserat* but also prior to the start of the year (see further 2n. *Compositum*).

This compound form of *colere* seems not to be found between Plautus and T.

unus 'the only one remaining'.

eoque: see 22.1n.; for the *uariatio* (here chiastic) of *apud bonos* ~ *iniquis* see 1.2n., 2.1n., 9.2n., 46.2n.

grauis: the adj. (*OLD* 10a) is explained by 33.4 'uirtus infensos habet, ut nimis ex propinquo diuersa arguens'.

68.2 Porcius Cato: suffect consul in 36 and *curator aquarum* in 38, the year in which he seems to have come to grief (*AA* 222–3). Little is otherwise known of the other three. Latinius Latiaris, whose first name is repeated at 71.1 below, is called Lucanius Latiaris at 6.4.1 in a cross-reference to this episode; while the latter is likely to be correct, Syme has argued that here T. himself may have made a mistake (*TST* 70).

non nisi per Seianum aditus: Sejanus' earlier influence (2.3) had increased because he now controlled physical access to Tib. too (as planned: 41.2 'sua in manu aditus'): see 70.1, 74.3, 6.8.2 'ut quisque Seiano intimus, ita ad Caesaris amicitiam ualidus', Juv. 10.91 'summas donare curules' (*RP* III 1148).

neque . . . quaerebatur 'and Sejanus' blessing was only acquired through crime' (*OLD quaero* 7a). *scelere* evokes the *certamen uitiorum* which had replaced the *certamen uirtutum* (Sall. *C.* 9.2) of earlier days (Walker 241–2). The repetition *non nisi . . . Seianum* ~ *neque Seiani . . . nisi* is emphatic, perhaps reflecting the fact that it was his name which was on everyone's lips.

Compositum: sc. *erat*: since the trial began at the very start of the year (1, 70.1), the following paragraphs, like *neque . . . omiserat* above (1n.), must also be a flash-back to an earlier period (a similar technique to that used for A.D. 23: above, p. 77). The main narrative is resumed at 70.1 with *Sed*.

qui . . . contingebat 'who came into contact with S. on a casual basis' (*OLD contingo* 2b).

strueret dolum . . . accusationem inciperent: the three stages of their plan correspond to this and the two following paragraphs (68.3–4, 69.1–2, 69.3). For the motif cf. 59.3 'subditis qui accusatorum nomina sustinerent . . .'

68.3 iacere: often used of conversations etc. (*OLD* 8).

florentis . . . adflictam: the (common) contrast derives from a metaphor of a tree or plant, once thriving but now laid low (cf. Colum. 2.16.2 'quod [sc. pratum] . . . tempestatibus adfligeretur'): so too 71.4 below. The change of fortune experienced by Germanicus' house mirrors that which began to overtake the emperor's at 1.1 (where, however, Germanicus' house was reckoned as part of his: see n.).

honora: 'Largely a poeticism, first attested in Valerius and Silius. In the *Annals* it seems to replace the decidedly unpoetical *honorificus*' (G. on 1.10.7).

ut sunt molles . . . mortalium animi: *ut* is used 'in parenthetic remarks . . . explaining an action by reference to a general tendency or characteristic' (*OLD* 20b): so e.g. 1.28.2 'ut sunt mobiles . . . mentes'. *molles* = 'easily influenced', 'sensitive' (*OLD* 12), or perhaps 'weak' (*OLD* 13); *mortalium* is as apposite here as at 40.1 (n.), 62.2 (n.).

onerat 'loaded', i.e. with accusations (*OLD* 6b); 'the return to the historical present marks the change of subject again to Latiaris' (F.).

saeuitiam, superbiam, spes: sc. e.g. *increpans* from *onerat* (by zeugma), and note the alliteration.

68.4 tamquam uetita miscuissent 'as though they had exchanged treasonable confidences' – which they had not, since Latiaris' were insincere: for *tamquam* see *OLD* 5c. The point is continued in *speciem* and *quasi* below. For *misceo* see *OLD* 10.

fidissimum: 'There is a clear stylistic distinction between *fidus* and *fidelis* in the poetry and prose of the late Republic. In poetry of the higher genres *fidus* is preferred almost exclusively . . . In the lower genres, however, *fidelis* is somewhat more frequent . . . In prose both Caesar and Quintilian avoid *fidus*, and Cicero has it comparatively rarely (and then usually in the superlative form, in which it may have retained a limited currency) in both the speeches and letters . . . Similarly various archaizing authors show a taste for *fidus*: it is preferred by 12:4 by Sallust' (Adams (2) 139 n. 22). Livy uses both words equally; T. in his historical works prefers *fidus* almost exclusively (46:1).

69.1 loco . . . facies 'their rendezvous had to maintain its appearance of being deserted'; *coibatur* = *coituri erant* (*NLS* §200 (ii)).

et si . . . erat 'and if they took up a position behind the doors, there was a risk of being seen, making a noise, or of Sabinus' becoming suspicious by accident'. *adsisterent* is subjunc. because the *si*-clause is in virtual *or. obl.* after *metus . . . erat. pone* is archaic (G. on 2.16.1).

tectum inter . . . tres senatores . . . turpi latebra . . . sese abstrudunt, . . . rimis aurem admouent: there is contempt in the imagery, and ridicule in the precision, of this description. The distinguished politicians are crammed like snakes into a disgusting lair (cf. Vell. 129.3 'uelut serpentem abstrusum terra'; *OLD latebra* 1b), and the author catches all three in the simultaneous act of putting an ear to every possible crack. For the position of *inter*, lodged (like the senators) between roof and ceiling, see 5.1n.

69.2 recens is adverbial (5.2n.).

narraturus: purposive (46.2n.).

praeteritaque et instantia 'past and present ⟨events⟩', as *H.* 3.36.1 'praeterita, instantia, futura' (and H.).

adfatim copia 'an ample supply': *adfatim* is adjectival (*OLD* a, c).

eadem ille et diutius . . . reticentur 'he ⟨echoed⟩ the same sentiments and at ⟨as much⟩ greater length as complaints, when(ever) they once flood out, are silenced with greater difficulty' (i.e. sc. *tanto* with *diutius*, cf. 18.1n.); or perhaps 'he ⟨echoed⟩ the same sentiments at even greater length, in proportion as complaints . . .' Either way, *prorupere* is frequentative (18.3n.). Lamentation was conventionally hard to control (Nisbet–Hubbard on Hor. *Odes*. 2.20.23).

69.3 ordinem fraudis: as 11.2 'ordo . . . sceleris' (n).

non alias magis . . . aduersum proximos: the conclusion of the flash-back is emphasised by a superlative expression of the type common in (esp.) Thucydides (*RICH* 31–2) and Livy (P. G. Walsh, *Livy* (1961) 200–1): in T. see also e.g. 2.46.4, 14.34.2, 15.47.1.

Here, however, the text is defective, since M's *egens* gives no acceptable sense. Lipsius proposed *tegens*, which, or a compound thereof (e.g. *obtegens*), has found favour with many editors. But since *tegere* is not normally used with persons as its object, it is difficult either to supply or to understand *se*: one would have to suppose a lacuna in which stood e.g. *sensus suos*. Such a lacuna is not impossible (cf. 53.1), but the proper word for being on guard against treachery is *cautus*, which is elsewhere followed by *aduersus* (Liv. 38.25.7 'consuli parum cauto aduersus conloquii fraudem', Val. Max. 3.8 ext. 5 'aduersus Heraclidem et Calippum . . . insidias ei nectentis cautior esset', cf. 6.5.1). A scribe might easily have omitted *cautissime* between *ciuitas* and *-gens* (by haplography), and T. is exceptionally fond of combining *agere* with an adverb; although he does not use the superlative form of *caute* elsewhere, the expression is otherwise unexceptionable (cf. Plin. *NH* 15.12 'qui cautissime agunt'), and the cynical suggestion that people were 'behaving most cautiously of all towards their nearest and dearest' is both distinctively Tacitean (18.1n. *amicitia*) and exactly right in the context of Sabinus' entrapment.

congressus . . . aures uitari: occasioned by suspicion and fear, as at 60.2. T.'s picture is of a society in which natural social groupings are collapsing and the isolation of individuals resembles that of the emperor himself (cf. 42.1): see further 70.2 below. In addition, society is servile, since people are unable to say what they want (cf. Phaedr. 3.34–5 'seruitus obnoxia | . . . quae uolebat non audebat dicere', Prop. 1.1.28 with Shackleton Bailey's n.): contrast the allegedly free society of T.'s own day, 'ubi . . . quae sentias dicere licet' (*H.* 1.1.4).

aures is used for *homines* (by synecdoche).

70.1 Sed resumes the narrative of 68.2 after the intervening flashback.

sollemnia . . . epistula precatus: the *sollemnia* are the *uota pro salute rei publicae*, offered on 1 Jan. each year (Weinstock 217–19; Scullard 52–4; also 17.1n.). *epistula* tersely reminds us of Tib.'s continued absence (cf. 39.1n., 41.2); and the way the letter changes subject to attack Sabinus (*uertit in Sabinum*) ironically foreshadows the same technique that Tib. will use in the letter denouncing Sejanus in 31 (Dio 58.10.1): see further below.

haud obscure: in contrast with his usual obscurity: 31.2n.

decerneretur: sc. *ultio*.

trahebatur: sc. *in carcerem* (cf. 68.1).

quantum . . . poterat qualifies *clamitans*. With *obducta* sc. *capiti* (the expression is discussed by Lyne (ed.), *Ciris*, Intro. p. 42); *adstrictis faucibus* is explained by *laqueus* at 3 below: see also Juv. 10.88 (and Courtney's n.). 'The picture of Sabinus, bound and helpless, . . . lives in the reader's mind when the circumstances of many other cases have been forgotten' (Walker 105).

has Seiano uictimas cadere: since the *sollemnia* (above) included the sacrifice of bulls to Jupiter, who was 'Optimus Maximus' and with whom Julius Caesar and Augustus had both been identified (Weinstock 302–5), Sabinus' cry indicates that the real power lay with the 'divine' Sejanus (2.3n. *facili*, 68.2n. *non nisi*, 74.3n. *erga S.*). Again there is an anticipation of Sejanus' own fall (Juv. 10.65–6 with Courtney, Dio 58.11.2 'they were now leading to execution the very man whom they had adored and worshipped with sacrifices as a god'). *cadere* is technical of sacrificial victims (*OLD* 9b); for religious language used in a legal context see also 36.3n. (*sacrosanctus*).

70.2 intendisset . . . acciderent: the subjunctives are frequentative ('wherever . . .'), cf. 6.4n. (*si quando*), 31.2; the distinction of tense perhaps indicates the order of events: looking preceded speaking, as *fuga* preceded *uastitas*. For the wasteland see also 69.3n. and above, p. 248.

id ipsum pauentes quod timuissent expresses, in a typically cynical manner (cf. e.g. 1.11.3 'quibus unus metus si intellegere uiderentur'), the fear to which the subjects of a tyrant are conventionally prone (18.1, 69.3, 74.1, cf. Plato, *Rep.* 578A, 579E, Arist. *Pol.* 1311a25–7). Yet while this fear is partly in the tyrant's interests (*oderint dum metuant*, cf. 7.1n.), it also generates a hostility towards him which makes him suspicious and afraid in his turn (53.2, 67.3, 71.2, cf. Plato, *Rep.* 579B, E, Xen. *Hiero* 2.18). The essence of the problem is elaborated in 3–4 below: 'non imprudentem Tiberium tantam *inuidiam* adisse . . .' ~ '*trepidam* sibi uitam, *suspectas* inimicorum insidias'; see further Tarrant on Sen. *Ag.* 72–3. Thus tyrant and subjects reflect each other (cf. also 69.3n.), as is the case under an ideal ruler (W. on Vell. 126.5), from whose régime fear is of course absent (Vell. 126.3 'non timet'). In T.'s work, on the other hand, 'fear holds domination' (Syme 545); cf. W.-R. Heinz, *Die Furcht als politisches Phänomenon bei Tacitus* (1975).

70.3 quem enim diem . . .: sc. *esse posse* (virtual *or. obl.* after *timuissent*: sc. 'they said to themselves').

quo tempore uerbis . . . profanis abstineri mos esset: a comment on the deterioration since 25, when Salvianus was criticised by Tib. for accusing during a ritual and exiled (36.1). The abandonment of respect for religious customs etc. is a sign of the breakdown of society (Thuc. 2.52.2). For the series of pres. subjunctives below see 2.1n.

adisse 'had met/incurred/submitted to' (*OLD adeo*[1] 11).

quaesitum meditatumque: sc. *id* (= *inuidiam adisse*).

70.4 adiecto: so too e.g. 1.35.5 'addito'; see 36.3n.

intendi: impersonal, and combining the notions of directing one's aim (*OLD* 7) and accusing (*OLD* 13). The accus. + inf. instead of *quin* + subjunc. after a negative expression of doubt is common in T., Nepos and Livy but rare in Cic. and absent from Sallust (cf. *NLS* §187 (b) *Note*, p. 143).

71.1 ni mihi destinatum foret . . . in tempore trademus: these two sentences do not mean that T. felt restricted by his annalistic format, which, as we have seen, he manipulates at will and to good effect;

rather, they well illustrate his characteristic technique of having his cake and eating it. By warning us of the accusers' deaths, he whets our appetites; by declining to reveal details, he preserves his annalistic format. Elsewhere he either refers briefly to items which lie beyond the current year (1.58.6, 2.4.3, 6.22.4, 11.5.3; cf. also 31.3n.) or he admits to having broken his traditional format (6.38.1, 12.40.5, 13.9.3). See also 5–6 above; and Ginsburg 2–4.

auebat: for the indic. see 30.2n.; here, however, the action clearly remains unattempted.

exitus quos . . . habuere alludes to the 'obituary' formula *hunc exitum habuit* (W. on Vell. 53.3, 72.1). Latiaris was killed in 32 (6.4.1); the fates of the others are unknown.

repertores suggests that Sejanus' henchmen resemble their master as he resembles Tib. (11.2n.); see also 34.1n. (*nouo . . . crimine*) and below.

postquam . . . potitus est: Gaius Caligula became emperor in 37.

scelerum ministros: a standard expression of abuse (*H.* 4.27.2 and H.; W. on Vell. 83.1), but see also next n. but one.

ut . . . ita 'although . . . nevertheless' (33.3n.).

satiatus suggests the focusing of a grotesque image. It is as though accusers, having invented new confections of crime (*flagitii . . . repertores*), then serve them up (*scelerum ministros*; *OLD minister* 1) for the emperor's gratification; but when he is glutted (*satiatus*, cf. 1.75.1, Cic. *Mil.* 3 'quos P. Clodii furor rapinis et incendiis et omnibus exitiis publicis pauit'; Fantham 133 n. 35), or offered practitioners of some other *nouvelle cuisine* (*oblatis . . . recentibus*; *OLD opera* 7a), he strikes down his former assistants like creatures past their prime and gone to fat (*ueteres et praegraues*, cf. Liv. 44.4.10 'Romanus imperator maior lx annis et praegrauis corpore'); the transformation of accuser into victim constitutes a further diversion for his tastes. Contrast Tib.'s retention of provincial governors (1.80.2 'taedio nouae curae').

sontium poenas . . . trademus: for *delatores* getting their just deserts see also 1.74.2; for the authorial plural, 11.3n.

71.2 Asinius Gallus: see 20.1n. To judge from *accepit* (3 below), his motion (*censuit*) was carried.

Agrippina: half-sister of Gallus' wife Vipsania, both being daughters of Agrippa: 'their relationship is added to aggravate the baseness of his conduct' (F.). His children included the consuls of 23 and 25.

71.3 ut rebatur: with *ex uirtutibus suis*: 'of his self-styled "virtues"' (see 38.1nn.).

dissimulationem diligebat: the verb is emphatic because rare in *A.*: at 6.51.3 of his affection for Sejanus, 15.63.2 of a man's for his wife (Syme 345). For *dissimulatio* see 1.2n.

eo aegrius accepit 'hence he was all the more upset to learn that what he was seeking to suppress was being exposed': i.e. he realised that his anonymous accusations were common knowledge (70.4). For *eo* see 22.1n.

ut . . . opperiretur 'to await the outcome of' (so 2.69.2 and G.); for the *uariatio* with *amore* see 8.2n.; for Tib.'s *cunctationes* see 11.1n.

ubi 'when(ever)': *prorupisset* = frequentative perf. indic. in *or. recta* (69.2, 18.3n.). The verb denotes a further link between Tib. and Sejanus (5.3.1, cf. 6.51.3).

dictis . . . facta coniungere: *dictum* (*ac*) *factum* is a proverbial expression of speed (e.g. Enn. *Ann.* 314 and Skutsch) and similar judgements to T.'s, but on other individuals, tend to emphasise speed and to be laudatory (e.g. Herodian 2.9.2 on Septimius Severus: 'sharp in making a decision and quick to execute it'): see e.g. Vretska on Sall. *C* 1.6, W. on Vell. 79.1 'consultisque facta coniungens'. But Tib.'s speed is counteracted by his *cunctationes* (above), his words are characteristically *tristia* (31.2n.), and his eventual actions heinous (*atrocia*: *OLD* 6).

71.4 Iulia: granddaughter of Augustus and sister of Agrippina: see *AA* 118–23, 486 (index). The placing of her obituary here, rather than at the end of the year, allows T. to give exclusive prominence to the marriage which concludes both the year and (in this case) the book: see 75n.

procul: preposition (2.1n.). For the abl. of duration of time (*annis* below), increasingly common from Livy onwards, see *NLS* §54 (ii).

quae florentes priuignos cum . . . subuertisset, misericordiam . . . ostentabat: for the former role see 1.3.3 and Suet. *Tib.* 22, where her complicity in the deaths of her stepsons Lucius and Gaius Caesar (in A.D. 2 and 4 respectively) and Agrippa Postumus (in 14) is alleged; the latter role seems reflected at 5.3.1. For the relationship between the two see esp. N. Purcell, 'Livia and the womanhood of Rome', *P.C.P.S.* 32 (1986) 95, who argues that the former 'is simply the inverse of the image of dynastic solidarity which Augustus was keen to project; Livia who was the lynch-pin of the family network is presented as the agent of the destruction within'.

The masc. *priuignos* here clearly includes the female ('stepchildren'), although there is no suggestion elsewhere in T. of any other intervention by Livia on behalf of any of her step-family.

72–3 Foreign affairs

T.'s narrative of the Frisian revolt lacks the drama and suspense of 23–6 or 46–51 above. Here, near the end of Book 4, he is principally concerned to point a moral: the Romans fail generally to live up to traditional ideals and at times seem almost to behave like barbarians (72.3n., 73.2–4nn.). This gloomy reversal of values and behaviour, more culpable and comprehensive than that of A.D. 24 (pp. 155–6), provides a fitting background to the section which follows.

72.1 Frisii: they lived in the area bordered by the IJssel Meer, the North Sea and the R. Ems, i.e. around Friesland in mod. Holland. See also *G.* 34.1.

exuere 'cast off', as if peace were oppressive (elsewhere in T. barbarians equate *pax* with *seruitus*: *H.* 4.17.2, cf. *H.* 4.25.3 'si exuissent seruitium').

nostra . . . auaritia: a frequent barbarian complaint (e.g. 45.3, 14.32.3, *Agr.* 15.4, 30.4): contrast 6.4 'sine auaritia'. *magis . . . quam* does not preclude the other traditional complaint of servitude (24.1n.), as *seruitio* below shows.

Drusus: Tib.'s brother had annexed the Frisians in 12 B.C. (Dio 54.32.2).

modicum pro angustia rerum 'modest in proportion to their straitened circumstances'.

penderent 'pay', sc. in dues (*OLD* 3).

non intenta . . . mensura 'without anyone having paid attention to what their strength or dimensions should be' (i.e. sc. *foret* with *quae . . . quae*).

e primipilaribus: sc. *unus* (42.2n.). Olennius is the first of four unfamiliar names in this section (73.3 Cethecius Labeo, 4 Baduhenna,

Cruptorix). From this unusual precision (compare above, p. 207) scholars have inferred that T. is indebted to an allegedly specific source such as the elder Pliny's *Bella Germaniae*, to which he refers by name at 1.69.2 (see G.). If so, it no more prevents the inclusion of conventional elements here than at 1.61–5 (see G.). See further below.

terga . . . acciperentur 'selected the hides of aurochs as a model for what would be acceptable' (lit. 'in accordance with the model of which they [i.e. the liable hides] would be accepted'): see *OLD ad* 34–8; for aurochs (wild oxen, now extinct) see below, 2n.

72.2 quoque 'even' (*OLD* 4).

beluarum denotes wildness and abnormality (*OLD* 1, 2a), which are conventional in descriptions of foreign animals: e.g. 2.24.4, *G.* 17.1, Caes. *G.* 6.25–8 (25.5 'genera ferarum nasci constat quae reliquis in locis uisa non sint', 28.1 'tertium est genus eorum qui uri appellantur . . .'). For *ferax* + genit., 'teeming (with)', see *OLD* 2a; for *quis*, 14.1n.

modica refers to size (~*ingentium* above): see *G.* 5.1 'numero [sc. armentorum] gaudent, eaeque solae et gratissimae opes sunt'.

seruitio: taken only with *corpora* (here almost = 'lives': *OLD* 8a, cf. 9).

72.3 postquam non subueniebatur 'when no relief was forthcoming'.

tributo aderant 'were at hand for ⟨the collection of⟩ the tribute'; the dative is purposive: cf. *OLD adsum* 4.

patibulo adfixi: typically of barbarians (1.61.4, 14.33.2).

haud spernenda . . . manus litora Oceani praesidebat: elsewhere (47.2, 49.1) it is barbarians who rely on a *castellum*. For *praesideo* + accus. see 5.1n.

73.1 pro praetore: sc. *legato Augusti*. For Apronius see 13.3n.

legionum: there were four on the Upper Rhine: V Alaudae, XXI Rapax, I and XX Valeria Victrix. See also 5.1n.

utrumque: i.e. his own from Lower, and that summoned from Upper, Germany.

soluto iam . . . rebellibus is almost parenthetic: *igitur* below continues the action of *intulit* above. *soluere obsidium* (also at 24.2 (n.), *H.* 4.34.1) occurs first in T. as a variant for *s. obsidionem*. *sua* = 'their own property'.

aggeribus et pontibus: so too at 1.61.1 'pontesque et

aggeres . . . imponeret' (see G.). *aggeres* are embankments for carrying roads (cf. *OLD* 4b).

traducendo grauiori agmini 'for the transportation of a more heavily armed column' (dat. gerundive of purpose: 1.3n.); *OLD grauis* 2c.

73.2 alam Canninefatem: the Canninefates lived west of the Frisii on the other side of the IJssel Meer.

quod peditum . . . merebat '⟨the element⟩ of German infantry which served with our men'.

turmas sociales 'the allied squadrons' (*OLD socialis* 2c).

subsidio is predic. dat. (*NLS* §68 *Note* (i)).

si simul incubuissent: failure to launch an organised attack is usually a barbarian characteristic (cf. 24.1).

per interuallum aduentantes neque . . . addiderant . . . et auferebantur: the choice of part. and variation of tense are deliberate: '⟨but⟩ by arriving at frequent intervals they had not brought resolve . . . and kept on being carried back. . .'

73.3 Cethecio Labeoni: for the form of name see *TST* 67.

quod: sc. *erat*. The subject of *tradit* is Apronius.

ille = Labeo.

in anceps tractus 'forced into a dangerous position' (*OLD anceps* 8b; G. on 1.36.2).

dux Romanus: this periphrasis for Apronius underlines his failure to behave like a true Roman general: for the horror of lying unburied etc. see esp. Cic. *Inu.* 1.108 'inimicorum in manibus mortuus est, hostili in terra turpiter iacuit insepultus' (also Pease on Virg. *Aen.* 4.620, Nisbet–Hubbard on Hor. *Odes* 1.28.23).

cecidissent: for the subjunc. see 4.1n. (*quamquam*).

73.4 Baduhennae: presumably a local goddess. Such *uocant*-clauses are a feature of ethnographical contexts (e.g. 1.51.1 'templum, quod Tanfanae uocant').

in posterum: sc. *diem* (as 45.2).

stipendiarii: i.e. a native, non-legionary soldier.

mutuis ictibus: ironical: they die in a barbarian manner (50.1, 3n.). The episode concludes with chiastic assonance: *pro- metue-* ~ *mutui- . . . pro-*.

74 Sejanus

In almost every respect the penultimate section of the year is the corollary of the first (above, p. 247). Still distracted by fear (74.1), the senators vote an *ara amicitiae* flanked by statues of Tib. and Sejanus, confirming and consolidating the relationship they have enjoyed since the very start of Book 4 (cf. 2.3), to which the present section is also a counterpart (above, p. 77). But whereas there Sejanus felt obliged to attract his own support (2.3–3), here, in contrast to the desolation in Rome itself (69.3, 70.2), the people go on a spontaneous mass pilgrimage to Campania and camp in the fields and on the sea-shore, hoping to catch sight of Sejanus as they might a god (74.3–4, cf. 70.1n.). These would-be *amici* are of course unaware that Sejanus is deceiving Tib. in the same way as his henchmen duped Sabinus (68–9). But there would come a time when, as the emperor's new son-in-law (40.7n.), Sejanus would be found guilty of even greater *impietas* than Vibius Serenus, whose attack on his own father (described in the second domestic section of A.D. 24: 28–30) represented the lowest point which the perversion of *amicitia* had then reached (above, p. 161). When that moment in 31 arrived, Sejanus' successful friends would pay as heavy a price for their misguided friendship as his henchmen had exacted from Sabinus for his (74.5 'infaustae amicitiae grauis exitus imminebat', cf. 69.3–70.1).

74.1 Clarum inde ... Frisium nomen: defeating Rome confers fame (e.g. *H.* 1.2.1 'nobilitatus cladibus mutuis Dacus', Liv. 9.1.1 'nobilis clade Romana', Vell. 105.1 'Cherusci ... nostra clade nobiles').

dissimulante Tiberio: as at the start of the year (71.3). His fear was that a successful general would win popularity and hence be seen as a rival.

imperii extrema: failure to defend the status quo is even more culpable than the absence of imperialism lamented at 32.2. The tone is that of the appeasers during the Munich crisis of 1938: 'A quarrel in a far-away country' (Chamberlain's broadcast of 27 Sept.). For an indir. qu. introduced by *in eo* cf. 40.1 (and cf. 4.3n.).

pauor internus links with the preceding episode (as often, e.g. 27.1n., 45 intro., 52.1n.) and implies a bitter reversal. In republican days *metus hostilis* was supposed to promote virtue at home, including *concordia* (Earl 13, 41ff.; see further 1.1n. *cum repente*); now even the reality of war is subordinate to domestic fear, which produces social isolation (69.3n., 70.2) and, as a psychological obsession (*occupauerat animos*, cf. *OLD occupo* 4a–b), is wrongly treated (*remedium*) by *adulatio*. By contrast it is the barbarian enemy who shows the traditional Roman response (72.3 *remedium ex bello*).

74.2 quamquam . . . consulerentur: for the subjunc. see 4.1n. (*quamquam*).

aram clementiae, aram amicitiae: the punctilious reference to each *ara* is ironic. The former was a high-point in Tib.'s claims to *clementia* (31.2n.), but entirely belied by his recent behaviour (70.1, cf. 71.1). The latter elevates still further the *amicitia* on which Sejanus' position as *socius laborum* (2.3n.) was based and which has been a major theme of Book 4 (1.1, 7.1, 39–41, 59.1–2); and it was as a betrayer of that *amicitia* that Sejanus was seen after his denunciation by Tib. in 31 (Val. Max. 9.11 ext. 4).

circum presumably = 'on either side' (cf. *OLD* 5).

crebrisque precibus efflagitabant, uisendi sui copiam facerent: T.'s language suggests that the prayers were cletic or 'summoning', in which deities were conventionally begged to 'leave' their present cult centre (cf. *degressi*, *omittere* below) and 'come' to another (*in urbem*) to 'reveal' themselves (*uisendi*, *aspici*): see e.g. F. Cairns, *A.J.Ph.* 92 (1971) 444–7 (whose remarks on *euocatio* are also relevant). The suggestion of Sejanus' divine status, already noted at 2.3 (*coli*; see also n. on *facili*) and emphasised by Sabinus' sarcastic cry at 70.1 and the *ara amicitiae* here, is also attested at Juv. 10.62 *adoratum*, Dio 58.4.3–4 and 11.2 (quoted 70.1n.). While it was common in the ancient world to ascribe divinity to a patron or (potential) benefactor (38.1n. *Ego me*; W. on Vell. 89.2, Fantham 64), T.'s extravagant treatment in 3–4 below is ruthless and contemptuous. For the importance of a ruler's appearance see also 34.2n.

74.3 uisum: sc. *est*.

omittere 'to leave' (*OLD* 3).

in proximo Campaniae 'in neighbouring Campania' (5.2n.).

eo uenire patres, eques, magna pars plebis: this reaction recalls the welcoming of a returning exile (e.g. Cic. *Pis.* 52 'senatum egressum uidi populumque uniuersum . . . omnes uiri ac mulieres omnis fortunae ac loci') or of a *triumphator* (e.g. Vell. 89.1 'quo concursu, quo fauore omnium hominum, aetatium, ordinum exceptus sit'), or the ancient equivalent of a pilgrimage to a religious centre (e.g. Gell. 12.5.1 'ad Pythia conuentumque totius ferme Graeciae'). Yet Tib. was in self-imposed exile (58.2n.), the Frisian campaign had been a disaster (above), and the emperor had given memorable expression to his disapproval of deification (38.1n.).

erga Seianum: not Tib. (see 68.2n., 70.1n., Juv. 10.92–3 'tutor haberi | principis'). Campania scarcely proves to be the *quies et solitudo* which Sejanus had promised Tib. at 41.3; but now it is Sejanus himself who has acquired the *populi adcursus*, *multitudinem adfluentium* from which he there pretended a desire to save Tib.

cuius durior congressus: sc. *erat*: 'was ⟨even⟩ harder' (i.e. than hitherto, cf. 40.5), explaining why they were compelled to resort to bribery etc. below. Hence *eo* ('therefore', cf. 22.1n.).

per ambitum: explained below by *ianitorum* (4), who were traditionally bribable (Hor. *S.* 1.9.57, Juv. 3.184–5).

societate consiliorum 'the sharing of advice/plans', or perhaps 'by taking part in his designs'.

parabatur = either 'was obtained' (in which case sc. 'only' with *per ambitum* . . .) or 'was prepared for'.

74.4 in propatulo is usually taken to mean 'in the open' (metaphorically) or 'within view of all' (*OLD* 2b), but since much of this passage is couched in language which suggests worshippers at the shrine of a god, the hopefuls are perhaps envisaged as suppliants in the forecourt of a temple (*OLD* 2a, cf. Cic. *Verr.* 4.110 'ante aedem Cereris in aperto ac propatulo loco'); similarly *iacentes* (below) may suggest religious prostration (*OLD* 3b). It is clear from *auctam ei adrogantiam* that their description as *foedum illud seruitium* coincides with the verdict of Sejanus himself.

sueti . . . incertum: sc. respectively *erant* and *erat*.

litore: being an archetypally marginal area (see T. E. J. Wiedemann, *PP* 190), the shore additionally suggests desperation (as in e.g. Archil. 79a.10–11 'lying powerless on the edge of the shore' [= Hipponax 115 West]). See also next n.

nullo discrimine . . . iuxta: these words reduce to sameness the three opposites of place (*campo aut litore*), time (*noctem ac diem*) and attitude (*gratiam aut fastus*): they therefore not only emphasise the desperate lengths to which the devotees will go (last n.) but also contrast with the diversity of city life above (*discursus*, *incertum*, *quisque*), underlining the slavish homogeneity of this instant community.

fastus ianitorum: doorkeepers were conventionally haughty (Sen. *Const. Sap.* 15.3 'ianitoribus turbam uenali fastidio derigentibus' and often in elegy), but Sejanus' reflected the *adrogantia* (above) of their *dominus* and were recalled bitterly after his fall (6.8.5 'libertis quoque ac ianitoribus notescere pro magnifico accipiebatur').

74.5 dignatus erat: the language again suits a divinity (cf. *G.* 40.3 'loca quaecumque aduentu hospitioque dignatur [sc. dea]'). The anaphora of *non* is emphatic, reflecting the inflexible refusals transmitted by the janitors.

male 'misguidedly' (*OLD* 9a), anticipating the dramatic reversal (*peripeteia*) to come (next nn.).

infaustae amicitiae brings to a simultaneous close both the main theme of the ch. and its religious language (*infaustus* is found first in Virg. and is esp. common in elevated poetry).

grauis exitus: though this expression occurs elsewhere, scholars have detected an echo of Juno's comment on her favourite Turnus (*Aen.* 10.630 'manet insontem grauis exitus'): similarly friendship with the 'divine' Sejanus would bring disaster to many who before his fall thought themselves blameless (5.6.2, 6.8.1, 6).

75 The end of the year

Just as the very first section of Book 4 ended with Sejanus' seduction of Livi(ll)a (3.3), whom Tib. later forbade him to marry (40.3–7), so the very last is devoted to the wedding of the younger Agrippina to Cn. Domitius Ahenobarbus, which Tib. officially blessed. The item 'is not dramatic in its formulation but sober and ostensibly innocuous'; yet 'the names were enough' (Syme 267). Their son will be Tib.'s counterpart in the last books of *A.*, the emperor Nero. 'an Neronem extremum dominorum putatis? idem crediderant qui Tiberio, qui Gaio superstites fuerunt, cum interim intestabilior et saeuior exortus est' (*H.* 4.42.5).

75 Agrippinam: see 53.2n. She was now about thirteen.

cum coram ... tradidisset 'after/although he had personally betrothed ...' Cn. Domitius Ahenobarbus, son of L. Domitius

Ahenobarbus (cos. 16 B.C.) and Antonia *maior* (44.2n.), was described about this time as 'nobilissimae simplicitatis iuuenem' by Vell. 2.10.2 (cf. 72.3) and later as 'omni parte uitae detestabilem' by Suet. *Nero* 5.1. He became consul in 32 (6.1.1), escaped various charges in 37 (6.47.2), and died in late December, 40. 'A nasty fellow' (*AA* 185, cf. 483 (index)).

celebrari nuptias: the marriage produced the future emperor Nero, of whom we have already been put in mind at 53.2 and of whom his father is said to have remarked that nothing could be born of himself and Agrippina 'nisi detestabile et malo publico' (Suet. *Nero* 6.1). For foreshadowing at the end of a year see esp. 3.29–30 (and Ginsburg 46–8); note, however, that here (unlike 3.30) T. has removed Julia's obituary to 71.4 in order to devote the final position in both the year and the book exclusively to the marriage notice, which thereby gains in emphasis and ominousness.

super uetustatem generis: three generations are summarised at 44.2 (nn.); see also Vell. and Suet. (last n. but one), and *AA* Table VIII. *super* = 'in addition to' (*OLD* 7).

sanguinem here combines the notion of 'blood regarded as running through a family and expressing relationship' (*OLD* 8a) and the common metonymy of a 'person standing in blood-relationship' (*OLD* 10).

Octauiam: sister of Augustus: hence *auunculum* = 'great uncle' (3.4n.).

praeferebat 'carried before him', i.e. as ancestor(s): so too 14.53.5 'longa decora praeferentes'.

REFERENCES AND ABBREVIATIONS

(1) All dates are A.D. unless otherwise stated.

(2) T.'s works are abbreviated as *A.* (*Annals*), *H.* (*Histories*), *Agr.* (*Agricola*), *G.* (*Germania*), *D.* (*Dialogus*). When referring to passages of the *Annals*, however, we omit *A.* altogether (e.g. 1.72.3).

(3) References to *A.* 4 omit the book number; references within the same chapter of *A.* 4 omit also the chapter number.

(4) Notes on *lexical* usage etc. (e.g. *glisco* at 5.4) are generally not cross-referenced after their first appearance in the commentary; they may be re-located by consulting the index. *Grammatical* and *syntactical* notes, however, are cross-referenced throughout.

(5) Periodical abbreviations are generally as in *L'Année philologique*; abbreviated references to other secondary works may be traced via the following list:

AA — Syme, R. (1986). *The Augustan aristocracy*. Oxford

Adams (1) — Adams, J. N. (1972). 'The language of the later books of Tacitus' *Annals*', *C.Q.* 22:350–73

Adams (2) — (1973). 'The vocabulary of the speeches in Tacitus' historical works', *B.I.C.S.* 20:124–44

Adams (3) — (1987). *The Latin sexual vocabulary*. 2nd edn. London

Bauman (1) — Bauman, R. A. (1967). *The crimen maiestatis in the Roman republic and Augustan principate*. Johannesburg

Bauman (2) — (1974). *Impietas in principem. A study of treason against the Roman emperor with special reference to the first century A.D.* Munich

Brunt (1) — Brunt, P. A. (1971). *Italian manpower 225 B.C.–A.D. 14*. Oxford

Brunt (2) — (1983). 'Princeps and equites', *J.R.S.* 73:42–75

Brunt (3) — (1984). 'The role of the senate in the Augustan régime', *C.Q.* 34:423–44

Campbell — Campbell, J. B. (1984). *The emperor and the Roman army*. Oxford

Crook — Crook, J. A. (1967). *Law and life of Rome*. London

Earl	Earl, D. C. (1961). *The political thought of Sallust.* Cambridge
EJ	Ehrenberg, V. and Jones, A. H. M. (1955). *Documents illustrating the reigns of Augustus and Tiberius.* 2nd edn. Oxford (references are to entries unless otherwise stated)
F.	Furneaux, H. (1896). *The Annals of Tacitus.* Vol. I. 2nd edn. Oxford
Fantham	Fantham, E. (1972). *Comparative studies in republican Latin imagery.* Toronto
G.	Goodyear, F. R. D. (1972–81). *The Annals of Tacitus.* Vols. I–II. Cambridge
Garnsey	Garnsey, P. (1970). *Social status and legal privilege in the Roman empire.* Oxford
Ginsburg	Ginsburg, J. (1981). *Tradition and theme in the Annals of Tacitus.* New York
Goodyear	Goodyear, F. R. D. (1968). 'Development of language and style in the *Annals* of Tacitus', *J.R.S.* 58:22–31
H.	Heubner, H. (1963–82). *P. Cornelius Tacitus: Die Historien.* Vols. I–V. Heidelberg
Handford	Handford, S. A. (1947). *The Latin subjunctive.* London
Hands	Hands, A. R. (1974). 'Postremo suo tantum ingenio utebatur', *C.Q.* 24:312–17
ILS	Dessau, H. (1892–1916). *Inscriptiones latinae selectae.* Berlin
Jerome	Jerome, T. S. (1923). *Aspects of the study of Roman history.* New York–London
K.	Koestermann, E. (1963–8). *Cornelius Tacitus: Annalen.* Heidelberg
Keitel	Keitel, E. (1984). 'Principate and civil war in the *Annals* of Tacitus', *A.J.Ph.* 105:306–25
Keppie	Keppie, L. (1984). *The making of the Roman army.* London
Levick	Levick, B. (1976). *Tiberius the politician.* London (repr. 1986)
Luce	Luce, T. J. (1977). *Livy: the composition of his history.* Princeton

Luttwak — Luttwak, E. N. (1976). *The grand strategy of the Roman empire*. Baltimore–London

Magie — Magie, D. (1950). *Roman rule in Asia Minor*. Vols. I–II. Princeton

Martin (1) — Martin, R. H. (1953). 'Variatio and the development of Tacitus' style', *Eranos* 51:89–96

Martin (2) — (1981). *Tacitus*. London

Millar — Millar, F. (1977). *The emperor in the Roman world*. London

Miller — Miller, N. P. (1968). 'Tiberius speaks. An examination of the utterances ascribed to him in the *Annals* of Tacitus', *A.J.Ph.* 89:1–19

MRR — Broughton, T. R. S. (1951–60). *The magistrates of the Roman republic*. Vols. I–II. New York

NLS — Woodcock, E. C. (1959). *A new Latin syntax*. London (repr. 1985)

OCD — Hammond, N. G. L. and Scullard, H. H. (1970). *The Oxford classical dictionary*. 2nd edn. Oxford

OLD — Glare, P. G. W. (1968–82). *Oxford Latin dictionary*. Oxford

PP — Moxon, I. S., Smart, J. D. and Woodman, A. J. (1986). *Past perspectives: studies in Greek and Roman historical writing*. Cambridge

Price — Price, S. R. F. (1984). *Rituals and power: the Roman imperial cult in Asia Minor*. Cambridge

RG — *Res Gestae Diui Augusti*

RICH — Woodman, A. J. (1988). *Rhetoric in classical historiography: four studies*. London

Rickman — Rickman, G. E. (1980). *The corn supply of ancient Rome*. Oxford

Rogers (1) — Rogers, R. S. (1935). *Criminal trials and criminal legislation under Tiberius*. Middletown

Rogers (2) — (1943). *Studies in the reign of Tiberius*. Baltimore

RP — Syme, R. (1979–88). *Roman papers*. Vols. I–V. Oxford

Scullard — Scullard, H. H. (1981). *Festivals and ceremonies of the Roman republic*. London

Seager — Seager, R. (1972). *Tiberius*. London

Shatzman — Shatzman, I. (1974). 'Tacitean rumours', *Latomus* 33:549–78

Sherk	Sherk, R. K. (1988). *The Roman empire: Augustus to Hadrian.* (*Translated Documents of Greece and Rome* 6.) Cambridge (references are to entries)
Sörbom	Sörbom, G. (1935). *Variatio sermonis Tacitei aliaeque apud eundem quaestiones selectae.* Uppsala
Starr	Starr, C. G. (1960). *The Roman imperial navy.* 2nd edn. Cambridge
Steele	Steele, R. B. (1904). 'The historical attitude of Livy', *A.J.Ph.* 25:15–44
Sutherland	Sutherland, C. H. V. (1951). *Coinage in Roman imperial policy 31 B.C.–A.D. 68.* Oxford
Syme	Syme, R. (1958). *Tacitus.* Oxford
Talbert	Talbert, R. J. A. (1984). *The senate of imperial Rome.* Princeton
Thomas	Thomas, R. F. (1982). *Lands and peoples in Roman poetry. The ethnographical tradition.* Camb. Philol. Soc. Suppl. 7. Cambridge
Traub	Traub, H. W. (1953). 'Tacitus' use of *ferocia*', *T.A.P.A.* 84:250–61
TST	Syme, R. (1970). *Ten studies in Tacitus.* Oxford
W.	Woodman, A. J. (1977–83). *Velleius Paterculus: The Tiberian narrative* and *The Caesarian and Augustan narrative.* Cambridge
Walker	Walker, B. (1952). *The Annals of Tacitus: a study in the writing of history.* Manchester
Wallace-Hadrill	Wallace-Hadrill, A. (1981). 'The emperor and his virtues', *Historia* 30:298–323
Weinstock	Weinstock, S. (1971). *Divus Julius.* Oxford
Wilkes	Wilkes, J. J. (1969). *Dalmatia.* London
Winterbottom	Winterbottom, M. (1974). *The elder Seneca.* Loeb edn. Vols. I–II. Cambridge, Mass.–London
Wiseman	Wiseman, T. P. (1979). *Clio's cosmetics.* Leicester
Woodman (1)	Woodman, A. J. (1972). 'Remarks on the structure and content of Tacitus, *Annals* 4.57–67', *C.Q.* 22:150–8
Woodman (2)	(1989). 'Tacitus' obituary of Tiberius', *C.Q.* 39:197–205
Yavetz	Yavetz, Z. (1969). *Plebs and princeps.* Oxford

INDEXES

1 GENERAL

2 LATIN WORDS

3 NAMES

All dates are A.D. unless otherwise stated. An asterisk indicates that an individual appears on the Stemma (pp. 282–3).

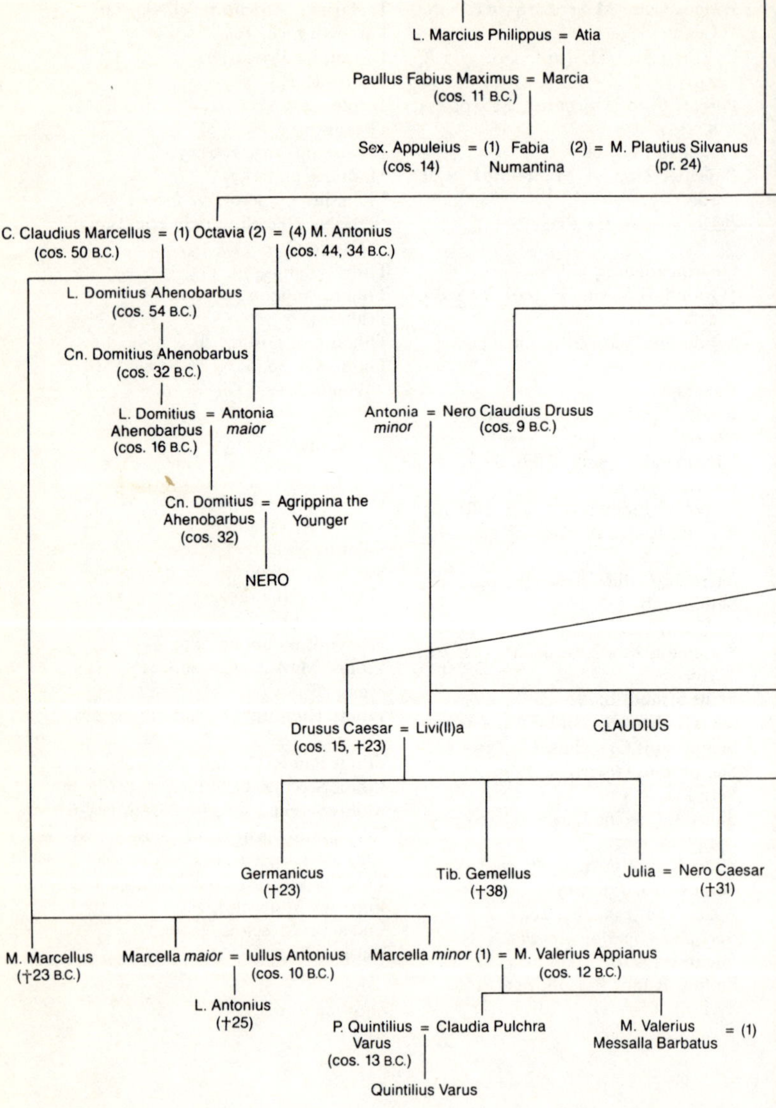

Ignota = (1) L. Marcius Philippus (2) = (2) Atia (1) =
L. Marcius Philippus = Atia
Paullus Fabius Maximus = Marcia
(cos. 11 B.C.)
Sex. Appuleius = (1) Fabia (2) = M. Plautius Silvanus
(cos. 14)
Numantina
(pr. 24)
C. Claudius Marcellus = (1) Octavia (2) = (4) M. Antonius
(cos. 50 B.C.)
(cos. 44, 34 B.C.)
L. Domitius Ahenobarbus
(cos. 54 B.C.)
Cn. Domitius Ahenobarbus
(cos. 32 B.C.)
L. Domitius Ahenobarbus
(cos. 16 B.C.)
= Antonia maior
Antonia minor = Nero Claudius Drusus
(cos. 9 B.C.)
Cn. Domitius Ahenobarbus
(cos. 32)
= Agrippina the Younger
NERO
Drusus Caesar = Livi(ll)a
(cos. 15, †23)
CLAUDIUS
Germanicus
(†23)
Tib. Gemellus
(†38)
Julia = Nero Caesar
(†31)
M. Marcellus
(†23 B.C.)
Marcella maior = Iullus Antonius
(cos. 10 B.C.)
L. Antonius
(†25)
Marcella minor (1) = M. Valerius Appianus
(cos. 12 B.C.)
P. Quintilius Varus
(cos. 13 B.C.)
= Claudia Pulchra
Quintilius Varus
M. Valerius Messalla Barbatus
= (1)